Covering American Politics in the 21st Century

Covering American Politics in the 21st Century

An Encyclopedia of News Media Titans, Trends, and Controversies

VOLUME 2: N–Z

LEE BANVILLE

An Imprint of ABC-CLIO, LLC
Santa Barbara, California • Denver, Colorado

Library of Congress Cataloging-in-Publication Data

Names: Banville, Lee, author.
Title: Covering American politics in the 21st century : an encyclopedia of news media titans, trends, and controversies / Lee Banville.
Description: Santa Barbara, California : ABC-CLIO, 2017. | Includes bibliographical references.
Identifiers: LCCN 2016020318 (print) | LCCN 2016032715 (ebook) | ISBN 9781440835520 (hardback) | ISBN 9781440846472 (vol. 1 : acid-free paper) | ISBN 9781440846489 (vol. 2 : acid-free paper) | ISBN 9781440835537 (ebook (set))
Subjects: LCSH: Press and politics—United States—Encyclopedias. | Mass media—Political aspects—United States—Encyclopedias.
Classification: LCC PN4888.P6 B36 2017 (print) | LCC PN4888.P6 (ebook) | DDC 070.4/49320973—dc23
LC record available at https://lccn.loc.gov/2016020318

ISBN: 978-1-4408-3552-0 (set)
ISBN: 978-1-4408-4647-2 (vol. 1)
ISBN: 978-1-4408-4648-9 (vol. 2)
EISBN: 978-1-4408-3553-7 (set)

21 20 19 18 17 1 2 3 4 5

This book is also available as an eBook.

ABC-CLIO
An Imprint of ABC-CLIO, LLC

ABC-CLIO, LLC
130 Cremona Drive, P.O. Box 1911
Santa Barbara, California 93116-1911
www.abc-clio.com

This book is printed on acid-free paper ∞

Manufactured in the United States of America

To the Big Room,
May you always have snacks.

Contents

Guide to Related Topics

BIOGRAPHIES

Ailes, Roger
Beck, Glenn
Block, Herbert (Herblock)
Breitbart, Andrew
Brock, David
Broder, David
Hannity, Sean
Huffington, Arianna
Ifill, Gwen
Jamieson, Kathleen Hall
Koch Brothers: Koch, Charles and Koch, David
Krauthammer, Charles
Lehrer, Jim
Limbaugh, Rush
Lippmann, Walter
Maddow, Rachel
Murrow, Edward
Oliver, John
O'Reilly, Bill
Palin, Sarah
Rove, Karl
Russert, Tim
Stone, I.F.
Steffens, Lincoln
Stewart, Jon
Sullivan, Andrew
Tarbell, Ida
White, Theodore
Winchell, Walter
Woodward and Bernstein: Woodward, Bob and Bernstein, Carl

CAMPAIGN ORGANIZATION AND STRUCTURE

Advance Teams
Commission on Presidential Debates
Direct Mail Campaigning
Federal Election Commission
Get Out the Vote (GOTV)
News Conferences
Opposition Research
Political Consultants
Rapid Response Teams
Surrogates
Trackers

INTEREST GROUPS AND POLITICAL ORGANIZATIONS

American Enterprise Institute (AEI)
Brookings Institution
Cato Institute
Center for American Progress (CAP)
Center for Public Integrity (CPI)
Congressional and Senate Campaign Committees
Conservative Blogosphere
Conservative Think Tanks
Dark Money Groups
Democratic Leadership Council (DLC)
Emily's List
Family Research Council
527 Organizations
Heritage Foundation
Leadership PACs
Liberal Blogosphere

Liberal Think Tanks
Media Watchdog Groups
Political Action Committees (PACs)
Super PACs

JOURNALISM ETHICS AND ISSUES

Advocacy Journalism
Balance
Citizen Journalism
Endorsements
First Amendment and Censorship
Government-Subsidized Journalism
Muckraking
Objectivity
Political Bias and the Media

MEDIA ORGANIZATIONS

ABC News
Air America
Al Jazeera America
American Communities Project
The *Atlantic*
CBS News
CNN
C-SPAN
The Daily Beast
Daily Caller
Daily Kos
Drudge Report
Face the Nation
FactCheck.org
FiveThirtyEight (538)
Fox News
Fox News Sunday
Frontline
Gallup
Gawker
The Hill
"The Hotline"
Huffington Post
McClure's Magazine
Media Matters for America
Meet the Press
Mother Jones
MSNBC
National Institute for Money in State Politics
National Journal
The *National Review*
NBC
New Republic
New York Times
Newsmax
NPR
Opensecrets.org
PBS NewsHour
Pew Research Center
Politico
ProPublica
Public Policy Polling
Rasmussen Reports
Real Clear Politics
RedState
Roll Call
Salon
60 Minutes
Slate
SurveyUSA
Talking Points Memo
TheBlaze
This Week
Time
Townhall.com
USA Today
Vox
Wall Street Journal
Washington Post
The *Weekly Standard*
Wonkette
Yahoo News
Zogby Analytics

MEDIA TRENDS

Aggregation
Anonymous Sources
Audience Fragmentation
Campaign Narratives and Dramatization
Campaign Strategy Coverage
Comedy, Satire, and Politics
Corporate Media Ownership
Data Journalism
Diversity in the Media
Echo Chamber Effect
Fact Checking
Fairness Doctrine
Feeding Frenzy
Horse-Race Journalism
Infotainment
Internet Advertising
Native Advertising
Newspaper Industry
Pack Journalism
Paywalls and the Free Flow of Information
Personalization and the Internet
Political Polarization and the Media
Primary Coverage
Public Interest Obligation
Public Opinion
Trust in Journalism
24-Hour News Cycle
Watchdog Journalism
White House Correspondents' Dinner
White House Press Corps
Women and the News Media

MEDIA TYPES

Alternative Newsmedia
Broadcast Television News
Cable News Networks
Daily Newspapers
Documentary Films
Newsmagazines
Non-Profit Journalism
Political Cartoons
Talk Radio

POLITICAL TRENDS

Access to Candidates
Ballot Access
Ballot Measures
Book Tours
Campaign Finance Reform
Campaign Narratives and Dramatization
Campaign Strategy Coverage
Citizens United
Comedy, Satire, and Politics
Cultural Conservatives
Damage Control
Disclosure
Early Voting
Grassroots Campaigns
Invisible Primary
Issue-Advocacy Advertising
Microtargeting
Negative Advertising
Photo Ops and Optics
Political Parties
Post-Truth Politics
Presidential Debates
Presidential Nominating Conventions
Primary Coverage
Red State-Blue State
Single-Issue Politics
Social Media and Politics
Sound-Bite Politics
Spin
Staging
Tea Party Movement
Television Advertising
Third Party Marginalization

Preface

Trying to explain the changing nature and scope of the shifting intersection between the media and American politics feels a bit like trying to carefully dissect and explain a jet plane in mid-flight. By its very nature, politics and the journalism that surrounds and informs that process are in the midst of the most significant transformation in the modern era, one that is still playing out during the 2016 campaign, when this work was written. To try and capture a sense of the change, I felt it was important to contextualize the issues and players shaping the modern political process by offering a look at the new developments fueled by technology and where they fit into the more than 200-year history of the republic.

To do this, *Covering American Politics in the 21st Century: An Encyclopedia of News Media Titans, Trends, and Controversies* offers more than 200 entries in two volumes. Each entry concludes with "See also" cross-references to other related entries and a bibliography of additional print and electronic information resources. Written for high school students, college undergraduates, and other interested nonspecialist readers, the entries in these volumes are loosely organized around the broad categories identified in the Guide to Related Topics, which will help readers easily and quickly trace related themes and topics across the entries.

Some entries cover the major trends that affect politics and the media. Some of these trends weigh more heavily on one sector than the other, but in some way they influence both. Whole works could be written about changes in the way we communicate and how they have separately affected journalism or the modern political campaign, but the goal of this work is to examine the trends that affect both in some way. These entries can be found listed under "Media Trends" and "Political Trends" in the Guide to Related Topics. An additional series of entries explores the ethical and legal issues within journalism and specifically political reporting and can be found under the "Journalism Ethics and Issues" category in the Guide to Related Topics.

Other elements of the book needed a deeper dive into specific types of organizations, be they think tanks that inform policy, forms of media, or elements of how campaigns are run. The goal here is to examine a specific kind of actor that influences politics and the media and explore how that type of organization functions and how it has changed over time. These categories of entries in the Guide to Related Topics include, on the political side, "Interest Groups and Political Organizations" and "Campaign Organization and Structure," and, on the media side, "Media Types."

Finally, political reporting and the modern world of campaigns are deeply affected by the major organizations that cover politics and supply the information the public consumes on political news, as well as the individuals who have come to play such a major role in the public conversations. Some of these organizations are polling firms, some traditional news outlets, and still others new forms of media and political persuasion. The groups can be found in the "Media Organizations" category of the Guide to Related Topics. For individuals, I sought to capture the people who helped create the modern form of political reporting and campaigning as well as the major voices in the public sphere. These are listed in the "Biographies" category.

Covering American Politics in the 21st Century also contains an Introduction that puts the topic into broad historical context, a Selected Bibliography of quickly accessed important general works in both print and electronic formats, and a detailed subject index to further help access information in the entries. Finally, all entries, except for those carrying a contributing byline, were written by me.

Lee Banville, February 25, 2016

Acknowledgments

Any project this large and this exhaustive (and exhausting) has a lot of people behind it who deserve the credit and to whom I owe much.

First, I need to start with the handful of contributors who helped write this work and who each brought a specialty and skill to their pieces. Michael Wright is a journalist with a fine sense of the narrative and a keen ability to craft a compelling story. I assume in the coming editions he is the kind of reporter for whom I will end up having to write a biography, but was happy to have him help me tackle everything from political cartooning to network news madness. Jule Banville brought her experience as a deputy managing editor of the *Washington City Paper* as well as her own background covering the alternative newsmedia for the Association of Alternative Newsweeklies to her exploration of the role of often-overlooked alt-weeklies to the political reporting landscape. And Jason Begay used his work as a reporter and editor as well as his experience as president of the Native American Journalist Association to help illustrate how the news media has often failed ethnic and racial minorities.

Of course the editors at ABC-CLIO deserve endless praise for working with me to help shape the prose and improve the collection. A special thanks needs to be said to Kevin Hillstrom who approached me with this project and helped me develop the entries (and come up with new ones as late as the end of 2015), and John Wagner for working on the tone and approach of the whole work.

There were also some critical institutions that helped with time and resources. On the time front, I owe a debt to the University of Montana School of Journalism. The school, especially Dennis Swibold and Larry Abramson, supported me through this project and scaled my teaching back a bit so I could tackle the scope of this project. As for resources, I had had wild visions of writing this work at the breweries and coffee shops of Missoula, Montana (of which there are quite a few of both), and nothing even close to that ever occurred. Instead, this book was written in the bowels of the Mike and Maureen Mansfield Library on the campus of the University of Montana. It seems wholly appropriate that I would be down here in a library named after the longest serving Senate majority leader in U.S. history and the man fabled political reporter David Broder once declared the politician he admired the most. I cannot tell you how invaluable the resources of a library are as you try to tell the wide variety of stories contained in this volume, and when I came across something I needed and they did not have, the staff of the library was always ready to go to any length to find it. I cannot ignore the contribution of the good folks at the UC Market who never judged just how much caffeine and how many bagels I purchased and consumed through the writing of this work.

I also need to thank the place that made me a political reporter and helped me become a professor: The *PBS NewsHour* (or *The NewsHour with Jim Lehrer* when I was there). They took a chance on a 22-year-old kid to help start their first digital news effort and for some 14 years I had the pleasure of getting up every day and trying to come up with the most compelling and relevant news I could. They let me launch podcasts and make video players, create Twitter feeds, and cook up crazy Election Day video projects with YouTube.

Finally, I have to thank my family who put up with my moodiness and crankiness while writing. Jule bore the brunt and still speaks to me. And my girls, Kate and Maggie, may be too young to know it, but they helped me step away from the book every day by insisting I play some elaborate pretend game with them.

To all of you and many more, thanks.

Introduction

It was a hell of a party.

That was what I remember of my first political convention. I was 23 and a newly minted member of the venerable PBS program that itself had just been re-minted—the *NewsHour with Jim Lehrer*. Upon joining the staff of the new digital version of the program, the Online NewsHour, I had set out to come up with some sort of project that would justify my attending one or both of the political conventions in 1996. I came up with one, a mix of website user-driven interviews with campaign officials in each location as well as a series of delegate-generated reports about the internal politics of the convention.

I had scored an invite to the biggest political story of the year and it was, literally, a party.

The sun was setting on another frighteningly perfect San Diego day as thousands of journalists strolled along the pedestrian paths of the Embarcadero. There were dozens of restaurants serving free food and beer. There was the Brian Setzer Orchestra playing as dusk settled in. This was just the media party. Sponsored by the still-thriving *San Diego Union-Tribune*, it was a testament to how a political convention was both a huge event and a source of civic and institutional pride. The major paper in the city of the convention always hosted such an event, and much of the real jockeying was to score invites to the best parties to be held that week.

But as great as the party was, it was just about over—or at least on the cusp of major changes.

The changes were everywhere. First of all, I was a reporter for the website of a television program. A website. That alone was a new phenomenon that year. Digital news was just at its beginning with a few large news organizations running their own sites, but they were still largely experimental. That year, the *New York Times* launched its first website. CNN was dominant and MSNBC was a month old. Fox News didn't exist, but it was coming. Still, the web was already rising in prominence. New digital-only publications were popping up—not Gawker or Buzzfeed, but sites like Suck and Salon and search engines like Web Crawler with its happy-looking spider that helped visitors find things on the web. The prototype of Google was still two years off. Looking back two decades later, Slate described the Internet this way: "It's 1996, and you're bored. What do you do? If you're one of the lucky people with an AOL account, you probably do the same thing you'd do in 2009: Go online. Crank up your modem, wait 20 seconds as you log in, and there you are—'Welcome.' You check your mail, then spend a few minutes chatting with your

AOL buddies about which of you has the funniest screen name (you win, pimpodayear94)" (Manjoo 2009).

The typical American with Internet access in 1996 averaged 30 minutes of web surfing a month. It truly was the dawn of the connected age, and most people were still living in the caves. But it was not just the Internet that was still in its infancy. Cell phones were still a luxury, not the norm, and those who had cell phones used them to really just make phone calls. There was no easy way to capture video or photos other than cameras, and broadcasters were still lugging U.S. Postal Service bins filled to overflowing with wide-mouth Betamax tapes. Still, that is not to say that things were not happening fast. While journalists lined the harbor to see Republican nominee Senator Bob Dole arrive with his vice presidential nominee, Internet gossip columnist Matt Drudge had already told us it would be former congressman Jack Kemp. That leak was only the beginning of a profound change in the way people communicate. Digital publishing and the explosion of mobile technology in the early 2000s would alter the news media and the world of political campaigns. Both fields are built on the idea of communicating with audiences—campaigns in hopes of inspiring voters and rallying support and journalists for attracting audiences and informing the public.

What would happen over the next 20 years is nothing short of a revolution. That year the three major campaigns—Ross Perot was running again and received federal matching funds—totaled $239.9 million. That is everyone running in the primary and the general election campaign. The presidential race in 2012 topped $2.14 billion, and that is not even counting the outside money. The average webpage took 30 seconds to load in 1996 and only 14 percent of Americans had Internet access. Now, near-ubiquitous Internet access is in most people's pockets.

You get the point. Things changed and they changed fast.

The political system is still in the middle of transitioning from what it was that night in San Diego in August 1996 to what it will be in a money-soaked, continuously connected world. The American political system has been in constant evolution, but the fundamental changes to communication have affected both that system and the media through which most of us see and understand that system. The bulk of my political reporting career has followed along with those changes, as I struggled to keep up and stay relevant in a digital media world adding new tools and possibilities all the time.

Covering American Politics in the 21st Century is an effort to document the things that appear to be shaping that transition of both journalism and politics and where the two meet. It is really the culmination of 20 years of political reporting, guiding digital news operations, and now teaching media history and modern reporting. Although the pages that follow have a lot (and I mean a lot) of information about the state of the media and politics, there is far more out there than can be captured in one piece of research and writing. Even as I wrote, venerable journals like the *New Republic* struggled to survive and apparently well-funded startups like Al Jazeera America suddenly evaporated. As I worked, a campaign unlike any other unfolded each day, with Donald Trump's 2016 White House run defying many of the long-held assumptions about momentum and negative media coverage. Still, as much as has changed, the American system remains surprisingly resilient in many ways, and so the idea of laying out the key players, the big questions, and the major controversies turned out to be more doable than it felt when I hunkered down to start writing.

You'll notice a lot of suggested readings for this book and that is on purpose. Each of these entries could be a book unto itself, so to the degree possible I have tried to identify sources and starting points for your own exploration of these topics.

As I said, a lot has changed in 20 years. I am no longer a giddy 23-year-old watching Brian Setzer on a balmy August evening as I got ready to head into my first convention, but for all the changes, the excitement of how the system works remains and I hope you'll find it on the pages that follow.

Further Reading

Manjoo, Farhad. 2009. "Jurassic Web." Slate. February 24. Accessed January 14, 2016. http://www.slate.com/articles/technology/technology/2009/02/jurassic_web.html.

N

NATIONAL INSTITUTE FOR MONEY IN STATE POLITICS

When it comes to tracking the money in national elections, reporters, voters, and political operatives can turn to many sources for raw data and analysis. When it comes to the money spent at the state level the National Institute for Money in State Politics, and their website FollowtheMoney.org, is the only game in town.

Based in Helena, Montana, the institute has tackled the unenviable job of sorting through the databases and often paper records at different state agencies in all 50 states to find out what information can be known about the funding of statewide and state legislative races. According to the nonprofit's own report, the institute maintains a "single-site, verifiable campaign-finance database of 26,000,000 records covering . . . 2000 forward. For each 2-year set of state elections, the Institute collects over 100,000 reports filed by candidates for state legislatures, high and appellate court judicial candidates and other statewide elected officials such as political party committees and ballot measure committees" (Guidestar Exchange 2013). The resulting database lives at FollowtheMoney.org, and allows reporters to search its extensive library of state-level campaign finance data. The group was organized to try and answer a simple question: Who funds politics at the state and local level? The answer turned out to be almost impossible to answer, as the institute's board member Samantha Sanchez explained, "50 different states that collect 50 different sets of data on 50 different schedules, 50 different forms and 50 different computer formats and we have to put all of that together" (MacArthur Foundation 2015). Once the group began cobbling together the reports from the different states, it was the only repository for tracking the increasing flow of money into state-level elections.

The institute is really a product of the MacArthur Foundation. The foundation in 1991 established five teams around the country to track down and digitize campaign finance records at the state level. One of those organizations was the Money in Western Politics Project and one of the people hired to run it was Ed Bender, a reporter who had worked in the Pacific Northwest. Bender would later recall, "No one had ever done this kind of stuff before: Profiles of who donated the most to legislatures as a body, as well as individuals. We had some pretty big stories, like the Nevada gaming industry. Everyone knew the gaming industry owned Nevada, but no one knew how much" (O'Connor 2012). By 1999, three of the original five groups merged at Bender's Helena location and the National Institute for Money in State Politics was born. The institute, according to its website, "does not receive financial support from government, corporations or corporate foundations; and we do not accept contributions from political parties or candidate committees" (National Institute on Money in State Politics). Although modeled on the Federal Election Commission's website and digital efforts, the institute does not receive any government support and lacks any enforcement function to require candidates or state agencies to report their numbers.

The service relies almost exclusively on foundation support—with some 95 percent of its 2014 budget coming from the Bauman Foundation, the California Endowment, the Energy Foundation, the Ford Foundation, the Hewlett Foundation, the MacArthur Foundation, the Mertz Gilmore Foundation, the Open Society Foundations, the Rockefeller Brothers Fund, the Rockefeller Family Fund, and the Sunlight Foundation. It raises the rest of the money through specific data analysis projects for media partners.

The Institute has become a focal point in the unfolding debate over the regulation of campaign spending. While the Supreme Court has struck down a number of limits on what entities can donate and spend to support or oppose a candidate, judges have often cited groups like the institute in ensuring the underlying fear of corruption needs not be a concern. In his 2014 decision in the *McCutcheon v. Federal Election Commission*, Chief Justice John Roberts wrote, "Disclosure of contributions minimizes the potential for abuse of the campaign finance system . . . [w]ith modern technology, disclosure now offers a particularly effective means of arming the voting public with information . . . Reports and databases are available on the FEC's website almost immediately after they are filed, supplemented by private entities such as OpenSecrets.org and FollowTheMoney.org." With a staff of 26, the institute continues to track donations to listed candidates but has struggled to bring the same reporting to so-called dark money groups that do not need to file official reports with most state agencies and are not required to disclose their donors.

For the most part, the institute's impact is seen through the reporting of existing news outlets. Although any interested individual can search the FollowtheMoney.org databases, the service primarily helps reporters and academic researchers more than the average voter. A 2014 report from the RAND Corporation found this to be the most effective part of the institute, arguing, "the Institute seeks to be a catalyst for greater integrity in the democratic process by providing more and better information on election funding to journalists, academics, voters, and other stakeholder groups. By collecting and facilitating access to state campaign finance information, the Institute aims to make that information more useful and, ultimately, to encourage others in sustained examination of the role and effect of money in politics" (McGovern and Greenburg 2014). But its database and datasets take some expertise to gather and analyze. Reporters who have been trained in computer assisted reporting are better equipped to search the database for connections, and many of the resulting searches need to be checked and the data cleaned up.

The site has clear strengths and a few weaknesses that are almost impossible to avoid. First on its strengths—it is the only free service that tracks money at the state level. A few states try to offer effective transparency, but no other group gathers the data from all the disparate datasets locked in state agencies across the country. Second, it does do in-depth research on the topic of money at the state level, connecting organizations and trends that may be difficult to identify in a single state or election cycle. Third, it aggressively seeks to train and work with news organizations and other groups looking to disseminate information on election spending. Despite these strengths, the key weakness is speed, or lack thereof. Because the institute must access, sort, clean and input thousands and thousands of state-based reports, data is usually at least one election cycle behind. Therefore, as opposed to telling a reporter or group what is happening in this election, it is more a resource for seeing what a group or donor or candidate has done in past campaigns.

See also: Campaign Finance Reform; Dark Money Groups; Data Journalism; Disclosure

Further Reading

GuideStar Exchange Charting Impact Report. 2013. "National Institute for Money in State Politics." November 6. Accessed June 16, 2015. http://www2.guidestar.org/report/chartingimpact/600214953/national-institute-money-state-politics.pdf.

MacArthur Foundation. 2015 MacArthur Award for Creative & Effective Institutions. Accessed June 15, 2015. http://www.macfound.org/maceirecipients/91.

McGovern, Geoffrey, and Michael Greenburg. 2014. "Shining a Light on State Campaign Finance: An Evaluation of the Impact of the National Institute on Money in State Politics." RAND Corporation. Accessed on June 16, 2015. http://www.rand.org/content/dam/rand/pubs/research_reports/RR700/RR791/RAND_RR791.pdf.

O'Connor, Maura. 2012. "National Institute on Money in State Politics: Tracking Political Donations and Their Influence in All Fifty States." *Columbia Journalism Review*. April 3. Accessed June 15, 2015. http://www.cjr.org/news_startups_guide/2012/04/national-institute-on-money-in-state-politics.php.

"Where Do We Get Our Money?" National Institute on Money in State Politics. Accessed June 14, 2016. http://classic.followthemoney.org/Institute/funding.phtml.

NATIONAL JOURNAL

For decades, *National Journal* and its family of D.C.-centric publications covered Congress and Washington with an eye toward the policy wonk side of politics, producing publications that offered lengthy and serious reporting about agencies and internal congressional matters. An effort in 2010 to reimagine the policy-focused magazine into a more politics-centered one eventually faltered and in 2015 the magazine ceased its print production to focus on its specialized set of digital products. The digital service claims to serve 3 million monthly readers and has more than 1,000 Washington-area organizations signed up as members.

National Journal built its reputation as a serious and exhaustive periodical that focused as much on the process as on the personalities and politics. And despite the many iterations and questions connected to the end of the magazine, the digital news service still provides the kind of detailed reporting that is aimed at helping lobbyists and legislative aides understand what is happening on Capitol Hill. The magazine has historically done the kind of reporting captured in one late 2015 story headlined, "The Senate Finally Passed Chemical Safety Reform. Here's How They Did It: 'Some good old fashioned legislating' helped end a years-long effort" (Plautz 2015). The mission of the publication was highlighted by editor Tim Grieve in a video aimed at advertisers, in which he said, "People hate Washington and everything they hate about Washington can be wrapped up in the way that the media covers Washington. It's the sound bites. It's the fierce partisanship that pervades both Capitol Hill and the media outlets that cover it. National Journal is different. We are not afraid to aim up rather than down. Our mission is simple, to equip lawmakers and civic-minded people all across America with the information they need to make this a better country" (National Journal).

The magazine began in 1969 and never aspired to be the popular journal of politics. With its muted, text-only covers and no-nonsense headlines, the magazine was intended for policy experts working within the capital and the federal bureaucracy. The magazine seemed intent on offering balanced, thoughtful coverage even as the nation's capital was still reeling from the violence and turbulence of the 1960s and bracing for the chaos of the Watergate scandal to come. Instead, *National Journal* would focus on the process of legislating and the facts needed to understand what was going on in the many branches of D.C. It was one of a handful of publications that sought to supply lawmakers with the information they needed to craft legislation. By 1996 the organization added The Hotline, the first real news aggregator that clipped daily newspapers and compiled a single report on the day's campaign and political news. The following year the National Journal Group was purchased by David G. Bradley. Bradley would go on to purchase the *Atlantic* in 1999 and merge the two organizations in the Atlantic Media Group.

The new organization tried several efforts to reboot the magazine, redesigning it and turning its focus to long-form reporting. But as the *National Journal* tried to move further away from its policy roots it moved closer to the turf of the *Atlantic*. Bradley would later acknowledge, "For the last five years, *The Atlantic* and *National Journal* have been in gentle competition, with two event staffs and two advertising staffs competing in this same Washington space. Serving both the membership and the general public, our editorial staff has been spread too thin" (Arana 2015). By the summer of 2015 Atlantic Media decided to pull the plug on the weekly magazine, with Bradley releasing a memo to his staff that read, "A few years back . . . distracted from *National Journal*'s work, I took both my eyes and hands off the task. In the long run, I don't think a weekly print magazine can thrive. Still, had I not failed for a time in my role, I think *National Journal* might have prospered longer" (Farhi 2015).

That decision triggered a reorganization within the entire Atlantic Media Group as the company considered how to deploy its reporting resources. Within three months, the company announced it would move almost 20 of the reporters who had worked a *National Journal* to the *Atlantic* to beef up that magazine's D.C. coverage, announcing the launch of a new Washington bureau for the remaining print publication. National Journal would complete its transformation into a digital, member-focused operation by focusing on election reporting through the National Journal Hotline and other member services, like its congressional monitoring service and leadership events aimed at serving lobbying organizations and party leaders.

Ron Brownstein, the former *Los Angeles Times* political correspondent and editorial director at *National Journal*, bemoaned the death of the magazine. Interestingly, he did not lay all the blame at the feet of the speed and demands of the 24-hour news cycle. Instead, he noted that the magazine had been "the ideal court chronicler for this extended era of bipartisan bargaining" but that the audience—Washington itself—had changed:

> I think the magazine's position deteriorated because the market for its core product eroded as our political system has grown more rigidly partisan. Fewer elected officials now follow the sequence of gathering objective information and then reaching a decision; usually they follow ideological or partisan signals to reach decisions and then seek talking points to support them. With that change, Washington reporting has evolved further toward sports reporting that partisans consult mainly to see whether their side is "winning" each day's competition. NJ could never entirely compete in that world. (Brownstein 2015)

See also: The *Atlantic*; "The Hotline"

Further Reading

"About National Journal." *National Journal*. Accessed June 14, 2016. https://www.nationaljournal.com/bp/48249/about-national-journal.

Arana, Gabriel. 2015. "The Atlantic to Launch Washington Bureau (Kinda Sorta)." Huffington Post. October 27. Accessed December 18, 2015. http://www.huffingtonpost.com/entry/the-atlantic-washington-bureau_562fb3dae4b0c66bae59aaa4.

Brownstein, Ron. 2015. "R.I.P. Facts." *National Journal*. December 11. Accessed December 18, 2015. http://www.nationaljournal.com/next-america/newsdesk/facts-r-i-p?mref=home_top_side_2.

Farhi, Paul. 2015. "Another Print Casualty: National Journal to End Print Magazine." *Washington Post*. July 16. Accessed June 14, 2016. https://www.washingtonpost.com/lifestyle/style/another-print-casualty-national-journal-to-end-print-magazine/2015/07/16/aa96607c-2bfc-11e5-a5ea-cf74396e59ec_story.html.

Plautz, Jason. 2015. "The Senate Finally Passed Chemical Safety Reform. Here's How They Did It." *The Atlantic*. December 18. Accessed June 14, 2016. http://www.theatlantic.com/politics/archive/2015/12/the-senate-finally-passed-chemical-safety-reform-heres-how-they-did-it/453069/.

NATIONAL POLITICAL CONVENTIONS

See Presidential Nomination Conventions

THE *NATIONAL REVIEW*

The year 1955 seems like it would be a conservative's dream. Ike was president. Media like the *Saturday Evening Post* espoused family-first views. Even Democrats were solidly behind national defense and the Cold War policies.

But a young conservative named William F. Buckley, Jr. was worried. He had seen staunch anti-Communist crusader Senator Joseph McCarthy taken down by the media and the political elites. So Buckley, joined by an array of elite thinking conservatives, organized the *National Review* as a magazine to give voice to political conservatism. He would write in the first edition, "Conservatives in this country . . . are non-licensed nonconformists; and this is dangerous business in a Liberal world, as every editor of this magazine can readily show by pointing to his scars. Radical conservatives in this country have an interesting time of it, for when they are not being suppressed or mutilated by the Liberals, they are being ignored or humiliated by a great many of those of the well-fed Right, whose ignorance and amorality have never been exaggerated for the same reason that one cannot exaggerate infinity" (Buckley 1955).

The magazine that took shape drew heavily from the anti-Communist ranks as well as from Catholic conservatives and libertarians. The tone was serious and intensely literate, as much about conservative philosophy as the day's events. It sought, even in the first edition, to outline a conservative vision for government, with Buckley writing, "It is the job of centralized government (in peacetime) to protect its citizens' lives, liberty and property. All other activities of government tend to diminish freedom and hamper progress. The growth of government (the dominant social feature of this century) must be fought relentlessly. In this great social conflict of the era, we are, without reservations, on the libertarian side" (Buckley 1955). And in this self-anointed role, the magazine and Buckley sought both to rally conservatives and to call out those aspects connected to conservatism that the editors saw as not true to the cause.

The magazine, with Buckley at the helm, would chart a course for the conservative movement. A lengthy report from the Heritage Foundation would cite Buckley and his magazine as one of the sources of modern political thought, finding that "slowly but steadily, Buckley constructed a strategy with the following objectives: Keep the Republican Party—the chosen political vehicle of conservatives—tilted to the Right; eliminate any and all extremists from the movement; flay and fleece the liberals at every opportunity; and push hard for a policy of victory over Communism in the Cold War" (Edwards 2010). This meant the magazine at times took on mainstream elements of its own party, criticizing President Eisenhower, rejecting the segregation arguments of George Wallace, and famously taking on the ultra-conservative John Birch Society.

Historian George Nash argues in his 1976 book *The Conservative Intellectual Movement since 1955* that "the history of reflective conservatism in America after 1955 is the history of the individuals who collaborated in—or were discovered by the magazine William F. Buckley Jr. founded" (Nash 1976). Indeed, the magazine helped champion many of the figures who would become the mainstays of the modern Republican Party. Whether it was supporting conservative Barry Goldwater in 1964 or giving future president Ronald Reagan space to explain the glaring Goldwater defeat by writing, "All of the landslide majority did not vote against the conservative ideology; they voted against a false image our Liberal opponents successfully mounted" (Reagan 2004), the magazine helped the conservative movement find its voice and develop its philosophy.

But the magazine is not just a tome of conservative philosophy, it is also a media entity that has been affected by the digital revolution. The magazine has adapted to appeal to a new wave of conservatives. It created the National Review Online (NRO) in 1995 as a new division of the *National Review* brand. By 2000, Howard Kurtz described the result as an effective use of the new media, writing, "While most media outlets essentially try and clone themselves on the Internet, National Review Online has created a split personality—with pop culture as the hook for drawing readers who may not be addicted to politics" (Kurtz 2000). The site, according to its 2015 media kit, attracts 4.5 million unique visitors a month, far more than the 150,000 subscribers to the magazine (The National Review Media Kit).

Still some have seen the magazine shift in its tone and coverage since its founding. They argue that to keep its position in the conservative ranks it must appeal to the more hardline social and cultural conservatives like those in the John Birch Society that Buckley once scorned. "The ideological descendants of the Birchers have since taken their revenge. Today they are the conservative movement's most passionate supporters and foot soldiers. But they demand a steady diet of red meat, and National Review now exists in part to provide it" (Linker 2014).

Although the magazine must continue to attract conservative subscribers, it has also diversified its offerings, aiming to connect with audiences in different ways. It spun off an institute to convene discussions and uphold the mission that Buckley espoused, seeking to bring together a diverse array of conservative voices, or as institute president Lindsay Young Craig wrote, "to unite a broad coalition of those who believed that a free society best nurtures the individual and the culture at large" (National Review Institute 2015). That original mission sits alongside a modern entity that lends its name to cultural offerings like the National Review Cruises and the National Review Wine Club.

Further Reading

Buckley, William F., Jr. 1955. "Our Mission Statement." *The National Review*. November 19. Accessed January 19, 2015. http://www.nationalreview.com/articles/223549/our-mission-statement/william-f-buckley-jr.

Edwards, Lee. 2010. "Standing Athwart History: The Political Thought of William F. Buckley Jr." The Heritage Foundation. May 5. Accessed January 19, 2015. http://www.heritage.org/research/reports/2010/05/standing-athwart-history-the-political-thought-of-william-f-buckley-jr.

Kurtz, Howard. 2000. "Online National Review Thrives on Offbeat View." *Milwaukee Journal-Sentinel*. July 13. Accessed January 20, 2015. http://news.google.com/newspapers?nid=1683&dat=20000713&id=fzUpAAAAIBAJ&sjid=ry8EAAAAIBAJ&pg=6836,1710247.

Linker, Damon. 2014. "Is National Review Doomed?" *The Week*. January 30. Accessed January 20, 2015. http://theweek.com/articles/451963/national-review-doomed.
Nash, George. 1976. *The Conservative Intellectual Movement in America since 1955*. New York: Basic Books.
National Review and National Review Online. 2015 Media Kit. Accessed January 20, 2015. http://www.nationalreview.com/sites/default/files/2015_NR-NRO_MediaKit.pdf.
National Review Institute. Accessed January 20, 2015. http://nrinstitute.org.
Reagan, Ronald. 2004. *Tear Down This Wall: The Reagan Revolution—A National Review History*. London: Continuum Publishing.

NATIVE ADVERTISING

Native advertising aims to break down the rigid separation between advertising and content, blending stories, messaging, and advertising together in a way many worry erodes the wall between editorial content and the business efforts to attract new money. For advertisers, it creates content that often resonates better with their target audience by being less aggressive in its sales pitch, building a sort of brand identity. For the media, it has emerged as one of the most profitable forms of advertising, helping struggling companies fill the void left by the flight of other advertising dollars. Both marketers and media firms have so far approached political native ads carefully, not wanting to cause a furor with readers or viewers, but the campaigns are exploring how to use this form of communication for their advantage.

The rise of native advertising has almost everything to do with the meager rate of return advertisers and publishers can garner from "traditional" digital ads. These ads, usually banners along the top of a webpage or display ads along the right side of the page, were the dominant form of Internet advertising for the first decade of the commercial web. Publishers can charge per view, a rate called CPMs (cost per thousand views), or by the number of times someone clicked on the ad (called a click-through). But the problem was they did not work that well. Click-throughs could be counted in the tenths of one percent and CPM rates usually hovered around 10 cents for a thousand impressions, meaning sites needed huge traffic to bring in the equivalent of a print or television revenue rate—more like $10 CPM for television and $5.50 for newspapers. Put simply, Internet advertising could only raise a small fraction of the traditional advertising revenue publishers counted on to turn a profit.

Enter native advertising, bringing in far more revenue and generating new business models for emerging digital publishers. The king of this world is BuzzFeed, the social media-focused news and information site known for its listicles and animated gifs. The site employs 40 people in its native advertising operation to work with brands to develop sponsored posts on the site like "15 People Share Tales of Living with a Computer-Illiterate Family" (sponsored by Best Buy) and "50 'Merica Things That'll Make You Say 'Merica" (sponsored by the U.S. Army). The model is the only source of revenue for BuzzFeed, but venture capitalists have poured money into the site as most see the model as set to succeed and grow. Jonah Peretti, the head of BuzzFeed, described its approach to advertising by looking at the behavior of his readers. Peretti told a conference in 2012, "With younger consumers, it's, 'I want advertising that I want to share or click, to engage with instead of advertising that forces me to watch it before I get what I want'" (Kim 2012). The concept has become such a major focus of digital advertising that the Interactive Advertising Bureau, the group that established regular ad units for the Internet from the very beginning of display ads, formed a task force to establish a uniform set of standards and to even come up with common definitions of what is native advertising. In its 20-page booklet on the subject, it explains the source of confusion about native advertising, saying it "is a concept encompassing both an aspiration as well as a suite of ad products. It is clear that most advertisers and publishers aspire to deliver paid ads that are so cohesive with the page content, assimilated into the design, and consistent with the platform behavior that the viewer simply feels that they belong" (IAB 2013).

Put even more simply, the idea that advertising on the Internet would be locked into the right side of a page or the top banner on a site is quickly becoming a thing of the past. The native advertising movement enables strong news brands to market themselves to advertisers as the kind of news and information source you want your product associated with, and the advertiser can try and more directly place their marketing messages within the content of major news brands. The IAB report, developed by a task force of 100 advertisers, publishers, and technology companies, outlined six forms of new merged advertising. These new forms, which included simply placing an ad in the middle of content or having it pop up at the beginning of a story, forced marketers and publishers to consider a handful of critical questions:

- Form—How does the ad fit with the overall page design? Is it in the viewer's activity stream or not in-stream?
- Function—Does the ad function like the other elements on the page in which it is placed? Does it deliver the same type of content experience (e.g., a video on a video page or story among stories) or is it different?
- Integration—How well do the ad unit's behaviors match those of the surrounding content? Are they the same, e.g., linking to an on-site story page, or are new ones introduced?
- Buying & Targeting—Is the ad placement guaranteed on a specific page, section, or site, or will it be delivered across a network of sites? What type of targeting is available?
- Measurement—What metrics are typically used to judge success? Are marketers more likely to use top-of-the-funnel brand engagement metrics (e.g., views, likes, shares, time spent) or bottom funnel ones (e.g., sale, download, data capture, register, etc.)?
- Disclosure—How is this ad product identified as such? (IAB 2013)

This all sounds fairly clear, but it is in the execution of native advertising that things get far more complicated and potentially far more damaging for media companies.

Take, for example, the *Atlantic* and the Church of Scientology. The *Atlantic* made a name for itself as a journal of letters begun in the finest traditions of New England intellectualism. As the company has moved aggressively to translate the slightly stodgy magazine to the frenetic Internet, the company added an aggressive native advertising division that accepted money to produce a piece for the church. The issue was that Scientology had come under fire in an exhaustively reported book by Lawrence Wright called *Going Clear*, which accused the church of abuse and intimidation of those who seek to leave the organization or who are too public in questioning the organization's leaders.

The Church of Scientology's response included the *Atlantic* native ad buy, which did not address the Wright allegations but rather hailed the work of the church's leader David Miscavige. The piece carried a small yellow banner that labeled the online story "Sponsored Content," but the controversial nature of the group and the heated politics of the moment meant the disclosure was not enough to prevent widespread criticism of the *Atlantic*. The company pulled the ad within 12 hours and offered up a profuse apology, saying, "We screwed up. It shouldn't have taken a wave of constructive criticism—but it has—to alert us that we've made a mistake, possibly several mistakes. We now realize that as we explored new forms of digital advertising, we failed to update the policies that must govern the decisions we make along the way. It's safe to say that we are thinking a lot more about these policies after running this ad than we did beforehand. In the meantime, we have decided to withdraw the ad until we figure all of this out. We remain committed to and enthusiastic about innovation in digital advertising, but acknowledge—sheepishly—that we got ahead of ourselves."

The problem of native advertising stems from the influence that the sponsor wields over the content decisions of the news organizations and the increasingly sophisticated efforts to essentially camouflage advertising content as editorial content. The Federal Trade Commission, the agency charged with regulating and punishing misleading commercial claims, has dealt with questions like native advertising for years. Long before the current fad of digital creativity, magazines and newspapers published what were called "advertorials," inserts that appeared like editorial content but were paid for by a supporter or advertisers. On television, the form of these early native advertising efforts was the infomercial, built to look like a talk show but strangely in love with a single product. These advertorials and infomercials triggered a wave of rules from the FTC that aimed to ensure that the readers and viewers would not be tricked into believing the material was objectively reported. So the FTC brings many of these same attitudes and beliefs to the question of native advertising. FTC commissioner Edith Ramirez summed up the main concern at a meeting with advertisers and publishers, "Critics argue that this practice improperly exploits consumers' trust in a publisher or deceives them outright to influence their purchasing decisions. While native advertising may certainly bring some benefits to consumers, it has to be done lawfully. The delivery of relevant messages and cultivating user engagement are important goals, that's the point of advertising after all, but it's equally important that advertising not mislead consumers. By presenting ads that resemble editorial content, an advertiser risks implying deceptively that the information comes from a non-biased source" (FTC 2013). It's more than just the FTC who has questioned the decision of traditional publishers like the *Washington Post* and *New York Times* to launch native advertising efforts. The effort has been criticized by journalists and professors, but caught even more flack when John Oliver took aim at it in a widely disseminated piece from his HBO comedy show *Last Week Tonight*. Oliver told his audience, "In news, that is seemingly the model now. Ads are baked into content like chocolate chips into a cookie. Except, it's actually more like raisins into a cookie—because nobody f—ing wants them there" (HBO 2014).

Despite these concerns, the concept of native advertising has swept digital and traditional media organizations. According to one survey of online publishers in late 2013, some 73 percent of publications offered some form of native advertising and another 17 percent said they planned to introduce those offerings. And some of the biggest media and journalism entities are fully embracing the new medium of content and marketing. The *New York Times* launched an internal studio called T Brand Studio to produce native advertising for its digital and print publications. The digital publications appear in a section called PaidPosts, but the people behind the effort say the section description and their sponsored nature of the content has done little to detract readers from engaging with it. In fact, a 2015 report found that the best performing PaidPost stories did as well as the traditional journalism on nytimes.com. The *New York Times* lead executive in charge of the effort, Michael Zimbalist, said, "'We've noted for quite some time that great stories can come from anywhere, and certainly from brands. This is part of the proof point that audiences will engage with great content regardless of its provenance, provided they have a sense of where it's coming from" (Wegert 2015).

So it's not surprising that campaigns, like any other marketing effort, are exploring how and when to use native advertising to try and reach potential voters. As early as 2012, BuzzFeed was diving into the political arena, running sponsored content from the presidential campaigns of Barack Obama and Mitt Romney. "For campaigns, it's relatively easy: They have something they stand for, they have something they want to say, and they have a specific message they want to get out," BuzzFeed Chief Operating Officer Jon Steinberg said that year, adding, "We've only had big traction with brands in the last nine months or so. Looking forward, there's a lot we hope to do in Washington" (Ellis 2012). But BuzzFeed is not alone in the world of campaign native ads, according to the *Washington Post*'s Eric Wemple, who called Politico must-read email newsletter "The PlayBook" a pioneer in native advertising. Wemple scoured the archives of the email newsletter composed by insider Mike Allen to find examples of sponsored sections of the electronic missives. Wemple reported in 2013, "Politico recently jacked up its 'Playbook' sponsorship rates and now collects around $35,000 for a weekly sponsorship. For that price, companies get a little blurb in 'Playbook' surrounded by a disclosure that it's a paid advertisement. Though not for sale, un-sponsored shoutouts from Allen are worth even more—the ultimate in Beltway earned media" (Wemple 2013). The Playbook mentions are not new, but Wemple's reporting points to the difficulty in sometimes differentiating the paid content of the email from the sponsored.

This is the question that campaigns and publishers will grapple with: finding a way to connect the marketing effects of native advertising (potentially very successful for the campaign and lucrative for the publisher) and the potential minefield of political missteps like the Church of Scientology brought to the *Atlantic*'s door in 2013. Advertisers increasingly want to connect their brand with the news and information outlet they are advertising within, but the outlet itself must balance profit motives with the desire to maintain editorial independence. Unlike traditional print and broadcast media that could only be altered so much—an infomercial is easy to identify even if it is a slick one—the digital world allows for much more sophisticated storytelling and seamless integration between editorial content and advertising content. Another thing to consider is that often marketers approach native advertising as a way to build their own brand, rather than an explicit plea to purchase a product or support a candidate. Their desire to use native advertising to build an affinity with the audience risks becoming more complicated and murky, and less easy to distinguish from unbiased reporting, as both politicians and lobbyists explore how to deploy these tools to shape public opinion and voter sentiment. The efforts of Barack Obama in 2012 were basic and largely transparent. The efforts of a potential dark money organization may not be so clear. With few formal rules in place and little experience in finding a middle ground, the area of native advertising should be one of rapid growth, but also potential abuse, in the years to come.

See also: Internet Advertising; Social Media and Politics; Television Advertising

Further Reading

Ellis, Justin. 2012. "BuzzFeed Adapts Its Branded Content Approach to Political Advertising, and Obama's In." Nieman Lab. October 24. Accessed August 13, 2015. http://www.niemanlab.org/2012/10/buzzfeed-adapts-its-branded-content-approach-to-political-advertising-and-obamas-in.

Federal Trade Commission. 2013. "Blurred Lines: Advertising or Content: An FTC Workshop on Native Advertising." Accessed August 13, 2015. https://www.ftc.gov/news-events/events-calendar/2013/12/blurred-lines-advertising-or-content-ftc-workshop-native.

Interactive Advertising Bureau. 2013. "The Native Advertising Playbook." Accessed August 14, 2015. http://www.iab.net/media/file/IAB-Native-Advertising-Playbook2.pdf.

Kim, Ryan. 2012. "BuzzFeed's Peretti: Design engaging ads made for sharing." Gigaom. April 17. Accessed August 13, 2015. https://gigaom.com/2012/04/17/buzzfeeds-peretti-design-engaging-ads-made-for-sharing.

"Last Week Tonight with John Oliver." 2014. August 3. Accessed August 14, 2015. https://www.youtube.com/watch?v=E_F5GxCwizc.

Wegert, Tessa. 2015. "Why the New York Times' Sponsored Content Is Going Toe-to-Toe with Its Editorial." Contently. March 27. Accessed August 14, 2015. http://contently.com/strategist/2015/03/27/why-the-new-york-times-sponsored-content-is-going-toe-to-toe-with-its-editorial.

Wemple, Eric. 2013. "Politico Boss: Mika, Joe & Co. Rock." *Washington Post*. October 3. Accessed August 14, 2015. https://www.washingtonpost.com/blogs/erik-wemple/wp/2013/10/03/politico-boss-mika-joe-co-rock.

NBC

The Peacock has seen it all, and it has shown it to the world. From World War II to the Kennedy Assassination, from the Watergate Scandal to the Iraq War, the National Broadcasting Company has been a leading outlet for Americans to turn to for their news. They tuned in first on their radios, later on television, and now online. NBC's storied past has been a boon for the network, but it hasn't been all sunshine and daisies. While its evening news program has kept its place as the biggest draw for nighttime network news audience, NBC is behind its competitors in other categories, like morning and news magazine show audience. And despite its still sizeable impact on broadcasting and news, the NBC of today is a shadow of the once dominant radio network.

The famous "Peacock" logo and iconic tones of the company are unmistakable, but NBC's impact on the world of journalism is even more memorable. It was the brainchild of the giant of American broadcasting—David Sarnoff. Sarnoff had worked for some of the earliest radio broadcasters, the Marconi Company, communicating with ships at sea. But Sarnoff saw a different future where people would have personal radios that could receive news, lectures, and music broadcast from a central network. Marconi passed, but another firm, the Radio Corporation of America (RCA), backed the young man and the National Broadcasting Company became the nation's first permanent radio network in 1926. RCA purchased a New York City radio station from AT&T for $1 million to place the cornerstone of what would become a national powerhouse. An RCA advertisement for the new network boasted of what it would be: "*National radio broadcasting* with better programs permanently assured by this important action of the *Radio Corporation of America* in the interest of the listening public" (nbcuniversal.com, n.d.).

At first, it was split into two separate networks. The Red Network was for music and entertainment, the Blue for news. Both focused on the East Coast, but not long after they were up and running, NBC expanded to the West. There, what were called the Orange and Gold networks ran many of the same programs. Yet, in the early days of network radio broadcasting, there were worries about allowing one company to hold a monopoly of the potentially potent broadcasting networks. Government pressure forced RCA to split from its parent General Electric in the 1930s. Later, and more significantly, RCA was forced to sell one of the networks in 1943. It chose the less popular Blue Network, which eventually became NBC's competitor, ABC.

By the time that happened, though, NBC had already established itself as a major player in television in addition to radio. In 1939, it broadcast the New York World's Fair's opening ceremonies, marking the beginning of its commitment to television. In the early 1940s, it showed the first televised newscast. But unlike the specialized and graphic-laden television newscasts of today, NBC simply simulcast Lowell Thomas' nightly radio news broadcast. It was a modest beginning, but the evening news would become a staple. NBC went through a few news-program iterations, like the *NBC Tele-News Reel*, which showed movie newsreels. The *Camel News Caravan*, which the R.J. Reynolds Tobacco Company sponsored, was a 15-minute show that used filmed NBC news stories, one of the first programs to do so. It was replaced by Chet Huntley and David Brinkley with the *Huntley-Brinkley Report* in 1956 (Shedden 2006). The new nightly news program launched just after two of the company's other signature programs—*Meet the Press* in 1947 and the *Today* show in 1952—expanded the news footprint in the broadcast schedule into the weekend and weekday mornings.

In the mid-1950s and into the 1960s the network's then-president Robert E. Kintner, former reporter and columnist himself, "pushed constantly for expanded budgets for news operations" (Smith 1980). Kintner wanted "round-the-clock" live coverage after John F. Kennedy was assassinated in November of 1963, a decision that led to NBC filming Jack Ruby shooting Lee Harvey Oswald to death (Smith 1980).

The *Huntley-Brinkley Report* helped cement the network's credibility in news, winning it back some of the momentum lost to Edward R. Murrow and CBS during World War II and the Red Scare. The anchor duo was chosen for the job after impressing network executives with their coverage of the 1956 political conventions. For 14 years, the pair garnered impressive ratings. With Huntley reporting from New York and Brinkley from Washington, D.C., the show often beat out formidable foes such as Walter Cronkite at CBS. The success helped inspire NBC to double the length of the evening newscasts from 15 minutes to 30. The Huntley-Brinkley team also fueled a national interest in politics. In a *New York Times* obituary for Brinkley, Richard Severo wrote that former president Bill Clinton had credited the show with spurring his own interest in politics (Severo 2003). But perhaps the team's most significant contribution to NBC was establishing one of its foundational programs—and the one that would produce some of its biggest stars. The *Huntley-Brinkley Report* was followed by *NBC Nightly News*, which Brinkley anchored until the 1980s. Tom Brokaw followed him as anchor, and Brian Williams came next.

The anchors of these evening programs offered the average citizen a window to the rest of the world and the inner workings of governments both in the United States and abroad. NBC remains the leader in that type of programming and is enjoying renewed audience growth, even as the digital age intensifies the competition for eyes. The Pew Research Center put NBC's average evening audience at 8.9 million in 2015, a 6 percent increase from the previous year and nearly a million more than ABC, which took second place (Pew 2015). The prominence of the evening program and its celebrity anchors is at least partially a result of their journalistic prowess and poise. Brokaw, for example, was one of the first journalists to report that the Berlin Wall was going to come down in 1989. He interviewed Russian presidents, the Dalai Lama, and helped anchor the network's coverage of the September 11, 2001, terrorist attacks.

But, however famous and trusted they may be, these anchors are not infallible. Brian Williams, who took over for Brokaw in 2004, came under fire in 2015 over revelations that he had fabricated an oft-repeated story from his coverage of the Iraq War in 2003. He was suspended from NBC for six months and later removed from the *Nightly News* anchor chair permanently. Throughout the controversy, the opinions on what exactly should be done with Williams ranged wildly. David Carr wrote in the *New York Times* that the unique combination of fame and national trust heaped upon nightly news anchors, the demand for them to be exemplary performers, is a lot to ask. "It's a job description that no one can match," Carr wrote (Carr 2015). Lester Holt became the new anchor in June 2015, and Williams was reassigned to MSNBC. Holt has kept the program atop the heap of network evening news, as it posted an average of about 8.7 million viewers in the last quarter of 2015 (Fitzgerald 2016).

Other offerings from NBC have been less successful than *Nightly News*. The newsmagazine program *Dateline NBC* is well behind CBS's *60 Minutes* in terms of audience. Two of the network's most famous and longest-running programs, *Today* and *Meet the Press*, have also been consistently behind their network competitors (Pew 2015). It has interests in two cable channels, the business network CNBC and the politics-focused MSNBC. While CNBC has been successful at establishing itself as one of the premier sources for financial news, MSNBC has lagged in ratings behind cable competitors CNN and Fox News. In its transition to the digital age, NBCnews.com has been one of the most popular destinations for news consumers to turn to, offering both video and written stories online, but hasn't emerged as a leader in that realm.

Still, some 90 years on, NBC remains one of the premier news organizations in the country, and is likely to keep that status for years to come.

Michael Wright

See also: Broadcast Television News; *Meet the Press*; Russert, Tim

Further Reading

Carr, David. 2015. "Brian Williams, Retreading Memories from a Perch Too Public." *New York Times*. February 8. Accessed January 6, 2016. http://www.nytimes.com/2015/02/09/business/media/brian-williams-and-memories-retread-from-a-perch-too-public.html.

Fitzgerald, Toni. 2016. "Surprise, the Nightly News Is Actually Growing." medialifemagazine.com. January 6. Accessed January 6, 2016. http://www.medialifemagazine.com/surprise-nightly-news-actually-growing.

Fletcher, Dan. 2009. "A Brief History of NBC." *Time*. December 4. Accessed January 6, 2016. http://content.time.com/time/arts/article/0,8599,1945408,00.html.
"Our History." nbcuniversal.com. Accessed January 6, 2016. http://www.nbcuniversal.com/our-history.
Severo, Richard. 2003. "David Brinkley, 82, Newsman Model, Dies." *New York Times*. June 13. Accessed January 6, 2016. http://www.nytimes.com/2003/06/13/us/david-brinkley-82-newsman-model-dies.html?pagewanted=1.
Shedden, David. 2006. "Early TV Anchors," poynter.org. April 4. Accessed January 6, 2016. http://www.poynter.org/2006/early-tv-anchors/74607.
Smith, J. Y. 1980. "Robert E. Kintner, Ex-Head of ABC and NBC Radio and TV, Dies." *Washington Post*. December 23. Accessed January 6, 2016. https://www.washingtonpost.com/archive/local/1980/12/23/robert-e-kintner-ex-head-of-abc-and-nbc-radio-and-tv-dies/dac9cafe-dcf4-4349-93ff-147d43eb9106.
"State of the News Media 2015." 2015. Pew Research Center. April 29. Accessed January 6, 2016. http://www.journalism.org/2015/04/29/network-news-fact-sheet.

NEGATIVE ADVERTISING

Every election cycle the negative tone of advertising comes under scrutiny from the media, voters, and academics. "Attack ads" that question the policies, personality, and qualifications of candidates are blamed for depressing voter turnout, increasing cynicism among the public, and cheapening the public dialogue. Efforts to regulate these ads included forcing the candidate to publicly state that they have "endorsed this message" in hopes toning down rhetoric and increase the quality of information produced. But as so-called dark money and other outside groups have poured money into campaign advertising, much of that spending has gone to negative advertising. The result is that for people living in states with competitive presidential, gubernatorial, or congressional elections, the deluge of negative ads has become a fact of life. Still, they remain a deeply divisive element of American politics.

Researchers and media commentators blast the use of negative campaigning, pinning much of the blame on advertising spots that flood television networks and are microtargeted to web users. These ads, which make hundreds of millions of dollars for local television broadcasters and cable companies, have been connected to lower voter turnout. Political scientists argue that the negative messages of the ads can depress support for the targeted politician, increase disenchantment with both parties, and diminish the civic activity of the viewer by increasing cynicism. The problem, two political science scholars noted in their book on the issue, is that negative advertising plays well within the media ecosystem of a campaign. They note, "The negative tenor of campaigns can be traced to the competitive nature of political advertising, to the activities of organized interests, and, last but not least, to the ways in which reporters cover the campaign. Politicians, interest groups, and journalists all act in ways that serve their own best interests. Few of these players really want to produce highly negative campaigns, but the interplay among them produces the kind of campaigns that voters have come to loathe" (Ansolabehere and Iyengar 1995). These researchers note that when one campaign runs an ad that seems to question the qualifications or positions of one candidate, that candidate almost inherently punches back, defending themselves and raising questions about their opponent. The news media plays into this as well, running the ad and dissecting its content, which often encourages campaigns to run the ad to begin with to benefit from the free media they expect to receive. Finally, outside groups, which have benefited from a series of Supreme Court decisions, are free to use their unlimited resources to attack a candidate.

Attack ads are not hard to spot. In the past 30 years they have come to often look the same—a grainy black and white photo of the offending politician, a damning quote or statistic, menacing music in the background, and tiny print at the bottom of the screen that sources the damning information. But to call the advertisement an "attack" implies that there is something aggressive, mean-spirited, and even untruthful in the information conveyed in the ad. This is one of the first problems with the tackling the issue of negative advertising: What is negative? The former editor-in-chief of *Campaigns & Elections* magazine, who has a more sanguine view of attack ads, notes that "what constitutes negative campaigning is usually a matter of perspective; tactics that to one voter may seem misleading, mean-spirited, and immoral can impart to another important and relevant information about how the candidate would perform under the pressures of public office. Negative campaigning, like beauty, is in the eye of the beholder" (Mark 2006). Negative ads often raise questions about the voting record of one candidate, criticize their public statements or accuse them of not living up to their public statements. In fact, David Mark, in his book *Going Dirty*, argues that all candidates must, to some degree, go negative to win an election. Challengers hoping to unseat an incumbent in a primary or general election must raise questions about how the current seat-holder has failed the voters because why toss them out otherwise? Similarly, an incumbent facing a serious challenge has to explain why they are better qualified to remain in office. Any ads that make these cases can be construed as negative because they argue one candidate is clearly better than the other. Marks's assessment aside, usually in public opinion polls it is personal attacks that the public reacts most negatively to; so-called issue ads, even if hard-hitting, are seen as within the bounds of a normal campaign.

But despite the hand wringing over negative ads there is one compelling fact that makes them a likely permanent part of the campaign—they seem to work.

A meta-analysis of past experiments and research papers connected to negative ads and campaigning noted that viewers clearly remembered the messages, and that there was no demonstrable effect on the likelihood of a person to vote in the election. This research seemed to conclude that negative ads will not keep someone from voting and that they can deliver key messages that will stay with a voter long after the airing.

But beyond the science, politicians also clearly imbue negative ads with real political power. One of the first ads that drew the attention of journalists for its hard-hitting tone and negative light it threw on the opponent was the so-called Willie Horton ad from the 1988 presidential campaign. The ad, released by a political action committee connected to Vice President George H. W. Bush, documented how a prison furlough program allowed under Democratic candidate Michael Dukakis had released a convicted murder for a weekend. Willie Horton then committed a brutal assault and rape while out, and the ad connected the attacks to Dukakis's prison policy and his generally being soft on crime. Dukakis dismissed the ad as so negative and potentially racist that the public and news media would reject it.

They didn't. The key message of being wrong on criminal justice issues stuck. It is a message that Dukakis said may have cost him the presidency. He later told NPR, "I thought people were tired of a lot of the polarization that was taking place . . . and basically just said, 'We're not going to respond to those attacks.' It was a terrible mistake . . . You can't do what I did . . . [because] if you do that, you're going to be hurt and you're going to be hurt badly" (NPR 2012).

But still, people express deep reservations about negative campaigns, telling pollsters they wish that candidates would choose to focus on positive messages of what he or she would do if elected. But those who have studied political communication stress that is not an easy case for most candidates to make. The reason often has to do with the voters themselves. It is easier for the campaign to make the case why the other candidate is bad—too liberal, too wealthy, too out-of-touch—compared to proposing a series of specific positions that the candidate intends to enact. Those who studied campaigning in both the United States and the newly democratic Russia noted that both Reagan and Yeltsin had been forced to cast their opponents in negative lights despite their very different systems and different campaigns. As they noted, "Because voters hold different views of how government should function, campaigners are driven to use negative messages rather than positive arguments. Positive statements of policy intent must be crafted as not to alienate people who might otherwise have voted for the candidate. But any clear policy statement is likely to alienate at least some voters. Therefore, at the first sign that such messages are costing support from more voters than are being attracted, the message must be abandoned" (Skinner, Kudelia, Bueno de Mesquita, and Rice 2008).

In the place of these messages, campaigns seek to find themes that will increase the public's positive perception of their candidate and raise potential doubts about their competitor. Therefore campaign messages are crafted that stress their candidate's personal biography and professional experience. Many ads in favor of a candidate offer little insight into their positions other than their support for families and the middle class. Instead, business experience is emphasized, their own families are noted, and connections to locally popular figures stressed. But as other research has noted, these messages do not stay with a viewer as much as the negative messages of why a voter should be concerned about the other candidate.

It is more than just the fractured nature of the electorate that facilitates negative campaigning. It is the media itself and how its coverage of the campaign can inadvertently serve the messaging goals of the campaigns. A negative ad can trigger a wave of reporting about the ad, its content, and its impact, all of which serves to amplify the original message. For example, one of the most powerful political ads ever developed was a "negative" ad that only aired once. The "Daisy" ad was conceived of by the campaign of President Lyndon Johnson as a way to emphasize the dangerous extremism of Republican senator Barry Goldwater. Goldwater, in accepting the Republican Party's nomination, had stressed, "Extremism in the defense of liberty is no vice. And let me remind you also that moderation in the pursuit of justice is no virtue." Two years earlier, the Soviet Union and United States had been at the brink of nuclear war during the 1962 Cuban missile crisis. Johnson and his team were well aware of the public's concern about the possibility of nuclear war and that served as the backdrop for the ad. The ad, which ran a full minute, aired during NBC's *Movie of the Week*. It opened, without voiceover or text, on a young girl plucking petals from a flower and counting from one to nine. When she reached nine the screen froze and began a slow zoom in on the girl's pupil as a mission control countdown started at ten. When the voice reached zero and the girl's pupil filled the screen the image changed to a massive hydrogen bomb explosion and then President Johnson's voice intoned, "These are the stakes: to make a world in which all of God's children can live, or to go into the dark. We must either love each other. Or we must die." Finally an announcer came on to add "Vote for President Johnson on Nov. 3. The stakes are too high for you to stay home." Professor of political advertising Drew Babb called the ad the "Mother of All Attack Ads" in the *Washington Post*, writing, "They used every weapon in their arsenal. They grabbed for viewers' hearts with an adorable little girl (commercial actress Monique Corzilius). They tapped into viewers' greatest nightmare with footage of a huge mushroom-shaped cloud. (Remember, this was less than two years after the Cuban missile crisis.) They reinforced the visuals with intrusive sound effects (provided by the genius sound engineer Tony Schwartz). They had Johnson read a snippet of spiritual poetry (by W.H. Auden). And they hired a voice-of-God baritone (sports announcer Chris Schenkel) to wrap things up" (Babb 2014).

The Johnson campaign expected Republicans would, well, go ballistic. And they did. They accused the Democrats of fear mongering and demanded they stop airing the ad. And this is where the media began factoring into the campaign's use of attack ads. The ad itself was suddenly a story and the other campaign was firing back. The Johnson campaign pulled the ad, but news segments on CBS, ABC, and again on NBC re-aired it. Now all three networks—there were only three—ran the ad and dug into the claims and counter-claims. The message of Goldwater's extremism was conveyed for free by news organizations covering the controversy. Campaign consultants saw the "Daisy" ad as both a powerful message and an effective way to earn "free" or "earned" media—the term often ascribed the journalistic media coverage. By going negative and prompting a response from the other campaign, these ads often serve as made-for-journalists stories that allow the campaign to amplify the message of the original ad without having to pay.

While media have worked to dissect negative ads through ad watches and fact checking, election laws and legislation have also profoundly affected the environment around which ads are developed and aired. When the long, tortured debate over campaign finance reform appeared headed to a historic victory in 2002, it included a reform-minded provision aimed at making candidates more responsible for the advertising aired by their campaigns. The "Stand by Your Ad" provision (SBYA) required:

> a statement that identifies the candidate and states that the candidate has approved the communication. Such statement—
> (I) shall be conveyed by—
> (I) an unobscured, full-screen view of the candidate making the statement, or
> (II) the candidate in voice-over, accompanied by a clearly identifiable photographic or similar image of the candidate; and
> (II) shall also appear in writing at the end of the communication in a clearly readable manner with a reasonable degree of color contrast between the background and the printed statement, for a period of at least 4 seconds.

The result was that ads aired by the campaign ended with some version of the candidate saying something like "I approve this message." This provision only applied to television ads, but it was still seen as a victory for connecting negative campaign ads directly to the candidate.

However, unintended consequences of the campaign reform act would ensue. The act triggered a wave of lawsuits that would also fundamentally change the campaign landscape and fuel a new wave of negative advertising, a wave not directly connected to the campaign. Lawsuits such as *Citizens United* created new Super PACs that could raise and spend unlimited funds in support of a candidate so long as they disclosed their donors and did not coordinate with the campaign. Campaigns have tried to test the idea of "no coordination" by uploading raw footage of their candidates to YouTube and releasing public schedules months in advance; the Super PAC then has all the material it needs to create ads and show up to support events. This process is easier with attack ads. Super PACs can work with research groups funded by other Super PACs to produce ads that attack the desired candidate's opponent. Beyond Super PACs, newer political nonprofits known as "dark money" groups can also produce issue attack ads that attack an issue and, by implication, a candidate. These ads cannot expressly call for the candidate's defeat, but can be funded by money anonymously donated to the "social welfare" groups.

Every campaign season sees letters to the editor, blogs, and candidates pleading for an end to the negative attack ads. Yet campaigns will always want to draw differences between the candidates' biographies, political beliefs, and professional experiences. A campaign's job is to convince the voter that candidate X deserves their vote and, just as importantly, that candidate Y does not. That process must be in part a negative casting of the opponent as not like the constituents they want to represent. The degree to which this criticism is merited and the way in which it is executed is where the debate over attack ads comes in. Media critics contend the current campaign system has intensified the negativity of campaigns. Most money for attack ads now flows not to candidates who must "approve" their attack ads on screen or in voiceovers, but to Super PACs or dark money groups that can spend enormous amounts on ads, lobbing heavy attacks while shielding their preferred candidate from responsibility. Candidates now routinely find themselves publically renouncing an advertisement being run by an independent group that has "crossed a line." Even as efforts to combat negative ads by forcing candidates to endorse them took hold, new laws around campaign finance have created a form of attack ads that the candidate cannot (or cannot appear to) control. What it all means is attack ads both online and on-air will continue.

See also: Campaign Finance Reform; Issue-Advocacy Advertising; Television Advertising

Further Reading

All Things Considered. 2012. "Putting a Positive Spin on Negative Campaigning." NPR. June 23. Accessed December 28, 2015. http://www.npr.org/2012/06/23/155636624/putting-a-positive-spin-on-negative-campaigning.

Ansolabehere, Stephen, and Shanto Iyengar. 1995. *Going Negative: How Political Advertisements Shrink and Polarize the Electorate*. New York: Free Press.

Babb, Drew. 2014. "LBJ's 1964 Attack Ad 'Daisy' Leaves a Legacy for Modern Campaigns." *Washington Post*. September 5. Accessed December 28, 2015. https://www.washingtonpost.com/opinions/lbjs-1964-attack-ad-daisy-leaves-a-legacy-for-modern-campaigns/2014/09/05/d00e66b0-33b4-11e4-9e92-0899b306bbea_story.html.

Mark, David. 2006. *Going Dirty: The Art of Negative Campaigning*. Lanham, MD: Rowman & Littlefield Publishers.

Skinner, Kiron, Serhiy Kudelia, Bruce Bueno de Mesquita, and Condoleezza Rice. 2008. *The Strategy of Campaigning: Lessons from Ronald Reagan and Boris Yeltsin*. Ann Arbor: University of Michigan Press.

NEW REPUBLIC

Almost since its inception the *New Republic* was the standard-bearer of modern liberalism in politics, emerging early in the twentieth century as a leading journal of progressive politics. The magazine had just marked its 100th anniversary in late 2014 when it went through the most violent internal shakeup in its history. A dispute between the owner, Facebook co-founder Chris Hughes, and the editorial staff prompted some two-thirds of the editors and writers to quit. In the wake of the changes, the magazine has re-emerged as a journal that, while adhering to its past interest in liberal politics, has narrowed its focus to a handful of topics like climate change and literature and more specific items like advocating for paid leave.

The magazine, originally founded to "bring sufficient enlightenment to the problems of the nation," faced a dire economic situation in 2014. For more than a decade the publication had been losing money and by 2011 the group of wealthy patrons who had kept the magazine afloat decided to sell. The new owner, Hughes, wanted to reinvigorate the magazine in much the same way that the *Atlantic* had overhauled itself from a stodgy magazine into a vibrant digital news venue. At the *New Republic*, most of the editorial staff viewed that transition with skepticism, worried that the in-depth reporting and investigative work would be cast aside in an attempt to draw clicks. The tensions had been mounting until the explosive shakeup in 2014. Hughes forced Franklin Foer, who had edited the magazine for a decade, out. In the same move, Hughes announced the magazine would leave Washington, D.C., for New York, and that the publishers would cut in half the number of print editions of the magazine, aiming to become a "vertically integrated digital-media company" (Folkenflik 2014).

The staff responded by quitting en masse—over two-thirds of the staff listed on the masthead resigned on the spot. The remainder headed into a surreal meeting with the CEO and Hughes joining via teleconference. The *New Yorker*'s Ryan Lizza, who had made a name for himself at the magazine he was now reporting on, described the chaos that ensued, writing that Hughes "sounded angry and emotional. Staffers in New York told me that he welled up as he spoke. He told colleagues later that he was unprepared for the scale of the resignations and depth of the protest, especially from people who he had spent the past two years cultivating. In the meeting, Hughes described the changes in the magazine's frequency and editorship, but insisted that a radical transformation into a digital-media company with a greater emphasis on profits did not mean that the *New Republic*, which was co-founded by Walter Lippmann, would devolve into a click-bait factory" (Lizza 2014).

Many in the media bemoaned the developments, accusing Hughes of casting aside what made the *New Republic* unique, trying to turn a small-circulation, erudite journal of politics and culture into a tech company more like Gawker than the *Utne Reader*. The magazine had to cancel its December edition since it did not have enough staffers to put the publication together, and the staff had to be rebuilt. Those who remained were given bonuses to help reorganize the publication and Hughes would later admit, "I f—ed up." Another magazine editor who was not involved in the turmoil would tell *Vanity Fair*, "Chris did what people have always done who bought magazines. He wants prestige; he wants acceptance. And he also wants to do good for the world. . . . He's not getting what he's entitled to under those rules. He's become the bad guy. And I'm sure he lies awake at night thinking, How did this happen?" (Ellison 2015). It was a stunning rebuke for Hughes, who had made enormous sums of money as a founder of Facebook and had helped build the wildly successful digital campaign for then-senator Barack Obama in 2008. It was an equally stunning development for a magazine long considered one of the pillars of the liberal establishment.

The *New Republic* was born of the Progressive movement of the early twentieth century. The magazine is said to have been organized in the Theodore Roosevelt's living room and was founded by Herbert Croly, author of the influential 1909 book *The Promise of American Life*, and journalist Walter Lippmann. The magazine's first edition sold less than 900 copies, but its smart writing, progressive politics, and skepticism of the Woodrow Wilson administration helped the magazine grow quickly, topping 43,000 copies a week during World War I. But it struggled in the post-war years and by 1924 filed for bankruptcy. The magazine would often struggle to turn a profit over its century of existence, but would often attract some of the most influential progressive voices. Henry Wallace, who had been vice president to FDR, served as the magazine's editor following his leaving public service, and Wallace used it to strengthen his credentials before launching an unsuccessful run for the White House on the Progressive Party ticket in 1948. Throughout the 1950s and 1960s, the magazine served as a major venue for debates about racial issues, anti-poverty causes, and the American role in Vietnam.

The magazine, while traditionally liberal on economic and domestic issues, carved out a more complicated worldview when it came to diplomacy and the use of the military. Although it would fluctuate from editor to editor, the magazine often bucked traditional liberal views internationally. Under Foer, the effort continued to evolve. The magazine backed Senator Joe Lieberman, who angered many liberals over his hawkish support for military action overseas, and even hailed his re-election as an Independent in Connecticut in 2006. It often backed decidedly pro-Israel foreign policy positions and at times appeared as much neo-conservative as liberal. Foer said this complexity was part of the magazine's mission, telling the *New York Times*, "It's very hard to put your finger on the magazine's ideological pulse, and that drives people up the wall, especially in this day and age," adding that the magazine "invented the modern usage of the term liberal, and it's one of our historical legacies and obligations to be involved in the ongoing debate over what exactly liberalism means and stands for" (Seelye 2007).

Throughout this period, the magazine was deeply influenced by its editor-in-chief, Martin Peretz. Peretz, a Harvard lecturer and veteran of political debates in the New Left, was among a group to purchase the magazine in 1974. Within a year, he replaced the editor of the magazine, annoyed at its continued deficit and sedate tone. He jettisoned many of the older writers, including Walter Pincus and Stanley Karnow, and replaced them with a who's who of young writers and editors. He hired Michael Kinsley as editor when Kinsley was only 28, and made it a practice to pick up writers on the rise. The magazine also hired homosexual conservative Andrew Sullivan to edit the magazine when he was 28 in 1991. This tendency to invest in its writers helped create the other major test in the magazine's modern history—the Stephen Glass plagiarism scandal. Glass was the 25-year-old associate editor at the magazine when Forbes Digital identified clear problems with one of his articles in 1998. The investigation by the online outlet and Glass's inability to document critical details, interviews, and sources for that piece and a series of others led to his firing. The magazine then investigated Glass's work and documented dozens of problems in the course of his reporting. Throughout the Glass controversy and other critical moments, Peretz was at the helm, a position he finally gave up in late 2010.

Since the upheavals that marked the reorganization of the magazine in 2014, the *New Republic* has focused on its digital footprint, expanding its reach in social networks to more than 100,000 followers on both Twitter and Facebook and overhauling the website to more aggressively market its content. It claims more than 100,000 email newsletter subscribers and in its pitch to advertisers, it almost solely relies on the appeal to digital ad buyers, offering an array of sponsored content and video options. Information about the print edition is only found buried on the same page that outlines the requirements for the tablet edition of the magazine. The journal still publishes 10 times a year, but its future seems to rely on its ability to reimagine itself as a digital news product.

See also: The *Atlantic*; Sullivan, Andrew

Further Reading

Ellison, Sarah. 2015. "The Complex Power Coupledom of Chris Hughes and Sean Eldridge." *Vanity Fair*. July. Accessed August 20, 2015. http://www.vanityfair.com/news/2015/06/chris-hughes-sean-eldridge-new-republic-congress-run.

Folkenflik, David. 2014. "New 'New Republic': A 'Vertically Integrated Digital Media Company.'" NPR. December 8. Accessed June 2, 2016. http://www.npr.org/2014/12/08/369276324/new-new-republic-a-vertically-integrated-digital-media-company.

Lizza, Ryan. 2014. "Inside the Collapse of the New Republic." *New Yorker*. December 1. Accessed August 21, 2015. http://www.newyorker.com/news/news-desk/inside-collapse-new-republic.

Seelye, Katharine. 2007. "New Republic Cuts Back, but Bulks Up Its Image." *New York Times*. February 24. Accessed August 24, 2015. http://www.nytimes.com/2007/02/24/books/24repu.html?_r=0.

NEW YORK TIMES

The *New York Times*, which has suffered many of the economic challenges that have buffeted the newspaper business in the past 20 years, has emerged as the nearly undisputed leader of American journalism. Its coverage of politics, like international and national affairs, is seen as the gold standard by many inside and outside the industry and has earned the paper 117 Pulitzer Prizes, more than any other news organization. It is also one of the largest circulation newspapers with a combined print and digital circulation of 2,178,674 for Monday-Friday and 2,624,277 for Sunday as of 2015.

There are rivals to the paper's position—a more nationally interested *Wall Street Journal*, an invigorated NPR, and a handful of large and increasingly influential websites like Huffington Post—but for now the *Times* stands as an unequalled force among the American press. It remains the so-called paper of record and its decisions about what and how to cover has demonstrated clear evidence of influencing other national and many regional news organizations.

The paper is generally considered left-of-center, although conservatives criticize it for being slanted heavily towards the Democratic Party and liberal causes generally. Even the paper's public editor once took to the op-ed pages to contend that the paper's coverage of gay marriage had demonstrated a clear bias in favor of permitting same-sex couples to wed. Daniel Okrent, himself a self-professed Democrat, wrote, "These are the social issues: gay rights, gun control, abortion and environmental regulation, among others. And if you think The Times plays it down the middle on any of them, you've been reading the paper with your eyes closed.

But if you're examining the paper's coverage of these subjects from a perspective that is neither urban nor Northeastern nor culturally seen-it-all; if you are among the groups the *Times* treats as strange objects to be examined on a laboratory slide (devout Catholics, gun owners, Orthodox Jews, Texans); if your value system wouldn't wear well on a composite *New York Times* journalist, then a walk through this paper can make you feel you're traveling in a strange and forbidding world" (Okrent 2004). Conservative blogs and commentators jumped on Okrent's description, but it also spoke to the core fact that the *Times* is based in New York City and covers the world from a major northeast, and politically liberal, city.

This is not to dismiss all of its coverage of politics and political issues. The paper has been known to take a hard edge in covering Democrats, as well. A story published in 2015 about former secretary of state Hillary Clinton's use of private email servers and a request for the Department of Justice to investigate was turned into a front page story in the *Times* that alleged she was facing a possible criminal probe. The story was corrected, but thousands of people commented on the article and accused the paper of being unfair to the Democratic candidate. The public editor once again took to the paper's own pages to write, "I talked to *Times* editors about their approach to covering Candidate Clinton. One top-ranking editor, Matt Purdy, agreed that she gets a great deal of scrutiny, but for good reason: 'We are dealing with a situation unique in American history: A leading candidate for president is not just a former senator and secretary of state, but she's also the wife of a former president and the two of them, along with their daughter, have a large global philanthropy.' There's a lot to explore, he said, and the *Times* owes it to its readers to do so" (Sullivan 2015). The issue of how the newsroom of 1,100 journalists employed by the paper covers politics is always a source of debate and as Margaret Sullivan noted in her 2015 column, the paper had not endorsed a Republican for president since Dwight D. Eisenhower.

It was not always that way.

In fact, the *New York Times* was begun by one of the founders of the Republican Party. Henry Jarvis Raymond was an influential leader of the anti-slavery wing of the Whig party and founder of the paper. Raymond was a sitting member of the New York State legislature and was angling for the lieutenant governor job when he decided the time was right to launch a new daily newspaper in the crowded New York City market. Raymond, with the help of journalist George Jones, decided that the reading population of New York City had grown large enough to support another member of the penny press, so in 1851 they put out the first edition of the *New York Daily Times*. The idea of the new paper was to carve out a position different than many of the other New York dailies. Those papers were either unabashed advocates of social change—like Horace Greeley's *New-York Tribune*—or salacious yellow journalism outlets like Joseph Pulitzer's *World* or William Randolph Hearst's *Herald*. Raymond and his team wanted the *Times* to be different, writing on the front page of the first edition, "Upon all topics,—Political, Social, Moral and Religious,—we intend that the paper shall speak only for itself;—and we only ask that it may be judged accordingly. We shall be *Conservative*, in all cases where we think

Conservatism essential to the public good;—and we shall be *Radical* in everything which may seem to us to require radical treatment and radical reform. We do not believe that *everything* in Society is either exactly right or exactly wrong;—what is good we desire to preserve and improve;—what is evil, to exterminate, or reform" (*New York Daily Times* 1851).

This idea of a more moderate paper with an anti-slavery bent seemed to work, and readers who were tiring of the preachiness of the reform journals and the scandal and crime of the yellow papers soon found a home with the *Times*. Raymond would continue his interest in politics and in the early years the paper had a clear anti-Democrat bent. Raymond would help organize the new Republican Party and would serve as its second chairman, and the paper often editorialized for pro-business and anti-slavery issues. By 1857 it decided to drop "Daily" from its name and became simply the *New York Times*. It also took great joy in launching investigations into the corrupt practices of the Democratic political machine, digging into the practices of Tammany Hall and Boss Tweed. The paper eventually became less predictable in its political stance and by the 1880s began supporting Democrats for elected office as well as Republicans. The editorial stances of the paper, though, unlike many other nineteenth century news organs, did not dictate coverage and the paper operate in a fairly unbiased way.

Still, by the 1890s the paper was struggling. With readership down and continued competition from other, more outspoken papers the *New York Times* was put on the sales block at a greatly reduced cost. News of its sale drew the interest of an enterprising young newspaper publisher from Tennessee, Adolph Ochs. Ochs, as a history of the paper would report, was uniquely positioned to try and save the paper. "He was thirty-eight years old; he had started in the newspaper business at the age of eleven as a carrier of papers, had graduated from that position to printer's devil, and had worked up through every position which either the news, the editorial, or the business department of Tennessee journalism had to offer until at the age of twenty he had become proprietor and publisher of the *Chattanooga Times*. In eighteen years he had brought this paper to a degree of prosperity remarkable in a city of that size, and to a position in public confidence perhaps still more unusual" (Davis 1921). Ochs formed the New York Times Co. to finance the purchase of the paper and in 1896 became the publisher. Like Raymond, Ochs saw a focus on straightforward news as a way to build and retain audience and the paper soon was back among the largest in the city.

Ochs's *New York Times* always had broad ambitions to be known nationally and internationally. The year after taking over Ochs introduced the slogan "All the News That's Fit to Print" in the upper left hand corner of the front page. The paper was also quick to embrace technology in its reporting. By 1904 the paper was using telegraphs to quickly transmit reporting from war zones, and its 1912 use of telegraphed survivor reports from the doomed *Titanic* helped cement the paper's reputation as a leading journal of the day. By its very nature, this powerful news organization became a sort of established power unto itself. Gay Talese would describe the world Ochs created at the *Times* as one where the reporters were made to feel they were protected from the world they reported about, writing in 1966, "They were secure at the *Times*. They were well paid, treated fairly, protected from the sham and uncertainties of the outside world. Economic recessions and depressions did not cut off their income, and threats to world survival seemed not to disturb the inner peace of the Times building. The *Times* stood apart, solid and unshakable. If it sometimes seemed a bit crusty and out of touch with popular trends, this was not so bad. It was, like Ochs, never frivolous" (Talese 2007). And this paper, which is still published under the watchful eye of the Ochs family in the form of Arthur Ochs Sulzberger, Jr., did earn a reputation of not kowtowing to the popular trends. The paper was one of the last to add color photos to the front page and was conservative in the creation of sections to divide up the newspaper. The organization added a website in 1996, much later than other news organizations like CNN and even other newspapers like the regional *Virginian Pilot-Ledger Star*.

But despite these slow additions, the paper still carved out a critical role for itself in its coverage of public policy and government, often by fighting and winning critical tests in court that would shape the relationship between the press and the state. For example, the 1964 libel case *New York Times v. Sullivan* created unprecedented legal protections for journalists covering public figures, making it almost impossible for those in the public eye to win libel suits against news organizations, unless the journalists knowingly publish false information with the intent of damaging the person. The paper also won the critical *New York Times v. United States* case in 1971 that found that the state could not stop the paper from running the controversial and top secret Pentagon Papers that detailed American involvement in Vietnam. This ruling by the Supreme Court severely limited the government's ability to exert prior restraint over news organizations.

In both its style of coverage and its role in the American media landscape, the *New York Times* represents a uniquely establishment enterprise. It is seen as one of the most cherished and valued news gatherers in the country and its launch of a paywall to access digital content has led more than 1 million subscribers to pay for web content, something previously considered nearly impossible. But even in this, the *New York Times* is somewhat unlike its fellow newspapers or broadcast outlets. NPR media reporter David Folkenflik outlined the modern reality of why the *Times* continues to hold such a unique place in American journalism, in part because the troubled economics of the modern media. He wrote in 2011, "The *Times* has few other national peers that match its aspirations. The audience for the nightly newscasts of national television networks has withered remarkably and enterprise reporting is rare. The *Washington Post*, the *Los Angeles Times* and *Time*, while each capable of illuminating work, have been forced by fiscal strains to make tough choices and scale back elements of coverage. Tens of millions of Americans continue to rely on the *New York Times* in print and online every month for the writing of grace, wit and insight, as well as photography of beauty and haunting pain" (Folkenflik 2011).

See also: Daily Newspapers; First Amendment and Censorship; Newspaper Industry; *Wall Street Journal*

Further Reading

Davis, Elmer Holmes. 1921. *History of the New York Times, 1851-1921*. New York: New York Times.

Editors. 1851. "A Word about Ourselves." *New York Daily Times*. September 18.

Folkenflik, David. 2011. *Page One: Inside the New York Times and the Future of Journalism*. New York: Public Affairs.

Okrent, Daniel. 2004. "Is the New York Times a Liberal Newspaper?" *New York Times*. July 25. Accessed October 15, 2015. http://www.nytimes.com/2004/07/25/opinion/the-public-editor-is-the-new-york-times-a-liberal-newspaper.html?pagewanted=all.

Sullivan, Margaret. 2015. "The Tortured Tale of Hillary Clinton and *The Times*." *New York Times*. August 1. Accessed October 15, 2015. http://www.nytimes.com/2015/08/02/public-editor/new-york-times-hillary-clinton-coverage-public-editor.html?_r=0.

Talese, Gay. 2007. *The Kingdom and the Power*. New York: Random House.

NEWS CONFERENCES

Part a realistic way to deal with the demands of the media and part a strategy for ensuring that a campaign's or politician's message gets out, the news conference has become an element of every election and all governing. It holds an almost ritualistic power in the media—that blue curtain and columns with the White House logo in the middle that marks the James Brady Press Briefing Room—and the expectation is that when something newsworthy occurs the politician or their spokesperson will make an appearance before the media to deliver a statement or take questions. Whether it is the century-old presidential press conference or a mayoral announcement, the idea of facing the press is a central part of the American political process.

The most recognizable and publicized of these events occur at the White House and began, inelegantly, with President Woodrow Wilson. Wilson, who as governor of New Jersey had had informal conversations with journalists, invited the reporters covering the White House to visit him soon after his election. The result was a surprise to the new president. "'I did not realize there were so many of you,' said Wilson after an awkward pause. It wasn't just that he was new to the job. At the time, the White House press room was barely bigger than the lavatory across the hall. 'Your numbers force me to make a speech to you en masse instead of chatting with each of you, as I had hoped to do, and thus getting greater pleasure and personal acquaintance out of this meeting'" (Dickerson 2013).

The effect on the media could be seen in the stories that came out from that first meeting, with the *New York Times* headline reading, "Wilson Wins Newspapermen" and the *Washington Post* describing the new president taking in the press corps "with a sweep of his kindly eyes and with a genial smile." Wilson would press the journalists to convey to him what was happening in the country while the newspapermen wanted to convey to the country what was happening in the White House. Or put another way, from the outset the press and politicians have wanted distinctly different things from these meetings. From the press perspective, they have stories to file, blogs to write, and quotes to tweet. The news conference is their chance to get on the record officials of the government or the campaign making their case. The politician's goal is more complex. He or she wants to shape the stories that will be written about the campaign or about the government, so the press conference offers a way to communicate with all the media at one time, delivering the same speech and talking points to all the newspapers, websites, and television networks in one fell swoop. This allows them to control their side of the story to a large extent, by carefully crafting the statement and dealing adroitly with any questions.

The press conferences themselves have evolved greatly since Wilson faced far more people than he had planned to that day in 1913. Before these events were broadcast—first on radio and later on television—the meetings were more informal. Franklin Delano Roosevelt was famous for inviting reporters in for a chat rather than delivering a formal address, and these sessions could be a mix of public on-the-record conversations or more informal discussions. In this scenario, the politician had much more control of the message that would emerge from the meeting as one episode with FDR's successor exemplifies. Harry Truman had been waxing on with the newspaper and wire service reporters about the growing power of Senator Joseph McCarthy and his anti-Communism crusade. Truman then offered up his thoughts of the Republican senator from Wisconsin, telling the assembled press in March 1950, "'I think the greatest asset that the Kremlin has is Senator McCarthy.' When one of the reporters commented that the president's observation would 'hit page one tomorrow,' Truman realized he had better soften the statement. He 'worked' with reporters and allowed the following as a direct quotation: 'The greatest asset that the Kremlin has is the partisan attempt in the Senate to sabotage the bipartisan foreign policy of the United States'" (Kumar). The juicier quote never saw the light of day because Truman asked the reporters to let him rephrase it and they did.

This earlier system was built on the unspoken arrangement between sources and the media: The press would have access to the president or some other key politician, and the politician would have some freedom to revise his comments before the press let them loose on the world. Looking back at this system, political scientists note that FDR and others benefited mightily from the pact, noting, "Because reporters did not quote him directly unless otherwise authorized, Roosevelt felt comfortable speaking much more candidly than do presidents today whose every word is immediately transmitted live to a vast audience. At the same time, reporters benefited because they received 'hard news' rather than the 'message du jour' that dominates most presidential responses today" (Dickinson 2009).

Broadcast changed all of that.

With the advent of radio and especially television, the press conference, by presidents and other leaders, became a completely different beast. Gone was the chummy, behind-the-scenes feel of the FDR chats and in its place emerged a more formal and very much on-the-record world of the televised press conference. John Kennedy and his use of the press conference created a new form of political communication. Aided by his comfort with the medium and his quick wit and mastery of the facts, Kennedy's televised press conferences created a vision of his presidency that fed into the mystique that would be called "Camelot." Looking back more than 20 years later, the *New Republic's* Henry Fairlie noted, "It was impossible not to be attracted again by the appearance of the man, to enjoy the nimbleness of the wit, the charm of his gaiety, and even to reflect that, for all the lengthy briefings with which he was prepared for these appearances, he displayed on his feet an intelligence which was wholly individual, and had to invite from all but the most skeptical a measure of trust and reassurance" (Fairlie 1983).

This form of communication was more formal and rehearsed. Gone were the off-the-cuff comments between newsmaker and reporter. In its place grew up a more dramatic and increasingly contentious beast where reporters shouted out questions and pushed for answers and spokespeople and politicians fired back or sought to duck the question. These back-and-forths have at times descended into gamesmanship where each side tries to "get" the other. Still, these more structured press conferences avoid some of the clubbiness that threatened the reporting of old. On camera there was no opportunity to walk a statement back. This more unforgiving medium has made the press less and less popular for politicians, who increasingly rely on surrogates to get up and deal with the press each day.

This aversion to the press conference becomes even more apparent when the politician is running for office. Politicians can still rely on the spokesperson to deliver their talking points for the day, but often the candidate can also point the reporter to the stump speech delivered that day for content, and any question shouted from the press line is more likely to distract from the message of the day rather than amplify the campaign's message. Candidates do rely on the press conference as part of a communications strategy on the trail, as two scholars have noted, "Political campaigns are communication events: communication of images, characters, and persona. Most campaign strategies are designed to do more than get votes. They are designed to project a certain image, alter a perception, or counter the opposition" (Denton and Kuypers 2008). Press conferences can help project that image, but on the trail the campaign tends to deploy them far less than senators, governors, and presidents do once elected. Unlike the campaigns, which have ads, banners, speeches, and surrogates to spread the word through the media, those attempting to govern often have far fewer tools at their disposal to get their message out and use press conferences more. Often on the campaign, candidate press conferences tend to be an effort at damage control, when a series of questions or allegations have reached a point that the campaign must address them. So to look back at press conferences from campaigns in the past is to see Gary Hart try to explain the visit of a young blonde woman to his D.C. home when his wife was out of town, or former senator Jim Webb answering questions about his failed quest for the Democratic presidential nomination in 2015.

The modern press conference has some clear advantages and disadvantages for both the press and the politician. From the politician's perspective, the clearest advantage is found in the simple fact that they don't have to repeat themselves. One statement made at one time can answer the questions of dozens or hundreds of reporters rather than dealing with each reporter on his or her own. The downside can come if the press asks questions that stump the politician or cause them to make a damaging impromptu comment. Additionally, refusing to answer questions can make the politician look unwilling to address the public on some matter of national or regional interest. Politicians can also increase the impact of the news event by ensuring that more reporters cover it and the comments get a wider distribution through the media.

For the journalists the benefits of a press conference is to gain access to the newsmaker that has refused to give him or her a sit-down exclusive interview. These events often also supply reporters with the necessary comment or sound bite they need to file a given story. Press conferences can also supply reporters with additional fodder for social media tweets and blogs that many news organizations demand from their political reporters. The downsides are pronounced for these journalists, though. There are no exclusives in the news conference. Everyone gets the same statement at the same time. Also, campaigns and government officials will call a press conference for an event that seems newsworthy, but may end up not to be and yet the press conference itself lends the story more weight than the reporter or editor would give it otherwise.

Still, despite their drawbacks for both campaign operative and reporter, news conferences remain a major force in how politics are covered. Although the televised press briefings remain the most visible manifestation of the form, increasingly campaigns have taken to using telephone conference calls as a modified form of updating the press. This has the benefit of being recorded but does not supply the visual element, meaning they are more often used by print journalists to document what is being said. Also, many organizations have taken to providing press briefings that are "on background" or even "off the record" so that their information can be supplied to the press, but none of the direct attribution or potential televised gaffes are a problem. As the types and number of news media have expanded in Washington and elsewhere, the need for candidates and those who govern to communicate one time to multiple outlets has expanded and so the press conference remains a central tool in political communication, even if it is one that carries with it inherent flaws.

See also: Access to Candidates; Photo Ops and Optics

Further Reading

Denton, Robert, and Jim Kuypers. 2008. *Politics and Communication in America: Campaigns, Media, and Governing in the 21st Century*. Long Grove, IL: Waveland Press, Inc.

Dickerson, John. 2013. "Meet the Press." Slate. March 3. Accessed November 14, 2015. http://www.slate.com/articles/news_and_politics/politics/2013/03/woodrow_wilson_held_the_first_presidential_press_conference_100_years_ago.html.

Dickinson, Matthew. 2009. "A Primer on Presidential Press Conferences." Middlebury University. Accessed November 15, 2015. http://sites.middlebury.edu/presidentialpower/tag/history-press-conferences.

Fairlie, Henry. 1983. "Television's Love Affair with John F. Kennedy." *New Republic*. December 26. Accessed November 16, 2015. https://newrepublic.com/article/115247/john-f-kennedy-television-presidency.

Kumar, Martha Joynt. "Presidential Press Conferences." White House Historical Association. Accessed November 16, 2015. http://www.whitehousehistory.org/presidential-press-conferences.

NEWSMAGAZINES

General newsmagazines—*Time, Newsweek*, and *U.S. News and World Report*—have fallen a long way from their former role as one of the most influential media platforms in shaping and informing public opinion. Built in an era of information scarcity, when people had access to handful of newspapers and long before people even had a dial of thirteen or fewer channels, these general magazines have struggled to find a role in a world flooded with information.

In response to the growth of broadcasting and later the explosion of digital publishing, magazines have become a specialized industry, focusing on narrow hobbies or specific political viewpoints and in this world, the general newsmagazine has floundered. The *Atlantic*'s Michael Hirschorn noted, "In the digital age, with its overabundance of information, the modern newsweekly is in a particularly poignant position. Designed nearly a century ago to be all things to all people, it Chaplin-esquely tries to straddle thousands of rapidly fragmenting micro-niches, a mainframe in an iTouch world. The audience it was created to serve—middlebrow; curious, but not too curious; engaged, but only to a point—no longer exists" (Hirschorn 2009). It is now a very different world. Originally, magazines served as an important counterpoint to newspapers, relying on the mail to reach people outside urban centers. Even once they became less critical as more people moved away from the rural world, they played the role of synthesizer of the mountains of print and news out there. A magazine like *Newsweek* could, in a simple feature like its "Conventional Wisdom" series of up and down arrows, introduce the reader to dozens of issues and news developments. The style of these periodicals tended to be breezier than the more somber and serious newspapers and often mixed news with fiction, photography, and commentaries.

Magazines emerged in America during the colonial era. These magazines often compiled the news from overseas and the other colonies for consumption in one region. In a real way, they were often the equivalent of the modern aggregator, taking snippets of information, stories, and repeated gossip and compiling them into weekly or monthly pamphlets that could be then mailed or sold in the growing number of newsstands in urban areas. By the late nineteenth century, magazines like the *Saturday Evening Post* were firmly established as popular outlets, landing in thousands of homes and doctors' offices each weekend. By the 1920s, even as radio began to sweep the land, a wave of publishers decided that the time was right for a new media form—the general newsmagazine. Henry Luce and Briton Hadden would launch the first of this new beast in 1923, *Time*. The prospectus of the first *Time* captured the ambitious goal of the new newsmagazine, noting, "People in America are, for the most part, poorly informed. This is not the fault of the daily newspapers; they print all the news. People are uninformed because no publication has adapted itself to the time which busy men are able to spend on simply keeping informed. *Time* is a weekly news-magazine, aimed to serve the modern necessity of keeping people informed, created on a principle of complete organization. *Time* is interested—not in how much it includes between its covers—but in how much it gets off its pages into the minds of its readers" (Muller 1988).

Time's launch would spawn an array of general news imitators—most notably *Newsweek* and *United States News*, both in 1933. The magazine would seek to address the challenge *Time* noted in that first prospectus, offering readers a simpler way to offer people a synopsis of the week that was. It had at its core a mission to inform the voting public in a way that sought to ensure that people would have a grasp of the major developments nationally and internationally. At Luce's death in 1968, the magazine he founded would focus on his vision of the role of the magazine in public life, noting in his obituary, "'As a journalist, I am in command of a small sector in the very front trenches of this battle for freedom'" (*Time* 1968).

From their outset, newsmagazines showed an enormous power to broaden the knowledge of the reading public by consciously seeking to organize volumes of news and information into erudite, yet readable copy and compelling photographs. These magazines differed from the more literary and political journals—*New Republic* or the *Atlantic* of the left and the *National Review* or later the *Weekly Standard* of the right. Those magazines never achieved wide circulation, instead serving the intellectual elite and the party philosophers more than the casual reader. The general newsmagazines were built for the average reader, so when the publication revolution that swept the newspaper industry in the early 2000s hit the magazine industry, many of the same challenges arose. Synthesizing news on a weekly basis made no sense when it was being done every minute by digital outlets or social media. The array of content that magazines relied on to attract readers could now be accessed at the swipe of a finger at any moment of the day, leaving structured publication and weekly distribution through the mail ridiculously outdated. General newsmagazines in particular struggled to find their way in this new news ecosystem, with many moving closer to the entertainment industry, others turning to specialized publications like college rankings, and others seeking to become like their thinker cousins. All the while, circulation and ad sales continued to dry up. These magazines had relied not just on the mail subscribers but also on thousands upon thousands of their periodicals being bought at the newsstand or the supermarket. *U.S. News and World Report* was the first to falter of the big three. Never the largest of the magazines, by June of 2008 it announced it would shift to a bi-weekly publication. By November even that was not working and so they slipped to monthly. By the end of 2010 the printed history of the magazine came to an end. The publication maintains a website and makes most of its money now through its branded rankings of colleges and graduate and professional programs.

By 2012, numbers were still plunging, leading one insider to tell the *New York Times*' David Carr, "When the airplane suddenly drops 10,000 feet and it doesn't crash, you still end up with your heart in your stomach. Those are very, very bad numbers" (Carr 2012). That year marked a major moment in the history of the newsmagazine as *Newsweek*, having been sold by the *Washington Post* to the website The Daily Beast, struggled no more and ceased weekly publication at the end of that year. Interestingly, the magazine would begin publishing again in 2014 with a far smaller staff and publication, and unlike the giant magazine of yore it soon claimed to be profitable. Still, many worry about these journals, noting that they struggle with one of the key elements necessary to succeed in the highly competitive modern media environment—uniqueness. In noting the newsmagazine's uneasy future, media commentator Ken Doctor, author of the book *Newsonomics*, noted, "*Time*'s fundamental problem is that the topics it talks about can be found in many places; whether they are bringing to them a sufficient aggregation of voices to differentiate themselves is in significant doubt" (Sasseen, Matsa, and Mitchell 2013).

For decades the political reporting of these three newsmagazines helped shape the perception of many voters about the campaigns and debates of Congress. The correspondents for these magazines had huge sway over the way the breathless news articles of daily newspaper reporters would be interpreted and, not surprisingly, these experts who spent their time considering the big picture of politics often appeared on television as experts on cable news and Sunday talk shows. These political reporters were the ones who often connected the dots of the campaign stories, offered the assessment that would become convention wisdom, and echoed that message in widely circulated magazines and on broadcast. Those voices have largely been replaced by the bloggers of the left and the right and the handful of remaining partisan columnists. Their role continues to be filled, but rarely by the reporters and columnists of *Time*, *Newsweek*, and *U.S. News and World Report*.

See also: Aggregation; Newspaper Industry; *Time*

Further Reading

Carr, David. 2012. "Wondering How Far Magazines Must Fall." *New York Times*. August 12. Accessed November 20, 2015. http://www.nytimes.com/2012/08/13/business/media/wondering-how-far-magazines-must-fall.html.

Hirschorn, Michael. 2009. "The Newsweekly's Last Stand." *Atlantic*. July/August. Accessed November 20, 2015. http://www.theatlantic.com/magazine/archive/2009/07/the-newsweeklys-last-stand/307489.

Muller, Henry. 1988. "A Letter from the Managing Editor." *Time*. October 17. Accessed June 2, 2016. http://content.time.com/time/magazine/article/0,9171,968673,00.html.

Sasseen, Jane, Katerina-Eva Matsa, and Amy Mitchell. 2013. "News Magazines: Embracing Their Digital Future." Pew Research Center. Accessed November 20, 2105. http://www.stateofthemedia.org/2013/news-magazines-embracing-their-digital-future.

NEWSMAX

Newsmax wasn't an overnight sensation like many of the meteoric websites and blogs that soon lose their steam (and audience), but the conservative news site headed by Christopher Ruddy has built a solid following and now ranks as the most visited right-leaning news site on the Internet.

In fact, in April of 2013, independent audience system comScore reported that Newsmax had topped its ranking of popular political news sites, beating out Huffington Post Politics, Fox News's political section, and CNN Politics. Ruddy said the news was "a testament to quality of our digital content that consumers online, on smartphones and on tablets continue to look to Newsmax for the latest political news" (Talkers 2013). The site has grown to include a magazine with a subscriber base of more than 200,000 and a satellite cable channel.

Much of the growth of Newsmax is credited to its ability to appeal to a wide range of Republicans and Independents. Unlike some of the more shrill partisan press advocates, Newsmax has offered more reasoned critiques of both Republicans and Democrats. But it still knows its core audience is a Republican one and Ruddy is quick to highlight his site's ability to reach critical members of the party. In a 2011 *New York Times* profile, Ruddy proudly cited that "Every major Republican committee has advertised at one point or another using our e-mails or Web sites. We're really the 800-pound gorilla if you want to reach Republican donors in the country. We've got the list" (Peters 2011). It's a list built not just through a political news website, but rather a suite of at-times seemingly random ventures, ranging from the magazine and website, to separate sites on health, business, and email newsletters on investing and specific health issues. The various business models have combined to create a media company that has seen revenues grow to more than $100 million a year.

The site's business strategy has also caused it some trouble. In early 2014, former U.S. senator Scott Brown cut ties with Newsmax after the company sent an email to his list of email supporters that was maintained by Newsmax. The email promoting the work of one of Newsmax's newsletter writers, Dr. Russell Blaylock, whose controversial views on some vaccines and the medical effects of MSG are at odds with most doctors, prompted Brown to end his relationship with Newsmax.

Despite these newsletter and email businesses, Newsmax's major role is in serving as a news source for those seeking conservative takes on the news. Regular contributors include Ruddy as well as other noted conservatives like George Will, Armstrong Williams, and economist Ben Stein. But the site also calls several liberals part of its team of "Insiders," including columnist Margaret Carlson, former Clinton attorney Lanny Davis, and lawyer Alan Dershowitz.

Ruddy launched the service in 1998, with the backing of his former boss, Richard Mellon Scaife. Ruddy had worked as a journalist at the *New York Post* before becoming a national correspondent at the *Pittsburgh Post-Gazette*. It was there he and Scaife developed the idea for Newsmax. Ruddy has often struck a more moderate approach to commenting on politics, taking shots at Republicans he sees as failing and at times even praising Democrats. He once told Forbes, "Let's face it, Bush was a horrible global statesman. Bill Clinton filled that void. If you read Clinton's book, *Giving*, you'd think it was written by Newt Gingrich. It's all about the value of public/private partnerships, microfinance and entrepreneurship. These are things that any Republican would want" (Smillie 2009). Ruddy has repeatedly told interviewers he is in the mold of former president Ronald Reagan, embracing Republicans of all stripes and espousing a conservative ideology he says comes more from the heartland rather than the beltway.

The site has drawn fire for at times bolstering the political efforts of some controversial politicians, most notably real estate mogul and television personality Donald Trump. Trump, who made waves for his repeated claims that he did not believe President Barack Obama was born in the United States, has often made comments that drew national attention to Newsmax. In 2011, as the Republicans jockeyed for attention in a crowded presidential field, Trump talked repeatedly with Newsmax, inserting himself as a potential contender and shaking up the race. Ruddy, who calls Trump a "friend," was all too happy to help him, saying, "Trump realizes the great potential of Newsmax and has been using it very adroitly. We're well aware he's using it . . . We are the platform for any Republican candidate that wants to articulate a vision to the American people and the Republican Party, and Trump is articulating a vision and idea and he's catching fire" (Bedard 2011). In the end that Trump candidacy failed to catch too much fire, but the ability of Newsmax to shape the tone and topics of the Republican primary was obvious.

It remains to be seen if the launch of Newsmax television on satellite and streaming will expand the reach and influence of the Florida-based news service. But with a mixed business model and Republican candidates lining up to reach Ruddy's list of thousands of potential donors as well as voters in the Republican primaries come election year, it stands a chance.

See also: Conservative Blogosphere; TheBlaze

Further Reading

Bedard, Paul. 2011. "Trump-Newsmax Conspiracy Is Real." *U.S. News and World Report*. April 19. Accessed February 3, 2015. http://www.usnews.com/news/blogs/washington-whispers/2011/04/19/trump-newsmax-conspiracy-is-real.

Peters, James. 2011. "A Compass for Conservative Politics." *New York Times*. July 11. Accessed February 4, 2015. http://www.nytimes.com/2011/07/11/business/media/newsmax-a-compass-for-conservative-politics.html?_r=0.

Smillie, Dirk. 2009. "The Great Right Hope." *Forbes*. March 6. Accessed February 4, 2015. http://www.forbes.com/2009/03/06/newsmax-christopher-ruddy-business-media-ruddy.html.

Talkers Magazine. 2013. "Wednesday, June 5, 2013." June 5. Accessed February 4, 2015. http://www.talkers.com/2013/06/05/wednesday-june-5-2013.

NEWSPAPER INDUSTRY

Given that newspapers still house a majority of the reporters working in America and generate most of the news reporting that people consume across print and digital platforms, the struggle of the newspaper industry to respond to the fundamental changes that have swept the information and advertising worlds has made this an era of uncertainty and change for all forms of reporting, including coverage of campaigns and politics. The newspaper newsrooms in America have shed nearly 40 percent of their staffs in the past decade, and this struggle to find a business model that can replace the loss of advertising revenue remains a daunting challenge for the industry.

The story of what happened to newspapers and, in particular, the business model of print journalism has been much discussed, but to understand the causes and effects of this change, it's important to understand the core idea of how newspapers work and make money. Newspaper publishing started more as an add-on source of revenue for printers in colonial America. In addition to being hired to publish books, currency, and official declarations, printers could make money by cobbling together news that had come across the Atlantic from Britain and elsewhere. These printers did not report, but really performed an early version of aggregation, gathering news and writing a version of it for the colonies. These papers catered to those interested in the happenings in Europe and cost a fair amount of money, making them more products for the wealthy. They were still risky affairs from a business and legal perspective. Publishers needed to operate within the bounds of royal permission and even if they did this, there was no guarantee of success. "Newspaper publishing could be a lucrative aspect of a printing business, supplementing competitive job printing, but it could also be disastrous—of the sixty newspapers begun in the colonies before 1760, ten failed before a year had passed and another ten closed after less than four years" (Smith 2012). That's not to say they were always well behaved. Newspapers were often battlegrounds for political parties seeking advantage or attacking their opponents and were highly partisan, in the tradition of many of the papers in England. But still they appealed primarily to the politically active and wealthy in their communities. The business would remain a wing of printers for the next 70 years as the American population—and literacy—grew.

By the early nineteenth century, the growth of larger urban centers with sizable literate populations created the atmosphere for a revolution in the newspaper business. In crowded New York City, a man named Benjamin Day had an idea for a publication that would not rely on the wealthy to subscribe, but would make money in a totally novel way, by selling itself at a low price to appeal to the widest possible audience. The paper would then make the bulk of its money by selling advertising to businesses wanting to reach people in the city where it was published. The idea came to be known as the "penny press," because Day and an array of publishers to follow would charge one cent for their paper, making it affordable to just about anyone interested in picking one up and learning about the day's news. The effect on the news business was profound. News became much more of a commodity, something that could be measured by the number of readers the paper could attract. It also helped birth a new form of writing, one that sensationalized the news to attract the reader. Businessmen entered the field trying to carve out unique niches for their paper, by adding more reporting, covering regular beats, and also hyping scandal and gossip. James Gordon Bennett would emerge as one of the early prototypes of the new newspaper publisher. He launched the first paper with a regular newsroom with reporters who regularly covered parts of the city. He also used his paper to attack opponents, advocate reform, and sensationalize the day's events. "At Bennett's death in 1872, Horace Greeley, editor of the rival *New York Tribune*, said of him, 'He developed the capacities of journalism in the most wonderful manner, but he did it by degrading its character. He made the newspaper powerful, but he made it odious'" (Farrell and Cupito 2010).

For Bennett's and the others' faults, the penny press model meant that newspapers would appeal to and communicate with the majority of citizens. One of the interesting elements is how this shift to a media that appealed more to the masses almost inevitably made it more of a platform for political debate and advocacy. The papers born of the penny press model became the newspapers that championed "yellow journalism," reporting that mixed the scandalous with an advocacy for the average worker. These papers would push for changes such as a cap on the number of hours per week, an end to child labor, and safer working conditions. They also became important political tools, with their publishers often trying to use the paper's influence to develop their own political career, or at least ruin the careers of the publisher's enemies. William Randolph Hearst was one of these barons of the press who used his paper to do more than comment on public matters, but to shape public opinion on matters foreign and domestic. These publishers created a new sense of what the paper was there to do. As one historian who explored the development of investigative reporting described it, "Through exposes and the editorials that commented on them, penny press editors conceived of and protected the public good, accepting a responsibility they would hand down to future editors of investigative journalism" (Aucoin 2007).

But it wasn't just a civic philosophy these papers handed down to those who would follow. The business philosophy of the penny press is what would shape the newspaper industry for the remainder of the nineteenth and all of the twentieth centuries. Newspapers operated with a simple model. In a given community, newspapers would offer news, commentary, and whatever would draw a sizable audience. They would provide this at an extraordinarily low price—as close to free as they could go, and they would make money by sprinkling throughout the paper advertisements for local businesses hoping to reach people. It was a model that, unlike the mixed success printers saw, worked again and again. Papers would compete against each other for readers, but once they had the readership, they could turn those eyeballs into real revenue by marketing their audience to businesses. Ironically, this did two things. It made attracting the most readers possible a core part of their business, and it made it the content that attracted the readers a separate thing than the businesses who wanted to advertise. The descendant of the penny press model helped solidify the separation of editorial and business, and it also ensured that most papers would be largely politically neutral—not necessarily because of any goal of objectivity, but because as a business model it did not make sense to alienate supporters of one party or the other.

Most papers became a sort of barometer of the general attitude of the community they served because they wanted to appeal to the widest possible cross-section of that community. The business worked so well that in most communities readers could choose from more than one paper, often being able to choose from morning and evening newspapers that could give the reader more up-to-date information.

But the newspaper would also reach its crest by the early twentieth century. The story of newspapers threatened by technology, so prevalent today, is actually, itself, already about a century old. As one historian of the newspaper concluded a decade ago (even before much of the current problems), "The story of American newspapers in the twentieth century is also one of decline, and as a result one of diminishing influence. In the 1920s, household newspaper penetration in the United States was higher than it would ever be again in the century. In the twentieth century Americans went from being a nation in which every household received an average of at least one newspaper to a nation where only half of all households did" (Wallace 2005).

Today's newspapers have to fight digital technologies; yesterday's had to survive the rise of broadcast. Radio and later television posed a major challenge to the newspaper industry and spurred a series of changes to the content and business of newspapering. It's no accident that the 1920s marked the high-water mark for newspaper subscriptions in the United States. It was also the decade that radio was began broadcasting. Broadcast media threatened to end the newspaper's dominance of information and advertising services. Radio's rapid rise from technological oddity to information and advertising juggernaut happened with stunning speed, and with it the slow decline in newspaper subscriptions began.

Initially newspapers competed by seeking to emulate the elements that were helping spur radio's growth. The newspapers sought to add more personality-style reporting, adding sections about sports and weather, lifestyle and food. This diversification of the paper helped broaden the appeal as many seeking instant news or entertainment were drawn to the radio, which provided many of the same updates for free once you purchased the device. Newspapers also responded by modifying their business models. In some markets, separately owned morning and afternoon newspapers merged into a single company. In others, newspapers sought to purchase and run radio or television stations. The idea was if you owned multiple ways to reach people, you could market yourself to advertisers more effectively. However, the purchasing of broadcast stations by newspapers raised questions about one company owning all the access to information in a single town, so by 1975 Congress moved to ban so-called cross-ownership.

Even throughout its slow slide in newspaper readership, twentieth-century newspapers continued to turn a solid profit. Despite the calls for tighter budgets, the newspaper business was big business and the industry was taking steps to make it bigger. First, once cross-ownership was off the table, many newspapers consolidated the business in each community. Pressed to compete with evening news, which was quickly overtaking newspapers as the primary source of news for the public, newspapers soon started closing afternoon papers. As newspaper analyst John Morton told the *American Journalism Review* in 1992, "Television has captured time that had been devoted to reading afternoon newspapers, [media analyst John] Morton says. Meanwhile, changes in the economy have produced more service and less industry, which means more white-collar workers who go to work later, a pattern favoring morning papers" (Mann 1992). The result could be clearly seen in the statistics. In 1950, there were 1,450 afternoon papers and 322 morning papers, while at the end of 1990 there were 1,084 afternoon papers and 559 morning papers.

But consolidation in communities was only the first form of merger that swept the newspaper business. Newspaper chains emerged as the primary business model for newspaper ownership during the 1980s and 1990s. This consolidation merged the newspapers across communities into a single business. Newspapers in given communities succeeded in spite of a drop in readership primarily because by the early 1990s only 90 communities had more than one paper. They became monopolies in their communities and therefore could charge advertisers a higher rate. Nevertheless, newspapers struggled to grow, which built pressure on businesses that had to show continued growth to potential investors. The way to grow, therefore, became buying other newspapers. "Many groups set high profit goals for their papers—as much as 40 percent before taxes—and these goals, in turn, push the companies to operate tightly budgeted, often miserly, news operations" (Ghiglione 1984). Profit margins of 40 percent are incredibly high when compared to other businesses. Wal-Mart, for example, operates a 3.1 percent profit margin. This need to deliver incredibly high profits forced many papers to slash budgets throughout the 1990s.

Then came the Internet. The explosive growth of the Internet and the changes it wrought on newspapers shook the business to its core and continues to force staff cuts and budget reductions at papers across the country. It is hard to overstate the way the web hit newspapers in essentially every major component of its business. First there was the impact on the core editorial thing about newspapers—being *the* source for daily news. Newspapers were born in an era of information scarcity, where finding out what happened today in your town, your country, or your world was a difficult task. They were built to tell you what had happened that day and helped you make sense of it. Although broadcast challenged that role, it was the World Wide Web that destroyed it. Now people could share news on social media, and readers could browse information from all over the world in an instant. A veritable endless library of facts and opinions were now a mouse click and later a finger tap away. Newspapers could no longer simply rely on being the only game in their given town.

Then there was the business tsunami that hit papers in the early 2000s. As Clay Shirky said in a film tracking an uneasy year and the venerable *New York Times*,

"The advertising market has turned upside down. So at the same time that revenue takes a hit, suddenly publishing has gone from being something done by a specialty class to being something that literally every connected citizen has access to . . . That reduction in revenue coupled with the competition for attention—both at the same time—has turned this from a transition to a revolution" ("Page One" 2010). The effect digital publishing has had on advertising is striking, especially for the economics of newspapers. Now, through web tools like Google or social media like Facebook, advertisers can target individuals who have expressed interest in their good or service specifically. Newspapers, on the other hand, could only offer a broad swath of geographically located individuals who may or may not be a potential customer. Advertisers no longer have patience for this lack of specificity. Additionally, most businesses have their own websites and social media campaigns to connect directly to customers and do not need to rely on mass media. This reality, in particular, has hammered newspaper businesses, causing once robust revenues to largely dry up and profit margins that in the 1980s and 1990s were north of 20 percent a year to dwindle.

As Shirky also notes, digital technologies have created a flood of new services that peel away the value of a newspaper to its potential readers. Sports fans now don't need to wait for the morning paper or the weekly *Sports Illustrated* to find out the latest on their team. Coupon clippers have thousands of sites devoted to helping people save 50 cents on yogurt, and political junkies can get the latest tweet or headline from Washington instantly on a smart phone from news services devoted to political reporting. The general newspaper has felt this change more than any other. It has most troublingly manifested itself in the shrinking of the American newsroom. Newspapers remain a primary source of information for the communities they serve. Generally, the paper is the first source for many stories that then get picked up and told on evening newscasts or echo into regional and national news outlets. The storm of business pressures on newspapers have clearly taken its toll on paper staffs. The American Society of Newspaper Editors reported that in 2001 there were 56,400 journalists working at daily papers in the United States. In 2015 the number was 32,900.

The bottom line of the revolution Shirky points out in his film is that American newspaper newsrooms are some 42 percent smaller today than 14 years ago. An open question remains as to whether the penny press model that built newspapers into major forces in their communities can keep functioning when the business elements have changed so radically, or if newspapers can alter the model to find a more stable mix of revenues. It's worth noting that in 2013 the *New York Times*, for the first time in its history, made as much money from its print and digital subscriptions as it did from traditional advertisers. But that reality, while interesting, has not become the norm in an industry still seeking its business model in a new world of content and advertising.

See also: Daily Newspapers; Internet Advertising; *New York Times*

Further Reading

Aucoin, James. 2007. *The Evolution of American Investigative Journalism*. Columbia: University of Missouri Press.
Farrell, Mike, and Mary Carmen Cupito. 2010. *Newspapers: A Complete Guide to the Industry*. New York: Peter Lang Publishing, Inc.
Ghiglione, Loren. 1984. *The Buying and Selling of America's Newspapers*. Indianapolis, IN: R.J. Berg & Company.
Mann, Cynthia. 1992. "Death in the Afternoon." *American Journalism Review*. April. Accessed July 30, 2015. http://ajrarchive.org/Article.asp?id=1443.
"Page One: A Year Inside The New York Times." 2010. Magnolia Pictures.
Smith, Lisa. 2012. *The First Great Awakening in Colonial American Newspapers*. Lanham, MD: Lexington Books.
Wallace, Aurora. 2005. *Newspapers and the Making of Modern America*. Westport, CT: Greenwood Press.

NONPROFIT JOURNALISM

As the digital publishing and advertising revolution economically pressured newspapers to cut staff and rein in their editorial ambitions, nonprofit news organizations, often focused on investigative and long-form reporting, have sprung up seeking to fill the void. These outlets, which often rely on personal donations or larger foundation grants, have become major sources of original reporting, winning Pulitzer Prizes and partnering with legacy media like the *New York Times* and CBS News. While some of these organizations aim to continue the best forms of investigative reporting, other organizations blur the line between objective journalism and advocacy, drawing funding from foundations and individuals more interested in ideological ends than the reporting itself. Both types of journalism nonprofits now are regular contributors to the news flow, but understanding the agenda of the funding agencies and goals of the organization itself become more difficult for the reader to know.

The interest in nonprofit journalism was born, at least in part, from a perceived failure of the for-profit media to adapt to the new digital realities. Newspapers, which had enjoyed wild profitability even after the dawn of the Internet age, seemed slow to embrace the web and other opportunities. Broadcasters were even slower to look toward the Internet in the early days before technology allowed for high quality streaming of media. Then as the economy slowed and advertisers found other outlets more effective for targeting and reaching potential customers, news organizations started to entrench, reducing the expenditures on long-term investigations and more civically minded—but perhaps less popular—coverage of policy and statehouses. With journalists increasingly concerned about the economics of their, business former *Washington Post* ombudsman and journalism professor Geneva Overholser penned a treatise, "On Behalf of Journalism," which argued that journalists needed to take the future into their own hands. She stressed, "The story of American journalism is undergoing a dramatic re-write. The pace of change makes many anxious, and denunciations are lobbed from all sides—and from within. It's easy to overlook the promise of the many possibilities that lie before us. Our focus here is on those possibilities" (Overholser 2006). Front and center in Overholser's document is the idea of nonprofit journalism—both in the form of new organizations to produce content and charitable foundations to support that work. The case came as many within journalism were arguing for a new wave of organizations to address the needs of the day. It was, in part, a return to some older ideas in journalism.

Nonprofit journalism groups are not new, despite the frenzy of interest in the digital version of these organizations. In 1846, five New York newspapers cut a deal to work together to get news from the battlefields of the Mexican-American War back to headquarters thousands of miles away. The project worked and a new nonprofit consortium was born, the Associated Press. The group would use whatever technology it could, from pigeon to pony express to Teletext, to deliver news to its members. The nonprofit model meant that the new organization would work in close collaboration with each of the member organizations and did not seek to compete with its own members. It also filled a specific need that each news organization faced—how to get reliable information quickly from far-flung locations. It made sense to work together to do it and not for each to try and send a reporter to cover a distant war.

Nonprofit journalism saw a second wave of interest grow around the concept of investigative reporting. In the wake of Watergate and Vietnam, journalists who wanted to dig deeply into stories sought ways to do that full time, and soon a new era of investigative nonprofits were born. In 1976 the Foundation for National Progress was organized to publish and run the activist liberal investigation magazine *Mother Jones*. A year later the Center for Investigative Reporting launched. A handful of other investigative operations followed, notably the Center for Public Integrity in the 1980s, but these nonprofit operations tended to be few and far between. It would take the dawn of the Internet to empower more organizations to start up in the nonprofit model.

One website, ProPublica, truly helped spawn the nonprofit journalism revival of the digital age. Although there were a handful of news nonprofits covering communities around the country, notably the Voice of San Diego and Seattle's Grist, ProPublica was part of a major new wave of nonprofit journalism. Like its predecessors of the 1970s and 1980s, ProPublica aimed to address a specific shortcoming in the mainstream media—a lack of thorough investigative journalism. The site stresses, "Investigative journalism is at risk. Many news organizations have increasingly come to see it as a luxury . . . New models are, therefore, necessary to carry forward some of the great work of journalism in the public interest that is such an integral part of self-government, and thus an important bulwark of our democracy" (ProPublica). The new organization stepped into that void, backed by $10 million from Democratic activists Herb and Marion Sandler, who made their fortune running the savings and loan firm Golden West Financial Corporation.

Unlike some of the earlier versions of nonprofits, ProPublica benefited from a changing attitude among the existing media companies. When the Center for Investigative Reporting or the Center for Public Integrity came onto the scene, few big newspapers or broadcast outlets were willing to work with the nonprofits to collaboratively produce stories. But media outlets had changed since then. ProPublica, and others that would follow, would be able to partner with existing media to produce reports, meaning that readers would encounter their work on the pages of the *New York Times* or see it on *60 Minutes* rather than only seeing it on the ProPublica site. These efforts helped bolster the amount of investigations news organizations were able to conduct. By the end of 2000s, journalism professor Jon Marshall said, "investigative reporters could see signs of hope: increased collaboration, creative Web-based ventures, new nonprofits, growing university support, and more help from foundations" (Marshall 2011).

Many of these organizations developed as the economic recession and advertising implosion swept across the newspaper industry. As newspapers shed staff, many of these journalists looked to create their own startups to cover the type of reporting they had done at their newspaper. Foundations, many worried by the economically shaky state of the newspaper newsroom, backed these new news entities. The period of 2008–2012 saw some 120 news organizations spring up. They ranged from national and statewide investigative reporting operations to regional and local news startups that aimed to cover communities left with weakened newspapers. Still, as the initial startup money started to run out, many of these newsrooms realized that they lacked sustainable business plans. Editors' focus was on content, and their business experience may have been minimal. A new organization could be kickstarted by a small section of the public concerned enough to donate money to back the new group, or foundations that wanted to support local information as a critical need to ensure good government and an informed electorate. But keeping the doors of the operation open becomes more difficult as the sense of urgency wanes.

Nonprofits must make their case to readers or foundations or organizations that may consider backing the group. Perhaps not surprisingly, many of these nonprofits are formally affiliated with a larger organization, often a foundation or university. But the very structures of foundations that support these groups have made it difficult to develop a plan for sustainability. According to groups that aim to help nonprofits function like the Nonprofits Assistance Fund, often "organizations starve themselves . . . There's an obsession with being able to say to [funders] that 80 to 90 cents of every dollar you give us is going to programs" (Mitchell, Jurkowitz, Holcomb, Enda, and Anderson 2013). Funders, from individuals to foundations, want to support content. They are inspired by the investigative piece that brings to light governmental corruption or casts a harsh light on where people are suffering because of the government actions or inaction. Few want to fund business development and planning. This puts many of these organizations in the unenviable position of continually seeking grants to continue their work. Some have worried that this may set journalists at the mercy of foundations with clear agendas. Yet this worry, to some, seems like a risk worth taking. Journalism professor Phil Meyer studied that potential problem in considering one of the oldest journalistic nonprofits, NPR, in his book *The Vanishing Newspaper*. He concluded that "(the) separation between funders and journalists works at least as well as the wall between the news and advertising departments at the newspapers most Americans read . . . So let us be blunt. Allowing charitable foundations to pay for news might be risky, but it can't be any worse than letting advertisers pay for it" (Meyer 2009).

Despite these challenges, nonprofits have been able to establish themselves around the country. By 2013, all but nine states had at least one nonprofit news group working in the state and many could boast more than that, often relying on various business models and backers to continue to operate. Take, for example, the sparsely populated state of Montana. With barely a million people and with Lee Newspapers owning most of the state's daily newspapers, one would not think the readership would exist to support a full-time nonprofit. But it actually had three running in 2015, each reflecting a version of what nonprofit news orgs look like. One, Last Best News, is run by a former Lee journalist who launched his own web news operation in Billings to fill the gaps he felt the paper left uncovered in the state's largest city—which only has a population of 100,000. Last Best News has only one fulltime staffer and a handful of contributors and relies on advertising and personal donations to fund its operations. A second news organization, the Montana Center for Investigative Reporting, aims to expand the amount of in-depth explorations of contentious issues not easily covered in the daily newspaper or nightly television news. These longer-term investigations are run by a single reporter/editor with the help of a couple contributors and the support of small grants that help it tackle specific investigations. The site is modeled after the national Center for Investigative Reporting and has partnered with the state's journalism school and Last Best News. A third operation, Montana Watchdog, is funded by the Franklin Center for Government & Public Integrity. The Montana branch of this operation is one of 40 state-based Watchdog.org sites that aim for "a well-informed electorate and a more transparent government." Watchdog.org, affiliated with the conservative Koch Brothers nonprofit Americans for Prosperity Foundation, has been accused by media observers of being a partisan stalking horse. Longtime political reporter Gene Gibbons worries, "At the forefront of an effort to blur the distinction between statehouse reporting and political advocacy is the Franklin Center for Government & Public Integrity, which finances a network of websites that focus on state government" (Gibbons 2010). Montana Watchdog covers the state, attends many reporting meetings and claims it is independent, but its funding source has raised questions from some. Still, these three organizations in a remote state offer a snapshot of the diversity and the varying roles of nonprofit news organizations at the state level.

In terms of political coverage, nonprofits have actually had more of an impact for a longer period than many other areas touched by these groups. For decades, news nonprofits and foundations have worked to increase the flow of information that voters and reporters have access to when considering public policy. (The idea of ensuring that voters can access information about their democracy seems to resonate with both charitable foundations and wealthy benefactors.) Sometimes these groups help reporters do their jobs in covering campaigns and governing. For example, the Sunlight Foundation, which seeks to open government to public scrutiny and has been essential to unlocking government documents and data, has emerged as both a recipient of foundation support and a backer of data journalism. Similarly the National Institute on Money in State Politics and the Center for Responsive Politics have worked at the state and federal level, respectively, to increase access to financial donor and disclosure reports on campaigns and lobbying. Other nonprofits have sought to play important roles in producing content for the public and interest media outlets. FactCheck.org, for example, emerged as a nonprofit aimed at consistently testing the claims made by politicians in campaign ads and on the stump.

Although Phil Meyer argued that the nonprofit model of journalism is no more dangerous than the old advertising-based system of for-profit reporting, the agenda of the organization and its funders can still be difficult for the public to easily decode. Unlike the commercial model where the bottom-line is usually to make the largest possible profits for the owners, nonprofits have a different and often less obvious agenda. Many nonprofits like National Public Radio or the Center for Investigative Reporting have long histories of negotiating the demands and agendas of their sponsors. They have a track record and institutional structures that create a wall between the fundraising and editorial arms of the organization. Although not always perfect, this system has worked well enough and allowed viewers and readers to feel comfortable that the organization is not simply serving as a mouthpiece for the funder. Other organizations have less experience and are often less transparent about their funding and any agreement they have signed onto to receive funding. These nonprofits may be producing content that aims to advance a specific policy agenda or even partisan end. This may not be, in itself, a problem as more and more media outlets take on clear partisan bents; the problem comes when that agenda is unclear to the reader. Nonprofit news organizations are not required to disclose their donors and so, as one adviser to nonprofit news operations noted, "As a nonprofit entity, your organization has to decide what your policy is with donors and the funds they give. Do you want to disclose funders' names and the amounts of money they give? How will you handle the role of donors who want to be involved in the editorial process? How will you handle anonymous donations? Will you accept anonymous donations and will you disclose that information to the public?" (Weiss 2011).

These decisions are in the hands of the media outlet, so news organizations can decide to hide their donor lists or only offer a list and not information about the grant or the amount. When nonprofit news stories are picked up by mainstream media or simply posted in a social media feed, they are largely treated as if they are a traditional piece of reporting, which may or may not be a fair description. Nonprofits are the source of some of the most important and revealing investigations and unbiased sources of data on the web, but they can also be a partisan front for organizations that hide behind nonprofit laws. The differences are up to the reader to find and know.

See also: Advocacy Journalism; Center for Public Integrity (CPI); FactCheck.org; *Mother Jones*; Newspaper Industry; ProPublica

Further Reading

"About Us." ProPublica. Accessed June 14, 2016. https://www.propublica.org/about/.

Gibbons, Gene. 2010. "Statehouse Beat Woes Portend Bad News for Good Government." Nieman Reports. December 15. Accessed October 3, 2015. http://niemanreports.org/articles/statehouse-beat-woes-portend-bad-news-for-good-government.

Marshall, Jon. 2011. *Watergate's Legacy and the Press: The Investigative Impulse*. Evanston, IL: Northwestern University Press.

Meyer, Phil. 2009. *The Vanishing Newspaper: Saving Journalism in the Information Age*. Columbia: University of Missouri Press.

Mitchell, Amy, Mark Jurkowitz, Jesse Holcomb, Jodi Enda, and Monica Anderson. 2013. "Nonprofit Journalism: A Growing but Fragile Part of the U.S. News System." Pew Research Center. June 10. Accessed October 4, 2015. http://www.journalism.org/2013/06/10/nonprofit-journalism.

Overholser, Geneva. 2006. "On Behalf of Journalism: A Manifesto for Change." The Annenberg Foundation Trust. Accessed October 4, 2015. http://www.annenbergpublicpolicycenter.org/wp-content/uploads/OnBehalfjune20082.pdf.

Weiss, Amy Schmitz. 2011. "Ethical Guidelines for the Nonprofit Journalism Organization." Journo.biz. August 15. Accessed October 4, 2015. http://journo.biz/2011/08/15/ethical-guidelines-for-the-nonprofit-journalism-organization.

NPR

With its iconic programs like *All Things Considered* and *Morning Edition* and an array of digital news and on-demand services, National Public Radio has grown from a consortium of educational and university-based local radio stations into a major force in American journalism. Although it has launched an aggressive website and podcasting strategy, NPR remains a service operated by hundreds of local public radio stations.

Public radio in this country began as a grassroots effort. Dozens of radio stations in the 1920s and 1930s were started at universities around the country, and these stations aired educational programs and were generally noncommercial. The Federal Communications Commission agreed in the 1940s to allot bandwidth at the lower end of the public airwaves to noncommercial stations, which is why most public radio stations are found in the 80s or low 90s on the radio dial. But the commission was careful not to be too specific about what kind of station would be considered for these noncommercial educational licenses. The FCC notes, "The Commission has intentionally left 'educational programming' undefined, describing public broadcasting instead in terms of what it is not: Public stations 'are not operated by profit-seeking organizations nor supported by on-the-air advertising,' with their 'positive dimensions' determined by 'social, political, and economic forces outside the Commission'" (FCC, n.d.). This set the stage for a period of expansion by local stations during the 1950s and early 1960s. Much of the growth of noncommercial radio was credited to growth of television, which put many commercial radio stations out of business.

Another government move began to build a national network out of these locally operated stations. When President Lyndon Johnson signed the Public Broadcasting Act into law, he created a publically funded nonprofit called the Corporation for Public Broadcasting. CPB helped fund early efforts at collaborative programs that mirrored the commercial networks on television and the radio. By 1970, 90 of these stations joined together and founded National Public Radio. The new network went into action the following year, broadcasting hearings into the Vietnam War for all member stations to air. By May 1971 the NPR operation in Washington, D.C., launched an afternoon news program called *All Things Considered*. It added the morning program a few years later and the network was up and running. From its outset, NPR sought to be different than commercial radio, which at that time still had sizable staffs and listenership. The new programs aimed to sound more informal and less like the historic, booming broadcasters such as Edward R. Murrow. Susan Stamberg, an icon of public radio and one of NPR's first employees, remembered NPR's first program director Bill Siemering castigating her for sounding too much like their commercial competitors. "'We want NPR to sound more relaxed,' Bill said. ' Conversational. We're going to talk to our listeners just the way we talk to our friends—simply, naturally. We don't want to be the all-knowing voices from the top of the mountain'" (Stamberg 2012). That tone would help make NPR and the hundreds of local stations unique on the radio. Its two daily newsmagazine programs soon drew millions of listeners.

Unlike commercial broadcasters and even public television, NPR is probably most unique for the amount of news not produced by the national network. Local radio stations across the country offer locally produced newscasts and discussion programs. The amount of content produced by these stations is enormous, and although some stories may be picked up by the national programs, the vast majority stays in the local communities they serve.

These stations rely on a mix of government funding received in grants from the Corporation for Public Broadcasting and local members. For many NPR-affiliated stations, the membership drives are the critical source of income, allowing the station to both license and run NPR's nationally produced content and pay for local reporters to cover the events in their community. This membership model has, itself, been undergoing changes as people's media habits and political realities evolve. As a long-time veteran of public radio noted in a 2015 article, "Though membership has always been a core part of public media, over the past several years, public radio has been grappling with new questions concerning membership and listener loyalty. The traditional form of building membership and leveraging organizational loyalty—the pledge drive—has declined in effectiveness, and new conversations are beginning about how to recruit and retain members who access content off-air" (Kramer 2015).

The network has found itself in the middle of political maelstroms from time to time, and some argue that has pushed the network more to the right. In 2010 a firestorm of protest erupted after the network abruptly ended its contract with commentator Juan Williams. The former host of *Talk of the Nation*, Williams had taken on more opinion-based assignments and had also begun working for Fox News as a paid, on-air commentator. It was during one of those appearances that Williams declared to host Bill O'Reilly, "I mean, look, Bill, I'm not a bigot. You know the kind of books I've written about the civil rights movement in this country. But when I get on the plane, I got to tell you, if I see people who are in Muslim garb and I think, you know, they are identifying themselves first and foremost as Muslims, I get worried. I get nervous" (Padilla 2010). The comments prompted NPR to sever all ties with Williams. NPR's CEO at the time, Vivian Schiller, said in an email to stations that Williams could no longer work as a "news analyst" for NPR, noting, "News analysts may not take personal public positions on controversial issues; doing so undermines their credibility as analysts, and that's what's happened in this situation . . . As you all well know, we offer views of all kinds on your air every day, but those views are expressed by those we interview—not our reporters and analysts" (Shepard 2010). The move angered many and prompted Republicans in Congress to propose eliminating public funding for public media. Williams himself would later call for NPR to no longer receive support from the government.

But the Williams controversy is just one of the stories that have caused NPR trouble. In 2011 a conservative filmmaker recorded a series of damning conversations with NPR fundraisers. In one, the outgoing head of NPR's money raising operation was recorded disparaging members of the tea party movement, calling them "xenophobic" and "seriously racist, racist people." The controversy, combined with the hangover from the Williams affair, cost the head of NPR her job and thrust the network into a crisis. About a week later the same conservative released a secret recording of the network discussing a grant it received from the liberal Open Society Institute, which is funded by billionaire philanthropist and controversial liberal George Soros. The recordings noted that OSI had given the network and local stations nearly $2 million without being mentioned on-air. Some worried that taking the funding without publically acknowledging the source could compromise the reporting of NPR. Maria Archuleta, a spokeswoman for the Open Society Institute, said "We haven't taken on-air credit for the last 10 years. We just don't feel the need to take credit. For us, it's about the issues" (Chiu 2011). The story still raised concerns that NPR was a liberal outfit. And the network has struggled to garner the trust of conservatives. According to a survey by the Pew Research Center, NPR is one of the most divisive news sources when it comes to trust. People who say they are liberal see the network as one of the most trusted sources of news while conservatives, especially strong conservatives, see it as particularly non-trustworthy.

Despite the trouble with conservatives and the occasional spat over funding in Congress, NPR has seen rapid growth in the post–September 11, 2001, era. NPR's official history of itself called the terrorist attacks "a turning point for NPR; a catalyst to shift our orientation even more fully to high-quality, contextual, timely news—both domestic and foreign. 9/11, Election 2004, the Iraq War, the primaries and Election 2008 led to spikes in audience, and most of these new listeners stayed with us" (NPR, n.d.). In the days before the attacks, the average listenership of NPR was about 16 million people. Soon after, it reached 20 million and by 2011 it was topping 25 million. This massive expansion of audience was accompanied by a massive expansion of the network's mission. As the American Journalism Review noted, "That day lit a spark under NPR to quicken its pace toward becoming a full-service, primary news source, but the movement had been underway for most of the network's existence. As FCC news requirements loosened and most radio stations pretty much abandoned journalism, NPR, aided by listenership growth and member stations' demands, became a formidable news operation" (Robertson 2004). NPR also stepped up its digital evolution, devoting more resources to the Internet. The audience has largely stuck with NPR, and the network has continued to expand.

Its growth in the digital arena is both a response to its expanded news role and an acknowledgement of the changing media environment. Radio, both commercial and noncommercial, was somewhat a product of the daily commute. The network's two most popular programs aired during what is called in the business "drive time"—the typical hours people spend in cars headed to and from work. As technology has evolved, some carmakers have begun to move away from installing radios in cars, instead allowing drivers to play their own mobile devices or streaming media. This uncertain future of the radio has helped spur NPR to deploy new programming and new ways of listening. The network hosts some of the most popular downloadable audio podcasts in the world, and it has tried to incorporate more experimental techniques of storytelling into its new on-air programs. In early 2015 the network launched a new program, *Invisibilia*, which mixes sound with interviews while exploring the intangible and its effect on behavior. Still, the network remains slow to change the model that has worked since the 1970s. And with an audience of more than 25 million listening, the NPR system remains a vibrant actor in the modern media landscape.

See also: Government-Subsidized Journalism; *PBS NewsHour*; Trust in Journalism

Further Reading

Chiu, Lisa. 2011. "Secret Recording Explores Relationship Between Billionaire Soros and NPR." *Chronicle of Philanthropy*. March 17. Accessed December 29, 2015. https://philanthropy.com/article/Secret-Tape-Explores/158703.

Kramer, Melody. 2015. "What, Exactly, Does It Mean to Be a Member of a Public Radio Station? Can That Definition Expand?" Nieman Lab. May 15. Accessed December 29, 2015. http://www.niemanlab.org/2015/05/what-exactly-does-it-mean-to-be-a-member-of-a-public-radio-station-can-that-definition-expand.

"Nonprofit Media." Federal Communications Commission. Accessed December 29, 2015. https://transition.fcc.gov/osp/inc-report/INoC-31-Nonprofit-Media.pdf.

"Overview and History." NPR. Accessed December 29, 2015. http://www.npr.org/about-npr/192827079/overview-and-history.

Padilla, Steve. 2010. "NPR Commentator Loses Job Over Muslim Remark." *Los Angeles Times*. October 21. Accessed June 14, 2016. http://articles.latimes.com/2010/oct/21/nation/la-na-juan-williams-20101021.

Robertson, Lori. 2004. "Quicker and Deeper." *American Journalism Review*. June/July. Accessed December 29, 2015. http://ajrarchive.org/article.asp?id=3700.

Shepard, Alicia. 2010. "NPR's Firing of Juan Williams Was Poorly Handled." NPR. October 21. Accessed December 29, 2015. http://www.npr.org/sections/ombudsman/2010/10/21/130713285/npr-terminates-contract-with-juan-williams?ps=rs.

Stamberg, Susan. 2012. "Introduction: In the Beginning There Was Sound but No Chairs." In *This Is NPR: The First Forty Years*. San Francisco: Chronicle Books.

O

OBJECTIVITY

Journalism, and in particular political reporting, is supposed to be the business of accuracy and precision. Words are important and what those words mean should be clear to the reader and to the reporter using them. So the strange and sordid history of the concept of objectivity is an odd object lesson in what happens when clarity of meaning becomes obscured.

Objectivity was conceived of as a way to push journalists to be more diligent and professional in ferreting out facts and information that could help voters and decision-makers make better-informed judgments. Over the years, the concept mixed with the growing concern about bias in the media, and objectivity came to mean that reporters should be devoid of opinions. An objective journalist did not secretly believe one side was right and the other was wrong. Some chose not to vote in an effort to prove their objectivity. But as readers became more sophisticated and some journalists came to reject the idea of reporters not expressing opinions, objectivity became a target of many politicians and advocacy journalists who called the whole concept of objectively reporting a joke.

The concept of objectivity and its importance for a journalist began emerging in the early twentieth century and found one of its strongest advocates and cogent philosophers in the commentator and author Walter Lippmann. Lippmann saw the country and democratic process in crisis of ill-informed voters and unregulated institutions and argued that journalists offered the most vital method of address both problems. If journalists could provide people with the facts and information necessary to make an informed decision in an election or other public matter, Lippmann felt the system could work. These same agents could help check against abuses of the system by politicians or corporations. It was a classically liberal argument that found an informed voter would inherently make effective decisions.

But there was a problem with Lippmann's proposal: many journalists of the day were driven more by emotion and bias than by what they discovered in their reporting. Throughout the nineteenth century many reporters and those who talked about reporting argued that journalists should be driven by a concept they called realism. In this construction of realism journalists simply collected the information and arranged it and presented it to the reader. The idea was that simply showing the reader what they had found would allow the truth to emerge almost naturally. The journalists Bill Kovach and Tom Rosenstiel would later explain, "Realism emerged at a time when journalism was separating from political parties and becoming more accurate. It coincided with the invention of what journalists call the inverted pyramid, in which a journalist lines the facts up from most important to least important, thinking it helps audiences understand things naturally" (Kovach and Rosenstiel 2001). But this new focus on realism often failed to help explain the core issues of the day. Realism could tell you that a fire at a factory had killed 146 workers in a New York City clothing factory. It could explain what people had seen and what the owners of the factory said afterwards. But it often failed to explain the bigger picture of how the company had treated these workers and ran their factory. It was less likely to question the underlying workplace safety regulations.

Lippmann wanted a more aggressive form of reporting that did not simply line up the basic surface of a story and show it to people. The solution, he argued, was for a new form of objective reporting that focused on reporting fact and data and relied less on the salacious or personal. He worried that journalism was likely to be overrun by "unenterprising stereotyped minds soaked in the traditions of a journalism always ten years out of date." Lippmann's solution was to train new journalists and promote their work as the best civic-minded experiment. He proposed "to send into reporting a generation of men who will by sheer superiority, drive the incompetents out of business. That means two things. It means a public recognition of the dignity of such a career, so that it will cease to be the refuge of the vaguely talented. With this increase of prestige must go a professional training in journalism in which the ideal of objective testimony is cardinal" (Lippmann 1920). Lippmann wanted to move beyond the "slick persons who scoop the news" and celebrate "the patient and fearless men of science who have labored to see what the world really is." This concept and its underlying value of professionalism and scientific work would create the structural foundation of objective journalism.

There did come a new ethic to journalism in the mid- and later-twentieth century that placed enormous value on the concept of objectivity. This led directly to certain professional tropes within journalism that would shape the profession for decades. First was the tendency of reporters to write with a detached, analytical voice. The result was often called "The Voice of God," where reporters covering hard news stories tended to sound like one another in print. To know a journalist and to read their work is like seeing two different versions of the same person, the latter formal and oddly disconnected from the events they are writing about. One journalist recalled the advice from their aged journalism professor, that their job was to "cope with the challenge of getting over ourselves. Didn't we understand that our calling was to reveal wrongdoing and tell other people's stories without muddying the waters with our own opinions or, worse, personal experiences? Writing in the third person, standing back from the material, maintaining objectivity, all were key. If we couldn't discipline ourselves to do this, we weren't news reporters, he said, gleefully humiliating us until we ironed any trace of our own voices out of our stories" (Heath 2012).

This tone of writing that sought to strip the voice of individual reporters from the story they were telling became one of the first major elements of objectivity to be challenged. Why did all news stories have to sound the same? Shouldn't experience and observations find their way into a story to add color or interest? As reporters became more experienced and their writing more crafted, the idea of fully expunging the individuality of a reporter from a story became a point of contention. Movements like New Journalism rejected the separation of reporter and story. Others critiqued it in less obvious, but no less powerful ways. The satirical news service *The Onion* made a name for itself by applying the same reporting voice to ridiculous stories such as "Evangelical Scientists Refute Gravity with New 'Intelligent Falling' Theory" or "Area Man Passionate Defender of What He Imagines Constitution to Be." These are funny because they faithfully reflect the formalized tone of so many news organizations. New Journalism declares that stories told in deeply personal ways can apply the concept of objective reporting, just as detached Voice of God stories can still easily lack such reporting. The American Press Institute makes the point clear: "Journalists who select sources to express what is really their own point of view, and then use the neutral voice to make it seem objective, are engaged in a form of deception. This damages the credibility of the craft by making it seem unprincipled, dishonest, and biased" (American Press Institute).

Many critics of the idea of objective journalism, especially on the conservative side of the spectrum, argue that objective reporting requires a journalist to be devoid of political beliefs. Andrew Kirell, senior editor of the politics and entertainment site Mediaite, argues, "Every journalist has a political point-of-view and they don't magically check that at the door the minute they land a job. Many pretend to pursue some noble cause of pure 'objectivity,' but it is truly in vain. Every good journalist is informed about what subjects they cover and it would be near-impossible to be informed and not have an opinion" (Kirell 2012). The question then becomes, if the reporter is going to vote for candidate X how can they possibly cover candidate Y fairly? The argument then follows that the reader should be allowed to understand the perspective of the person writing the story. If the reporter thinks what a candidate is saying is bunk, shouldn't the reader know that and use that in their evaluation of the story?

It seems like a logical and fair request, but it's muddier than it may appear. Objectivity does not require nor expect a reporter to be devoid of opinions. In fact, the argument for objectivity is based on the inherent opinions the writer will bring to a story. Objectivity pushes the reporter to acknowledge their opinions and then pursue the information wherever it leads, even if it challenges their perceptions. The idea of objectivity is that it should apply to the process of *reporting*, not to the *reporter*. To clarify this, Lippmann and other defenders have often turned to science for inspiration and implementation. A scientist may enter an experiment with a presumption of what is going to happen when they conduct the process, but they still go through the experiment and document it objectively. This ensures any information they provide based on that theory is backed up with information they obtained. The bias of the scientist, while helpful in organizing the experiment and perhaps formulating a hypothesis, has little to do with what they discover. The difficulty in translating this to journalism is that, unlike the scientific process, there is no established and accepted form of what the objective reporting process looks like. It is far easier simply to lump objectivity into the same concern as bias.

More than just media critics and those who see inherent bias in reporting see objectivity as a problem. Many journalists have argued that the quest for "fairness" in the name of objectivity can neuter the reporting process by enabling the manipulation of media. In this construction objectivity often merges with balance to create anemic "he-said/she-said" stories—each side makes their case without the media pushing back and challenging the claims. Reporters can simply quote official sources of both sides of a debate in Congress and call that objective, because one Democrat and one Republican was interviewed.

Such reporting places more value on an official than on other sources and can lead to either deliberately or inadvertently misleading stories. For example, in the months leading up to the invasion of Iraq in 2003, news organizations reported on the official accusations of the Bush administration that Iraq was working to develop weapons of mass destruction. Stories about Iraqi efforts to purchase uranium for possible nuclear weapons appeared in the *New York Times*. Press conferences with President Bush occurred where the president made reference to the September 11 attacks 14 times in a one-hour event. In the wake of the invasion many would revisit the press coverage to question where they fell down, and some pointed part of the blame at the use of objectivity to justify weak reporting. Brent Cunningham, in particular, argued that too tight an adherence to "objectivity" allows reporters to get away with shallowly reported and poorly understood stories. He adds that many journalists fear that pushing back too hard against a source may make them appear biased and lacking objectivity. He concludes by arguing that "journalists (and journalism) must acknowledge, humbly and publicly, that what we do is far more subjective and far less detached than the aura of objectivity implies . . . [and that] we need to free (and encourage) reporters to develop expertise and to use it to sort through competing claims, identify and explain the underlying assumptions of those claims, and make judgments about what readers and viewers need to know to understand what is happening" (Cunningham 2003).

The reporter, in this model, might look more like Glenn Greenwald, the controversial journalist who broke the National Security Agency surveillance programs story and who has advocated against government secrecy. Greenwald clearly has the opinion that the NSA's electronic data tapping programs are wrong, but like Cunningham wants, he also has the technical know-how to write about these issues in a way that a less experienced reporter would not. That less technically proficient reporter would likely be forced to interview an official from the NSA and a critic from outside and then present that in an objectively balanced story, but would struggle to combat potentially false claims by either side.

This has downsides too, however. The reporter risks becoming simply another voice in the debate, not a fact-checker but an advocate. Will people now believe that Glenn Greenwald would accurately portray the government's argument for the surveillance program when he himself has clearly made it his cause to fight? This is the struggle of modern objectivity—without a clear sense of process that allows an opinionated reporter to cover a controversial story in a fair way, the idea of objectivity becomes itself a source of debate. Objectivity cannot be reduced to interviewing both sides of a debate. Political reporting is particularly prone to this, as candidate X attacking candidate Y can be covered fairly easily, but that does not get at the facts of the case. Add increasingly fragmented audiences for these publications, and the tendency of readers to see facts themselves as subjective, and the objective reporting approach becomes even more difficult to achieve.

It seems notable that a century ago Lippmann in his work *Liberty and the News* made the subjectivity of facts such a point of crisis. He noted, "Everywhere to-day men are conscious that somehow they must deal with questions more intricate than any that church or school had prepared them to understand. Increasingly they know that they cannot understand them if the facts are not quickly and steadily available. Increasingly they are baffled because the facts are not available; and they are wondering whether government by consent can survive in a time when manufacture of consent is an unregulated private enterprise. For in an exact sense the present crisis of western democracy is a crisis in journalism" (Lippmann 1920). The same words could be used today to describe a chaotic world inundated with (mis) information on digital platforms. The issue remains, but Lippmann's solution of objectivity has become less an answer and now more part of the debate itself.

See also: Balance; Echo Chamber Effect; Lippmann, Walter; Political Bias and the Media; Post-Truth Politics

Further Reading

Cunningham, Brent. 2003. "Rethinking Objectivity." *Columbia Journalism Review*. July/August. Accessed February 1, 2016. http://www.cjr.org/feature/rethinking_objectivity.php.

Heath, Jena. 2012. "The Voice of God Is Dead." *American Journalism Review*. April/May. Accessed December 21, 2015. http://ajrarchive.org/Article.asp?id=5283.

Kirell, Andrew. 2012. "There Is No Such Thing as 'Objective' Journalism—Get Over It." Mediaite. November 5. Accessed December 21, 2015. http://www.mediaite.com/online/there-is-no-such-thing-as-objective-journalism-get-over-it.

Kovach, Bill, and Tom Rosenstiel. 2001. *The Elements of Journalism: What Newspeople Should Know and the Public Should Expect*. New York: Crown Books.

Lippmann, Walter. 1920. *Liberty and the News*. New York: Harcourt, Brace and Howe.

"The Lost Meaning of 'Objectivity.'" American Press Institute. Accessed December 21, 2015. http://www.americanpressinstitute.org/journalism-essentials/bias-objectivity/lost-meaning-objectivity.

OLIVER, JOHN (1977–)

As the star of a cable comedy show that lampoons the media, John Oliver is not beholden to the Federal Communications Commission. It may be the other way around.

Oliver, the host of HBO's *Last Week Tonight*, has quickly become one of the sharpest critics of, well, everybody. From the world soccer governing board to federal sentencing guidelines, the profanity-laden program has made it its business to explain complex policy questions with biting commentary and often a call to action.

That's where the FCC thing comes in. In late 2014 it appeared the commission was nearing approval of a plan to allow cable companies to charge certain content providers a premium to deliver content more quickly over the Internet. The move would end a long-time federal policy of "Net Neutrality." It was a policy debate thick with technical and legal details. That is, until Oliver let loose with a 13-minute rant on the subject. Oliver took special aim at the chair of the FCC, former cable lobbyist Tom Wheeler, telling his audience and more than 10 million online that "the guy who used to run the cable industry's lobbying arm is now running the agency tasked with regulating it. That is the equivalent of needing a babysitter and hiring a dingo. . . . 'Make sure they're in bed by 8, there's 20 bucks on the table for kibbles, so please don't eat my baby'" (Last Week Tonight 2014).

Oliver then dispatched the "trolls" of the Internet to comment on the proposed rule change at the FCC website. Tens of thousands did that night and crashed the website. Millions more would follow suit over the coming weeks and soon the FCC reversed itself, ruling to maintain the net neutrality policy. Twitter spokesperson Nu Wexler said that those groups arguing to maintain the policy had felt Oliver's take had done more to help their cause than almost anything else, telling the *New York Times*, "We all agreed that John Oliver's brilliant net neutrality segment explained a very complex policy issue in a simple, compelling way that had a wider reach than many expensive advocacy campaigns" (Carr 2014). Even Wheeler made note of the tidal wave of comments Oliver triggered, saying, "I think that it represents the high level of interest that exists in the topic in the country, and that's good. You know . . . I would like to state for the record that I'm not a dingo."

It was a triumph for the Birmingham, England-born comedian. Oliver had built up a reputation for standup comedy when he interviewed for a spot on Comedy Central's *Daily Show with Jon Stewart*. It was 2006 and it was also his first trip to America. Oliver got the gig and was within days serving as the program's "Senior British Correspondent." Oliver would go on to win Emmys as part of the writing team in 2009, 2011, and 2012. He would also spend two months hosting the *Daily Show* in 2013 as Stewart directed a film. By the end of that run, cable giant HBO had announced plans to give Oliver his own late-night program.

Oliver takes his role as outsider seriously, although he has been careful to avoid connecting his comedy to journalism. Still, he told public radio's Terry Gross, there are similarities between the two jobs, saying, "There should be a kind of awkward tension whenever a journalist walks into a room that politicians are in, because you should've done things that annoyed them in the past. It's the same as a comedian. You're no one's friend" (NPR 2014).

Oliver's program is somewhat unique in the pantheon of late-night comedy programs not for its satire but for its approach of explaining complex, often seemingly dull public policies in ways that connect with viewers. He has explored problems with the civil forfeiture laws and the cycle of bail and poverty. His segments have sparked legislative debates and helped spur cities to ease certain policies. The reports air on the premium cable channel, but have been seen by millions more on the program's YouTube channel, allowing many of the policy-heavy sketches to go viral through social media. *Vanity Fair* labeled Oliver the country's most "disruptive journalist"—although Oliver rejects the label "journalist"—and *Time* magazine went so far as to label the real-world impact of the program "The John Oliver Effect."

The label makes Oliver groan, but he admitted in a CBS interview, "There are a lot of absurd public policies to shine a light on. That is generally what we look for, things that have not been covered too much but are inherently ridiculous." And he continues to focus on American politics, but stressed he hopes to look at stories and not just run clips of politicians saying stupid things. Still, he reflected, "No one can say that the American democratic process is not long, or indeed, way too long. And there's a lot of balloons involved. American democracy looks like a 4-year-old's birthday party" (Song 2015).

See also: Comedy, Satire, and Politics; Stewart, Jon

Further Reading

Carr, David. 2014. "John Oliver's Complicated Fun Connects for HBO." *New York Times*. November 26. Accessed December 29, 2015. http://www.nytimes.com/2014/11/17/business/media/john-olivers-complicated-fun-connects-for-hbo.html?_r=0.

"John Oliver Is No One's Friend on His New HBO Show." 2014. NPR. June 19. Accessed December 29, 2015. http://www.npr.org/2014/06/19/323335539/john-oliver-is-no-ones-friend-on-his-new-hbo-show.

"Last Week Tonight with John Oliver: Net Neutrality." YouTube. June 1, 2014. Accessed June 14, 2016. https://www.youtube.com/watch?v=fpbOEoRrHyU.

Song, Jean. 2015. "John Oliver, a 'Disruptive Comedian.'" CBS News. October 30. Accessed December 28, 2015. http://www.cbsnews.com/news/last-week-tonight-john-oliver-effect-american-politics-donald-trump.

OPENSECRETS.ORG

It's hard to imagine that two U.S. senators who retired more than 30 years ago could be responsible for one of the most powerful tools for tracking money in American politics, but that's the story of Opensecrets.org.

Opersecrets.org is a public database of financial disclosure data and Federal Election Commission reporting that allows visitors to track donors, candidate spending, and publicly available information on political parties, campaign organizations, and PACs. The site is run by the Center for Responsive Politics, a nonpartisan, nonprofit group based in Washington, D.C., that former U.S. senators

Frank Church (D-Id.) and Hugh Scott (R-Penn.) started in 1983. The pair of senior legislators had grown increasingly concerned about the role of money and the cost of campaigns and organized CRP to help create a better source of information for the public.

The center maintains a clear mission, stating on its website it hopes to:

- Inform citizens about how money in politics affects their lives
- Empower voters and activists by providing unbiased information
- Advocate for a transparent and responsive government (Center for Responsible Politics 2015)

Throughout the early work of the center this included developing and publishing major works on the state of campaign financing, including tracking the growing importance of so-called soft money contributions to political organizations and the role of independent political spending going back to the late 1970s. These reports often offered groundbreaking insights into the funding and expenses connected to running political campaigns and often advocated for increased disclosure of political funding.

The center's bipartisan founding has continued to this day with sources from across the political spectrum endorsing the information and, usually, the work of CRP. The center took a major step forward in 1996, launching Opensecrets.org, a searchable database of donors, candidates, parties, and political groups. The site has built a reputation among investigative journalists and scholars as the go-to source for political finance data, offering more user-friendly data often accompanied by explanatory material lacking from the Federal Election Commission and other sources. It even provides workshops on how to do research online and how to report data. It also offers a suite of tools that allows data reporters to sift through reams of political data quickly and digital tools that can automatically sort the latest material published at the site. This training and database system that makes up the backbone of Opensecrets.org came into being as both data reporting and campaign financing became more significant forces within modern political reporting.

Much of the information in the center's website comes from FEC reports filed by candidates, but the center also tracks politically active nonprofit groups—the so-called Super PACs and dark money groups. Although far more difficult to monitor, dark money groups have become an increasing focus on Opensecrets.org, with the center reporting in 2015, "These organizations can receive unlimited corporate, individual, or union contributions that they do not have to make public, and though their political activity is supposed to be limited, the IRS—which has jurisdiction over these groups—by and large has done little to enforce those limits. Partly as a result, spending by organizations that do not disclose their donors has increased from less than $5.2 million in 2006 to well over $300 million in the 2012 election" (Opensecrets.org 2015). The center also employs analysts who generate original reports and analyses that track trends within publically disclosed data and those resources that may be published but are far more difficult to find, decipher, and translate for the general public.

Although the center does its own investigations and has partnered with news organizations like NPR in the past to conduct campaign finance series, Opensecrets.org has successfully steered clear of crossing into advocacy or partisanship. *New York Times* reporter Ian Urbina praised the service as "a rare thing in Washington. It does the heavy lifting of true research, not just spinning information" (Opensecrets.org 2015). The center and the site they operate garner most of their funding from other nonprofits, including major grants from the Ford and MacArthur Foundations, but they also accept money from some more controversial foundations, including liberal activist George Soros's Open Society Foundation and two other members of the Soros family. Donors are disclosed on the site in an effort to live up to the transparency it seeks in politics.

Opensecrets.org continues to evolve its offerings, trying to expand its coverage to take in more of who pays to influence the political process and what firms benefit from the explosion in campaign spending. In early 2015, the site launch a new effort aimed at exploring the media and consulting firms that so much of the money raised now flows toward. Andrew Mayersohn explained that expenditures have "always been the poor stepchild of campaign finance, typically receiving far less attention than the other side of the ledger. They're often ignored simply because of the size and complexity of the data set" (Mayersohn 2015). The new focus on expenditures highlights both the complexity of tracking data—for example, many filings from campaigns simply label things "media" or "postage," offering little insight into what the spending actually covered—as well and the explosion of data in the campaign coverage realm.

Opensecrets.org and the Center for Responsive Politics continues to work to decode and translate these dense and often deliberately vague campaign filings, offering the public and the media a critical service in informing campaign coverage and knowledge about the positions and supporters of given campaigns.

See also: Campaign Finance Reform; Dark Money Groups; Data Journalism; National Institute for Money in State Politics

Further Reading

Center for Responsive Politics. 2015. "Our Mission: Inform, Empower & Advocate." Accessed February 17, 2015. http://www.opensecrets.org/about.

Mayersohn, Andrew. 2015. "OpenSecrets.org Unveils New Section on Expenditures." Opensecrets.org. February 11. Accessed February 18, 2015. http://www.opensecrets.org/news/2015/02/opensecrets-org-unveils-new-section-on-expenditures.

Opensecrets.org. 2015. "Political Nonprofits." Accessed February 19, 2015. https://www.opensecrets.org/outsidespending/nonprof_summ.php.

Opensecrets.org. 2015. "What People Are Saying about OpenSecrets.org and the Center for Responsive Politics." Accessed February 18, 2015. https://www.opensecrets.org/about/testimonials.php.

OPPOSITION RESEARCH

Opposition research, often known simply as "oppo," is the work done by campaigns and outside groups to vet candidate statements, identify political weaknesses that may be attacked in ads, and find vulnerabilities in their own side that can be alleviated through public statements and the work of surrogates.

This type of work has existed since long before there was a term to describe it, and since the formalization of investigative teams, the money that has poured into research efforts has exploded. Much of the research is often done by groups associated with campaigns—be it national party organizations or so-called dark money groups and Super PACs. The work can appear in public through a variety of venues. Much of the more straightforward political research—looking for controversial votes or apparent flip-flops on critical issues—appears in ads funded often by technically independent organizations. The juicier stuff—infidelities or stories from far in the past—often is leaked to reporters to dig into further. The work of these groups has always been controversial, seen as a "dark art" of campaigning and a sort-of modern equivalent of the dirty tricks teams of President Richard Nixon that led to Watergate. Even in the wake of Watergate, though, the work of outing stories that might damage an opponent or digging into every past public document produced by an individual continued and continued to grow. Just a decade after attempts to cover up the work of a particularly aggressive opposition research team led to the resignation of President Nixon, the efforts continued on the Democratic side in an incident that highlighted the dangers to both the attacked and the attacker.

The 1988 campaign was setting up to be a crowded field of Democrats seeking the nomination for the presidency, hoping to end the Republican control of the White House since 1981. Party leaders and veteran members of Congress vied with activists and governors for the nod. One of the ones at the forefront of the race was Senator Joe Biden, who was in the national spotlight at the time chairing the controversial nomination hearing of Judge Robert Bork to the U.S. Supreme Court. Bork was seen as too conservative by many on the left, and Biden's strong leadership of the Senate Judiciary Committee put him in a position to turn the hearing into a powerful platform for his campaign for the nomination. As the hearings were set to open a video showed up in the hands of several political reporters. In it, Biden's stump speech from the Iowa fair in 1987 was juxtaposed with a campaign speech by Neil Kinnock, who had run unsuccessfully for prime minister in Britain against conservative Margaret Thatcher. The video highlighted Biden using excerpts of Kinnock's speech without crediting him. The story exploded in the press, but reporters at the time noted that the video itself was a product of some nefarious campaign also running that year. Richard Ben Cramer's exhaustive account of the 1988 campaign, *What It Takes*, captured the moments when the story first appeared and Biden press spokesman Larry Rasky went on the attack because of the video. "The story showed up in Iowa. David Yepsen, the big-foot-on-a-small-pond for The Des Moines Register, had done the piece the same day . . . but Yepsen made sure to note: a tape (the 'attack video,' he dubbed it) of Biden and Kinnock had been provided by a rival campaign. So Rasky was pushing that, too: Who would be so dastardly as to attack Joe Biden, Defender of the Constitution, on the eve of the most important hearings of the century? Was White House skullduggery behind this?" (Cramer 1992).

But once in the bloodstream, a story like the plagiarism scandal tends to lead to more reporters doing more digging. Soon other stories appeared outlining plagiarism in law school and lifted passages from past Democratic candidates. The story would not die, so the Biden campaign died instead. He withdrew from the race. But the story was also cast as a sleazy political attack from within the Democratic Party. R.W. Apple wrote of the incident in the heat of the feeding frenzy, that "the Biden disclosures are another disturbing development in a campaign season in which, other things being equal, they should have a good chance of recapturing the White House. The disclosures weaken a potentially strong candidate, and more: They suggest, because reporters were tipped off in some cases by aides to other contenders, that a season of intraparty guerilla warfare may be about to unfold" (Apple 1987). The opponent in this case was eventual nominee Michael Dukakis. Dukakis's chief adviser, John Sasso, had actually put the video together and was forced to resign from the campaign days after that fact came out. Dukakis spent weeks trying to undo the damage the incident had caused. But in the end, Dukakis won the nomination that year and Biden was forced to watch from the sidelines.

The Biden story highlights the techniques of opposition research, but also the controversial nature of the work. Campaigns want to find out stories about opponents, and that is far from a new trend. Partisan newspaper editors lobbed researched—and some simply rumored—stories about candidates as far back as the bitter campaign of 1800 between President John Adams and Vice President Thomas Jefferson. Adams papers accused Jefferson of sleeping with slaves and Jeffersonian outlets said Adams imported British prostitutes. Things got more specific in the campaign to keep Andrew Jackson out of the White House. That year, 1824, political opponents tracked down the marriage certificate of Jackson and Rachel Robards and discovered she had not been legally divorced when she married Jackson. The opponents circulated stories that year (and four years later when he ran again) accusing Jackson of being an adulterer. Every election cycle, this type of work continued and even after the outing of Sasso in 1987, four years later it was reported that "there were more than 50 firms explicitly engaged in various kinds of opposition research. As the campaign has heated up, more have undoubtedly joined the fray. According to published sources, the Democratic National Committee has employed private investigators and outside researchers to comb through public records and interview potential sources. The Republicans have denied using private investigators, but have employed a variety of outside research and consulting firms, some of whose staff members have backgrounds in investigation and law enforcement" (Basch 1992).

Opposition research has always been part private investigator and part librarian. It mixes political science work aimed at tracking every vote on every bill and every public statement ever made by a politician, law enforcement-style investigations of the candidate and anyone associated with the candidate, and a new era of digitally capturing everything that happens on the campaign trail. The work employs journalists, document experts, and law enforcement veterans and has stayed largely under the radar. A little-read book about the art, *We're with Nobody*, was published in 2012 and written by two veterans of the opposition research efforts who had spent nearly 20 years in the field. One of them, Alan Huffman, admitted that one friend had convinced them to write the book after he told Huffman, "This is just fascinating that there are these two, kind of quirky guys just driving around in a rented Hyundai looking for trouble on politicians all over the country and that this is one of the sort of underpinnings of our political system" (BookTV 2012). The craft Huffman and his colleague Michael Rejebian describe in their book is a surprisingly thorough system that vets candidates' obvious record—did they get a DUI while serving in the state legislature? How did they vote on abortion?—and their far less obvious record—did they plagiarize their Master's thesis? They dig up dirt and test the honesty of the opponent and their candidate, identifying weaknesses in both and passing the information back to their employers. This work has occurred for more than 100 years in the field of politics, but that is not to say recent technological and legal developments have not fundamentally altered the work of oppo teams.

First on the technology front, the volume of information gathered by opposition researchers has soared in recent campaign cycles. The Internet has made available reams of data formerly locked away in county courthouses or buried in files kept at state political enforcement agencies. A click of the mouse can bring up scores of publicly available documents from national, state, and local agencies. These documents may be difficult to locate—just because it is on the Internet does not mean a simple Google search will suffice—and so some opposition researchers have become highly skilled in locating specific documents. One opposition researcher's list of places to search on a given candidate runs more than 300 websites long. Databases connected to financial contributions have also made it easier for researchers to dive into the potential controversies of candidates accepting donations from organizations or individuals with a politically dubious history. In many ways, the trick of this aspect of opposition research is to find the connection to the controversial figure or statement or find a vote on a broader piece of legislation that includes a locally unpopular element.

The Internet has also created a subterranean sector of data hacked from third-party sources that can serve as a potential gold mine (or minefield) for politicians. For example, one can now expect political researchers to be culling through the files that were hacked from Ashley Madison, an adult site that helps married people cheat on their spouses. The Canadian site admitted its security had been breached and in August of 2015 the data was posted on a hacker site. The information is encrypted and difficult for an average web user to find, let alone decipher, but political organizations on both sides no doubt dive in to find dirt on their candidates or their opponents. Digital technology has also given rise to so-called trackers who monitor and record the daily goings-on of the campaign trail. With the ability to easily record from cheap digital devices, campaigns and other groups have deployed trackers to follow candidates to every public speech, sometimes pushing their way to keep their lens on the candidate at all times. These trackers aim to record flubs, mis-statements, and impolitic utterances that the campaigns or organizations opposed to the candidate can use in a campaign ad or distribute to the press. Opposition research wings can now amass thousands of hours of video, gigabytes of documents, and thousands of public records in their quest to know everything about a candidate that may help or hurt them.

But the story of Joe Biden's fall in 1988 included bad news for the campaign that leaked it and this raises the other important element of opposition research. Often campaigns or even political parties do not want their fingerprints on the research that topples a candidate, hoping to seem above the fray of nasty politics even while benefiting from it. Recent Supreme Court and Federal Election Commission decisions have given birth to a new array of organizations that can more freely raise and spend money independent of a campaign. And do its dirty work. Much of that money is going into increasingly sophisticated and omnipresent opposition research work. Perhaps the best known of this new type of organizations is American Bridge 21st Century, a Super PAC created by mega-consultant James Carville and other Democratic strategists. Unlike Super PACs and dark money groups that fund a variety of different campaign work—including advertising and direct mail campaigns—American Bridge is solely focused on opposition research. The group employs dozens of trackers, and was the first national outlet to identify Missouri Senate candidate Todd Akin's comments to a local television station as potentially explosive. In 2012, Akin told local station KTVI that, "From what I understand from doctors, (pregnancy from rape) is really rare. If it's a legitimate rape, the female body has ways to try to shut that whole thing down. But let's assume that maybe that didn't work or something. I think there should be some punishment, but the punishment ought to be on the rapist and not attacking the child" (Marcotte 2014). Because of American Bridge's extensive media gathering operation, they were able to flag the "legitimate rape" comment and post it on YouTube. The clip and the comment went viral and Akin, who had been leading in the polls, lost 15 points and the race.

Despite the success of American Bridge, some worry the growth of independent outside groups is leading to an arms race in the opposition field game. A campaign must report how much money they raise and what they spend it on. Even the most savvy political campaign can only do so much to keep its work hidden. For example, one campaign professional cited a post from campaign manager Ty Harber that advised fellow campaign officials to be as vague as possible when reporting how they spend money, saying, "Instead of reporting that you spent $3,000 on a 'Background check and public records search on Congressman X,' list the expenditure as 'Issue research' or simply 'Research'" (Barksdale 2009). But outside groups like American Bridge add a whole new level of secrecy. Robert Maguire, a researcher at the Center for Responsive Politics, said new independent groups "are raising these pools of unlimited money, and none of it is going toward elevating the political debate. The aim of these groups is to embarrass the candidates they don't like, whether it is by publishing books full of opposition research or this creepy tracker element" (Halper 2015). These groups can deploy dozens of researchers to scour a candidate's life and then supply the information to other independent groups to run in ads or mailings. Interestingly, these groups are required to not coordinate with the campaign they want to help and so the work of American Bridge or another oppo Super PAC must be directed either to other independent groups, the public, or the media.

Not all opposition research is being done by groups unconnected to campaign. One of the biggest coups of oppo research in 2014 had little to do with trackers and reams of data gathered by secretive groups. It was the result of one curious guy. The rare glimpse into the opposition research world came at a gathering organized by the political news organization Politico just ahead of the midterm election that year. During the lunch, the executive director of the National Republican Senatorial Committee recalled how his staff researcher, Mark McLaughlin, had happened to read the thesis of the Democratic U.S. Senate candidate from Montana, John Walsh. The NRSC's Rob Collins said that as McLaughlin read the thesis Walsh had submitted to the U.S. Army War College, "What caught his attention was it was a very pro-Bush NeoCon thesis that Senator Walsh had written, so he was investigating it. He just put it through a translator that checks for plagiarism and the entire last five pages turned bright red. So he said: 'Boy, we got something here'" (Schultz 2014). What they had would lead to Walsh dropping out of the race and the Republicans picking up their easiest win in 2014.

As the Walsh and Akin cases clearly demonstrate, the power of opposition research has become one of the abiding realities of the digital age of politics. Any statement, vote, or donation now can be fodder for researchers and campaign ads and any off-the-cuff comments can be tomorrow's attack ad. With more sophisticated oppo gathering tools and teams, the amount of material these groups miss appears to get smaller and smaller with each cycle. Candidates must now operate under the assumption that if there is something out there in their past that can hurt them or they do something stupid on the trail, it will come out.

See also: Damage Control; Feeding Frenzy; Negative Advertising; Super PACs; Trackers

Further Reading

Apple, R.W. 1987. "Biden's Waterloo? Too Soon to Tell." *New York Times*. September 18. Accessed August 20, 2015.

Barksdale, Brent. 2009. "TMI Can Sink Your Campaign." *Campaigns & Elections*. June 19. Accessed August 20, 2015. http://www.campaignsandelections.com/campaign-insider/1284/tmi-can-sink-your-report.

Basch, Reva. 1992. "Sex, Lies, and Politics: The Opposition Research Wars." *Information Today.* October. Accessed August 20, 2015. https://www.questia.com/magazine/1G1-12831945/sex-lies-and-politics-the-opposition-research-wars.
BookTV. 2012. "Alan Huffman and Michael Rejebian, 'We're with Nobody.'" C-SPAN. February 21. Accessed August 20, 2015. https://www.youtube.com/watch?v=S1_i6GyD0pk.
Cramer, Richard Ben. 1992. *What It Takes: The Way to the White House.* New York: Random House.
Halper, Evan. 2015. "Once a Dark Art, Opposition Research Comes Out of the Shadows for 2016 Campaigns." *Los Angeles Times.* May 27. Accessed August 19, 2015. http://www.latimes.com/nation/la-na-opposition-research-presidential-election-20150521-story.html.
Marcotte, Amanda. 2014. "Todd Akin: 'Legitimate Rape' Doesn't Result in Conception, Unless You're One of My Staffers." Slate. July 17. Accessed June 14, 2016. http://www.slate.com/blogs/xx_factor/2014/07/17/todd_akin_on_msnbc_a_number_of_people_on_my_staff_were_conceived_by_rape.html.
Schultz, Marisa. 2014. "GOP Researcher Responsible for Exposing Montana Senator." *New York Post.* October 30. Accessed August 20, 2015. http://nypost.com/2014/10/30/gop-researcher-responsible-for-exposing-montana-senator.

OPTICS

See Photo Ops and Optics

O'REILLY, BILL (1949–)

The host of Fox News's most popular program is not shy about picking a fight with someone. Bill O'Reilly, the sharp-tongued host of the *O'Reilly Factor,* has made a career of asking in-your-face questions and calling out people when he finds the answers incomplete or not to his liking. Usually right-leaning in his critiques of political issues and candidate, O'Reilly has also angered fellow conservatives with his blunt assessments of some of their iconic leaders. It is a somewhat odd place for a local television reporter-turned-tabloid news host to end up, but O'Reilly has become a highly successful syndicated columnist and a best-selling author of a series of historical books on assassinations and assassination attempts.

O'Reilly was born in New York City and grew up in modest means in Fort Lee, NJ. He attended Marist College and afterward moved to Florida to teach English. After a couple of years he moved back north, earning a Master's degree in broadcasting journalism from Boston University. He actually climbed the traditional career ladder of commercial television news, starting at a small market station in Scranton, Pennsylvania, before moving to Dallas, Denver, Portland, Hartford, and then Boston. He ended up back in New York City in 1980. He joined the national CBS network team in 1982 as a correspondent and covered breaking news like the war in the Falklands and violence in Central America. In 1986 he went to ABC, then three years later joined the syndicated tabloid news program *Inside Edition.* O'Reilly served as the host of the program for nearly six years and then left to pursue another Master's degree, in public administration, at the John F. Kennedy School of Government at Harvard University.

It was while he was at Harvard that he was recruited to join a new network being developed by Rupert Murdoch and Republican campaign adviser Roger Ailes. The *O'Reilly Report* went on air with the dawn of the Fox News network in October 1996. The program has been the most popular on the network for years and features fiery interviews between O'Reilly and guests of the right and the left. The general consensus is that O'Reilly is a conservative who looks for opportunities to dismiss or disparage Democrats, a charge O'Reilly rejects. In one interview he said, "I don't look at it ideologically. We try to run a straight show. The far right doesn't like me at all. They attack me routinely. I don't evaluate it. I let the chips fall as they may. It's not about ideology for us at *The O'Reilly Factor*. It has worked for 19 years. There is an authenticity to what we do. At the same time, the left isn't going to like it. I don't believe capitalism is bad. I don't believe in a welfare system" (Steigard 2015). Despite his claims, O'Reilly has often been the target of liberal critics and served as the primary inspiration for Stephen Colbert's Comedy Central program about an egocentric conservative talk show host.

O'Reilly has recently drawn fire from the right for a historical book on the assassination attempt on President Ronald Reagan. In the book, *Killing Reagan*, O'Reilly claims that Reagan was nearly removed from office in the wake of the shooting under the 25th Amendment to the Constitution. Many scholars have dismissed it for lacking the necessary depth of research, and conservative columnist George Will accused O'Reilly of slandering Reagan. Will and O'Reilly brawled on the *O'Reilly Factor* about the accusation:

> *George Will:* You say that that memo he wrote is the centerpiece of a book. It's a memo that you have never seen. It's a memo that you didn't even ask to try to see from the Reagan library, until after the book was in print. It's a memo that the Reagan library doesn't have, and you should know it doesn't have, because the author was not a member of the White House staff . . . The memo was presented to Howard Baker, Howard Baker took one look at it and said to the man who wrote it, "This is not the Ronald Reagan I know," and that was the end of the influence the memo ever had.
>
> *O'Reilly:* That was not the end of it. You're not telling the truth. You are actively misleading the American people, you are lying.
>
> *Will:* You're something of an expert on actively misleading people.
>
> *O'Reilly:* You are lying . . .

O'Reilly caught heat from historians and conservatives who accused him of not doing enough research. He has produced a series of *Killing* . . . books including Jesus and Lincoln, and the pace of the book production has caused some to question how well researched the works are. He has also been criticized for exaggerating his wartime reporting exploits, but the books have continued to sell and O'Reilly remains the top-ranked host on cable news, drawing some 3 million viewers on some nights. Only Fox's Megyn Kelly has come even close to his numbers.

O'Reilly remains a hard man to pin down or pigeonhole. He is outspoken and, at times, belligerent. He angers the left and sometimes the right. He is and entertainer and yet claims the mantle of journalist. One liberal television critic took on the task of trying to write his biography and in so doing found himself struggling to categorize a man who many of his critics dismiss as, at best, a television entertainer who seeks to provoke for the sake of attention. *Newsday*'s Marvin Pittman decided that those who label O'Reilly an entertainer miss the point. "He is a TV newsman, who is in the rare, envied position of being able to express his opinion while reporting and analyzing the news. He is a man who spent twenty-five years learning his craft before become a success . . . He has the background and the credentials that make him more than just a shouting head on a cable network" (Pittman 2007).

See also: Fox News; Hannity, Sean

Further Reading

Pittman, Marvin. 2007. *The Man Who Would Not Shut Up: The Rise of Bill O'Reilly*. New York: Macmillan Books.

Steigard, Alexandra. 2015. "Media People: Bill O'Reilly." *Women's Wear Daily*. June 3. Accessed January 11, 2016. http://wwd.com/media-news/media-features/bill-oreilly-interview-media-10137732.

P

PACK JOURNALISM

Pack journalism is the idea that groups of reporters covering the same story—especially a political campaign—will begin to act as a herd, writing stories that sound the same, including the same quotes and offering readers essentially the same take on an event. The pack concept pressures reporters to adhere to the same approach to the story and for editors to demand their reporters deliver pieces that line up with what other news organizations are reporting. It is a common boogeyman of political reporting, seen as an agent that fuels media feeding frenzies and limiting the scope and diversity of campaign coverage.

The idea was a major theme of the gonzo journalists who covered the 1972 presidential campaign—especially Timothy Crouse and Hunter S. Thompson. These reporters saw themselves as fundamentally different than the reporters who worked for traditional news outlets and they blasted the idea of the pack, but it is Crouse who is credited with coining the term "pack journalism." In his 1973 book, *The Boys on the Bus*, he wrote, "They all fed off the same pool report, the same daily handout, the same speech by the candidate; the whole pack was isolated in the same mobile village. After a while, they began to believe the same rumors, subscribe to the same theories, and write the same stories. Everybody denounces pack journalism, including the men who form the pack" (Crouse 2013). Crouse's book goes on to explain the blame for this campaign coverage goes beyond the reporters who simply make up the pack. The pack was shaped by a campaign operation that fed them very little information and kept them on a rigid schedule of events that limited the reporters' ability to interview sources or expand their story. This shaping of the message deeply influenced the pack. There was also pressure from editors to have their stories essentially line up with what the editors would read in other outlets, and then there was the dynamics of the media group itself. Certain reporters would be the ones leading the pack and others would feed off their conversations with the reporters who were seen as the smart ones.

The pack was a common enemy that reporters, professors, and scholars all railed against. One journalism professor offered this assessment, "We do not lack information. What we lack is the assurance that the information that is selected for our newspapers and news broadcasts is selected with independent, intelligent judgment; that the selection is free, not only from the influence of special economic, social, and political interests but also from the poison of pack journalism" (Cunningham 1987). This "poison" really boils down to a version of groupthink. If a group of reporters are tracking a story—especially one where the sources try to control information as tightly as a campaign does—those reporters become a cohesive group and that fact begins to influence the work they do. The pack can cover more than just politics. For example, one takedown of business reporting around Apple in 2013 concluded, "The punditry—indeed, even the purportedly 'factual' reporting on Apple—has been little more than myth-making. . . . The prevailing yarn about Apple through mid-September 2012 was that it was a juggernaut. Could do no wrong. Would eventually grow to consume the entire Earth and everything on it. Yet even stories of world domination begin to pale after time, so this one was duly succeeded by another: Apple knocked off its perch. Its best days were visible only in a rear-view mirror. No longer 'cool'" (Hiltzik 2013). This take on Apple could be used to describe almost any campaign of a major candidate. Reporters and commentators tend to follow one another, maybe not in their direct analysis, but in their general topic selection. A campaign is up. A campaign is on the rocks. A move to bring in a new team means the candidate is changing strategy or realizes things are not working.

When digging into what is so very bad about pack journalism, most scholars denounce that it fosters journalistic laziness, offers the public a skewed version of events, and does little to challenge the dominant media "narrative" of a campaign. It becomes much harder to report about stories that do not adhere to what the majority of other reporters and commentators are discussing. This leads to a public informed by what the pack believes to be the case rather than what may actually be happening. Admittedly, while few journalists endorse the idea of the pack, the most heated criticism comes from outside the field. These critics see the pack as a monolith of lazy reporters feeding off one another rather than reporting a story for once. The pack becomes a living, breathing entity that is reduced to the least skilled reporters in the group. In fact, the academic industry of commentators about pack journalism has even taken to criticizing journalists who criticize pack journalism, with one writing, "Whether pejorative depictions of pack journalism should be regarded as a genuine move toward greater accountability or mere lip service is debatable. Either way, reflexive media criticism constitutes significant evidence that an occupational culture with a reputation for ignoring external criticism has begun to recognize that its image is in need of repair" (Frank 2003).

Several contributing factors continue to fuel elements of pack reporting when it comes to campaigns. First, there are the tight message controls placed on those reporters who are traveling with the candidate. Even back to the 1972 campaign Crouse followed, the campaign bus was a tightly scheduled affair. Reporters had to adhere to the schedule set down by the campaign or risk being left behind, literally. Also, most campaigns do not make available the candidate or senior members of the campaign except at carefully coordinated events—either with voters or background briefings for the press. Reporters have access to few other sources to confirm what is being told to them. Often no other campaign officials will discuss the matter other than those who have been authorized, and prospective voters at campaign events tend to be handpicked and made available to the press by the campaign. In this way, pack journalism is often the result of what the campaign wants.

Another critical component of the modern pack is the public opinion poll. Polls, and the interpretation of what those polls mean, are offered to reporters as a separate source of information they can incorporate into their reporting. As all reporters have access to the same data, these stories also feel like a product of pack journalism. When the access to candidates and outside information is deliberately limited by the campaign, the similarity of stories coming out of the campaign bus or plane can only partially be blamed on lazy reporting or bad editors.

Although the campaign will foster a pack journalism approach by limiting the flow of information and carefully coordinating events and access, these same elements of pack reporting can also explode in their face when the story grows beyond their control. Scandals like President Clinton's possible perjury in an investigation into his affair with a former White House intern led to his impeachment, but exploded into the public through an Internet gossip site that then turned into a massive case of pack journalism. *Newsweek* magazine had been investigating the ongoing work of a special prosecutor, Kenneth Starr, whose investigation into Clinton's behavior had shifted from financial questions to those of sexual infidelity and lying under oath. *Newsweek* reporters had spent more than a year on the story and the magazine was getting ready to publish when it received a copy of a taped conversation featuring the intern, Monica Lewinsky. The magazine could not confirm the veracity of the tape and due to the explosive nature of the story, it waited.

Then it leaked via the gossip site "The Drudge Report."

The ensuing flurry of stories about everything from a possible semen-stained dress to whether oral sex should be considered adultery flew across the media—from the most tabloid gossip sites to the national network news. Add to it the few public pronouncements from the prosecutor and a White House in full damage control mode and the result was a furious flurry of stories. The day the news broke, President Clinton hedged in an interview with Jim Lehrer:

Jim Lehrer: The news of this day is that Kenneth Starr, independent counsel, is investigating allegations that you suborn perjury by encouraging a 24-year-old woman, former White House intern, to lie under oath in a civil deposition about her having had an affair with you. Mr. President, is that true?

President Clinton: That is not true. That is not true. I did not ask anyone to tell anything other than the truth. There is no improper relationship and I intend to cooperate with this inquiry, but that is not true.

Jim Lehrer: No improper relationship, define what you mean by that.

President Clinton: Well I think you know what it means. It means that there is not a sexual relationship, an improper sexual relationship or any other kind of improper relationship.

Jim Lehrer: You had no sexual relationship with this young woman?

President Clinton: There is not a sexual relationship. That is accurate. We are doing our best to cooperate here, but we don't know much yet, and that's all I can say now. What I'm trying to do is to contain my natural impulses and get back to work. It's important that we cooperate. I will cooperate, but I want to focus on the work at hand.

And then there is the part of the story impossible to ignore. Throughout his campaign for the presidency and in many times since then, reporters had been deeply frustrated by the carefully opaque responses to direct questions. Reporters found themselves having to grapple with a question of tense—the president saying there is no relationship and not directly answering whether there had been one. From Clinton down, the White House personnel helped fuel the media frenzy by refusing to clearly address the questions, but the pack was already loose upon the land and the reporters found themselves breathlessly reporting unsubstantiated rumors based on less-than-reputable sources. Also, digital technology had progressed so that Internet blogs and 24-hour news channels could pick up a rumor and repeat it without verification or additional reporting and add to the pack. Author and journalist Jules Witcover would bemoan, "Such mixing of journalistic pretenders side by side with established, proven professional practitioners gives the audience a deplorably disturbing picture of a news business that already struggles under public skepticism, cynicism, and disaffection based on valid criticism of mistakes, lapses, poor judgment, and bad taste" (Witcover 1999). Witcover's argument hammered home one of the new dangers of the old pack: when pack journalism was made up of journalists all working on the same story or taking similar approaches to what the story meant, that was bad. When the pack had come to include those who operated on the fringes of modern journalism—the blogger, the gossip columnist—then the pack would be reduced to its lowest common denominator. Matt Drudge would be on the level of the *Wall Street Journal* in the eyes of the reader.

Although the development of digital journalism appeared only to amplify and speed up the behavior of pack journalism, as the media matured and consumers began to turn to search and aggregators for their information, the most effective weapon in the war against groupthink may have been born—Google News and other aggregators. In pleading with journalists to get beyond the spin that followed a 2012 debate, the *Columbia Journalism Review* noted, "Legitimacy questions aside . . . it's worth noting that the economic incentives that supported pack journalism are disappearing. Media outlets need to differentiate themselves in an increasingly crowded marketplace" (Nyhan 2012). That is, in the era when readers can scan hundreds of sources quickly before selecting the piece of reporting they want to actually read, news sources face increasing pressure to stand out and offer a different take on the day's news. This is attractive to aggregators as it gives them another voice to add to their mix of coverage and helps the original source by providing something different to their readers.

Pack journalism is the result of many factors, including the group dynamic of journalists on the campaign trail, efforts by campaigns to control the message and access to the candidate, polling data that creates a common set of data to gauge the narrative of a campaign, and a growing bastion of online commentators and bloggers who can contribute to the pack. But even as the idea of pack journalism remains a fear among journalists and academics, the economics of the Internet are building a counter-pressure that encourages and rewards journalists and others who buck the pack and craft stories that add new perspectives on the campaign. This does not signal the coming demise of pack journalism, but it does make countering the pack story easier. That, coupled with the fact that fewer reporters are actually traveling with campaigns—this job has now been handed off to production assistants and interns—means that the pack mentality is not as potent as it once was in day-to-day campaign coverage. Still, scandals and simple gaffes will likely always spark a journalistic feeding frenzy. And with the need to sate hungry blogs and news sites, reporters will stay pressured to quickly turn around sparsely sourced stories that continue to feed the perception of "a bunch of boys on the bus."

See also: Damage Control; Feeding Frenzy; News Conferences; Spin

Further Reading

Crouse, Timothy. 2013. *Boys on the Bus*. New York: Random House.

Cunningham, Richard. 1987. "Journalism: Toward an Accountable Profession." *The Hastings Center Report* 17, no. 1 (February). Accessed July 15, 2015. http://www.jstor.org/stable/3562451.

Frank, Russell. 2003. "'These Crowded Circumstances': When Pack Journalists Bash Pack Journalism." *Journalism*. November.

Hiltzik, Michael. 2013. "How Apple Invites Facile Analysis." *Los Angeles Times*. March 22. Accessed July 15, 2015. http://articles.latimes.com/2013/mar/22/business/la-fi-hiltzik-20130322.

Nyhan, Brendan. 2012. "Breaking the Pack Journalism Paradigm." *Columbia Journalism Review*. October 3. Accessed July 16, 2015. http://www.cjr.org/united_states_project/how_to_avoid_pack_journalism_at_debates.php.

Witcover, Jules. 1999. "Where We Went Wrong." In *The Media and Morality*. Edited by Robert Baird, William Loges, and Stuart Rosenbaum. Amherst: Prometheus Books.

PALIN, SARAH (1964–)

Not many people knew who Sarah Palin was in 2008. Then, in August, John McCain changed all that. The self-identified maverick Republican presidential nominee tapped the first-term governor of Alaska to be his running mate, seeking to change the dynamic of the election. The result was electric. "When Palin took the stage with McCain, jaws dropped and eyes popped across the country and around the world," wrote John Heilemann and Mark Halperin in *Game Change*, their gossipy tell-all on the 2008 election (Heilemann and Halperin 2010).

The choice got the Republican nominee's campaign a lot of media attention, with Palin even outshining the man at the top of the ticket at times. Dubbed the "Palin Phenomenon," the Pew Research Center tracked this spectacle in 2008. In October of that year, a Pew researcher wrote that she had become a "lightning rod for coverage of everything from her family life to her public record to her potential impact on the presidential race" (Pew 2008).

But the coverage was mostly unflattering and at times downright mean. Her sometimes-shaky answers to substantive questions in media interviews on foreign or domestic policy or what newspapers and magazines she read frequently overshadowed the campaign. Stories about her unwed pregnant daughter and fashion budget made headlines over policy discussions. In the end, Barack Obama and Joe Biden beat them soundly. A question that lingered both during and after the 2008 campaign was just how this one-time Wasilla, Alaska, city councilwoman became the first woman to appear on a Republican presidential ticket—and a national media sensation. And she would turn a failed national campaign into lucrative television contracts and a one-woman conservative movement.

She was born Sarah Heath in Sandpoint, Idaho, on February 11, 1964. Within a few months, the family moved to Alaska, eventually settling in Wasilla, a town with fewer than 10,000 residents where Sarah would first make her mark. Her father was a high school science teacher, and her mother was a school secretary. Palin's childhood was filled with the exploration of the great outdoors. "When I was a kid, my family's idea of a great vacation was to hike the Chilkoot Trail, the rugged thirty-three mile path between Alaska and British Columbia that the pioneers used to travel to seek their fortune back when we were just a territory," Palin wrote in her 2010 memoir *America by Heart* (Palin 2010).

After helping her high school basketball team win the 1982 Alaska State championship, Palin went to Hawaii for college. But, after just a short time there, she transferred to a junior college in Idaho. She eventually landed at the University of Idaho, just a few hours south of her birthplace. In 1987, she graduated with a journalism degree and returned to Alaska as a sports reporter for an Anchorage television station. She married Todd Palin in 1988 and began her foray into politics shortly after that.

She was elected to the Wasilla city council in 1992. In 1996, she unseated an incumbent mayor. And, in 2006, she ran for governor and won. Just 20 months into her term in that position, Palin had another, much higher profile, gig. After throwing out other possibilities, including a cross-ticket pairing with Senator Joseph Lieberman, McCain settled on Palin for the vice presidency, something that earned him criticism from both sides of the aisle. "The reaction to her selection in much of the GOP Establishment ranged from stupefaction to scorn," Heilemann and Halperin wrote (Heilemann and Halperin 2010).

At first, the McCain campaign was sold on Palin. But it wouldn't be long before the campaign started to worry. She feuded with some of the campaign staff and often tried to do things her own way. Staffers probing her background found that some claims she had made about her past were rosier than the truth. Media interviews didn't go well—one with CBS's Katie Couric was famously bad—and her gaffes and non-answers dominated news cycles throughout the final months of the race. *Saturday Night Live* skewered Palin as well, with actress Tina Fey's uncanny Palin impersonation. With that as a backdrop, Barack Obama and Joe Biden won a decisive victory.

After the election, Palin continued to bask in her newfound fame. She wrote memoirs, appeared frequently on Fox News, and seemed to toy with the idea of making a presidential run in 2012. But some wished the Palin phenomenon would end. After a speech Palin gave in Iowa in January 2015, Charles C.W. Cooke wrote for the *National Review* that she shouldn't have a role in GOP politics in the future, and that her appearances give the impression that she is working more to "ensure her name remains in the news" rather than help the Republican Party (Cooke 2015).

Still, Palin, with her own PAC and popularity among some Republicans, continues to be a figure that helps inspire tea party groups and pressure more moderate wings of the party not to compromise with Democrats. Her 2016 endorsement of Republican nominee Donald Trump was widely seen as a boost to the real estate mogul's campaign to attract tea party and conservative Republicans over to his side. She still grabs the spotlight when on the campaign trail, even if the light is dimmer than it was in 2008.

Michael Wright

See also: Comedy, Satire, and Politics; Tea Party Movement

Further Reading

Cooke, Charles C.W. 2015. "Sarah Palin Slips into Self-Parody." *National Review.* January 26. Accessed December 28, 2015. http://www.nationalreview.com/article/397238/sarah-palin-slips-self-parody-charles-c-w-cooke.

Heilemann, John, and Mark Halperin. 2010. *Game Change: Obama and the Clintons, McCain and Palin, and the Race of a Lifetime.* New York: HarperCollins.

"The Palin Phenomenon." 2008. *Pew Research Center.* October 3. Accessed December 28, 2015. http://www.journalism.org/numbers/the-palin-phenomenon.

Palin, Sarah. 2010. *America by Heart: Reflections on Family, Faith, and Flag.* New York: HarperCollins.

PAYWALLS AND THE FREE FLOW OF INFORMATION

The American political system has always placed great value on the role of journalism in informing voters about matters of public concern. This value manifested itself in legal protections and financial incentives for publishers, but the ability of reporters to keep their local communities informed was also based on an economic model that allowed publishers to profit from the number of readers they could attract by selling advertising. Subscriptions were hugely subsidized to attract more readers, and news outlets were able to produce news for free or nearly free to consumers. But it wasn't free and as the digital revolution exploded the old model of media, especially newspapers, new business models began to develop that forced readers to incur more of the costs of producing the publication. It is now the era of the paywall on many sites, a fact that could change the amount of information available to the general public unless they are willing to spend more money for that journalism.

The growth of either nearly free or free information has never been a given in the United States. The Founding Fathers invested enormous power in the concept of an informed electorate and while that electorate was far from everyone—it really amounted to the white, land-owning men—the men who drafted the Constitution and organized the government stressed the value of information in the new governing system they proposed. Thomas Jefferson, writing to a colleague during the Constitutional Convention argued famously:

> The people are the only censors of their governors: and even their errors will tend to keep these to the true principles of their institution. To punish these errors too severely would be to suppress the only safeguard of the public liberty. The way to prevent these irregular interpositions of the people is to give them full information of their affairs thro' the channel of the public papers, & to contrive that those papers should penetrate the whole mass of the people. The basis of our governments being the opinion of the people, the very first object should be to keep that right; and were it left to me to decide whether we should have a government without newspapers or newspapers without a government, I should not hesitate a moment to prefer the latter. But I should mean that every man should receive those papers & be capable of reading them. (Cogan 2015)

The idea that newspapers, or more generally, information, was more important than government is central to the American conception of governing. The system is built around the idea that voters, if informed, will far more often than not make rational and effective decisions about who should represent them and how they should be governed. But embedded in that bold declaration of Jefferson is a concern about those same voters being able to access the information. Those concerns helped fuel the idea of public education as well as an interest in the flow of information. During the early years of the new country, news was seen as something that the government was keenly interested in circulating to the fledgling nation. As early as 1792, Congress passed and George Washington signed the law establishing the U.S. postal service. Included in that law was a cash subsidy that made it cheaper for newspapers to send copies of their editions to subscribers. The subsidy continues to this day, but is far smaller than its eighteenth century predecessor. Newspapers were still expensive and generally aimed at the wealthier class, but these were the same men enfranchised by the new system and so ensuring that the new postal service could deliver news to all of the new states represented a revolution. While traveling the still-new country in 1831 Frenchman Alexis de Tocqueville would note the importance of this new, government-backed system, writing to a friend, "There is an astonishing circulation of letters and newspapers among these savage woods . . . I do not think that in the most enlightened rural districts of France there is intellectual movement either so rapid or on such a scale as in this wilderness" (John 2009).

As the country evolved and urbanized and the electorate expanded to include free men, the issue that Jefferson highlighted once again emerged. In the growing middle and working classes the price of newspapers often seemed too high and so readership remained among the more educated and wealthier classes. A business revolution, not a government policy, changed this. In the 1820s and 1830s the average paper cost 6 cents. Publisher Benjamin Day modified the printing for his paper, the *New York Sun*, and began selling it on street corners for just a penny, making it far more affordable. To make up the lost revenue, Day would sell space in his publication to businesses that sought to reach workers in New York. The idea of the penny press was born and with it, the idea of advertising being the primary source of newspaper revenue. Competitors soon followed suit. And while many of these early papers had clear political leanings, they curbed them in order to appeal to the most people possible, as more readers equaled more money from advertisers.

This was the model of the modern newspaper. Attract readers by making the end product as inexpensive as possible and make revenue through the advertising. For the next 180 years it worked and worked well. Newspapers, especially those who survived the coming of television, operated often as monopolies in their communities and could charge healthy fees for both display ads and classified ads. With profits of 20 percent or higher, business was good. When the Internet came along in the mid-1990s many newspaper publishers applied a basic cost analysis to the new platform. If they could publish the same content online and not pay to print and distribute it, they could attract more readers, even from beyond their home community, and raise the fees on advertisers. Many newspapers began publishing their content that they had already created for free to attract readers. Some executives and journalists, however, equated this to The Fall of Man. As one journalist bemoaned, "The Original Sin among most (but not all) publishers was permitting their content be consumed for free on the web . . . Life today would have been easier if newspapers, magazines and other print-to-web media had recognized in the first place that their content was too valuable—and too expensive to create—to simply give it away on the Internet" (Mutter 2009). Essentially the Internet changed the way people accessed information; it made readers and news consumers less faithful to one source and therefore devalued each reader when it came to monetizing them through advertising. Advertising online only cost a fraction of print ads, and many advertisers could turn to websites that supplied better advertising returns than the traditional mass media did. Newspapers were no longer the only game in town, and often found they weren't even the best player in a now-crowded field. To cap it off, readers who had always received news at a deeply discounted rate soon found themselves getting it for free, and came to expect that.

Revenues crashed, and next came an inevitable wave of layoffs and newspaper closings. According to the American Society of News Editors, the number of journalists working around the country plummeted from 42 percent between 2001 and 2015. That meant far fewer people covering government as well. The Pew Research Center found the number of newspaper journalists credentialed to cover Congress fell by 30 percent between 1997 and 2009. Major papers like the *Rocky Mountain News* and *Seattle Post-Intelligencer* closed and others like the *Ann Arbor News* went completely online. Others scaled back to print only a few times a week. Former *Wall Street Journal* assistant publisher and ProPublica president argued in a 30-page ebook, entitled *Why American Newspapers Gave Away the Future*, "The business model that had fueled the golden age of American newspapers broke somewhere around 2005. Total advertising revenues began dropping, and, at least at this writing, it seems unlikely they will rise appreciably again, at least until print newspapers have literally disappeared and been replaced by some digital future that is still emerging" (Toefel 2012). The overwhelming sense was that publishers and journalists had allowed news to be devalued and a new business model had to be built in its place, but many were uncertain how that could happen when consumers had quickly come to expect news and information to be readily available and free.

While newspapers, and to a lesser extent television and radio, struggled to find a business model that would support the journalism and turn a healthy profit, a quieter revolution was happening in the field of policy reporting. While newspapers slashed D.C. bureaus and new startups like Politico focused on the campaigns and back-and-forth of political debate, a section of journalism was thriving—trade publications and specialized digital news services. These news organizations charged high fees to access their content, all of which was put behind paywalls for subscribers only. Their reporting was solid, if specialized, and often filled a gap left by the scaling back of general reporting in Washington. As specialized political reporting focused less on the function of government and more on the dramas of political intrigue and leadership fights, these publications not only survived but grew. The political news that lobbyists, lawyers, politicians, and policy makers need is often not the type of reporting that appears in the *Washington Post* or Politico.

The dual trend of paywall journalism thriving while general audience reporting dwindles does have some worried. A veteran of the paywall press wrote in *Washington Monthly* in 2015, "This sector of the Fourth Estate is booming, and its coverage of government has never been more robust." But he worried, "The rise of the paywall press and the decline of mainstream media coverage of government aren't causally connected. But the two trends coincide with a palpable populist outrage, in which average Americans are suspicious of how their tax dollars are being spent and observe Washington insiders operate at ever-greater levels of power and secrecy. The irony is that policy journalism in Washington is thriving. It's just not being written for you, and you're probably never going to read it" (Heltman 2015). Several of the established mass media, like Politico and the *Atlantic*, have maintained or launched "Pro" versions that offer insiders more up-to-date and thorough analysis on what is happening in Congress and throughout the federal government, hoping to catch on to the same profitable business that has fueled other trade publications.

Perhaps inevitably, centuries-old penny press newspapers and others have begun moving toward a paywall model themselves. The *New York Times* moved first, launching a metered paywall that allowed the public to view a certain number of stories—it started with 20 and soon dropped to 10—and then to view more they would have to purchase a subscription. The move was quickly emulated by many smaller and regional papers, to mixed effect. By 2015, the *Times* could report that it had 1 million people subscribing to its digital content across the web and mobile, and by 2013 the paper was making as much money from subscribers as it was from advertisers. But a lengthy report from Columbia University cautioned other publishers and the public against mixing the fate of the *Times* with that of journalism. The authors noted, "In the last generation, the *Times* has gone from being a great daily paper, in competition with several other such papers, to being a cultural institution of unique and global importance, even as those papers—the *Washington Post, Chicago Tribune, Los Angeles Times, Miami Herald*, among others—have shrunk their coverage and their ambitions. This puts the *Times* in a category of one. Any sentence that begins 'Let's take the *New York Times* as an example . . .' is thus liable to explain or describe little about the rest of the landscape" (Anderson, Bell and Shirky 2014). Despite these cautions, several companies have dived into the paywall business after the venerable *Times*. Lee Enterprises, which owns papers throughout the Midwest and Rocky Mountains, launched paywalls, meaning members in their smaller communities will only be able to read a handful of stories a month without subscribing. The papers' revenues were still off some 4 percent in 2015, but that was far better than recent years.

While paywalls have slowed the bleeding of revenue from some papers, they have not stopped it. Advertising revenue continues to fall, subscription rates continue to inch up, and digital subscriptions have done more to remove content from the Internet than to add to the newspapers' subscriber base. Many worry that the efforts of news organizations to prop up still flawed business models with additional subscriber revenue will slowly turn local news into a model of what has happened in D.C. Newspapers will continue to report on their communities, documenting key debates, covering local events, and offering important information for voters, but the pool of people receiving that information may become smaller and smaller. Like the trade publications in the nation's capital, reporting will be done and stories written, but the assumption is that those stories will only be for the wealthier residents, the people willing to fork over hundreds of dollars for a print subscription or a digital door in the paywall. Heltman, that paywall journalist, for one is worried about the resulting gap in coverage, writing, "That vacuum provides an opening for outlets that peddle in the kind of bias, treachery, and quackery that we have always been afraid of . . . [M]isleading or conspiratorial ideas about government activities can spread more easily when the public lacks credible information to counter it. And instead of solving that problem, the market is directing more and more journalistic resources and talent toward figuring out how to keep insiders better informed and at a greater convenience" (Heltman 2015). It has driven some who focus on online news to consider other alternative business models that might not place content out of the reach of people looking for it, but unwilling to pay the cost of seeing it. These journalists and academics have cooked up ideas to expand nonprofit outfits like ProPublica or the semi-public programs like PBS and NPR.

But for many it comes down to a core question: Is journalism a business or a public service?

The answer historically was it was both. The business model of journalism almost inadvertently turned it into a social good by pushing its publishers to convince the most people possible to read it. Now, the business model appears to be pushing it toward a specialized service that may become tailored more and more to the wealthy. One analysis of the potential impacts of paywalls said that the paywall itself is only the manifestation of the existential question about news and information. This author noted, "Democracy still requires journalism . . . If news is treated as only a commodity, then it is rational to maximize profits by any means possible, like asking the government to allow for greater media concentration and policing online content. But if journalism is seen as primarily a public service, then democratic society should try to minimize market pressures, return media production to local communities, and sustain public service media into perpetuity, just as we preserve permanent spaces in society for museums, libraries, and schools" (Pickard 2014). This model of journalism as equivalent to public education seems a radically different vision of media and journalism than is at work in America today, and would represent a significant shift in the way Americans view and value work. Still, the depth of division over how to solve the economic crisis of journalism speaks to the level of concern with which many who observe the intersection of civic need and media view the current state of affairs.

See also: Corporate Media Ownership; Daily Newspapers; *New York Times*; Newspaper Industry

Further Reading

Anderson, Chris, Emily Bell, and Clay Shirky. 2014. "Post Industrial Journalism: Adapting to the Present." Tow Center for Digital Journalism. December 4. Accessed December 29, 2015. http://towcenter.org/research/post-industrial-journalism-adapting-to-the-present-2.

Cogan, Neil. 2015. *The Complete Bill of Rights: The Drafts, Debates, Sources, and Origins*. Oxford, UK: Oxford University Press.

Heltman, John. 2015. "Confessions of a Paywall Journalist." *Washington Monthly*. November/December. Accessed December 29, 2015. http://www.washingtonmonthly.com/magazine/novemberdecember_2015/features/confessions_of_a_paywall_journ058444.php?page=all.

John, Richard. 2009. *Spreading the News: The American Postal System from Franklin to Morse*. Boston, MA: Harvard University Press.

Mutter, Alan. 2009. "Mission Possible? Charging for Web Content." Reflections of a Newsosaur. February 8. Accessed December 29, 2015. http://newsosaur.blogspot.com/2009/02/mission-possible-charging-for-content.html.

Pickard, Victor. 2014. "Salvation or Folly? The Promises and Pitfalls of Digital Paywalls." *Digital Journalism* 2, no. 2. Accessed December 29, 2015. http://repository.upenn.edu/cgi/viewcontent.cgi?article=1439&context=asc_papers.

Toefel, Richard. 2012. *Why American Newspapers Gave Away the Future*. n.p.: Now and Then Reader.

PBS NEWSHOUR

Often heralded as the most substantive nightly news program on American television, the *PBS NewsHour* has served as a counterpoint to the shrill arguments that mark cable television programs. The program has for 40 years offered viewers lengthy discussions and reporting, often proudly claiming that they "dare to be boring."

The program that would become the *NewsHour* grew out of the Watergate scandal and the commitment of the still-young Public Broadcasting Service to offer live coverage of the hearings. To do this, PBS tapped NBC veteran Robert MacNeil to anchor the coverage and paired him with a print journalist who had been anchoring the news at KERA in Dallas, Jim Lehrer. The 1973 coverage was unprecedented in its gavel-to-gavel reporting, earning the pair an Emmy and sparking increased interest in news programs across public television. By 1975 MacNeil launched a nightly 30-minute program from the New York City PBS station. Within two months the program was recast as the *MacNeil/Lehrer Report* and began airing nationally.

The format of the program was unique. Following a brief summation of the day's news, the anchors would spend the remaining time exploring one issue in depth, inviting experts, political leaders, and activists to offer different takes on the one story. With MacNeil in New York and Lehrer based in D.C., the program offered extensive coverage of political issues, hosting debates between congressional leaders, lengthy interviews with presidents and other national figures, and serving as a counter-point to the shortened stories reported on broadcast news program. At the time, the program advertised itself as a complement, telling viewers "Watch Walter Cronkite and then watch us." In 1983, the program expanded to an hour and began covering multiple stories in depth every night. MacNeil would later write, "As we expanded to an hour, cable news was emerging. More cable news followed, and then every imaginable kind of program was selling news from everywhere: Wall Street, Hollywood, supermarket-scandal magazines. So the audience began to fracture. Competition intensified, and more and more tabloid values were introduced to hold on to viewers" (MacNeil 2010). The program sought to differentiate itself, but remained far behind the broadcast nightly news in terms of viewership. Still the program dwarfed cable news viewership and as broadcast numbers shrank the *NewsHour* was able to keep much of its audience.

The program made political reporting a staple of its daily fare, hiring some of the best-known political reporters, like Judy Woodruff and Cokie Roberts, to cover Congress. The program also featured regular weekly political roundtables that brought together liberal and conservative commentators. The Friday evening discussion was initially made up of liberal columnist Mark Shields and Republican adviser David Gergen. The cast would change from time to time, but Shields remains a cornerstone of the segment, now joined by *New York Times* columnist David Brooks. Although this long-standing regular political talk segment sets partisans against one another, those who have studied its commentary note that the *PBS NewsHour* offers an appreciably different approach than most programs on cable television. One scholar says, "Opinion on the *NewsHour* is more like print opinion than cable television opinion" (Jacobs and Townsley 2011). This is an insightful finding about the way the program approaches the idea of political analysis. Instead of seeking provocation and confrontation, the program takes a more passive role, allowing intelligent partisans to offer their views in depth and then allowing viewers to juxtapose those ideas with the other guests' and their own. It's a style of program and interviewing that has made the program a source for many of the moderators who would be tasked with running presidential and vice presidential debates organized by the Commission on Presidential Debates. Lehrer has been called the "dean of moderators," having been asked to moderate 12 of the presidential debates including the first debate of 2012. Lehrer's low-key, "this is not about me" style made him a favorite of candidates who did not want moderators seizing the spotlight, and of the commission that sought informed and effective questioners. But Lehrer is not the only member of the team to be asked to participate, with current anchors Gwen Ifill having moderated two vice presidential debates and both Judy Woodruff and Margaret Warner having served as panelists in past meetings.

The program entered its latest iteration in 2013 when it, now called the *PBS NewsHour*, became the first nightly news program to have two lead female anchors in Ifill and Woodruff. The program's last two executive producers have also been women, a fact that still stands out in contrast from many news operations. In introducing the latest iteration of the program, Lehrer said one thing would remain despite the new set and different anchors, outlining what he called "MacNeil/Lehrer journalism." He told the audience that brand of reporting should live by certain standards, saying:

> Do nothing I cannot defend. Cover, write and present every story with the care I would want if the story were about me. Assume there is at least one other side or version to every story. Assume the viewer is as smart and as caring and as good a person as I am. Assume the same about all people on whom I report.
>
> Assume personal lives are a private matter, until a legitimate turn in the story absolutely mandates otherwise. Carefully separate opinion and analysis from straight news stories, and clearly label everything. Do not use anonymous sources or blind quotes, except on rare and monumental occasions. No one should ever be allowed to attack another anonymously.
>
> And, finally, I am not in the entertainment business. (Lehrer 2009)

The program has been cited as one of the most balanced on television, often going to great pains to offer opposing sides opportunities to engage. But this has also led to criticism of the show from those who question its choice of experts and the tendency to offer too much balance on some topics. For example, the program continued to debate global warming into the late 1990s, offering deniers of the science significant airtime. That said, the program has also done extensive coverage of the crisis, using scientific experts to cover its multiple angles. From the sources side, liberal media watchdog group Fairness and Accuracy in Reporting (FAIR) targeted the program in 2006 as giving too much airtime to governmental and military experts and marginalizing critics. Still, the program was hailed for its efforts to offer viewers a more diverse array of guests; a 2015 study of nightly news programs found the program was by far the most progressive in offering a range of guests in terms of gender and ethnicity. Woodruff said it's no accident, telling Huffington Post, "It's a matter of being deliberate about it and saying, 'This matters, this is a priority.' If you don't do that, it's so easy to slip back into the trap and just say, 'Well, we used so-and-so last time we did this topic, so let's use them again.' Frankly, there's no excuse for that" (Taibi 2015).

See also: *Frontline;* Government-Subsidized Journalism; Lehrer, Jim

Further Reading

Jacobs, Ronald, and Eleanor Townsley. 2011. *The Space of Opinion: Media Intellectuals and the Public Sphere*. New York: Oxford University Press.

Lehrer, Jim. 2009. "Another Chapter Begins for NewsHour." *PBS NewsHour*. December 4. Accessed September 17, 2015. http://www.pbs.org/newshour/bb/media-july-dec09-pbs newshour_12-04.

MacNeil, Robert. 2010. "No Blaring: MacNeil on Emmy, Keeping a Reasonable Tone in Broadcast News." *PBS NewsHour*. September 27. Accessed September 17, 2015. http://www.pbs.org/newshour/rundown/no-blaring.

Taibi, Catherine. 2015. "The Media Is Failing Women, But One Network Is Leading the Fight to Change Things." Huffington Post. June 18. Accessed September 10, 2015. http://www.huffingtonpost.com/2015/06/18/pbs-women-media-newshour_n_7587852.html.

PERSONALIZATION AND THE INTERNET

Most major digital news sites and search services offer a level of automatic personalization that seeks to create a more relevant and useful experience for the website visitor. This personalization is often invisible to the user, leaving some to worry that such an algorithmic news-curating system could further insulate citizens from information and points of view that challenge their worldviews. The personalization itself is a product of the enormous volume of information on the Internet and engineers' increasingly sophisticated tools for understanding what people are looking for from a given web search.

Personalization has become a critical selling point for Internet services as the volume of material these services could pull from erupted. The Internet is big and getting bigger at a mind-boggling rate. For example, YouTube, a single site, adds 300 hours of video every minute of every day (McConnell 2015) and another study found that some 571 new websites launch in that same 60 seconds (Wollaston 2013). With this level of growth, offering people some level of guidance through an ocean of content has become an increasingly important element of services like Google, Netflix, and Apple. But the result is a surprising reality. To put it simply, no one Google search generates the same results from person to person and region to region. If you are a hockey fan and you hop on Google and type "Sharks," chances are you mean the San Jose Sharks hockey team and so, if that is what you have clicked on before or if you are in northern California, Google will make an educated guess as to what you meant to search for and feed back those results. The idea is this makes the search more useful because you receive the information you wanted even if you were not very specific in your original query.

This usefulness has made companies enormous amounts of money as they recommended products and shared reviews of things people were considering purchasing. From economic and usability points of view, the development of increasingly personalized searches and recommendations makes enormous sense in a universe of content that is continually expanding. But some worry what effects this helpfulness may have on the democratic process. In 2011, liberal activist and digital democracy advocate Eli Pariser raised some eyebrows when he published *The Filter Bubble*, which documented how different individuals searching for items in the news—from the BP oil spill in the Gulf of Mexico to the Arab Spring uprisings in the Middle East—could receive very different results in their Google searches based largely on what they had clicked on before and what websites they search. Pariser, who helped form the web activist site Moveon.org, said his concern was that much of this personalization was invisible to the reader and manifested itself on many of the most important sites from which people access information, including Google and Facebook. He said, "Being a politically-minded person, my biggest fear is probably that important but un-sexy problems—from homelessness to the war in Afghanistan—fall out of view entirely. [Digital thinker] Clay Shirky points out that while most newspaper readers read the internal sections (Sports, Home and Garden, whatever), at least they had to flip by the front page which let them know if something important was going on that they should know about. Now it's possible to live in a bubble where that stuff doesn't ever show up—you'd never know it's happening" (Catone 2011). Pariser's debate has trigged revisions to both the Facebook news feed and a globe icon on most Google results that allow you to de-personalize your results—somewhat.

Although its impact on society is still debated, personalization is a core economic reality of the Internet. It's nearly as old as the commercial World Wide Web and was an early part of what made Amazon such a success as a digital store. Amazon invested millions of dollars and thousands of engineering hours in building a technological infrastructure that could create an effective recommendation engine. They began with a system called "BookMatch," which required users to answer some 20 questions about genres and types of books. It worked fairly well, but was limited by the amount of work it required the visitor to do to make it functional. So the company began working on an invisible recommendation tool. It began mapping what you bought, what you clicked on, read a free chapter from, as well as what other people who purchased the same books did. It dove deeper, recognizing that what you bought and shipped to other people probably did not reflect your taste as much, but could reflect the recipient's. This data ocean created a much more predictive system that allowed Amazon to create a recommendation list without the user even knowing they might like the books the engine would generate. The results were clear when sales soared, and people accepted and came to rely on the invisibly generated list as a tool for finding new albums or volumes.

It wasn't just Amazon on this quest for finding relevant connections on the Internet. At Google, the idea of creating a better search engine drove two Stanford students—Sergei Bryn and Larry Page—to come up with a new way of ranking pages that included how popular they were and how often people link to them as a source. The search engine blew the others out of the water. But as the company grew, they realized that search also opened up new avenues for the startup. As one former employee explained it, "Every search is in some sense an expression of intention. It's an expression of what you want to do, where you want to go, what you're looking for. And that maps very nicely with the desire of advertisers to target their messages towards people at the moment when they are intending to go buy something" (Frontline 2014).

Although the shift toward a more personalized version of the Internet has been underway since the 1990s, it also marked a fundamental shift in the electronic media. As far back as the 1920s electronic media—first radio and later television—had created what Canadian media theorist Marshall McLuhan famously referred to as a "global village" in which time and distance were eliminated by the power of broadcast technology. He described the change this would have on culture as a new form of tribalism, saying, "The world is now like a continually sounding tribal drum where everybody gets the message all the time. A princess gets married in England and boom, boom, boom go the drums. We all hear about it. An earthquake in North Africa, a Hollywood star gets drunk, away go the drums again . . . we're retribalizing. Involuntarily we are getting rid of individualism. Just as books and their private point of view are being replaced by the new media (of television and radio) so the concepts that underlie our life and our social actions are changing" (CBC 1960). This emergence of a broadcast world meant that international events, as McLuhan described, would be seen and heard and responded to in almost every corner of the globe. The potential power of a global concept, that superseded the individual, to generate soapboxes for political figures and demagogues has always been a concern of policy makers. When the government considered regulations of the possible political elements of broadcasting they took a strong stand to ensure information of public interest would be broadcast, would be balanced, and would convey multiple viewpoints, in rules like the Fairness Doctrine of the 1940s.

The Internet, on the other hand, was seen initially as a democratizing force in the electronic media. First via websites and later through social media, the ability of voters, politicians, experts, and others to offer their views on the political issues of the day represented the most revolutionary development in media since, most people contend, the printing press. No longer would the media be the sole gatekeeper of information; the Internet would be a counterweight to the global village-driven consensus and hierarchy of broadcast. Joe Trippi, an early evangelist of this new way of doing politics, followed the development in the late 1990s, writing, "For me, the most promising thing about the Internet in those days was the way it transformed communication, the way it actually reversed some of the more insidious aspects of television. It was making people *talk to each other* again" (Trippi 2004). This vision of an equal, open community would hopefully push back against political parties that stifled their members, and a media that censored and gated the conversation.

However, Pariser and others argue that the push for personalization and individuality actually re-imposed a new hierarchy on communications. Trippi's idea of the Internet as a great library and crossroads was lost in a quest for personalization and relevance. Pariser, in a controversial TED Talk about the filtering of the Internet, challenged, "This is how the founding mythology goes— in a broadcast society, there were these gatekeepers, the editors, and they controlled the flows of information. And along came the Internet and it swept them out of the way, and it allowed all of us to connect together, and it was awesome. But that's not actually what's happening right now. What we're seeing is more of a passing of the torch from human gatekeepers to algorithmic ones. And the thing is that the algorithms don't yet have the kind of embedded ethics that the editors did" (Pariser 2011). Much has now been written about the idea of algorithmic filters. Facebook conducted a survey of some 10 million politically active users, finding that on average 23 percent of these users' friends represented the other political view and about 29 percent of the information these users saw represented something that would conflict with their viewpoint. This both demonstrated that Pariser's fears were true, but also were true to a much smaller extent than the worst-case scenarios. (Some researchers questioned whether the results represented the average user who would not declare themselves liberal or conservative.)

The Internet was also expected to make the public dialogue more democratic, by making it so easily to publish. This effort still has many supporters who argue that "net roots" movements have the power to reach beyond geographic and other barriers. The concept of a democratized political voice spoken by a "global village" has clear appeal, but even this powerful concept is affected, experts have found, by the emergence of filters and algorithmic search criteria. One professor of media and public affairs has concluded, "From the perspective of mass politics, we care most not about who posts but about who gets read—and there are plenty of formal and informal barriers that hinder ordinary citizens' ability to reach an audience . . . [T]his study finds powerful hierarchies shaping a medium that continues to be celebrated for its openness. This hierarchy is structural, woven into the hyperlinks that make up the Web; it is economic, in the dominance of companies like Google, Yahoo and Microsoft; and it is social, in the small group of white, highly educated, male professionals who are vastly overrepresented in online opinion" (Hindman 2008).

That is, in the modern world, it is not enough to be able to speak on politics. The question is who gets heard and who are the gatekeepers who can elevate or ignore certain voices? Are they algorithms that may benefit the more extreme voices because they draw more shares on social media or are linked to more often by other bloggers?

Embedded in all of these debates about personalization and democratization is a bigger, difficult question: What role and responsibility does the individual have to challenge the personalization pressures? People like to be surrounded by those things they normally seek out—be it a type of movie on Netflix, a regular entertainer like John Oliver or Rush Limbaugh, a group of "real" friends on Facebook. Is it the Internet's job to force people to confront information that challenges this habit? There is a surprisingly paternalistic element of this conversation that contends people are too simple to do this on their own and they will never get beyond the first few links of a Google search or the regular feed of friends on Facebook. Since Pariser's book was published, many of the Internet personalization tools have become a bit more transparent, allowing people some controls over the basic ways the Internet is filtered for them. But most investigations into these tools find they are almost like a "Terms of Use" for an Internet site—people may know it exists and may even recognize the importance of it, but rarely choose to engage it or truly consider it. That reality, while empowered by the technologies of personalization, actually represents a far more difficult question and one no digital tool can fundamentally alter. If people have the choice to avoid difficult questions or things that challenge their beliefs are *they*, not the digital tools, willing to face that challenge?

See also: Aggregation; Social Media and Politics; Yahoo News

Further Reading

Catone, Josh. 2011. "Why Web Personalization May Be Damaging Our World View." Mashable. June 3. Accessed July 28, 2015. http://mashable.com/2011/06/03/filters-eli-pariser.

CBC. 1960. "Marshall McLuhan: The Global Village." CBC Digital Archives. May 18. Accessed July 27, 2015. http://www.cbc.ca/player/Digital+Archives/Arts+and+Entertainment/Media/ID/1565028215.

Frontline. 2014. "United States of Secrets: Part Two." PBS. May 20. Accessed July 27, 2015. http://www.pbs.org/wgbh/pages/frontline/government-elections-politics/united-states-of-secrets/transcript-61.

Hindman, Matthew. 2008. *The Myth of Digital Democracy*. Princeton, NJ: Princeton University Press.

McConnell, Fred. 2015. "YouTube Is 10 Years Old: The Evolution of Online Video." *Guardian*. February 13. Accessed June 2, 2016. https://www.theguardian.com/technology/2015/feb/13/youtube-10-years-old-evolution-of-online-video?CMP=fb_gu.

Pariser, Eli. 2011. "Beware Online 'Filter Bubbles.'" TED. February. Accessed July 25, 2015. http://www.ted.com/talks/eli_pariser_beware_online_filter_bubbles/transcript?language=en.

Trippi, Joe. 2004. *The Revolution Will Not Be Televised*. New York: Harper Collins Publishers.

Woollaston, Victoria. 2013. "Revealed, What Happens in Just ONE Minute on the Internet: 216,000 Photos Posted, 278,000 Tweets and 1.8m Facebook Likes." *Daily Mail*. July 30. Accessed June 2, 2016. http://www.dailymail.co.uk/sciencetech/article-2381188/Revealed-happens-just-ONE-minute-internet-216-000-photos-posted-278-000-Tweets-1-8m-Facebook-likes.html.

PEW RESEARCH CENTER

The Pew Research Center is an independent polling and analysis firm based in Washington, D.C. Widely seen as the most nonpartisan and scientifically solid polling firm in the country, the group researches a wide array of subjects, from horserace-style polls on the state of the presidential campaign to in-depth analyses about Americans' views of race, religion, and work.

The center started in 1990 as the public opinion research arm of one of the largest newspapers in the United States—the *Los Angeles Times*—and its parent company, Times Mirror. The company ran an array of newspapers, magazines, and television stations and that year they formed the Times Mirror Center for the People and the Press to supply its publications with a variety of public opinion products. The firm did a lot of polling for the 1992 election, covering Americans' views of their own country, polling the Russian public about their views of the collapsing Soviet Union, and assessing the thoughts of the press about politics. The Times Mirror Center hired Andrew Kohut as its first director of surveys. Kohut had already built a widespread reputation for his solid methodology and entrepreneurialism in finding new projects. He had spent a decade at the Gallup Organization as its president before leaving to start Princeton Survey Research Associates, an attitude and opinion research firm specializing in media, politics, and public policy studies. By 1993, Kohut was running the Times Mirror project, but the question was how long it would be around. The parent company had suffered sluggish advertising revenues and falling readership at several of its larger papers. Following a series of internal reorganizations, the Times Mirror Center was on the block to be shuttered by 1994.

This is when the heirs of an oil fortune stepped in and began to build the Pew Research Center. The Pew Charitable Trusts was formed by the children of Joseph Newton Pew and his wife, Mary Anderson Pew. Pew founded Sun Oil, the crude giant that would become Sunoco, in 1886. The trust formed in 1948 and was the sole beneficiary of seven charitable trusts of the Pew's children. According to the trust's own history, "Honoring their parents' religious conviction that good works should be done quietly, the original Pew Memorial Foundation was a grantmaking organization that made donations anonymously" (Pew Charitable Trusts). This religious element and a strong belief in unbiased reporting to the country fueled much of the trusts' work, including its support for the Red Cross and historically black colleges. Despite its philanthropic work, the trusts have not been free from internal conflict or external pressure. When it first formed, the chief architect of the trusts was one of Joseph's sons, J. Howard Pew. J. Howard was a strong conservative and made it clear that organizations that were considered too liberal would never receive funding from the trusts. According to the *Philadelphia Inquirer*, "For his J. Howard Pew Freedom Trust, the second largest of the seven, J. Howard left guidelines for grants that included a diatribe against 'Socialism, welfare-state-ism, Marxism, Fascism and any other like forms of government intervention'" (Fleeson 1992). But as the trusts expanded and the Pew family members grew more distant from the conservative past and developed a more diversified set of interests, the group expanded its work to include support for the arts, environmental causes, health rights, and consumer policies. Bolstered by those seven trust funds, the total assets of the trust have topped $5 billion.

It was this organization that decided in 1994 to take over the research operation from Times Mirror and the Pew Center for the People and the Press was formed. Over the years, the organization added specialized research projects that included a center that focused on the state of the American news media, an examination of the changes wrought by the Internet, as well as projects that focused on religion, the role of Hispanics in America, and a survey of global attitudes. By 2004, Pew decided to centralize all of these research projects under one umbrella, the Pew Research Center. The center operates almost exclusively on a nearly $40 million annual grant from the Pew Charitable Trusts. According to its tax returns, the center does raise funds through independent work, but these sums usually are less than $1 million a year and never include money from campaigns or any political organization.

Throughout these changes, the center remained under the leadership of Andrew Kohut. Under Kohut's guidance, the Pew Center continued to conduct an array of survey projects, fulfilling its specific philanthropic goals, as outlined in its mission: "Our public opinion surveys allow the voice of the people to be heard, and our demographic, economic, and political analyses provide context to understand how the world is changing. We are nonprofit, nonpartisan and nonadvocacy. Our mission is to inform, not to prescribe. We believe that better information can build a better world" (Pew Research Center, n.d.). That effort to inform means much of its research is distributed through the news media, where the Pew Center allows the press to access its survey work and often partners with media companies to conduct specific research. The center does not charge for any of the research it produces, but it also does not work under the influence of any media outlet. The group has partnered with news organizations in the past, like a project with Judy Woodruff that sought to understand the interests and pressures facing the millennial generation, but these projects are not the core of its efforts.

Its long-standing work and financial independence have created a real brand of trust among journalists who use the poll. Stories or blog posts raising questions about Pew's integrity are few and far between in the media coverage. Instead, the poll results are seen as the best and most accurate gauge of public sentiment on an issue. The only caution raised by the press in recent years was focused on the evolution of polling itself. A 2012 report on *Slate* noted that response rates to Pew's surveys have dropped precipitously, down to about 10 percent of the public—from 35 percent some 15 years ago. Questions linger on how representative that 10 percent actually is (Oremus 2012). Nevertheless, Pew remains the gold standard in public survey research reporting and the center's data will remain a core go-to for journalists covering politics and a wide array of other subjects.

See also: Gallup; Public Opinion; Public Policy Polling; Rasmussen Reports; Real Clear Politics

Further Reading

Fleeson, Lucinda. 1992. "How a Foundation Reinvented Itself: The Children of Sun Oil's Founder, Heirs to Great Wealth, Could Have Financed a Dynasty. What They Chose Instead Was Quiet, Conservative Generosity. They Likely Wouldn't Recognize the Pew Foundation Today." *Philadelphia Inquirer*. April 27. Accessed July 27, 2015. http://articles.philly.com/1992-04-27/news/26001700_1_pew-grants-pew-officials-foundation.

Oremus, Will. 2012. "Minority Opinion." Slate. May 17. Accessed July 27, 2015. http://www.slate.com/articles/news_and_politics/politics/2012/05/survey_bias_how_can_we_trust_opinion_polls_when_so_few_people_respond_.html.

Pew Charitable Trusts. "History." Accessed July 27, 2015. http://www.pewtrusts.org/en/about/history.

Pew Research Center. "Our Mission." Accessed July 27, 2015. http://www.pewresearch.org/about/our-mission.

PHOTO OPS AND OPTICS

For more than a century, politicians have used the image—either still or video—to convey themselves in certain ways, playing off deeply held American symbols to create the image of a leader who connects with his or her constituents or evokes certain desired characteristics. Campaign strategists have become so adept at staging the perfect moment that news reporters have often made the coverage of how and why the campaigns manufacture such images a core part of their campaign coverage. The photo op has come to symbolize how efforts to control the message of a campaign have sparked a sort of intellectual arms race between journalists and consultants to have the final say in what gets reported and how it looks.

The setting of a speech or a presidential or candidate appearance is almost never left to chance. Careful planning goes into organizing the event, the content of a speech or set comments, and all of what will appear in the camera frame. The results can be intoxicating. It can turn a president to a Top Gun as it did with George W. Bush in 2003. President Bush was looking for a way to announce what the United States believed to be the end of "major combat operations" in the invasion of Iraq. The president and his advisers decided to make the speech a memorable affair, given the relative ease with which American forces had ousted the former dictator of Iraq Saddam Hussein. A former ABC producer was hired to work with White House communications director Dan Bartlett to put together what would become known as "the mother of all photo ops." In their plan, President Bush would fly out to the USS *Abraham Lincoln*, a massive aircraft carrier that was approaching San Diego after concluding its tour of duty near Iraq. Bush, who had served in the Texas Air National Guard during Vietnam, would pilot the plane some of the way, land on board, and then would deliver his speech to the ship's thousands of sailors. The idea stemmed from the wildly popular film *Top Gun*, starring Tom Cruise, and aimed to demonstrate the president's tenacity and fierceness.

When the first draft of the president's speech was completed it included the line "mission accomplished," so when the producer read it he chose to have a huge banner created that could hang behind the president. The visual team left nothing to chance. The White House team ordered the ship to delay its return so it was further out to sea when the president flew to meet it, and then the producer ordered the ship to turn so that no land would be visible in the background. The president would look like he was aboard an aircraft carrier in full battle mode and not one idling outside its naval parking garage. When Secretary of Defense Donald Rumsfeld, who was in Iraq, read the draft speech, he said the phrase "mission accomplished" should come out to ensure that it did not sound as if all fighting was over in the country. But the people coordinating the event never got that edit and the massive banner was printed and hung from the ship's superstructure. All the coverage of the speech went off without a hitch. The president was filmed flipping the thumbs up from the cockpit, sailors wildly cheered the president's address, and the images were dramatic as the sun set on the ship. The images dominated even the print reporting of the event, with, for example, the *Washington Post*'s Dana Milbank describing the moment in a way anyone in the White House would have been pleased to read, writing, "Bush emerged from the cockpit in full olive flight suit and combat boots, his helmet tucked jauntily under his left arm. As he exchanged salutes with the sailors, his ejection harness, hugging him tightly between the legs, gave him the bowlegged swagger of a top gun" (Milbank 2003).

Of course that speech, the backdrop, and especially the banner would haunt the Bush White House in later years. Bush's "swagger" would appear less genuine as insurgent attacks would claim thousands of American lives and American forces would still be in Iraq in force more than a decade later, but the images really never lost their power. They just as powerfully captured the degree to which the White House failed to understand what was happening in Iraq years later as they did evoke the patriotism and military power they had in 2003.

For more than 100 years politicians have used the power of the image to bolster their position and try, without saying a word, to convey core principles about their character and their connection to important American ideals. Theodore Roosevelt often had photographs taken of his hunting trips and campaign stops. In his archive is a photo he had in the White House on one of his trips out West capturing a band of thieves. As a PBS documentary about the president would later note, "The incident was real but the photograph was staged: Friends posed as the bad guys. And while Theodore built the White House's first press room and loved to have cameras around, [Documentary writer Geoffrey] Ward said, no photos were unearthed of him playing his daily tennis match. He thought the game would make him look effete" (Jensen 2014). These images, whether staged or not, helped influence the men who would come and sit with him during his frequent meetings with the press. Roosevelt recognized that to implement many of his policies and even to maintain his political position he needed the support of voters more than the political establishment that had historically opposed him within the Republican Party. To maintain this popularity, Roosevelt relied on the press and the popular image of him as maverick and man's man.

It would take several more years for the photo op to become a standard fare for presidents, as news images became a regular part of news coverage. Ironically it would be a president known for his somber moods and sour expression to first fully embrace the photo opportunity. Calvin "Silent Cal" Coolidge would build a reputation for himself of being a photo-friendly president. The *Wall Street Journal* would later recall, "'It was a joke among the photographers that Mr. Coolidge would don any attire or assume any pose that would produce an interesting picture,' one Washington reporter noted. One summer vacation in the Black Hills, Coolidge donned an Indian headdress to address 10,000 members of the Sioux tribe. Another time, he dressed up in garish cowboy regalia—from chaps and silver spurs to a flaming red shirt and blue bandanna—while being feted by local South Dakotans" (Greenberg 2016).

As presidents became more comfortable in front of the camera and campaigns became more sophisticated about how and when to use photos, communications experts began to develop more of a strategic approach toward stage-craft. Rather than relying on chance or, frankly, the journalists to convey the image the campaign wanted, communications experts deployed many of the same tools used in advertising. Images were constructed not only to convey the individual in his or her best possible light, but often the scene or the surroundings were composed to play off of contemporary stories and myths of the day. President Bush, in part, wanted to play off of the movie *Top Gun*, but he also could be seen as the leader at a time of war, the commander-in-chief and a modern-day action hero. Not everyone would see every message, but the messages were there for those who were receptive to them.

Photographer Charles Hagen would write about these images in the *New York Times*, explaining, "The underlying strategy of photo ops is the same as that of most ads: pose the candidate (or the product) with symbols of appealing values, in the hope that viewers will equate the two . . . For a Presidential candidate, the values include patriotism—where there's a candidate, there's sure to be a flag—as well as physical vigor, compassion and honesty. Photo ops can also be used to send subtle messages about the candidate's class allegiances" (Hagen 1992). And so, candidates often appear at events or while touring factories out of their suit coats and in rolled up sleeves. Such a candidate will get things done and is more like me than those buttoned-up politicians. Campaigns often call these visual impressions the "optics" of the campaign. Research has found that voters need only one-tenth of a second to develop some impressions of a candidate based only on a photo. More attractive and friendly looking candidates are ranked as more competent, trustworthy, and qualified and so those public events and the images that are distributed by the campaign are carefully considered to ensure the right sense is conveyed.

Journalists are keenly aware of how carefully campaigns control their visual aspects. Photographers, either still or television, are rarely allowed to capture unplanned images of the candidate. More and more, press are herded up like cattle and positioned where campaigns want them to be positioned to capture the same image from the same angle at the same time. Many journalists chafe at being handed such a tightly scripted story. Those that pride themselves on their ability to research topics, interview people, and analyze data often become frustrated in the highly controlled campaign world. For these reporters often the story shifts from what the campaign is saying to why they are saying it—seeking to contextualize the story in a larger narrative about the campaign or strategy for winning. Harvard scholar Kiku Adatto would explore these tensions, finding, "Politicians became so adept at manipulating television images that the reporters who covered them had to find a way to strike back, to bring the attention of their viewers and readers all the contrivances and manipulations behind the images they were seeing. This desire to remind the viewers and readers of the behind-the-scenes attempts to control the pictures fundamentally changed the way politics and especially political campaigns have been covered over the last three decades" (Adatto 2008). Presidents as far back as Ronald Reagan adeptly focused on the visual presentation of their news, often worrying less if the television reporter's narrative was critical of the president's claims so long as the right video accompanied the report. This hostility between press and campaign escalated throughout the age of television news, where often reporters would balk at reproducing a story that had been stage-crafted for them. The term "pseudo-events" soon entered the modern campaign dictionary, and reporters rejected completely staged campaign moments. Some journalists even refused to attend national party nominating conventions, citing the highly controlled, infomercial quality of the four-day events. Instead reporters focused on the political thinking behind the messages, staged photos, and speakers. Rather than relaying what was said, they exerted their independence by focusing on the "Why" and not the other core reporting questions.

From the campaigns' perspectives, this journalistic rebellion often led to still-more increased efforts to control the campaign, reducing the times in which reporters could ask questions and even more tightly minding the available visuals for photojournalists to capture. Campaigns invested in their own photographers to shoot events and then made those images available to the media and the public. Many journalists refused to use them, but campaign communications staff members continued to produce set images. The press continued to dissect the crass political calculations behind those images, and the game went on. As British professor Mick Temple tried to explain to the BBC about the British wave of photo ops with prime minister candidates feeding sheep or cuddling with their newborn child, "People aren't stupid. They can see through the pictures." He continued, "They'll base their decision on other areas. The idea they're going to vote for someone who looks best feeding a lamb is risible. But, on the other hand, the more pictures you've got out there not presenting negative images of you, the better. Plus the media has an insatiable appetite for this stuff and almost infinite space to put it" (Smith 2015). The basic equation is thus reduced to this: We all know candidates standing in front of flags is a base attempt to convince us that the candidate in question loves America and is a good person. But even though we all know why they put the photo out, they will still do it because that photo is better than a photo of the candidate asleep at a congressional hearing.

This is where the uneasy relationship between campaigns and the media stood until the Internet came along and mucked things up, shifting the balance of power in two ways. First, the economic impact of the digital revolution has decimated many newsrooms, leading to a reduction in reporting and photography staffs. These reporters must often generate multiple stories on different topics during a typical day on the job. This is especially true at the state and local level, but even for national reporters there is an expectation of a daylong feed of tweets and other social media in addition to the major piece for the paper or nightly news. Add to this the need for more content—in particular, photo content—to feed website slideshows and Facebook posts. News organizations need visuals to run their websites, and yet usually have fewer people to produce those visuals. So the photos and videos produced by the campaign have become something many news organizations feel compelled to use. In exploring how this tension plays itself out in their elections, Canadian professor Alex Marland found that "digital handouts reinforce centralized messaging and respond to the economic realities of the information business. When authentic photos are received effortlessly, they address a newsroom's growing need for new visual content. Second, technology continues to shift the rules of the game. Visual handouts and their Web platforms seem poised to displace other forms of institutional accommodation of the political press and to disrupt the business model of wire services. Journalists are now fighting for the right to document the pseudo-events that were scoffed at in the television age" (Marland 2012). American journalists too face the same pressures, and have come to use the campaign-provided images and videos with more frequency. And why not? For years, photographers found themselves assigned to the same location to shoot the same photograph with the same people in it from the same angle. Is that, really, all that different than the same photo from the same angle taken by a campaign photographer?

Campaigns at all levels have come to realize that photo opportunities are an essential element of campaign communication strategies. These tools allow campaigns to connect their candidates to core myths and beliefs held by the constituents they hope to woo. A candidate walking into church holding hands with his or her spouse can convey, regardless of what the reporter is saying or writing about the campaign, that the candidate is a good, God-fearing person. And that can be far more powerful than any speech about their faith. Campaigns are keenly aware of this, so they carefully organize those events that may be photographed by journalists and often document it themselves and offer those images to the press. And the press, hungry for new information to feed out across digital news platforms, are often susceptible to the temptation of a good photo op.

See also: Campaign Narratives and Dramatization; Campaign Strategy Coverage; News Conferences

Further Reading

Adatto, Kiku. 2008. *Picture Perfect: Life in the Age of the Photo Op*. Princeton, NJ: Princeton University Press.

Greenberg, David. 2016. "A Century of Political Spin." *Wall Street Journal*. January 8. Accessed January 11, 2016. http://www.wsj.com/articles/a-century-of-political-spin-1452267989.

Hagen, Charles. 1992. "The Photo Op: Making Icons or Playing Politics?" *New York Times*. February 9. Accessed January 11, 2016. http://www.nytimes.com/1992/02/09/arts/the-photo-op-making-icons-or-playing-politics.html?pagewanted=all.

Jensen, Elizabeth. 2014. "White House Photo Ops, Old School." *New York Times*. September 14. Accessed January 11, 2016. http://www.nytimes.com/2014/09/14/arts/television/the-roosevelts-documentary-series-on-pbs.html.

Marland, Alex. 2012. "Political Photography, Journalism, and Framing in the Digital Age: The Management of Visual Media by the Prime Minister of Canada." *International Journal of Press/Politics* 17, no. 2 (April): 214–33.

Milbank, Dana. 2003. "The Military Is the Message." *Washington Post*. May 2. Accessed January 11, 2016. https://www.washingtonpost.com/archive/politics/2003/05/02/the-military-is-the-message/f1911e8e-8bc2-445f-818b-f807ef079e7c.

Smith, Jodie. 2015. "Election 2015: Is There Any Sense Behind Political Photo Ops?" BBC News. April 26. Accessed January 11, 2016. http://www.bbc.com/news/election-2015-england-32302152.

POLITICAL ACTION COMMITTEES (PACs)

The influence of political action committees, usually simply referred to as "PACs," is essentially proof of the law of unintended consequences.

The first PAC formed in 1944 when the Congress of Industrial Organizations formed a political account to support the reelection of President Franklin Roosevelt. The fund was allowed to operate because it did not receive money from the CIO and relied on donations volunteered by union members. Several other early political funds formed in similar ways, but efforts to reform campaign funding spurred their rapid growth in the 1970s and 1980s. Fueled in part by an effort to rein in the rising costs of campaigns and further accelerated by the financial shenanigans uncovered inside President Richard Nixon's reelection campaign, Congress passed the Federal Election Campaign Act (FECA) of 1971 and amended the law in 1974, 1976, and 1979 in an effort to "clean up campaigns."

The laws put in place disclosure requirements and donation limits, and also codified PACs as the way in which corporations, unions, and other organizations could give money directly to candidates running for federal office. From the start they were controversial. PACs could donate up to $5,000 to a candidate per election—meaning a candidate could get $5,000 in a primary campaign and another $5,000 for the general election. This total was substantially larger than the cap of $1,000 for an individual during each election cycle.

Soon most organizations and many corporations had established PACs as a way to fund candidates that supported their industry or backed their ideology. Hundreds of PACs were organized, from MINEPAC of the National Mining Association to the Target Citizens Political Forum to the National Pro-Life Alliance PAC and Planned Parenthood Action Fund.

Most PACs registered with the Federal Election Commission fall into one of two categories—so-called connected PACs and nonconnected PACs. Connected PACs in the parlance of the FEC are called "separate segregated funds." These funds are administered by a union or corporation and can only solicit and receive donations from a restricted list. In the case of unions this would be the membership and in the case of corporations it is the shareholders, executives, and their families. The unions and corporations themselves are not allowed to donate to the PAC, but can help cover the cost of administering the funds. These funds must include the name of the sponsoring organization in the name of the "connected" PAC.

Nonconnected funds are those linked to associations, nonprofits, or issue advocacy groups (as well as members of Congress). These groups are free to solicit funds from the general public as well as organizations, but these groups must pay their own expenses from funds that are donated and disclosed (FEC 2015). According to the Center for Responsive Politics, eight of the top 20 PACs in 2012 were connected to unions, four were affiliated with corporations, and the remaining eight were "nonconnected." These 20 groups funneled some $50 million to candidates for federal office during the 2012 primary and general elections (Opensecrets.org 2015).

Both the connected and nonconnected organizations quickly emerged as tools to channel significant funds to House and Senate candidates and as a way of affixing a sort of seal of approval for campaigns. But as a result of this explosion of new funding, "political action committees superseded the 'fat cats' of old as the public focus and symbol of the role of money in politics, and PACs inherited the suspicions that go with the territory" (Sabato 1984, p. 186). In fact to read the political science or reporting of the time, PACs took on an almost super-power ability to influence democracy. Candidates could come under real scrutiny for accepting support from PACs from one side of an issue, and there was a growing sense that either through supporting key officials at specific committees or by backing certain candidates, corporations or advocacy groups could essentially purchase political access. One political scientist summed it up in 2002 as essentially, "a PAC can manipulate government policies either by buying policies directly from legislators or by buying elections. In the latter case, interest groups attempt to sway the elections in favor of the candidates whose views are most in line with their own" (Magee 2002, p. 373). Some, including former Federal Election Commission chair Lee Ann Elliott, rejected this characterization of PACs, arguing that "saying 'PAC money buys votes' is the equivalent of looking at the obituary page and concluding that people die in alphabetical order. There is not a quid pro quo . . . The presumption is that congressmen are dishonest and on the take, that the PAC givers are all sleazeballs, in the business of bribery—and neither is the case" (Sabato 1984, p. 122).

Attention paid to PACs has waned in recent years following the rise of independent expenditure groups and so-called Super PACs. It should be noted, Super PACs, although they share a name with their older campaign finance cousins the "connected" and "nonconnected" PACs, are fundamentally different organizations. PACs have much more stringent disclosure requirements both in the donations they accept and the contributions they make to candidates, political parties, and other PACs.

Although it is early to tell what the rise of the Super PAC may mean to traditional political action committees, some experts predict PACs may become a less useful tool. The Bipartisan Campaign Reform Act of 2002 doubled the donations individuals could make to candidates but kept the 1970s cap of $5,000 in place for PACs. Now with unlimited spending possible through Super PACs and dark money issue advocacy groups, the role of the traditional PAC may be coming to an end.

See also: Campaign Finance Reform; Dark Money Groups; 527 Organizations; Super PACs

Further Reading

Center for Responsive Politics. "Top 20 PAC Contributors to Candidates, 2011–2012." Accessed February 13, 2016. https://www.opensecrets.org/pacs/toppacs.php?Type=C&cycle=2012.

Federal Election Commission. 2008. "Separate Segregated Funds and Nonconnected Committees Fact Sheet." May. Accessed December 30, 2014. http://www.fec.gov/pages/brochures/ssfvnonconnected.shtml.

Magee, Christopher. 2002. "Do Political Action Committees Give Money to Candidates for Electoral or Influence Motives?" *Public Choice* 112, no. 3/4. Accessed February 13, 2016. http://www.jstor.org/stable/30026312.

Sabato, Larry. 1984. *PAC Power: Inside the World of Political Action Committees*. New York: W.W. Norton and Company.

POLITICAL BIAS AND THE MEDIA

The American public has come to see media in general as politically biased in its coverage of campaigns, elections, and government. That belief in reporting bias permeates the discussion of the media by candidates as well as watchdogs and comedians. And the view continues to grow. A 2013 survey from Pew Research Center found that 76 percent of people believe "the media" tends to favor one side in their reporting, up from 53 percent in 1985. That same survey found that nearly half of the people saw the media as generally biased toward liberals while only a quarter of respondents said there was a conservative bent. In short, the public assumes the media has a political agenda and is using its reporting to advance those beliefs.

But the question of bias is more complex than simply a liberal reporter deciding they like one candidate over another and then writing pro-one sided articles. The media is a complex set of news organizations—some that represent the views of one blogger and others that are huge corporations often owned by even larger corporations.

Still, the vast majority of Republicans and a sizable majority of independents see a liberal bias in the media, a reality that fuels not just growing distrust of what is reported but also an increasing number of attacks on the press by candidates on the trail. During one particularly disastrous Republican primary debate in 2015, candidates sparred repeatedly with the CNBC moderators, attacking the questions as "nasty" and "propaganda." Candidate Marco Rubio won huge applause when he declared, "The Democrats have the ultimate Super PAC. It's called the mainstream media." Senator Ted Cruz also drew attention by attacking the moderators, saying, "The questions that have been asked so far in this debate illustrate why the American people don't trust the media." The line drew applause in the room, but for a group of potential Republican voters watching the debate in Colorado, the argument also resonated. GOP pollster Frank Luntz tweeted out during the debate, "Ted Cruz's focus group dials [hit] 98 with his attack on media bias. That's the highest score we've ever measured. EVER" (Luntz 2015). Academics have come back with similar claims. One analysis of how the press frames political issues, not necessarily campaigns, found that the media, in a general way, creates a set of parameters of positions that are seen as moderate and representative of the way most people think. Jim Kuypers, a professor in communications studies, used an examination of 700 newspaper articles about five controversial speeches to declare, in sweeping tones, that the press accepts only a "narrow band of correct political thought," adding that, "Essentially put, the politics represents liberal, upper middle class, white baby boomer activist politics. This narrow band of press acceptable politics is clearly to the left of the political center and substantially to the left of the majority of Americans. The practical implications of this are clear. Those to the right of this band of liberal politics will be ostracized, ignored, or demonized. However, just as perniciously, those to the left of this narrow band will suffer the same fate" (Kuypers 2002).

But there's real bias, and there is perception of bias. In his exhaustive analysis of bias research on media coverage of campaigns from 1948–2008, professor Dave D'Alessio concluded that people perceive bias through their own political prism. For example, a Pew report from 2013 noted that 66 percent of people thought the entire media tended to get the story wrong; but in the same report, when asked about the news organizations the individual read or watched the number dropped to 30 percent. So the entire media may be off base most of the time, but my media usually gets it right. D'Alessio also pushes back against individual stories or news coverage of a single event as proof of bias, because true bias must be systematic and sustained. Finally, he highlights that there should be a distinction made between news content and commentary. His analysis of more than 100 research reports on bias found that essentially the press tends to end up in the political middle. Why? Not because of some glorified sense of objectivity but "because that's where the people are, and that's where the [advertising] money is. . . . There's nuance there, but when you add it all and subtract it down, you end up with nothing" (D'Alessio 2013).

But this general finding that the press does not overtly side with one presidential candidate or another does not eliminate the underlying concern that media coverage tends to skew the public perception of an issue. On the core question of whether certain policy or political biases affect coverage of controversial issues, the answer is more complex. Many of those within and outside of the media find that there is a power within the press to contextualize issues and cover them in certain ways that alter the public's understanding of that issue. In what became a lightning rod of a story, the *New York Times* public editor, Daniel Okrent, examined the question of bias in his paper. After having examined the way it covered a series of hot-button social issues like gay rights and gun control, Okrent told readers, "If you think the *Times* plays it down the middle on any of them, you've been reading the paper with your eyes closed." Okrent's column actually raises one of the critical issues many press critics often ignore when making general claims about the content of "the media," which is that each news organization tends to reflect the audience it serves as much as seeks to change their opinions. For a paper like the *New York Times* that audience is an urban, east coast one. Okrent closed his column by pushing the *Times* to consider whether it is a national news organization or a New York one, writing:

> On a topic (gay marriage) that has produced one of the defining debates of our time, *Times* editors have failed to provide the three-dimensional perspective balanced journalism requires. This has not occurred because of management fiat, but because getting outside one's own value system takes a great deal of self-questioning. Six years ago, the ownership of this sophisticated New York institution decided to make it a truly national paper. Today, only 50 percent of the *Times*'s readership resides in metropolitan New York, but the paper's heart, mind and habits remain embedded here. You can take the paper out of the city, but without an effort to take the city and all its attendant provocations, experiments and attitudes out of the paper, readers with a different worldview will find the *Times* an alien beast. (Okrent 2004)

To understand if the news is reflecting the biases held by its readers or viewers, or seeking to impose the reporters' and editors' views on that same audience, it is important to consider ways in which bias may appear in reporting. Media watchdogs on both the left and the right have sought to catalogue the manner in which the press may overtly or inadvertently skew their reporting. These biases may appear through what assumptions the reporter brings to a story. For example, if the reporter starts with the premise that homelessness is a problem a community ought to be doing more to address and then finds stories of those suffering on the streets to illustrate their position, that would reflect a bias. And yet the same story arrived at by the reporter observing the problem and then documenting the manner in which the community has neglected the individual in question may simply be good reporting. The difference? Intent. Bias may also crop up in who the reporter interviews for a given story. Are the most articulate sources quoted or are the views balanced? Additionally, bias can appear in how different stories are featured in the publication. The *New York Times* again came under fire in 2012 for handling Mitt Romney and Barack Obama differently, as Politico noted, "On the front page of its Sunday edition, the New York Times gave a big spread to Ann Romney spending lots of time and tons of money on an exotic genre of horse-riding. The clear implication: The Romneys are silly rich, move in rarefied and exotic circles, and are perhaps a tad shady. Only days earlier, news surfaced that author David Maraniss had unearthed new details about Barack Obama's prolific, college-age dope-smoking for his new book, *Barack Obama: The Story*—and the Times made it a brief on A15" (VandeHei and Allen 2012).

Although the intensity of media bias claims may have grown, the idea of politicians attacking the press as a campaign tactic is anything but new. In 1948, President Harry Truman, who was not seen very favorably, made the idea of inherent media bias one of his main campaign themes. The embattled Democratic president accused the Republican-led legislature of being a "Do-nothing Congress" and accused the media of being lined up against him, calling them the "one-party press." It might be odd to consider that one party being the Republican Party given the current right-wing skepticism of the mainstream media, but Truman claimed that the newspapers of the United States were overwhelmingly backing Republican Thomas Dewey. Often the claims of bias are a tactic for campaigns that appear to be struggling. Richard Nixon famously castigated the press for their coverage of his failed 1962 California gubernatorial campaign, but made no such claims during his successful 1968 presidential run. Howard Dean accused the press of repeatedly running his concession speech in 2004 where he yelled and whooped at supporters to damage his campaign, especially once he lost.

But bias is more than just a claim of those campaigns that have received negative coverage. There are inherent biases within the media that can alter coverage of stories, but often they may appear political when they are actually more structural. For example, the media are drawn to stories—narratives—that are compelling and interesting. The 2008 campaign may be one of the most pronounced examples of this bias. Senator Barack Obama had first exploded onto the national stage in 2004, delivering a powerful post-partisan speech at the Democratic National Convention. A state senator when he delivered that address, the speech was about being raised as a young black man by his white grandmother and his powerful message that "the pundits like to slice and dice our country into red states and blue states: red states for Republicans, blue states for Democrats. But I've got news for them, too. We worship an awesome God in the blue states, and we don't like federal agents poking around our libraries in the red states" (Washington Post 2004). The press took notice of this up-and-coming politician. That interest in a compelling personal narrative and a possible historic election of the nation's first black president drove many of the stories about the Obama campaign. If one asked political reporters whether they wanted Obama to win over Hillary Clinton or later John McCain, most would express a degree of objectivity or at least would be slow to publicly declare their allegiance. But ask a reporter which story is more compelling to write about or cover and the answer was clear—the junior senator for Illinois.

The result was clearly positive coverage of the Obama campaign, and when he rolled to victory that fall it set up an unforeseen problem of impossibly high expectations. As Rodger Streitmatter noted in his book about the power of the press, "Journalists had played a role in getting *candidate* Obama elected but their favorable coverage might ultimately work against President Obama succeeding" (Streitmatter 2015). For Streitmatter the obsession with the story of Obama led to volumes of stories focused on his compelling personal narrative and the historic nature of his campaign. This focus turned Obama from a politician to something more—a trailblazer and an instant historical figure. The coverage helped propel his nomination within the Democratic Party and election in the general campaign, but that same coverage established him as someone with the power to change Washington and politics. It set him up to fail or at least to fall far short of the hopes he carried into the White House.

The Obama story raises two issues about the bias within the press. How much does the media focus on a candidate or a story because of a deep-seated political objective and how much does it focus on certain stories because of the accepted styles of reporting and the drudgery of covering the same issues year after year? For some who study the press and the way reporters cover politics, the question of bias is too often focused on questions of partisan interest and not enough on the real tendencies of the media. Lance Bennett, who has written about fundamental biases within the media, tries to dismiss conventional political bias debates, writing, "There are at least two ironies in this ongoing and inherently unresolvable debate about ideological bias. First, even if neutrality or objectivity could be achieved, citizens with strong views on particular issues would not recognize it. Second, even if the news contained strong ideological or issue biases, people with a point of view (who are most likely to detect bias in the first place) would be well equipped to defend themselves against such biases" (Bennett 2003). For Bennett, the biases within the media that harm the public discussion come from a place far more troubling than the political leanings of a given reporter or publication. Instead, he sees the press as too interested in stories about individuals rather than issues, drama over information, and the sometimes-artificial authority invested in public figures and sources. These biases can affect the way journalists think about and report stories, turning hard policy decisions into heart-rending stories of individuals and changing political debates into life-and-death struggles for power.

Biases exist in any system or organization, especially one made up of flawed humans. So the media certainly contains them. But to approach the media itself as a single organism is itself a bias of those who are prone to see any news organization as an agent of some political agenda other than one's own. The media, in many people's minds, combines incendiary talk shows with straight news reporting, *The Daily Show* with *PBS NewsHour*, and Rush Limbaugh with the local government reporter for the local daily newspaper. Each of these organizations suffers from biases that affect their reporting, but to assume they are the same or all inherently political in their goals is to misunderstand the fragmented nature and business of modern media.

See also: Balance; Objectivity; Post-Truth Politics; Trust in Journalism

Further Reading

Bennett, W. Lance. 2003. "Four Information Biases That Matter." In *News: The Politics of Illusion*, 5th ed. New York: Longman.

D'Alessio, Dave. 2013. *Media Bias in Presidential Election Coverage 1948–2008: Evaluation via Formal Measurement*. Lanham, MD: Lexington Books.

Federal Document Clearinghouse. 2004. "Transcript: Illinois Senate Candidate Barack Obama." *Washington Post*. July 27. Accessed June 2, 2016. http://www.washingtonpost.com/wp-dyn/articles/A19751-2004Jul27.html.

Kuypers, Jim. 2002. *Press Bias and Politics: How the Media Frame Controversial Issues*. Westport, CT: Praeger.

Luntz, Frank. 2015. "Ted Cruz's Focus Group Dials Hits 98." Twitter. October 28. Accessed June 2, 2016. https://twitter.com/frankluntz/status/659532219069763584.

Okrent, Daniel. 2004. "THE PUBLIC EDITOR; Is *The New York Times* a Liberal Newspaper?" *New York Times*. July 25. Accessed January 8, 2016. http://www.nytimes.com/2004/07/25/opinion/the-public-editor-is-the-new-york-times-a-liberal-newspaper.html?_r=0.

Streitmatter, Rodger. 2015. *Mightier Than the Sword: How the News Media Have Shaped American History*. Boulder, CO: Westview Press.

VandeHei, Jim, and Mike Allen. 2012. "To GOP, Blatant Bias in Vetting." Politico. May 31. Accessed January 8, 2016. http://www.politico.com/story/2012/05/to-gop-blatant-bias-in-vetting-076898.

POLITICAL CARTOONS

Distilling complex issues into often simple drawings accompanied by a few spare words, political cartoons have skewered the powerful and given voice to the less powerful. They've ruffled figures from Boss Tweed to Barack Obama and created lasting political symbols, like the Democratic donkey and the Republican elephant. But with their power has come controversy, like decisions made by European newspapers to publish cartoons depicting the prophet Muhammad, an action considered blasphemous by some Muslims.

Whether laugh-inducing or incendiary, the form has captured the attention of the public for nearly two centuries, calling attention to corruption and hypocrisy, and despite the huge changes to the media landscape, political cartoons continue to have an impact today.

The exact origins of the political cartoon are hard to know, but they are sure to go a long way back. "Wherever there had been a cave wall and a sharp-edged rock or a city wall and a piece of coal, political wits can be presumed to have declared a conviction masked as drollery," Donald Dewey wrote in his book *The Art of Ill Will* (Dewey 2007). Cave drawings aside, the first cartoon to appear in an American newspaper came in 1754. That's when Benjamin Franklin, already an established figure in the colonies, went to the Albany Congress as the representative for Pennsylvania. He proposed a "Plan of Union" for the colonies to unite and defend themselves from French and Indian forces. He drew a serpent divided into eight parts, each representing a different colony, and wrote underneath it "Join, or Die." The *Pennsylvania Gazette* printed the image, and the other papers on the continent soon followed suit. It would be recycled a few times in the following years, including as the colonies prepared to revolt against the British in 1774 (Hess and Northrop 1996). But that was just the very tip of the iceberg.

Franklin wouldn't be considered the father of the modern American political cartoon. That title has been bestowed upon Thomas Nast. Nast drew cartoons for *Harper's Weekly* in the mid- to late 1800s. His work helped to make both the magazine and himself famous during the Civil War, as its readership reached both ends of the still-growing nation. Victor Navasky wrote in his 2013 book *The Art of Controversy* that Nast "had an infallible ability to get swiftly to the heart of an issue" (Navasky 2013). Nast is most famous for putting fear into New York's most powerful and corrupt politician, Boss Tweed, with his drawings. In the fall of 1871, as the corruption of the Tammany ring became more public, Nast drew a series of cartoons skewering the political machine's bosses. One, called "Who stole the people's money?" showed the top Tammany officials pointing the finger at other people. Another showed New York being crushed under a giant thumb meant to represent the political machine. Quite famously, Tweed urged the paper to "Stop them damn pictures!" The articles didn't really matter, he said, because his constituents couldn't read—but they could see pictures, and most certainly ones featured on the front page of a major weekly publication. Nast also deserves credit for at least one of the two symbols for America's major political parties: the Republican elephant. He drew the first party elephant in a November 7, 1874, cartoon called "Third Term Panic," which he drew as President Ulysses S. Grant considered running for a third term. The symbol remains iconic to this day. (The Democratic donkey predated Nast and had been used since the time of Andrew Jackson [Hess and Northrop 1996].)

Nast was just the first of a number of cartoonists who contributed to the national conversation in important ways. The Pulitzers started awarding a prize for the form in 1922, offering a higher level of legitimacy for great cartoonists. The first one was won by Rollin Kirby, who went on to win two more. Kirby became known for his attacks on prohibition, largely focusing on the hypocrisy of prohibition forcing drinking to occur behind closed doors. One soldier-turned-cartoonist, Bill Mauldin, became a prominent anti-war voice. With his World War II series "Willie and Joe," for *Stars and Stripes*, he showed everyday frustrations of "two bedraggled soldiers serving on the front lines, who each day belied any thought that war is noble" (Hess and Northrop 1996). He became the youngest cartoonist ever to win a Pulitzer and grew famous as he cartooned from a war zone.

Mauldin, like many cartoonists who tackled controversial topics, drew some sharp criticism from those who found his opinions unpatriotic. And his post-war work about the hardships faced by returning soldiers or racism or the Cold War found a less receptive audience. Meanwhile, Herbert Block was gaining prominence. Herblock, as he was known, drew for the *Washington Post* for most of his career, which spanned seven decades. He coined the term McCarthyism, won three Pulitzers and shared in a fourth, and was also known for his garish drawings of President Richard Nixon. Aside from Thomas Nast, Herblock could be the most famous master of the single panel.

But the single panel isn't the only place where political cartooning exists. Many magazines feature editorial cartoons, with *New Yorker* covers being among the most prominent and enduring examples. In the 1970s, Ralph Steadman, with his distinctive drawing style, drew a famous caricature of Richard Nixon for a book Hunter S. Thompson was writing. And, political cartooning has existed in the same realm as such favorites as "Peanuts" or "Garfield"—as a strip. Garry Trudeau created "Doonesbury" while still an undergraduate at Yale, and it was syndicated soon after he started it. In 1975, it became the first comic strip to win a Pulitzer for editorial cartooning, and it has been a finalist three other times since. Its expansive cast of characters caused Chip Kidd, writing in *Rolling Stone* in 2010, to compare the entire body of Doonesbury cartoons to Leo Tolstoy's *War and Peace*, crediting Trudeau with building "a large cast of complex and intriguing characters whom the reader comes to care about, then letting the great tsunami of current events envelop them all" (Kidd 2010).

Cartoonists typically have no worse repercussion for their work than an angry reader or two, but that's not always the case. Cartoonists have faced legal battles, kidnappings, and death threats for doing their jobs. In 2005, a Danish newspaper printed 12 cartoon images of Muhammad in one issue. That decision caused widespread protests by Muslims because Islam prohibits drawings of the prophet. More than 100 people died because of the protests, and the cartoonists responsible went into hiding. American cartoonist Molly Norris received threats after promoting an "Everybody Draw Muhammad Day" with a poster and a website. Navasky noted that she is now in a witness protection program.

In 2015, armed gunmen attacked the Paris offices of the French satirical newspaper *Charlie Hebdo*, killing 12 people. The paper had a history of showing images of Muhammad, often in aggressively provocative scenes. Past acts had already prompted protesters to burn down their offices four years earlier. In the aftermath of the 2015 attack, some journalists and free speech advocates rallied around the paper, with the phrase "Je Suis Charlie"—French for "I Am Charlie." Some, like *New York Times* columnist David Brooks, criticized the rallying cry, equating the magazine's actions to hate speech. He argued the rallying cry was disingenuous because most journalists "don't actually engage in the sort of deliberately offensive humor that that newspaper specializes in" (Brooks 2015). Many rejected criticisms like Brooks's, instead applauding the organization for its bravery in publishing the images.

In the digital age, the form hasn't lost its significance. But it does have more competition from other satirical pictorial forms like memes and GIFs. Some of the most recent Pulitzer Prize winners produce animated web cartoons rather than the traditional form. In 2012, Farhad Manjoo argued in Slate that cartoons had totally become irrelevant, noting that aside from controversy over the use of Muhammad, "it's hard to remember the last time a single-panel cartoon entered the political zeitgeist" (Manjoo 2012).

In response, Matt Wuerker, the Politico cartoonist who won the 2012 Pulitzer Prize, wrote in the *Columbia Journalism Review* that the shift to a more digital media landscape doesn't mean the traditional political cartoon should disappear, and especially not the cartoonists, who are poised to thrive in the new reality. "Cartoonists were creating memes before anyone had a clue what a meme was. They were the original tweeters, long accustomed to boiling a thought down to 140 characters. We've been around a long time and like the rest of journalism, we are adapting to all the current changes" (Wuerker 2012).

Michael Wright

See also: Block, Herbert; Comedy, Satire, and Politics

Further Reading

Brooks, David. 2015. "I Am Not Charlie Hebdo," *New York Times*. January 8. Accessed January 17, 2016. http://www.nytimes.com/2015/01/09/opinion/david-brooks-i-am-not-charlie-hebdo.html?_r=3.

Dewey, Donald. 2007. *The Art of Ill Will: The Story of American Political Cartoons*. New York: New York University.

Hess, Stephen, and Sandy Northrop. 1996. *Drawn and Quartered: The History of American Political Cartoons*. Montgomery, AL: Elliot and Clark.

Kidd, Chip. 2010. "Doonesbury Turns 40." *Rolling Stone*. December 2. Accessed January 17, 2016. http://www.rollingstone.com/politics/news/doonesbury-turns-40-20101027.

Manjoo, Farhad. 2012. "Editorial Cartoons Are Stale, Simplistic, and Just Not Funny." Slate. April 19. Accessed January 17, 2016. http://www.slate.com/articles/technology/technology/2012/04/political_cartoons_don_t_deserve_a_pulitzer_prize_give_one_for_infographics_instead_.html.

Navasky, Victor. 2013. *The Art of Controversy: Political Cartoons and Their Enduring Power*. New York: Knopf.

Wuerker, Matt. 2012. "A Picture Is Worth a Thousand Memes." *Columbia Journalism Review*. April 23. Accessed January 17, 2016. http://www.cjr.org/behind_the_news/pulitzer_prize_winner_matt_wue.php.

POLITICAL CONSULTANTS

Political consultants are professionals who aid candidates in developing and deploying aspects of a campaign. Although their work focuses heavily on messaging, the development of advertising, and voter engagement, political consultants can play a variety of roles, from in-house pollster to social media strategist. Many also work with the media, serving as commentators and editorial advisers. Critics of consultants argue the professionalization of politics has led to more cynical strategies that deepen citizen frustration with politics.

The growth of consulting as a full-time job reflects the increasingly complicated and expensive task of running a modern political campaign. Campaigns were historically staffed and run by local and statewide parties. The party would select the candidate and then help them stump for votes, organize speeches, and motivate voters to get out to the polls. But the reforms in the early twentieth century that weakened the political parties and created more popular participation in contests for the U.S. Senate and the presidential nomination left the parties poorly positioned to run campaigns. Add to this reality the increasingly sophisticated elements of running a campaign and American politics had entered a time when, in the words of political journalist Theodore White, "The old bosses are long gone and with them the old parties. In their place has grown a new breed of young professionals whose working skills in the new politics would make the old boys look like stumblebums" (Trent and Friedenberg 1983). These new campaigns were a mix of salesmanship and social science, using political polling and television advertising to package the candidate and sell him or her to the voters.

By the 1960s, presidential campaigns, and increasingly statewide campaigns for governor and Congress, began to hire specialists. The growth in polling and television advertising in particular fueled the need for campaigns to bring in people with specific skill sets who could field the survey to find out what messages might resonate with voters and could turn those messages into powerful and memorable campaign ads. Add to this the increasingly complicated task of raising and reporting money, building field operations to mobilize voters, and targeting voters with direct mail appeals, and the campaign was quickly becoming highly specialized. With this specialization, smaller sub-industries formed to tackle these challenges and the number of consultants grew.

They also began to appear more and more in congressional contests, and politically active young people saw the opportunity to move into a professional field of campaign work. By 1969 the number of professional campaign workers had grown to such a point that they formed a nonpartisan organization to promote their work and put forward a common set of principles. Their organization, the American Association of Political Consultants, published a mission statement that reads, "We set the standard for American political campaigns because we are driven to be the best and make a difference for our clients and America. We craft effective strategies and employ best practices so our clients win at the ballot box and in the halls of government. We fight to defend political free speech as an essential foundation of democracy, while promoting excellence by recruiting and recognizing the best in our profession. We share the skills, resources and network our members need to thrive and win" (AAPC). The association also tried to enforce a loose set of standards around what kind of causes they would work for—none that were based on racism or sexism—and a handful of controversial campaign techniques, such as a cautious rejection of so-called push-polls that masquerade as surveys but are intended to attack a candidate.

But as working on campaigns has become a full time job for more and more, concerns for how this affects American politics has also grown. First, the fact that campaigning is now a job means for consultants the actual beliefs or leadership of a candidate come in second in what they seek in a candidate. A campaigner and political scientist surveyed his consultant colleagues and found most valued willingness to work hard and ability to stay on message higher than the traits voters sought—like leadership or integrity. But for the consultants, he argued, that makes sense, writing, "If my professional livelihood rests on the back of a candidate who is either a great person or willing to knock on a few extra doors to get out the vote on election day, I am going with the candidate with more mud on their shoes" (Johnson 2012). This focus on the skills of the candidate over the beliefs they seek to convey may be the most significant element of the consultant relationship with a candidate compared to the supporters or volunteers. Consultants are in the campaign to win, or at the very least, to get paid, and there is always an element of self-motivation in their participation in a campaign. The message they are spreading is just one element of their thinking and, according to their own survey results, it's not the most important element.

Some have accused the growing profession of creating a cookie-cutter approach to politics, where the same negative campaigns play out time and time again. They argue that this reduces politics to a basic math equation where money and negative ad buys equal victory. Consultants reject this argument, but will admit that they do bring their experience to each campaign and that this history has an influence on their thinking. Because of this, as one consultant explained, "Candidates have to realize that when they put their team together, that team, just by their past experiences, will shape the final strategy even before that strategy is written. As the candidate considers his race, he ought to ask himself what it is he wants to do, what kind of race he wants to run, and whether the background of his consultants is appropriate for that purpose" (Luntz 1988).

Consultants have been blamed for many of the ills of the current political system. Their sometimes-exorbitant fees and strong use of television advertising contributes to the skyrocketing cost of politics. Their tendency to demonize the opponent to rally their base contributes to the polarized state of American party politics. Their work for dark money groups and Super PACs means these destructive tactics are now as likely to show up when Congress is debating a law as they are in the heat of the campaign year. Experts like Stephen Medvic argue you can't really blame the consultants for all of these realities. They did not weaken the party system, they filled the void left after the parties faltered. They did not create the political divisiveness in the country, but Medvic will admit, "Consultants have actively sought to capitalize on the disorders that exist (e.g., the weakening party system, the pervasiveness of television, a corrupt campaign finance system, etc.). The arrival of political consultants on the political scene did not improve the system and may have even solidified its deficiencies" (Medvic 2001). And so the consultant has become a major source of attention within the press. Political reporters study their histories and past strategies to inform their current story about the current campaign, turning many into household names even where politics are not the main source of dinner table conversation.

Consultants, until recently covered by a handful of industry-style publications, have now become their own brand thanks to coverage by large national news organizations. Take Politico's coverage of the 2015 British election, which pitted two former advisers to President Barack Obama against each other: "The surprisingly decisive victory for Prime Minister David Cameron and his Tories also delivered a big win to Jim Messina, President Barack Obama's 2012 campaign manager, who advised the Conservative Party and triumphed over his fellow Obama aide, Axelrod, who advised the Labour Party" (Gass and Robillard 2015). This coverage highlights two realities of the modern top-tier consultant world: first, the media's interest in their efforts in the British election merited such a story and second, that two consultants from the same presidential campaign could be hired on competing sides of a foreign election. This is the modern world of the political consultant.

In this modern world of the celebrity consultant, the press covers the moves and actions of consultants like Axelrod and Messina as though they themselves are on the ballot. It is somewhat a product of the fact that some of these top-level consultants turn to punditry, cutting lucrative deals with cable networks to offer on-air commentary on other campaigns. It is also a fact that some of these consultants have emerged as powerful forces behind new politically active nonprofits that pour millions of ad dollars into critical campaigns.

In this world, conservative consultant Karl Rove is royalty. Rove started his career in direct mail, helping Republican candidates in Texas and the South raise serious money and using targeted mailing to attack opponents in primaries and general elections. He soon began working with up-and-coming GOP star and son of a Republican statesman, George W. Bush. With Rove's help, Bush won election to governor and then went on to take the presidency twice. He did it by crafting a campaign that appealed to conservatives in key states while attacking their opponents through various means. In the days that followed the fairly easy re-election of Bush to a second term in 2004, Democrats expressed a deep frustration and respect for Rove's strategy. But at least one told the *Washington Post* Rove was the meanest man in politics. Rove responded by saying, "This is a town that runs on myths. That's one of the myths. The evil Rasputin Rove. There's nothing I can do about it. If you want to rage against the system, blame Rove" (Balz and Allen 2004). But Rove was also one who, like a consultant will do, took advantage of the system to help his side.

Following the key Supreme Court decisions around campaign financing that opened up the possibility for new organizations to take and spend enormous sums, Rove launched his own groups, American Crossroads and Crossroads GPS, to spend huge amounts of money on key races. In 2014 alone, the group spent some $100 million in critical contests. Rove, who remains an adviser to the group he founded, has carved out a new role for the consultant, one where he can work across multiple campaigns at the same time to shape messages and launch major ad blitzes without being limited by campaign finance regulations. Rove is far from alone. Many dark money and Super PAC groups have connections to consultants on both sides of the political spectrum.

Rove and other consultants who run or are affiliated with these big-spending groups are just the latest step on the road of the professional consultant. The modern consultant often fits a pattern, as Dennis Johnson explained in his seminal work on the profession, *No Place for Amateurs*. Johnson noted, "Many campaign consultants have politics in their blood: They volunteer for candidates and causes while they are in college, work for their political parties in their state capital or in Washington, work for a member of Congress, or toil away at a variety of statewide and local campaigns before striking out on their own. Over 95 percent of political consultants are white and 81 percent of the principals in campaign firms are men" (Johnson 2007). This professional political class consists overwhelmingly of privileged white men. Most hold degrees from elite grad programs in campaign management and few have worked up from anything lower than middle class. This class of campaigners has become as important as the candidates they represent, often carrying with them from campaign to campaign important endorsements, lucrative donors, and affiliated connections to independent groups.

During the so-called invisible primary where candidates for the major parties' presidential nominations jockey for media attention and financial support, the role of the powerful consultants has only increased. Where once consultants sought to be hired by rising political stars, now an agreement by a certain consultant to sign onto a certain candidate is seen as a major endorsement of a campaign's gravitas. Especially in years where multiple candidates compete for one party's nomination for president (or governor or U.S. senator), this vetting by consultants weighing what campaign is worth their time is part of the political conversation. Although the competition between candidates is what makes a consultant's stock truly rise, the press also plays a role in bolstering a consultant's political capital, turning to him (almost always a him) to serve as an expert on campaigns, seeking interviews on the record, and willingly offering these sources anonymity for a glimpse of what is truly going on. In states with large capital press corps and certainly in Washington, D.C., these two groups—the consultants and the political press—often socialize together and trade shoptalk on the state of campaigns. In this way, the consultant class of political workers helps shape the political reporting, not by going on the record to out a campaign's troubles, but by sharing them over a beer, supplying a tip to a reporter, texting an update to an editor. Especially at the highest levels of politics, it has become a game that frustrates some, is invisible to most, and has a clear impact on how many of the largest newspapers, websites, and cable news networks cover the politics of governing and the major campaigns.

See also: Negative Advertising; Public Opinion; Rove, Karl

Further Reading

Balz, Dan, and Mike Allen. 2004. "Four More Years Attributed to Rove's Strategy." *Washington Post*. November 7. Accessed July 17, 2015. http://www.washingtonpost.com/wp-dyn/articles/A31003-2004Nov6.html.

Gass, Nick, and Kevin Robillard. 2015. "Jim Messina Trounces David Axelrod in British Elections." *Politico*. May 8. Accessed July 16, 2015. http://www.politico.com/story/2015/05/british-elections-jim-messina-david-axelrod-117759.html.

Johnson, Dennis. 2007. *No Place for Amateurs*. New York: Routledge.

Johnson, Jason. 2012. *Political Consultants and Campaigns*. Boulder, CO: Westview Press.

Luntz, Frank. 1988. *Candidates, Consultants, and Campaigns*. New York: Basil Blackwell.

Medvic, Stephen. 2001. *Political Consultants in Congressional Elections*. Columbus: The Ohio State University Press.

Trent, Judith, and Robert Friedenberg. 1983. *Political Campaign Communications*. New York: Praeger.

POLITICAL PARTIES

Perhaps more than any single electoral institution, political parties, their growth, period of dominance, and modern weakening, have done the most to shape the role and importance of media coverage of politics. When political parties were the primary way in which electoral politics were fought and won or lost, the media's role in shaping popular public opinion was only marginally important, but as Progressive Era reforms shifted power away from party officials and to individual voters, journalism saw its role and importance expand. Political parties remain vital instruments of partisan identification, fundraising, and voter mobilization, but the modern political party only exerts a limited amount of control over the politicians who represent that party and the voters who cast their ballot in key elections.

Unlike many western democracies that support several major parties, the United States has since its founding viewed political parties as, at best, a necessary evil and at worst a potential agent for the dissolution of the American experiment. In the United States, political parties have been organized to be the broadest possible coalition of like-minded voters and organizations, rejecting regional and single-issue parties through the ballot and the very structure of the American political system. From the outset, parties, or factions as they were interchangeably called during the early days of the Republic, were viewed as destabilizing, but inevitable tendencies in a democratic system. James Madison, one of the critical builders of the American system, saw the development of political factions as inherent in a population given the freedom to express opinion or exert political influence. He also saw it as "a dangerous vice." But Madison also saw the U.S. Constitution and the new republican form of government it proposed as a solution to the danger by creating a system that forced factions into a system of dispersed authority and repeated elections. As he wrote in the *Federalist Paper Number 10*:

> If a faction consists of less than a majority, relief is supplied by the republican principle, which enables the majority to defeat its sinister views by regular vote. It may clog the administration, it may convulse the society; but it will be unable to execute and mask its violence under the forms of the Constitution . . . A religious sect may degenerate into a political faction in a part of the Confederacy; but the variety of sects dispersed over the entire face of it must secure the national councils against any danger from that source. A rage for paper money, for an abolition of debts, for an equal division of property, or for any other improper or wicked project, will be less apt to pervade the whole body of the Union than a particular member of it; in the same proportion as such a malady is more likely to taint a particular county or district, than an entire State. (Madison 1787)

For Madison and the other authors of the U.S. Constitution, the solution to the evils of parties was to create a system that would punish those organizations that only represented a minority of voters. With its separation of powers and winner-takes-all electoral results in presidential and congressional elections, the American system was built on an antiparty philosophy and that reality has forever shaped what parties existed and how they operated.

Although the founders viewed factions as a potential agent of chaos in the emerging American system, those who have studied the early growth of parties in the United States would later say the first wave of American parties played a critical role in establishing the American system. In his exhaustive, four-volume work on the history of political parties in the United States, historian Arthur Schlesinger noted that parties helped unify the nation beyond the provincial interests of the former colonies, offered representation to general groups of voters across a spectrum of issues, and helped recruit and train the leaders who would implement the new system. The parties also helped unify the government between the divided branches and became agencies of compromise when it came to making critical decisions in the early Congresses. In short, Schlesinger notes, "What political scientists have agreed to call the first American party system was thus both the creation and the creator of a national political order. As the first thing of its sort in the world, it was a remarkable invention" (Schlesinger 1973).

These parties helped establish the nation and guided it through its turbulent early decades. But they were far from static things. As the country evolved and the issues that would divide the country crystallized, the party system was tested. Early parties were the products of the landed interests of the wealthy men of the United States. These parties struggled to change as a growing middle class and then an enfranchised working class pushed different issues. This struggle was most sharply seen in the sudden implosion of the Whig Party and the birth of the Republican Party in the mid-nineteenth century. The Whig Party had grown out of opposition to President Andrew Jackson and had advocated for a strong Congress to stand up to the president. The party flourished briefly in the 1830s and 1840s, but the coalition struggled over the issue of slavery. Efforts by Congress to negotiate compromises over the issue had failed and the party was unable to unify around a central concept. As the nation lurched toward a civil war, the Whig Party fell apart and within 10 years disappeared.

What is striking about the political system, though, is it seems to require two parties, for as soon as the Whigs faltered and then collapsed, the modern Republican Party came swiftly into being and became the second political party in the country. These two parties—Democrat and Republican—would become the two parties of the United States for the next 150 years. They would continue to evolve as America urbanized, but through their internal organization and the use of political jobs and government money, the two parties established themselves as the dominant forces of American politics, selecting candidates, guiding policies, and running elections.

Throughout these years the relationship between the media and political parties was one of mutual cooperation. Most of the newspapers and many magazines had direct connections with established parties, often supporting that party's candidates and policies on the editorial pages (and sometimes on their front pages). Media bias was an accepted concept. But the maturing of the press and critical institutional changes to the political system would combine to fundamentally alter this relationship, turning the media into a more powerful institution in the political system at the direct expense of parties. The media began to develop its own business strategy that no longer relied on a select few subscribers who were willing to pay the substantive subscription costs. The rise of the so-called penny press in the mid-nineteenth century meant that the modern newspaper now sought the widest possible audience, aiming to appeal to people from different political factions and economic backgrounds. Newspapers, and media generally, moved toward mass media, and away from serving a party.

At the same time, an even more important political change was developing within the parties themselves. Around the dawn of the twentieth century, reformers within the Republican Party pushed to take power away from the party leaders—who for decades had decided who would win elections and who would receive the benefits of ruling, including countless political appointments and lucrative government contracts. This manifested itself first in Wisconsin where a progressive Republican Robert LaFollette sought to change the policies of his party. He ran into countless roadblocks from party bosses who could undermine his efforts through their entrenched party machine. LaFollette knew that to change the party he had to change the way the party ran. "The only hope for true democracy, he argued, was to take the nominating power away from the bosses and restore it to the people by means of the direct primary; for democracy dies when any self-selected organization is allowed to intrude itself between the sovereign people and their free choice of public officials" (Ranney 1975). As Madison had argued earlier, systems needed to be put in place to limit the influence of the party in the governing process, and the growth of the party machines and bosses of the nineteenth century led to the reforms spearheaded by LaFollette.

These reforms did not occur overnight. In fact, the role of the voter in the primary system would not truly catch fire until some 60 years later following the disastrous Democratic campaign of 1968, where the chasm between the mainstream party leadership and the party activists reached its widest. A reform commission spread the use of direct primary elections to select party nominees. Now, party officials could only hope to influence the process, through supporting a given candidate or working through the media to create the sense that the party favorite is the clearly better candidate. These progressive reforms were the latest effort to weaken the leadership of the major parties at both the national and state level.

Putting the question of which candidate the party preferred into the hands of the party voters also spawned a new national media effort that turned the primary campaign into the first round of the national elections. The media, through its reporting ahead of the direct primaries, began to exert more influence on the campaign by serving as a public vetting of candidates. A 1976 study of the primary system noted that in the campaigns between 1936 and 1972 thirteen of the fourteen frontrunners when the primaries began were the nominees at the end of the process. Parties wanted their perceived frontrunner to be their nominee, so the process tended to favor those candidates. Still, that same 1976 report noted, "Primaries provide the best available arena in which to challenge front-runners. The chances of destroying the initial leader are forlorn. But there is some chance, the costs of trying to do so are not prohibitive, and the potential pay-offs of an unexpectedly strong showing are very large" (Keech and Matthews 1976).

With party nominations decided by party voters—and in many states, any registered voter can cast a ballot in a party nomination fight—the desires of the party are now only one factor in shaping the contest. In the wake of that 1976 report, more insurgent candidates have been able to knock off the perceived frontrunner. In 2008, Senator Barack Obama overcame former First Lady Hillary Clinton. In 1976, 1988, and 1992, little-known Democratic governors mounted successful campaigns against party leaders who had higher name recognition. The new system allows outsider candidates to make direct appeals to voters through organized campaigns and pre-primary media coverage.

But the parties still wield influence, because they are more than just tools of selecting candidates and mobilizing voters. Because of their broad base, the Democratic and Republican Parties serve as a shorthand way of thinking about the political philosophy of the nation. Although the parties themselves are not static—Republicans taking a more conservative bent and Democrats drifting left in recent decades, the performance of these parties in elections serves as a sort of philosophical barometer of American political preference. The health of the party's performance in elections is often directly connected to the political views of the country. It is almost funny to read old accounts of party performance and see the unfortunate generalizations authors and journalists derived from the effectiveness of the party coalition.

For example, in 1978, just two years before the election of Ronald Reagan and rise of a newfound conservatives within the Republican ranks, one political scientist noted, "The United States lacks a competitive two-party system at present time because of the exceptional weakness of the Republican Party. The now-common observation that the two-party system in the U.S. has been replaced by a 'one-and-a-half-party system' does not contain much exaggeration" (Ladd and Hadley 1978). The Republican Party was, at the time of that book, actually building a potent combination of anti-tax groups, social and cultural conservatives, and pro-business activists to electoral victories.

As machine politics weakened throughout the twentieth century, party leaders sought other ways to maintain their importance and role in the political process. In this media age, parties began to focus less on the individual candidate primaries and instead sought to bring together a new coalition of voters who were not driven by the old self-interest of political patronage and were instead inspired to participate in politics due to their strong belief in a single issue—like protecting gun rights or supporting a woman's reproductive freedom. This new party organization aimed to harness the political activism of these voters, but for parties it was a careful balancing act, seeking to tap into the fervor and activism of the group without, when possible, alienating other voters who did not feel as strongly about the single issue. So Democrats sought, for years, to protect economically liberal Catholic voters who opposed the party's pro-choice positions. Republicans aimed to keep cultural conservatives who were focused on issues like prayer in school in the same coalition as the chamber of commerce-style groups that sought limited government and pro-business policies.

In a strange way the modern political party tried to carve a role for itself where each would claim the general mantle of partisanship—Democrats were the moderately liberal party and Republicans, the moderately conservative. Why this is strange is that at the same time partisanship was decried as one of the core problems with the American political system. Despite this, some argued that the parties were the only thing keeping a lid on the increasingly shrill voices of the conservative and liberal groups. By 2016, this was particularly true on the Republican side of the aisle where fights over the party's presidential nomination and leadership ranks in Congress spilled over into the media. Maverick members of the Republican majority in the House of Representatives forced Speaker John Boehner to resign, and then the leadership fight to replace him tested the ability of these single-issue groups, especially cultural conservatives and tea party activists, to work with the party leaders. During one of the contentious fights about whether to shut down the government in 2013, some columnists opined that the factions within the Republican Party spoke to the need for stronger political parties. Political scientist Mark Schmitt took to the pages of the liberal *New Republic* to argue for partisanship, writing, "[Parties'] long-term goal is in winning elections, at many levels, now and in the future. So long as they are organized around a reasonably coherent philosophy . . . parties are a stabilizing force in American politics, pulling it towards the median voter and offsetting the many other forces and interests that pull in other directions. The current Democratic

Party, which trims and disciplines the aspirations of its core progressive activists, is a good example of a fairly strong party, which is why it's consistently frustrating to the left" (Schmitt 2013). This potential weakness of the Republican Party leadership to control its own rank-and-file became a major theme of the 2016 nominating contest. As real estate mogul and reality television star Donald Trump stayed atop the public opinion polls while making inflammatory comments about immigrants and Muslims, some within the Republican Party worried publicly that the nomination of a divisive figure like Trump could damage the party and affect its ability to maintain control of the House and Senate. For months senior members of the party remained largely quiet about the campaign, hoping that Trump's inflammatory language and negative press coverage would derail his campaign. But by the end of 2015, with Trump still leading in most polls, state party officials began to make their own anxiety public through the media. One story in the *New York Times* summed up the fear that the Trump campaign provoked, noting, "With his knack for offending the very constituencies Republicans have struggled with in recent elections, women and minorities, Mr. Trump could be a millstone on his party if he won the nomination . . . 'If he carries this message into the general election in Ohio, we'll hand this election to Hillary Clinton—and then try to salvage the rest of the ticket,' said Matt Borges, chairman of the [Ohio] Republican Party" (Martin 2015).

The Trump candidacy and the public hand wringing it prompted from party officials actually offer keen insight into the modern phase of political parties. Political parties of years gone by would never have let a figure that could harm the party's vulnerable candidates for Congress or governor become a leading contender for the party nomination, let alone the nominee. But the Republican Party lacks any mechanism for disqualifying Trump and its job of being a coalition builder pushes it to tread carefully with the candidate. Overtly attack or punish Trump and his sizable voter base could turn away from the party or refuse to back another GOP candidate; do too little to rein him in and the party may struggle for years to attract voters whom Trump angered with his comments.

Political parties remain a central organizing structure of American politics, helping voters orient themselves in elections, offering core political perspectives, and running political campaigns at the local, state, and federal levels. But as candidates have become the center of most national and federal campaigns and parties have sought to stitch together fragile and often deeply divided coalitions of interest groups, instilling discipline and offering a unified front has become more difficult.

See also: Invisible Primary; Political Polarization and the Media; Primary Coverage; Single-Issue Politics; Third Party Marginalization

Further Reading

Keech, William, and Donald Matthews. 1976. *The Party's Choice*. Washington, DC: The Brookings Institution.

Ladd, Everett Carll, and Charles Hadley. 1978. *Transformations of the American Political System*. New York: W.W. Norton & Company, Inc.

Madison, James. 1787. "The Utility of the Union as a Safeguard against Domestic Faction and Insurrection." The Constitution Society. Accessed December 16, 2015. http://www.constitution.org/fed/federa10.htm.

Martin, Jonathan. 2015. "Wary of Donald Trump, G.O.P. Leaders Are Caught in a Standoff." *New York Times*. December 1. Accessed December 16, 2015.

Ranney, Austin. 1975. *Curing the Mischiefs of Faction: Party Reform in America*. Berkeley, CA: University of California Press.

Schlesinger, Arthur. 1973. *History of U.S. Political Parties*. New York: Chelsea House Publishers.

Schmitt, Mark. "More Partisanship: What We Need to Fix Congress." *New Republic*. October 1. Accessed December 16, 2015. https://newrepublic.com/article/114950/government-shutdown-2013-democratic-republican-are-too-weak.

POLITICAL POLARIZATION AND THE MEDIA

The intensified partisanship of the American political system has become one of the dominant themes of the twenty-first century. Debilitating debates over critical issues like health care policy and arguments over government funding for family planning have led to stalemates that either threatened to or actually did shutter the federal government. Deep and profound differences over the size and cost of the government have complicated what were once routine votes over the federal debt and have jeopardized the country's credit rating. This rise in partisan behavior comes at the same time that the media have moved from a relatively limited number of mass outlets that aimed to appeal to as many people as possible to more niche publications and broadcasts that aim to reach elements of a fragmented audience. The question that has come with these developments is, to what degree is the media fragmentation feeding this political trend versus reflecting the modern reality of the American public and its political systems.

The electoral causes of this increasing polarization are numerous—political gerrymandering has carved up states into more politically homogenous regions, party structures have become more beholden to harder-edged, single-issue voters, and most members of Congress face greater campaign threats from people within their own party as opposed to the competing party—but the result is clear. Political scientists have developed a complex statistical analysis of congressional voting that examines the voting patterns of senators and representatives along a liberal/conservative continuum and overlays regional differences over certain political issues. This research has generated a telling image of Republicans and Democrats moving further away from one another politically. As one of the researchers noted, "since the mid-1970s, Democrats and Republicans in Congress have continued to move away from the ideological center and toward their respective liberal and conservative poles . . . The result is that the parties are now ideologically homogenous and distant from one another. With almost no true moderates left in the House of Representatives, and just a handful remaining in the Senate, bipartisan agreements to fix budgetary problems of the country are now almost impossible to reach" (Poole

2012). But this analysis, while compellingly explaining the crippling partisanship that has made even electing a new Speaker of the House among Republicans a process fraught with ideological bickering, does little to explain why the American voters elect these increasingly ideological figures. Is it because the country itself is deeply polarized over politics, or could it be the parties represent fewer and fewer voters in their district? This is where most political science falters, according to some researchers who point the finger of blame either partially or mainly at the modern media.

The power of media to shape culture has been a debate among parents and academics for decades. This conversation often landed on the idea that the media could move behavior and content from the extremes to something more socially acceptable. The arguments in the 1980s about sex and violence on television or in video games often gravitated around the idea of "mainstreaming." If television showed two men kissing or was awash in blood and mayhem, people became used to the idea and it became less taboo. Mass media, in this interpretation, created a common culture and this, some political scientists argue, had a huge effect on politics in the United States. In fact, if you go back along the history of that same partisanship index that highlights the gulf between the parties now, there is a period where the two parties moved toward the middle, essentially the 50 years between 1920s and the 1970s.

Some researchers argue that is no accident.

The 1920s represented the introduction of the radio to the American home and that pressure to create a common political culture only increased after World War II with the growth of television. Television, for all its problems, researchers say, brought people together and brought the parties with them. Radio and later television expanded the basic level of political information people had, expanding the pool of politically informed Americans. But television also operated as a true mass media, making its money by appealing to as many people as possible and so the information conveyed in those political news reports tended to be cast in a moderate light, not advocating one side or the other and actually championing the political middle. This moderate news source, researchers argue, informed the political system in a way that tamped down polarization and forced politicians to appeal to the masses as well. One group found that they could show statistically that "places where TV was introduced earlier displayed a decrease in different measures of the extremism of their representatives, relative to latecoming places . . . The results we find suggest that TV operated as an important moderating force, bringing members of Congress toward the political center" (Campante and Hojman 2013).

Although most researchers see the growth of broadcasting as the great unifier, it is important to note that the introduction of these new outlets, in particular television, affected the media in most communities in ways that likely reinforced this mass media reality. When television swept America in the post-war period many communities supported multiple newspapers, usually a morning and afternoon paper at a minimum. These papers, in addition to relying on the time of day to differentiate themselves from one another, often aligned themselves with one party or the other. As the evening news on television took off, many newspapers struggled to stay open and most communities over the next 30 years moved from multiple-newspaper towns to one paper. The result was most media in communities followed the same model of seeing their audience as essentially everyone in a geographic area. This either overtly or subtly kept the news media as less partisan, not wanting to alienate a large swath of their potential audience.

Until the growth of cable in the 1980s and the birth of the commercial Internet in the 1990s, the business of journalism was built on appealing to as many people as possible. But when news sources multiplied in the cable and Internet ages, audiences started fragmenting, attracted to different styles of reporting. News outlets either deliberately or over time came to see the partisan audience as a consistent one. They did not need to appeal to everyone, but instead could succeed as a business by focusing on a smaller section of the public, one likely to turn to them on a regular basis. Also, as cable and digital outlets evolved and the cost of production plummeted, political information could become more specialized and focused on still smaller segments, and the political media has done that. Those who are interested in the inside baseball of campaigns and strategy now have outlets like Politico. Talk radio filled a need of conservatives who were disenfranchised by the mainstream media and a caustic approach to politics mixed with humor. The same could be said of liberals and programs like *The Daily Show*.

The effects of this new form of reporting and content have, according to those who have studied it, undone the moderating force that broadcasting helped usher in nearly a century ago. It is not that all people now turn to more partisan media, but rather a subsector of the population. Political scientist Matthew Levendusky is among those who argue that partisan media is fueling polarization, seeing this new media as appealing to those who seek a so-called confirmation bias—they want information that agrees with their already-held beliefs. By repeating the views and offering commentary that embraces those partisan beliefs, viewers and readers are less challenged in their worldviews. As Levendusky said in an interview about his research,

> Partisan media—particularly reinforcing media—tend to make people a little more extreme, a little less positive toward the other side, more unwilling to compromise . . . But there's an important caveat: a lot of these findings are centered on those who are more likely to encounter that type of media. It's not that [these media] take people who are uninterested and uninformed and polarize them; people who are somewhat polarized go to these sources, and it pushes them further out. (Kim 2014)

Still, political observers worry that this pushing outward of those already on the far edges has an out-sized impact on the political process because of the politically active nature of these voters. These are the people most likely to vote on Election Day as well as to show up at the high school gym to participate in the caucus process. They are the volunteers for campaigns and the small donors who help fledgling candidates.

When television and radio first offered their political reporting, a tool that observers argue expanded the universe of politically educated Americans, those viewers that were engaged in the new, primarily entertainment, mediums of radio and television were Americans who were generally disinterested in politics. Those who have seen their partisan biases intensified and affirmed by the modern fragmentation of media were never unengaged, argues Princeton professor Markus Prior. He wrote in his book on media and polarization that "broadcast television helped the less educated learn more about politics, whether or not they were particularly motivated to follow the news. The current high-choice environment concentrates political knowledge among those who like the news—largely independent of their levels of education or cognitive skill" (Prior 2007). Interested and informed individuals—whether that information is accurate or not—are the ones who have responded to the explosion of political information unleashed by the rise of cable and the web. These people seek out information that may confirm their bias but still is additional information. In many ways the rise of fragmented media has affected the information flowing to the voting public in at least two critical ways. Some members of the public who want to seek out partisan, confirmation-biased information are edged further to the extreme, more disconnected from the information that flows to those in the middle and the other partisan extreme. Additionally, the explosion of political news and commentary has diminished the value and quality of political reporting on the major outlets, meaning that those who do not seek out political reporting often find themselves less informed than before the change in the media.

Today's media environment is a complicated soup of audience fragmentation and partisan bias. But there may be hope—social media. Social networks like Facebook and Twitter offer people a different door through which to access political news, one affected not just by their behavior, but by the network of people they have chosen to follow or friend. The idea that Facebook may actually help spur polarization caught the public's attention in a significant way following the publication of the book *The Filter Bubble*, by Eli Pariser. Pariser, one of the organizers of MoveOn.org, was troubled by the way the social network chose to organize his newsfeed. He explained, "I'm progressive, politically—big surprise—but I've always gone out of my way to meet conservatives. I like hearing what they're thinking about; I like seeing what they link to; I like learning a thing or two. And so I was surprised when I noticed one day that the conservatives had disappeared from my Facebook feed. And what it turned out was going on was that Facebook was looking at which links I clicked on, and it was noticing that, actually, I was clicking more on my liberal friends' links than on my conservative friends' links. And without consulting me about it, it had edited them out. They disappeared" (Pariser 2011).

Pariser's critique prompted an outpouring of questions about how Facebook manipulated its feed and helped spur a series of changes. Facebook added more features that encouraged people to see information from different connections—not just your close friends, but those people you knew in high school or that uncle who is so different than the rest of the family politically. Facebook explored what their feed did to the information flow people saw on a typical day and came back with a conclusion that countered Pariser's concerns, writing, "The information we consume and share on Facebook is actually much more diverse in nature than conventional wisdom might suggest. We are exposed to and spread more information from our distant contacts than our close friends. Since these distant contacts tend to be different from us, the bulk of information we consume and share comes from people with different perspectives" (Bakshy 2012). Given the breadth of most people's social networks on a site like Facebook, the argument goes, you are likely to run into information from people who are unlike you more often than in real life or in your own web usage. This fact, while subtle, offers a ray of hope in the continued concerns that technology is marching the public further and further apart.

Still, most trends point to a continued pressure away from the moderate middle. A massive study of polarization by the Pew Research Center in 2014 delivered worrying information about the gulf between conservatives and liberals when it comes to news and political participation. Conservatives turn overwhelmingly to a single source for their news, investing trust in only a handful of news outlets, primarily conservative-oriented websites and Fox News. Liberals turn to a variety of news sources and invest public broadcasting with enormous trust. Few news sources are held in trust by both groups. Just as worrying is the depth to which each side distrusts the information from news sources used by the other side. Liberals reject most of the content on Fox News, even if it is straightforward reporting, and conservatives see liberal bias in most news sources used by Democrats. This gulf in trust has helped perpetuate the idea of post-truth politics, where facts reported accurately by either side may be rejected or opened for debate by the other side.

The same report found that those who are consistently conservative and consistently liberal are more politically active and post and discuss politics on social media more than those who are more moderate, adding to the argument that these polarized groups are driving much of the discussion of politics on their social networks. As the report's authors note, "Those whose political views are solidly on the left or right—and especially those on the right—have a much greater tendency than others to have politically like-minded friends. Two-thirds (66%) of consistent conservatives say most of their friends share their political views, more than twice the number who say only some of their friends do (29%) . . . Consistent liberals are somewhat less likely than consistent conservatives to have politically like-minded friends. About half (52%) say most of their friends share their views—though that is still twice that of those in the middle" (Mitchell, Gottfried, Kiley, and Matsa 2014).

This means political polarization affects people's information lives regardless of whether they intend it to or not. Those who are strongly partisan one way or the other read different news, have different friends on social networks, and view information differently than those individuals who are more moderate or have mixed political views. Media and technology tools allow people to seek out information and reject facts that they find uncomfortable, in part based on their pre-conceived bias. The media helps them deepen their distrust of the other side of the political aisle, but much of the research notes that these biases exist outside the media. Therefore, polarization may be the core idea that is aided and abetted by the modern fragmented media, rather than the other way around.

See also: Audience Fragmentation; Echo Chamber Effect; Personalization and the Internet; Political Bias and the Media; Post-Truth Politics; Social Media and Politics

Further Reading

Bakshy, Eytan. 2012. "Rethinking Information Diversity in Networks." Facebook. January 17. Accessed January 15, 2016. https://www.facebook.com/notes/facebook-data-science/rethinking-information-diversity-in-networks/10150503499618859.

Campante, Filipe, and Daniel Hojman. 2013. "Media and Polarization: Evidence from the Introduction of Broadcast TV in the United States." *Journal of Public Economics* 100 (April).

Kim, Anne. 2014. "Do Partisan Media Add to Political Polarization?" Republic 3.0. June. Accessed January 15, 2016. http://republic3-0.com/partisan-media-add-political-polarization.

Levendusky, Matthew. 2013. *How Partisan Media Polarize America*. Chicago: University of Chicago Press.

Mitchell, Amy, Jeffrey Gottfried, Jocelyn Kiley, and Katerina Eva Matsa. 2014. "Political Polarization & Media Habits." Pew Research Center. October 21. Accessed October 31, 2016. http://www.journalism.org/2014/10/21/section-3-talking-politics-leaders-vs-listeners-and-the-views-people-hear/.

Pariser, Eli. 2011. "Beware Online 'Filter Bubbles.'" TEDTalk. March. Accessed January 15, 2016. https://www.ted.com/talks/eli_pariser_beware_online_filter_bubbles?language=en.

Poole, Keith. 2012. "Picture of a Polarized Congress." *UGAresearch*. Athens: University of Georgia.

Prior, Markus. 2007. *Post-Broadcast Democracy: How Media Choice Increases Inequality in Political Involvement and Polarizes Elections*. Cambridge: Cambridge University Press.

POLITICO

It takes a certain chutzpah to look at the crowded field of political reporting and blogging—especially as the already sluggish economy started to nosedive into the housing crisis—and say, "Let's start a political newspaper." But that is what former *Washington Post* reporters Jim VandeHei and John F. Harris did in 2007.

Since then, Politico has become one of the must-reads for the Washington set and those wanting to understand D.C. politics. It has become big business as well. In fact, even as many traditional newspapers continue to struggle with dwindling readership and sagging profits, Politico's business has boomed. The online-first publication has added a monthly magazine and now has announced plans to move the Politico model to Europe.

Why it's worked is a combination of journalistic style, niche publishing, and luck.

Describing their journalistic approach, the founders stressed the idea that this news service would be unique, not adopting the formal style taken by most Washington reporters or the legislative blow-by-blow of the congressional journals. As they put it in their mission statement, "Reading a story should be just as interesting as talking with the reporter over a sandwich or a beer. It's a curiosity of journalism that this often isn't true. The traditional newspaper story is written with austere, voice-of-God detachment. These newspaper conventions tend to muffle personality, humor, accumulated insight—all the things readers hunger for as they try to make sense of the news and understand what politicians are really like" (Politico 2007). What emerged was a news source as interested in process and personalities as in legislation and policy. Politico has become a barometer of the politically relevant and important, a cherished status for many in the nation's capital.

But that is not to say the coverage is without its critics. Mike Allen, the White House correspondent, composes a daily email blast ad blog, dubbed "The Playbook," that has drawn the ire of Mark Leibovich in his work *This Town* for its part-vapid, part-sycophantic reporting about top-tier journalists and politicians. Michael Wolff's story in *Vanity Fair* went even further, calling the entire news service "obsessive-compulsive." He wrote two years after its launch that Politico "exalts, and fetishizes, in breathless, even orgiastic news flashes, the most boring subject in the world: the granular workings of government bureaucracy. It is, arguably, in its hyperbolic attentions and exertions, in its fixations on interests that could not possibly interest anyone but the person doing it and the writer writing about it, something like a constant parody of itself" (Wolff 2009).

It was built to be more "inside baseball" than any publication before it and with features like "The Playbook," a job board called "PowerJobs," and a professional subscription area for real-time coverage of D.C., the multi-faceted news service has flourished.

By Politico's own count the site draws some 83 percent of its viewers from outside the capital and yet 60 percent of its profits still come from the weekly paper printed only in D.C. (Politico 2014). It has succeeded, in part, because it understands the niche it wants to reach, cultivates that audience, and then aggressively pursues advertisers wanting to reach senior media- and government-types. As VandeHei said in a promotional video aimed at advertisers, "We don't focus on the masses. We are focusing almost exclusively on an elite audience and the smart set is not that big."

The paper launched with backing from Allbritton Communications, a media company that operated the *Washington Evening Star* before that newspaper went under in 1978. Robert Allbritton financed the beginning of Politico, but required that VandeHei and Harris include an actual printed publication in addition to their planned website. By 2009, the newspaper profits were outpacing online, bringing in 60 percent of the news service's profit (Politico 2014). The news service is now the envy of other media properties, with the former CEO of Huffington Post saying, "They've been doing quite well, not only in terms of numbers but in terms of being able to establish an almost purely digital brand . . . A brand that had no prior legacy has established itself as a real player in the media business in [Washington, D.C.], which is really quite a feat" (Shaw 2011). Within four months of its founding, the paper was hosting primary debates in the presidential campaign and was being cited as one of the leading voices in political reporting.

By 2011, the service expanded, launching a subscription service "Politico Pro" with "the goal of providing readers real-time intelligence on the politics, process and personalities involved in policy." It has developed a steady audience of more than 1,000 subscribers shelling out a minimum of $3,295 a year—but normally more like $8,000—to access early and exclusive reporting (Lafrance 2012). The effort, similar to projects from the *National Journal* and *Congressional Quarterly*, takes the Politico approach to reporting on Capitol Hill and the White House and turns it into a 24-hour live stream of political and journalistic research, reporting, and gossip.

The mixed business strategy has been so successful that the company announced in the fall of 2014 that it would launch a European equivalent in partnership with one of the continent's largest publishers, Germany's Axel Springer SE. Media observers welcomed the news, with the *Columbia Journalism Review* saying, "Though media precedent in the region suggests that it's hard to grow an audience for European, as opposed to country-specific coverage, the qualities that constitute Politico's appeal—an ability to turn dry policies into narratives that are passionately followed by core readers—just might be a formula for success" (Sillesen 2014).

The move to Europe is a major risk for the still-young Politico. They are seeking to recreate a magical combination of political power reporting, niche audience development, and aggressive advertiser recruitment in a far more diverse and politically divided region. Whether it will be able to recreate the D.C. success in Brussels, Belgium, will be a tall order, but the success of its American project was far from what experts predicted when VandeHei and Harris launched their effort. Despite their relative success in the chaotic media marketplace, internal divisions over the future direction of the company eventually led to a major shakeup at the organization in 2016, with VandeHei and key leaders announcing they would depart the eight-year-old news organization to pursue new projects.

Further Reading

Lafrance, Adrienne. 2012. "Politico Pro, One Year In: A Premium Pricetag, a Tight Focus, and a Business Success." Nieman Lab. April 17. Accessed September 10, 2014. http://www.niemanlab.org/2012/04/politico-pro-one-year-in-a-premium-pricetag-a-tight-focus-and-a-business-success.

Politico. 2007. "Mission Statement." Accessed August 22, 2014. http://www.politico.com/aboutus/missionstatement.html.

Politico. 2014. "Advertising." Accessed September 10, 2014. http://www.politico.com/about/advertising/audience.

Shaw, Lucas. 2011. "D.C. Drama Has Been Very Good for Politico." TheWrap. August 29. Accessed September 1, 2014. http://www.thewrap.com/media/column-post/political-climate-has-been-very-good-politico-30429.

Sillesen, Lene Bech. 2014. "Will Politico Fill a Media Void in Europe?" *Columbia Journalism Review*. September 12. Accessed September 24, 2014. http://www.cjr.org/behind_the_news/will_politico_fill_a_media_voi.php?page=all#sthash.9o8uKVqc.dpuf.

Wolff, Michael. 2009. "Politico's Washington Coup." August. Accessed August 21, 2014. http://www.vanityfair.com/politics/features/2009/08/wolff200908.

POST-TRUTH POLITICS

The idea of post-truth politics stems from the concept that in the current political and media climate no statement can be rejected as inaccurate because the facts themselves have become subject to political debate. A commentator or politician can clearly misstate the facts. They can lie. And the fragmented media and polarized audiences they serve are unable to dispute the facts, turning to opposing commentators to offer a form of balanced coverage that offers little factual critique of the original statement. It is the era where Barack Obama's birth, although legally documented by the state of Hawaii, can be covered in a story where one side repeats a claim, regardless of its factual accuracy. The idea of post-truth politics has challenged political reporters, who tend to find balance in their stories by seeking comment from one side of the debate and then the other to push back and increasingly challenge the core honesty and accuracy of the public officials they are covering.

The he-said, she-said approach to political reporting is far from new and represents a deeply entrenched way of covering political debates. Programs like CNN's *Crossfire* built themselves up as venues where the different political parties came together to discuss—or sometimes shout at one another—about the issues being debated in Congress or the upcoming election. Other programs like the *PBS NewsHour* also followed this model of inviting different sides of a debate, but focused on choosing substantive policy experts who could tackle the nuance of a debate versus the heat and verbal bombast that fueled many of the cable news talk shows.

But then something changed in the debate, and the competing arguments model of reporting became more difficult to execute. As James Fallows noted in a 2012 article in the *Atlantic*, "when significant political players are willing to say things that flat-out are not true—and when they're not slowed down by demonstrations of their claims' falseness—then reporters who stick to he-said, she-said become accessories to deception" (Fallows 2012). In this model, the basic truths that underlie political issues are open for debate and if a fact is misstated or simply fabricated by a candidate and repeated by the media it is covered as Republicans (or Democrats) say X and Democrats (or Republicans) reject that notion.

Part of this new reality is a result of the deeply fractured media environment where increasingly partisan news outlets will pick up messages from their politically aligned party's candidates and repeat them with little fact checking. In particular, liberal activists have accused conservative media outlets and Republican candidates of fostering this form of reporting. This accusation emerged in 2012 when both Nobel Prize–winning economist and columnist Paul Krugman took to the pages of the *New York Times* to accuse Republican candidate Mitt Romney of simply inventing the positions of President Barack Obama. Krugman, who traditionally supports liberal and Democratic policies, wrote about how Romney had accused the president of endorsing widespread economic redistribution, going so far as to claim that President Obama wanted the government to ensure "equal outcomes" in the economy. Krugman countered by saying that President Obama's positions are essentially that of moderate Republicans from the past four decades. He went on to opine, "Won't Mr. Romney pay a price for running a campaign based entirely on falsehoods? He obviously thinks not, and I'm afraid he may be right. Oh, Mr. Romney will probably be called on some falsehoods. But, if past experience is any guide, most of the news media will feel as though their reporting must be 'balanced,' which means that every time they point out that a Republican lied they have to match it with a comparable accusation against a Democrat—even if what the Democrat said was actually true or, at worst, a minor misstatement" (Krugman 2011).

Krugman's argument captures the two facets of the post-truth critique. First, politicians feel that they can outright lie about the positions of their opponents. In this case, Republicans can lie about the positions of a Democrat and the media won't call out the fabrication, instead couching their reporting as assertions made by one side about the other. By 2016 the rhetoric of the left had become increasingly shrill as columnists and writers took an increasingly hard line on the claims of the right. One Salon columnist summed up the state of post-truth politics in late 2015 by writing, "The passion for political incorrectness on the right has had some rather unfortunate consequences for the GOP candidates. To begin with, it's put constant pressure on people like Donald Trump, Ben Carson, and Carly Fiorina to stretch the truth, to say very stupid things that very stupid people want to hear, regardless of the facts" (Illing 2015).

The concept of lying politicians is also a trope that has existed for decades. Books have been written about how Franklin Roosevelt misled Congress and his advisers about deals he struck with Joseph Stalin to get Russian help to win the war with Japan. Or how President Johnson sold the American public on the idea of the Gulf of Tonkin incident to garner support in Congress for an expansion of America's role in Vietnam. Or how President Clinton lied to the public about the nature of his relationship with a former intern. In each of these incidents the press reported the lies, and in the case of Johnson would repeat the lies for decades. As John Dean, who famously worked for President Nixon and expressed concern that Nixon's lying about Watergate amounted to a "cancer on the presidency," wrote of the Tonkin situation, Johnson and his senior advisers spoon-fed the story of the clash between North Vietnamese gunboats and an American warship, writing, "*Time* magazine dramatized this incident (that, in fact, never occurred) down to the smallest details: 'Russian-designed 'Swatow' gun boats armed with 37-mm and 28-mm guns . . . opened fire on the [American] destroyers with automatic weapons, this time from as close as 2,000 yards.' Similarly, *Newsweek*'s creative writers described a non-existent North Vietnamese 'PT boat burst[ing] into flames' and other boats that were never there sinking or scurrying into the shadows nursing their wounds. The *New York Times* likewise provided a minute-by-minute account" (Dean 2004).

Why did the press not call out the politicians for misleading them and the public, in the past as well as now? Is there something about the American press corps that makes it unable to respond to a specific untruth? It may be respect for the office these public figures hold, or that they empathize with the policy objectives that may prompt the falsehood.

Still, in an era before the media fragmentation of cable news and the Internet, if caught in the lie, campaigns and politicians would still face a media and public backlash. Investigations might be launched, fact checking done, and the campaign would be forced to correct the statement, stick by it, or hope the entire incident would blow over. Today, as the media became increasingly fragmented and trust in reporters and the work they do plummets, some politicians have pushed misleading statements further, seeing how far they could stretch the boundaries without political cost. By 2010, some liberal media observers began to identify a specific trend within the Republican Party to use politically loaded terms and accusations against any policy or politician they opposed. A columnist for the environmental news and commentary site Grist took to the web in 2010 and said the debate over a federal climate change legislation had very little to do with the facts of the bill or the problem; instead, whatever Democrats proposed was accused of being thinly veiled socialism. David Roberts wrote that the environment in Washington, D.C., had reached the point where, "We live in post-truth politics: a political culture in which politics (public opinion and media narratives) have become almost entirely disconnected from policy (the substance of legislation). This obviously dims any hope of reasoned legislative compromise. But in another way, it can be seen as liberating. If the political damage of maximal Republican opposition is a fixed quantity—if policy is orthogonal to politics—then there is little point to policy compromises. They do not appreciably change the politics" (Roberts 2010). This version of politics, where the factual accuracy of a claim bears little connection to reality, has quickly become the norm. Krugman would adopt the term "post-truth politics" to describe the campaign developing in 2012, and by 2016 the concept had become a rallying cry of liberals who accuse the Republican Party of being essentially dishonest.

While liberals and conservatives hash out which party was more blatantly dishonest, journalists have struggled to adapt to the more aggressive claims of politicians on both sides of the aisle. Journalists have been trained to make sure to seek multiple sides of a story, to interview a proposal's author and its detractors and to cobble together a story that explains the different sides. Inherent in this model of balanced reporting is the idea that an argument has two rational sides; the journalist does not draw a conclusion but instead allows the reader or viewer to draw their own conclusion. This idea of balance, to most people, sounds like an admirable trait. Fox News made "Fair and balanced" its marketing motto and even critics of Fox News bash it for being neither.

But as politicians pressed the limits of what they claimed, a growing chorus of journalists have raised real reservations about the concept of "balance." *New York Times* public editor Margaret Sullivan has argued the newspaper should be a "vigilante" for truth, not fearing to call a lie a lie. She also came out against was she called a " false balance," writing, "Simply put, false balance is the journalistic practice of giving equal weight to both sides of a story, regardless of an established truth on one side. And many people are fed up with it. They don't want to hear lies or half-truths given credence on one side, and shot down on the other. They want some real answers" (Sullivan 2012).

But executing an accurate balancing of the legitimacy of different sides of an argument is far easier said than done. Take Krugman's column helped spur the use of "post-truth politics" as a term. His column focused on a speech where Mitt Romney's claimed that "President Obama believes that government should create equal outcomes. In an entitlement society, everyone receives the same or similar rewards, regardless of education, effort, and willingness to take risk. That which is earned by some is redistributed to the others." To Krugman, this was patently absurd. The president had made no policy proposal that amount to such a radical redistribution of wealth. That, for Krugman and many others, would amount to proof that President Obama does not believe the things that Romney claims. But how, exactly, do we know that President Obama does NOT believe this? Do we know that President Obama, if given full control of all of the nation's lawmaking, would not advocate a system that leveled the playing field? To truly disprove what Romney said a journalist would need to be able to say categorically what the president actually believes, not what he has proposed. This may sound too much like a philosophy paper, but this push back against post-truth politics is leading to an increasing debate between reporters and those who distrust the mainstream media.

In 2015 an incident that would seem ripe for the post-truth politics police erupted in the Republican primary race. It developed when then-frontrunner Donald Trump claimed that on September 11, 2001, thousands of Muslims in New Jersey had celebrated the attacks that destroyed the World Trade Center. This factual claim seemed easy enough to check. Trump cited the work of a then-*Washington Post* reporter who reported that several communities in New Jersey had investigated several people holding parties on rooftops to celebrate the attack. Trump reiterated that he had seen thousands and thousands celebrating in Jersey City, N.J. Reporting has piled up against his claims and the reporter of the *Post* story said the Republican's characterization is inaccurate. Even Fox News's Bill O'Reilly fact checked the claim and found no evidence of the celebrations. But another reporter, Sharyl Attkisson, pushed back against the media, demanding, "Reporters may believe it's untrue or unlikely that thousands in New Jersey cheered-on the World Trade Center attacks. They may not know anybody who participated in such a thing and they may not be able to locate videotape of it. But that's quite different than knowing, unequivocally, that it didn't happen. Knowing that it didn't happen would require a magical mix of omniscience and clairvoyance. Reporters who claim to know that it didn't happen are committing a journalistic error more serious than the offense of which they accuse Trump" (Attkisson 2015).

Attkisson's demand, that a reporter rejecting a claim of a presidential candidate should have clear and convincing proof to justify the rejection, is the difficult position that reporters pushing back against the idea of post-truth politics face. A reporter documenting the claims and counter-claims of politicians does not have any real intellectual skin in the game. They may be criticized for choosing a poor source or not interviewing the correct sources, but that is an error of reporting. To stand up and declare a politician is wrong or, even more provocatively, lying puts the reporter squarely in the political debate rather than on the side documenting it. It's a role few reporters relish, but as the post-truth political world moves from the realm of the presidential stonewalling to a full-blown continuous campaign of factually tenuous claims, it is one that more political reporters are having to face.

And even as American reporters find how they will balance debatable political claims from flat lies, post-truth politics appears to be spreading beyond the Americas to other democratic systems. In each society where fractured media collides with aggressive partisan claims, writers have taken to the pages of papers, magazines, and blogs to decry the dangers of the relative truth of politicians. A columnist for one of the largest Australian papers felt compelled to question the state of political dialogue in their own country in a fit of concern that sounds very much like those in America, writing, "The minority of Australians who are interested in politics for the most part seem to be talking among their own kind, so often consumed with rage, yelling 'liar, liar' before basic details are known, unable to see merit in any other point of view . . . Trust is essential in a democracy. Politicians will spin, put the best gloss on things, and even deceive at times. But it's gone beyond that in the past few years—the very basis of our system seems to depend on deliberately misleading the public" (Alcorn 2012).

Reporters and editors are pushing back with increasing force, outlining that candidate claims are without factual basis and fact checking more stump speeches and campaign ads. But in an era of eroding trust in the media and fewer outlets that serve a broad audience, the concern about post-truth politicians on the right is relegated to liberal blogs, columns, and magazines and those claims of politicians that infuriate Democratic media commentators are often repeated widely by conservative-facing talk radio, websites, and talk show hosts. The truth, often, is left to the individual and whom he or she chooses to watch or read.

See also: Balance; Fact Checking; Objectivity; Political Polarization and the Media; Trust in Journalism

Further Reading

Alcorn, Gay. 2014. "Facts Are Futile in an Era of Post-Truth Politics." *Sunday Age*. February 28.

Attkisson, Sharyl. 2015. "The 'Post Truth' News Media." Sharylattkisson.com. December 2. December 11, 2015. https://sharylattkisson.com/the-post-truth-news-media.

Dean, John. 2004. "The Post-Truth Presidency." *Washington Monthly*. November. Accessed December 11, 2015. http://www.washingtonmonthly.com/features/2004/0411.dean.html.

Fallows, James. 2012. "Bit by Bit It Takes Shape: Media Evolution for the 'Post-Truth' Age." *Atlantic*. August 29. Accessed December 11, 2015. http://www.theatlantic.com/politics/archive/2012/08/bit-by-bit-it-takes-shape-media-evolution-for-the-post-truth-age/261741.

Illing, Sean. 2015. "The GOP's House of Lies: Ben Carson, Carly Fiorina & the Era of Post-Truth Politics." Salon. October 12, 2015. http://www.salon.com/2015/10/12/the_gops_house_of_lies_ben_carson_carly_fiorina_the_era_of_post_truth_politics.

Roberts, David. 2010. "Post-Truth Politics." Grist. April 1. Accessed December 11, 2015. http://grist.org/article/2010-03-30-post-truth-politics.

Sullivan, Margaret. 2012. "He Said, She Said, and the Truth." *New York Times*. September 15. Accessed December 11, 2015. http://www.nytimes.com/2012/09/16/public-editor/16pubed.html.

PRESIDENTIAL DEBATES

The 1992 debates were destined to be remembered.

First, there was a serious third party alternative, Texas businessman Ross Perot, whose quirky and quixotic campaign had already made the presidential contest one filled with one-liners. In fact, Perot had been declared the winner for the first debate in a CNN/USA Today poll conducted that first night (CNN 1996). Then there was the format of the second debate. For the first time ordinary Americans sat on stage and asked questions of President George H. W. Bush, Perot, and Democratic candidate Bill Clinton. This town hall-style debate allowed pre-selected audience members to ask the candidates a question in an effort to help undecided voters choose a candidate.

"Tonight's program is unlike any other Presidential debate in history . . . An independent polling firm has selected an audience of 209 uncommitted voters from [Richmond, Va.]," moderator Carole Simpson said, adding those undecided voters would be allowed to ask questions "on a topic of their choosing—anything they want to ask about."

But that's not what President Bush remembers. For him, that debate is all about a watch.

About half way through the contest, as a woman asked the candidates about how the debt had affected their lives, the camera cut away from the questioner to show the full stage and there, on the far left of the screen, was President Bush, glancing at his watch.

"Oh God, do I remember," he said later. "I took a huge hit. That's another thing I don't like about debates, you look at your watch and they say that he hasn't any business running for president. He's bored and he's out of this thing, and he's not with it and we need change," he added, raising a fist of protest (Lehrer 2000).

Coverage from after that debate does confirm the former president's assertions. One piece, under the headline "Bush's demeanor raises GOP concern," quoted one Republican official as saying it seems the "president now believes he is going to lose" (Devroy and Marcus 1992). Looking back the reaction, Bush is still irked by what he calls a focus on "show business" over substance, saying, "I mean, they took a little incident like that to show that I was, you know, out of it . . . Now, was I glad when the damn thing was over? Yeah, and maybe that's why I was looking at it, only 10 more minutes of this crap."

President Bush may feel like they are "crap," but presidential debates have emerged as one of the major milestones and critical tests during the general election campaign. Part-televised drama, part-collective job interview, these are high stakes moments, according to Jim Lehrer, the journalist who has moderated or participated in more debates—12—than anyone else. He has written, "The consequences can be enormous from those final critical events in the process that ends with the selection of the president of the United States. Everybody involved, from the candidates to the ticket takers, knows it and that is why anxiety rules all minds—and stomachs" (Banville 2013).

Presidential debates are fairly new spectacles in campaigns to win the White House. It's true that the 1860 presidential campaign between Republican Abraham Lincoln and Democratic senator Stephen A. Douglas referenced a lot of claims and statements the two men had said while debating one another, but the debates themselves had occurred two years earlier when they met seven times in an effort to sway Illinois state legislators to send one of them to the U.S. Senate. It would be another 80 years before candidates even got around to challenging one another to publicly debate. Republican Wendell Wilkie, hoping to highlight incumbent President Franklin Delano Roosevelt's stranglehold on the presidency, challenged Roosevelt to debate. FDR passed and, according to polls at the time, the public was evenly split on whether that mattered or not (Trent, Friedenberg, and Denton 2011, p. 262).

Eight years later Republicans Thomas Dewey and Harold Stassen did meet, debating live on the radio ahead of the Oregon primary. The clash, broadcast nationally, was hailed as an "historic occasion" (*New York Times* 1948) and helped solidify the campaign of New York governor Thomas Dewey. Democrats had their own primary debate eight years later and by 1960 interest in a presidential debate had reached a new level.

That was the year Vice President Richard Nixon accepted a challenge from Democratic senator John F. Kennedy to debate on live television. The mythology of this debate continues to affect the way candidates and media consider these meetings. The myth goes something like this: the junior senator from Massachusetts entered the debate largely unknown by the public. He performed well, answering the questions with substance, but even more importantly appearing calm and cool under the hot television lights. Vice President Nixon was ill and had injured his knee that afternoon and so appeared pale and sweaty as the debate dragged on. The result was Kennedy appeared more "presidential."

But it goes even further. Read most accounts of the debate and someone will tell the anecdote about how radio listeners had thought Nixon had done better and television viewers believed Kennedy had bested the vice president. In his book on televised debates, Alan Schroeder dug into the facts behind the myth and found it all started with a stunt organized by the publisher of the *Atlanta Constitution*, Ralph McGill. "He arranged for 'a number of persons' to listen to the first Kennedy-Nixon debate on radio, to see if they would react differently than television viewers did.

'It is interesting to report they unanimously thought Mr. Nixon had the better of it,' McGill concluded. Despite later, more-scientific data to the contrary, this early finding took root as a shibboleth. McGill's poll, specifying neither sample size nor methodology, reflects the casual approach the news media of 1960 took towards the audience reaction story" (Schroeder 2000, p. 246).

This importance of appearance—Kennedy's dark suit looking better, Nixon's lack of makeup making him appear unshaven—over substance has pervaded views of the debates since. As debatable as the importance of the visual component of the debate is, the 1960 meetings did include one more documented fact that should not be overlooked. They helped Kennedy win. Research done at the time by CBS found that six percent of voters said the debates had been a major factor in their decision that year and of those voters Kennedy won 2-to-1. "I think the evidence is convincing that the debates were the determining factor," historian Richard Norton Smith said. "What the debates allowed JFK to do was, if nothing else, establish himself on the same footing, an equal footing in terms of experience, command" (Banville 2013).

Debates appeared so potentially powerful that after this, most incumbents saw little reason to open themselves up to the challenge, so for the next several elections there weren't any. It was not until the post-Watergate campaign of 1976 that debates returned, and they have been a staple of the presidential campaign ever since.

But why do they loom so large on the presidential stage?

First, they are one of the few moments that are not carefully scripted. That's not to say there aren't preparations, but when the lights turn on and the questions start flying, things are no longer under the control of message makers or handlers. "The presidential debates are the one time that the leading candidates for this office come together in the same place, answering the same questions without the involvement of any advisers or pre-produced segments. It is unlike anything else that happens during the election period in that regard," said Janet Brown, head of the Presidential Debate Commission, adding that they are also one of the few events not paid for by any partisan interest (Banville 2013). That may be why candidates, advisers, and consultants will spend weeks preparing for these brief affairs. Candidates often hole up in a resort with a raft of advisers and other pols there to act as the competition to go over answers, possible questions, and videos of past performances to try and create the right mix of detailed information, likability, and gravitas. Schroeder said it is a delicate mix of skills that can help bolster a candidate's chances, writing, "A winning debate strategy hinges in large measure on how well a candidate apprehends the experience as televised drama. Smart debaters understand that their mission, at least in part, is to stage a performance for an audience—an audience that expects to be simultaneously enlightened and entertained" (Schroeder 2000, p. 77).

The second reason debates are so important is that they fuel a flurry of media coverage, both before and after the debate itself. The process begins before a single question is asked, as campaigns use the media to lower expectations for how their candidate will perform and raise them for the opponent.

Debates may set the agenda for the media narrative around the campaign, but we have also seen incidents where media coverage of the debate can shift perceptions of what happened on that stage for 90 minutes. It is a role that academics who have studied the events agree is critical to the public digesting the clash of ideas and making sense of the underlying importance of what is said. As Schroeder wrote in his work, "The power of the press reaches its apogee in the aftermath of a debate, when two things happen: First, the pundits have their say in the period immediately following the broadcast, and second, the ninety-minute event is reduced to a collection of sound bite highlights that will be played over and over as a kind of shorthand for the complete program" (Schroeder 2000, p. 243).

This power came to the fore during the 1984 confrontations between incumbent Ronald Reagan and former vice president Walter Mondale. Headed into the first meeting, Reagan had been enjoying a double-digit lead in most polls. Still, an unnamed adviser warned the *New York Times* that they still had some concerns going into the debate. The strategist cautioned they knew their man could sometimes go off on tangents or get mired in facts and so the advisers boasted that they were prepared for a stumble in the re-election effort, but were confident, "If we make a mistake, it won't take 10 days to deal with it. It will be over in 12 hours" (Raines 1984).

Then they debated. Reagan repeatedly got lost in details of specific answers, appearing confused and distracted throughout. Still, he was affable Ronald Reagan and the instant reactions, while not effusive, called the event more of a draw. But over the next few days a drumbeat of negative press coverage would shift the public's perception of what had happened on the stage in Louisville, KY. As the press asked increasingly hard questions about President Reagan's performance the public's perception of the debate began to shift, from one of a draw to one of a clear win by former vice president Walter Mondale. In fact, Reagan's weak performance only became a larger issue about his age—he was already the oldest president in history—until two mornings after the debate when the *Wall Street Journal* ran a story with the headline "New Question in Race: Is the Oldest U.S. President Now Showing His Age?"

But the heated and largely negative press reaction to the president's performance in some ways aided his comeback by lowering expectations of President Reagan and raising new expectations that Mondale would struggle to meet. So many questions were raised about Reagan's ability to perform that ABC's Sam Donaldson predicted ahead of the second meeting, "People will be watching tonight because of Louisville, to see whether the president stands up, makes sentences that make sense from the standpoint of not stammering and stuttering, and doesn't drool."

Just about halfway through the second debate the *Baltimore Sun*'s Henry Trewhitt went directly at the president about his debate performance two weeks earlier.

The experienced newsman told the president he wanted to address an issue that had been "lurking out there" and went right after the issue, asking Reagan, "You already are the oldest President in history… I recall, yet, that President Kennedy had to go for days on end with very little sleep during the Cuba missile crisis. Is there any doubt in your mind that you would be able to function in such circumstances?"

Reagan, who said that his team had not prepared a canned answer for such a question, nevertheless ripped off a one-liner that would echo throughout the history of presidential debate—and dash any hopes the Democrats had of unseating the popular Reagan.

With a hint of a smile and without missing a beat, the former actor responded, "Not at all, Mr. Trewhitt and I want you to know that also I will not make age an issue of this campaign. I am not going to exploit for political purposes my opponent's youth and inexperience."

The line, the audience's roar of approval, and even Mondale's laugh ended the larger discussion of the president's age, even if years later some would wonder if the first debate had been an early warning sign of the Alzheimer's that would devastate the president's health later.

Debates also play a larger role in the democratic process according to some experts. One that may surprise the reader is that these contests help the public be more comfortable with the candidate they did not intend to vote for. In 1976, a panel of communications professors looked at the impact on the voters' attitudes toward both candidates. These researchers found that "the debates stimulated exposure to various kinds of communication about the campaign without, at the same time, causing voters to balance their increasing support for their own candidate by becoming more negative toward the opposing candidate" (Becker, Pepper, Wenner, and Kim 1979, p. 396). Put more simply, debates create a moment when voters learn about the candidate they didn't plan to vote for and see them not as the enemy, but as a largely legitimate option. The debates, unlike negative ads or a stump speech, help voters see the other candidate as a viable president.

Still, in the 40 years since Presidents Carter and Ford restarted the presidential debate, this role may be increasingly important, according to presidential historian Michael Beschloss. Beschloss said that with the increasing cost of campaigns, "$1 billion is basically spent to show the candidate they're backing in a completely airless environment that shows him at his best . . . and to the extent they deal with the opponent, it shows the opponent as Satan or someone who's not worthy of being elected. The debate is one of the very rare opportunities where the two candidates are forced to get into a situation where they have to confront their accuser, their opponent, and they also have to be asked questions that are not scripted" (Banville 2013).

Given their role in the process it is not surprising that debates have also been at the center of criticism for decades. The organization behind them—the Commission on Presidential Debates—has been criticized for being too secretive, and for making it too difficult for third-party candidates to participate. The formats of debates have been attacked for not allowing actual discussion, but instead allowing candidates to stick to set talking points. And moderators have often faced questions about their questions and the fairness of their approaches.

It's a recipe for televised drama as much as it is a civic function.

Further Reading

Banville, Lee. "Debating Our Destiny: Presidential Debate Moments That Shaped History." MacNeil/Lehrer Productions. 2013.

Becker, Samuel, Robert Pepper, Lawrence Wenner, and Jin Keon Kim. 1979. "Information Flow and the Shaping of Meaning." In *The Great Debates: Carter vs. Ford, 1976*, ed. Sidney Kraus. Bloomington: Indiana University Press.

CNN. 1996. "All Politics: The 1992 Debates." Accessed September 29, 2014. http://www.cnn.com/ALLPOLITICS/1996/debates/history/1992/index.shtml.

Devroy, Ann, and Ruth Marcus. "Bush's Demeanor Raises GOP Concern; Some Sense Resignation in Debate Remarks, Less-Aggressive Style." *Washington Post.* October 17, 1992.

Lehrer, Jim. "Debating Our Destiny." PBS. 2000.

Raines, Howell. 1984. "Lapses by Reagan Please Democrats; Tendency to Misstate Is Seen as 'Wild Card' in Campaign." *New York Times.* October 1, 1984.

Schroeder, Alan. 2000. *Presidential Debates: Forty Years of High-Risk TV*. New York: Columbia University Press.

Trent, Judith, Robert Friedenberg, and Robert Denton. 2011. *Political Campaign Communication: Principles and Practices.* Lanham, MD: Rowman & Littlefield.

"U.S. Hears Stassen and Dewey Debates." 1948. *New York Times.* May 18.

PRESIDENTIAL NOMINATING CONVENTIONS

Presidential nominating conventions are held every four years to select the major party nominees for president and vice president. Once the scene where delegates debated among several candidates and sometimes took dozens of votes to select a nominee, reforms in the 1970s shifted the fight for the nomination away from multi-day conventions to the primaries and caucuses held in the states. The conventions remain a major event in the presidential campaign, serving as a platform for parties to present their issues, introduce rising stars, and, at times, air their political dirty laundry in front of the American public, which still tunes in by the millions to watch. Coverage of these multi-day spectacles has always been intense, but as they became more choreographed for the television cameras, some journalists balked at investing so much time and money covering a political infomercial.

Conventions developed in the early nineteenth century as a way to combat the increasingly insular ways in which the nation's two major parties—the Democratic-Republicans (soon to become the Democratic Party) and the Federalists (soon to collapse)—selected their nominees for president. Beginning in 1796 after George Washington announced his retirement, the two parties would hold caucuses among the party's elected members of Congress and they would select the party's nominee. But this system began to falter fairly quickly. By 1820 the Federalists did not even nominate a candidate for president. Four years later when the

Democratic-Republicans met, only a quarter of the party's members of Congress showed up. The group selected the Secretary of the Treasury William Crawford, passing over far more popular candidates like Andrew Jackson, John Quincy Adams, and Henry Clay. All four candidates ended up running—and Adams was elected in a contested Electoral College vote in Congress—but the idea of the "King Caucus" was on the ropes.

Two campaigns later a new party, the Anti-Mason Party—which was opposed to, not surprisingly, the power of the secret society the Freemasons—met in September 1831 to select a candidate. Rather than caucusing with its elected party or specific leaders, the Anti-Masons invited members of the party to come and discuss the positions of the party and select a nominee. The other major parties followed suit and by 1832 conventions had been born. The idea was to select a candidate that better represented the interests of the party from across its geographic ranks. With this new structure, state parties were empowered to select delegates to the nominating convention, decentralizing power in the political party and somewhat inadvertently turning the conventions into arenas where the party hashed out differences and debated major internal issues.

A major case in point was the Democratic convention 12 years later in 1844. When the convention delegates gathered in Baltimore there were three primary candidates—former president Martin Van Buren, Senator James Buchanan, and retired general and ambassador Lewis Cass. Van Buren had been the frontrunner until he cautioned against a quick annexation of Texas—a political issue that threatened to raise real debate over slavery. Van Buren's position cost him the support of southerners, who saw Texas as a critical new pro-slavery state, and threw the contest in the convention into chaos. Cass wanted to annex Texas and so won those votes and Van Buren and Buchanan split the remainder. The party was deeply divided and the southerners controlled enough delegates to ensure Van Buren would not get the nod. Party leaders had to look for another candidate that could unite the party and they found one in the famous "dark horse" (meaning "little known" in racing parlance) James Polk. Polk, who had supported the Texas move but had not blocked Van Buren, emerged as a compromise candidate.

The Polk nomination and other party fights—like the notorious 1924 Democratic convention that took 103 ballots to select their candidate—created a mythology of the contested convention. This idea of the party going into the convention without a nominee and the ensuing jockeying for position is a narrative that crops up every election cycle, especially if there are multiple candidates vying for the mantle of frontrunner. The closest to a brokered convention that has occurred recently was in 2008 when Senator Barack Obama surpassed the needed number of delegates in the final primary contests. But even in this closely fought battle with Senator Hillary Clinton, Clinton appeared at the convention and ended the delegate counting, handing all her delegates to Obama and making the nomination vote a unanimous affair. But long before the 2008 contest, observers had seen a clear shift in the nomination process. As the media covered the fight for the party's nod more and more, and polling that assessed public opinion about candidates became a regular part of that coverage, the idea of party delegates gathering in a fabled smoke-filled room to select a candidate of their choosing became more difficult to fathom.

Even as primaries took on more importance in the selection process, party leaders sought to maintain the importance and relevance of the convention—and themselves. Still, an unmistakable shift was happening in the selection of the nominee that had nothing to do with party structure or leaders versus rank-and-file. By 1960 observers would argue, "Presidential nominating campaigns have been subject to real and significant changes, for which the combined impacts of the primaries, the public opinion polls, and the mass media of communication seem to be mainly responsible. The effect can be seen in many elements of the campaigns—in the augmented efforts of candidates (and their managers) to prove they have popular support; in the marked rise of voter participation; and in the number of candidates already billed as popular national favorites that the conventions increasingly find at their doors on opening day" (David, Goldman, and Bain 1960).

The process itself was also being overhauled along the way to de-emphasize the convention and shift more power to the primary contests. In particular, the ugly Democratic convention of 1968 precipitated a wave of reforms that completed the shift away from conventions as the epicenter of the nomination fight. That year, Eugene McCarthy, an anti-Vietnam War senator from Minnesota, and former attorney general Robert Kennedy opposed Vice President Hubert Humphrey for the nomination of the Democratic Party. The party itself was in deep turmoil, fundamentally split over President Lyndon Johnson's handling of the Vietnam War. That split exploded at the convention. The party, already on edge due to the assassination of civil rights leader Martin Luther King in April and Kennedy that June, arrived in Chicago under the watchful gaze of mayor Richard Daley. Daley had planned to use the convention to highlight the achievements of his administration but when anti-war protesters descended on Chicago, he sent police to force them away from the convention. The result was chaos in the convention hall and bloodshed on the streets. Television cameras caught it all, showing protesters chanting, "The whole world is watching" as Chicago police used heavy-handed techniques to clear the streets. Television also captured the troubles inside the hall when Dan Rather of CBS News tried to interview a delegate being thrown out of the hall. Security guards scuffled with Rather whose microphone was on. After the altercation Rather said to anchor Walter Cronkite, "Walter . . . we tried to talk to the man and we got violently pushed out of the way. This is the kind of thing that has been going on outside the hall, this is the first time we've had it happen inside the hall. We . . . I'm sorry to be out of breath, but somebody belted me in the stomach during that." Cronkite then replied, "I think we've got a bunch of thugs here, Dan" (Johnson 2009).

Other media moments from the convention included cameras showing Daley cursing at podium speaker Connecticut senator Abraham Ribicoff who, while nominating another anti-war candidate George McGovern, angrily denounced the violence saying, "And, with George McGovern as President of the United States, we wouldn't have to have Gestapo tactics in the streets of Chicago." The media coverage of the 1968 convention helped highlight the divisions of the party, which began a series of reforms aimed at ensuring the will of the party members was better reflected in the convention. The reforms guaranteed that the vast majority of the delegates to the convention would be selected by party members in primaries or caucuses and not picked by the party elites.

Ever since the reforms were fully enacted the focus of the nomination fight has been the primaries; the conventions have become more ceremonial in function. Scholars say this has had several effects on the process. First, it empowered the voters to become more involved in the selection of the nominees by allowing them to vote or caucus for candidates at the local level. Second, it created a less heated and momentum-driven process by spreading it across many contests. In addition to the ability of candidates to appeal to the rank-and-file party members, "Delegates chosen over the 105-day period from the New Hampshire to the California primary are much less susceptible to the bandwagon psychology that in the past sometimes enabled a 'favorite son' or 'dark horse' candidate to stampede the convention" (Davis 1980). The creation of the modern primary system also completed the decentralization of party power in the selection of the nominee, moving first from the "King Caucus" to the convention and then from the convention to a series of votes by party members in most states.

All of this meant that the actual nominating power of the conventions has weakened considerably since the 1960s. Even the hotly contested Democratic and Republican contests of 2016 did little to test the highly structured and closed nominating process at the conventions. Instead the conventions have become carefully stage-managed pageants about the party, its positions, and its standard-bearers. From their creation, conventions have always been partly outward facing, explaining to the public and to its potential supporters what a party stood for. This has become particularly true as mass media allowed the events inside the hall to be broadcast to listeners and viewers nationwide. And this also helps explain why the convention has been the epicenter of bruising fights, most often, although not always, among Democrats. These clashes have generally been about the divisive issues of the day—slavery in the Polk nomination, anti-Catholicism and the power of the Ku Klux Klan in 1924's epic fight, or the Vietnam War in 1968. One of those divisive, as well as decisive, moments played out at the Democratic Party convention to nominate Harry Truman for a full term in 1948. It occurred as Hubert Humphrey stood before thousands in Philadelphia, PA. It would be a speech of spectacular impact, fracturing the party for years, but also fundamentally shifting its direction.

Humphrey was only the mayor of Minneapolis at this point and was tasked with issuing a report to the party faithful on the divisive issue of civil rights. The Democratic Party had been the party of the South since the Civil War and had created an electoral bloc—"the Solid South"—that had emerged as one of the true powers of the modern political era. But Humphrey stood to deliver the minority argument about why the party platform on civil rights was still off. He boldly declared, "To those who say that this civil-rights program is an infringement on states' rights, I say this: The time has arrived in America for the Democratic Party to get out of the shadow of states' rights and to walk forthrightly into the bright sunshine of human rights. People—human beings—this is the issue of the twentieth century." The Alabama delegation marched out of the convention during the speech and most of Mississippi followed. Humphrey would become one of the party's national leaders and would be elected that fall to the U.S. Senate. And the Dixiecrat Party would splinter off of the Democrats to compete against them. But the Democratic Party was shifting from the states' rights party of the post–Civil War to the civil rights party it would become in the 1960s and 1970s. Humphrey's convention speech did not precipitate all of those changes, but it marked a public moment when the Democratic Party began its march to the left.

This is not to say that Republicans never had high drama or critical speeches at their convention. In fact, the 1976 convention had historic doses of both. The Republicans gathered in Kansas City and it was the last time that, as the convention opened, no candidate had enough delegate support to claim the nomination. President Gerald Ford had won more delegates and earned more votes, but a tough challenge from the more conservative former governor of California Ronald Reagan had left Ford short of the nomination. Coverage at the time cast it as either man's to win. Both Ford and Reagan jockeyed for support, with Reagan promising to nominate a member of the party's liberal wing as vice president if he got the nod. Analysts said the move may have backfired as many conservatives expressed anger with the announcement and few moderates changed their mind on Reagan. Still, when the first ballot was cast, either man could still win, making for the most dramatic roll call of states ever televised. Ford ended up narrowly defeating Reagan, but Reagan may have gotten the real last word.

With many in the country watching, Reagan took the podium to endorse Ford and in so doing overshadowed the party's nominee. Speaking largely off the cuff, Reagan talked of writing something for a time capsule set to be closed until the country's tercentennial in 2076. He told a rapt audience, "Those who would read this letter a hundred years from now, will . . . they look back with appreciation and say, 'Thank God for those people in 1976 who headed off that loss of freedom, who kept us now 100 years later free, who kept our world from nuclear destruction'? And if we failed, they probably won't get to read the letter at all because it spoke of individual freedom, and they won't be allowed to talk of that or read of it." Reagan's speech rallied the convention delegates and became a central argument in his successful campaign four years later.

Reagan had mastered what conventions had really become, media moments that could be choreographed and made compelling for the home viewer. Increasingly, media coverage of the conventions became high-priced affairs with networks spending millions to cover the four-day extravaganza. Coverage each night went on for hours as the party's carefully selected speakers appeared at critical moments when coverage started or came back from a commercial break. And with the fact that these events became media-oriented moments, critics began to question the manner in which the media—television in particular—covered them. Many of the journalistic crimes political reporters are accused of are only intensified and amplified in coverage of an event like the presidential nominating convention. Many argue the media, still interested in attracting advertising even as it spends millions to cover the conventions, will focus on any scrap of controversy to create excitement at the event. Two political scientists were already grumbling 30 years ago, "Only the most dramatic speeches from the podium are given more than cursory attention; the speaker who delivers a careful, cerebral discourse offering complex solutions to the nation's ills is not likely to be heard at home. Those who create and perpetuate conflict and uncertainty are given constant coverage" (Crotty and Jackson 1985).

The media itself seems split over the modern convention. Throughout their history, conventions have drawn throngs of press to cover them. As broadcast technology allowed, convention coverage dominated radio and later television news for the two weeks they occurred every four years. But as conventions moved away from scenes of confrontation and party debate to much more orchestrated affairs, some journalists began to balk at the idea of spending millions of dollars and hour after hour of airtime to present what some called a political infomercial. By 1996, ABC had had enough and in a dramatic turn, ABC's *Nightline* host Ted Koppel told his viewers they were leaving because there was no news at the 1996 Republican National Convention to cover. Other ABC officials, like ABC vice president Joanna Bistany, backed Koppel up, telling reporters, "We were all sitting around saying, 'My God, there's no news here. What will it be like at the Democratic convention?'" Although she added that ABC's *World News Tonight* would be there to report anything newsworthy (O'Neill 1996).

Koppel's decision, although no other network followed his lead that year, still resonates with many reporters who see the event as too choreographed and too built for television to offer the public anything more than an ad for each party. Many other journalists disagree, arguing the conventions allow reporters a chance to delve into what each party and candidate stand for and debate the matters before the country. It also offers reporters a chance to talk to party activists from all corners of the country and a wide variety of backgrounds. And even as broadcast coverage has dwindled to usually about an hour a night except for the final night, cable networks and the Internet have moved to fill the void and the media spots. The number of media dwarf the number of delegates, with about 3,000–5,000 party members and alternate delegates seeming modest compared to the 15,000 credentialed reporters, bloggers, producers, and crew that swarm the host city.

Coverage of these events continues to offer candidates a rare opportunity to reach potential voters in ways that can help a candidate. The media coverage of conventions, while different than the excitement and chaos of the brokered conventions of old, still is one of the few times millions of Americans will see the candidate outside of a 30-second ad and remains a major element of modern campaign coverage.

See also: Political Parties; Primary Coverage

Further Reading

Crotty, William, and John Jackson. 1985. *Presidential Primaries and Nomination.* Washington, D.C.: CQ Press.

David, Paul, Ralph Goldman, and Richard Bain. 1960. *The Politics of National Party Conventions.* Washington, D.C.: Brookings Institution Press.

Davis, James. 1980. *Presidential Primaries: Road to the White House.* Westport, CT: Greenwood Press.

Johnson, Ted. 2009. "Walter Cronkite: Ten Top Moments." *Variety*. July 17. Accessed June 1, 2016. http://variety.com/2009/biz/opinion/walter-cronkite-ten-top-moments-40723/.

O'Neill, Helen. 1996. "Koppel's Departure Leaves Media Questioning Future Convention Coverage." Associated Press. August 14. Accessed July 5, 2015. http://www.apnewsarchive.com/1996/Koppel-s-Departure-Leaves-Media-Questioning-Future-Convention-Coverage/id-72dc20dd8fc6dae5678b9b7f95faa4cb.

PRIMARY COVERAGE

As presidential campaigns have come to skip over the mass media, connecting campaigns directly to specific voters through microtargeting and messaging, the power of the press to influence the political process has shifted to the primaries. Here campaigns generally lack the financial power and name recognition that comes with the nomination. It is during this period that reporters have the most influence to shape the perceptions of candidates, helping craft the idea of how viable a candidate is and offer insights about their personality and presidential abilities.

Although only a portion of the electorate will live in the states or be registered as members of the right party to actually influence the nomination contests, the press follows the primary campaigns with almost the same intensity they invest in the general election campaign, covering the debates, stump speeches, and pancake breakfasts with surprising intensity. Reporting from the presidential campaign announcement through the capturing of enough delegates to secure the party's nomination focuses on both big picture issues that may drive a candidate's quest for the presidency and the tactical ability of campaigns to raise funds and organize supporters in key states, and the candidate's ability to connect with voters in early primaries. Especially in recent years this coverage has also come to include performance in often packed and somewhat chaotic debates that come up during the pre-primary campaign. As the media coverage of the primary process has grown, so has the tendency of the media to cover it in much the same way as the general election campaign—an odd fact given that in most states only party members will cast a primary ballot or attend a caucus. National media heap attention on the primary contestants, judging campaigns by the quarterly fundraising reports, electoral strategy, and perhaps most notably the explosion in the number and coverage of debates.

Unlike the general election debates that are governed and run by the Commission on Presidential Debates, the primary debates have no set rules or independent entity to monitor them. Broadcast and cable networks, websites, and campaigns have instead stepped into the void to host and run these events. This lack of control over the debate process helps highlight the ongoing weakening of political parties to shape events. In one of the few formal examinations of the primary debate process, political adviser Mark McKinnon interviewed Republican National Committee chairman Reince Priebus, who assumed his role in January 2011. He described a process driven by campaigns seeking exposure and media seeking viewers where the goals of the party played little role, saying, "When we came in the door, I put together a debate commission committee made up of six members of the RNC and six others. We would agree that the candidates would only do one debate a month starting in July or August, that we would spread out debate partners and there would be a fundraising component for the RNC. We wanted to have the Party play a meaningful role that would inform our voters who share the goal of defeating Obama. The media wants to create news, I want to defeat this president" (McKinnon 2012). His plans didn't play out.

Although this commission aimed to organize the Republican debate schedule so to optimize the chances of selecting a viable candidate (and minimize the chances of their candidate saying something that could come back to haunt them), the campaigns simply refused to listen, agreeing to more debates. The minor candidates agreed so they would receive exposure. The major candidates agreed because they felt they had to or face public backlash. In the end 2011–2012 saw a total of 30 debates, with wildly different rules around who would be allowed to participate, the number of candidates, and the length of response. By 2015 parties had begun to re-exert more control, and both parties set a far more rigid schedule. In fact, former Maryland governor and long-shot Democratic candidate Martin O'Malley blasted the limited number of Democratic debates, saying, "This is totally unprecedented in our party's history. This sort of rigged process has never been attempted before. Whose decree is it exactly? Where did it come from? To what end? For what purpose? What national or party interest does this decree serve? How does this help us tell the story of the last eight years of Democratic progress?" (Healy and Haberman 2015).

Beginning in 2012 and then continuing into the 2016 campaign, primary debates took a larger and larger role in shaping not just the media coverage but also voter perceptions of the candidates, particularly on the Republican side. From 2012 many would cite the 54-second brain freeze by Texas governor Rick Perry as one of the reasons his once-hyped campaign faltered and 2016 saw an equally pivotal exchange between Republicans battling for votes in New Hampshire.

While businessman Donald Trump was well ahead in most polls and Texas senator Ted Cruz was basking in the glow of a win in Iowa, Florida senator Marco Rubio was hoping to turn a surprisingly strong third place finish in Iowa into major momentum headed into New Hampshire.

Then he ran into New Jersey governor Chris Christie.

Christie, who had bet his campaign on a strong showing in New Hampshire, took the stage of their pre-primary debate and took dead aim at Rubio. Christie said Rubio lacked the experience necessary to be president. He accused Rubio of being little more than a robot. He told the crowd to listen for his "memorized 25-second speech" that was "exactly what his advisers gave him." A *New York Times* article described what happened next, writing, "Mr. Rubio—inexplicably—seemed to fulfill Mr. Christie's prediction, repeating the main idea of that same memorized-sounding speech about Mr. Obama. Almost word for word . . . Mr. Christie pounced. 'There it is,' he said icily, turning to Mr. Rubio and jabbing his finger at him. 'There it is, everybody' (Barbaro 2016). Many in the crowd started to boo Rubio and the Florida senator, clearly flustered, struggled to right his ship.

Rubio would go on to finish a disappointing fifth in New Hampshire, and looking back at his failed candidacy he cited that debate as a critical moment. He would tell the *Guardian* newspaper that "I don't think it impacted voters, but I do think it impacted media coverage in the days leading up to the New Hampshire vote, which I think ultimately hurt us, . . . I think we would have finished very strongly in New Hampshire had it not been for that, and it might have led to a different outcome in South Carolina and maybe changed the trajectory of the race" (Siddiqui 2016). The reason a primary debate can have outsized impact on the ability of a candidate to make a serious run at the presidency is only partially understood. It's odd primary debates have become such a major component of the campaign in recent cycles, namely because they have been around so long. The first debate was broadcast on radio between Republican candidates Thomas Dewey and Harold Stassen in 1948. The first televised primary debate came 20 years later when Eugene McCarthy and Senator Robert Kennedy met in 1968, just four days before Kennedy's assassination. And despite more than five decades of debates, political scientists have done far fewer studies of presidential primary debates than of general election clashes. Still, these limited examinations offer some important insights into why these debates matter.

In 1988, two researchers watched as viewers gauged their opinion of the Democratic candidates for president. Viewers were given the ability to rate each candidate using a "thermometer" to gauge their level of interest and support of a given candidate. The results were striking. One candidate, then-Tennessee senator Al Gore, saw support among the audience increase 26 points out of 100 over the 90-minute debate. The two concluded that primary debates were more volatile than other clashes because partisanship doesn't come into play as a limiter to how much opinion can change (being all in the same party, any candidate could be "viable" to the voter); many voters are getting their first chance to hear little-known candidates in their own words; and the face-to-face contest allows voters to make comparisons (Lanoue and Schrott 1989).

So why do primary debates elicit such strong reaction among viewers? Research indicates that it is a mix of factors, including the fact that party identification—THE key lens through which people watch the general election debates—is not an issue in the primary debate since the clash here revolves around who is the "true" conservative or represents the "real" Democratic Party. Essentially the partisan bias is eliminated from the equation. Secondly, most of the candidates are not widely known by the audience. So for many, this is the first time they are sizing up a candidate.

Although these debates have taken on real significance, they are far from the only element of the modern primary coverage.

Which brings us to the actual voting in the primaries and power and mystique of two states with outsized influence on the nomination fight—Iowa and New Hampshire. Both states have unique political and demographic realities that make them odd bellwethers. First off, Iowa is not even a primary, but rather a caucus—a very different creature. Unlike a primary where a voter can cast a ballot in secret at any time during the day the polls are open, caucuses require the voter to attend a specific meeting at one location at one time. Once there, backers offer speeches and literature in support of different candidates. Then the caucus-goers vote with their feet, physically joining the other supporters of a given candidate. The voter has to publicly align themselves with one candidate in front of his or her neighbors. The caucus then tallies the votes and if one or more candidate does not have enough support, they are eliminated and the remaining campaigns try and persuade them to back one of the remaining candidates. It is a unique affair and has historically benefitted campaigns with the most ardent supporters. The caucuses have often been the place where candidates thought to have little chance of winning can sneak up on a frontrunner and either beat them or at least show momentum. Pat Robertson used his 1988 second-place finish, where he beat Vice President George H. W. Bush, as a huge victory for his Christian conservative campaign. Senator Barack Obama scored a huge upset in Iowa in 2008 over his better known, and once thought inevitable, nominee Senator Hillary Clinton.

As unpredictable as Iowa is, the campaign calendar then shifts to a state that could not be more different—New Hampshire. New Hampshire is the first primary contest the candidates face and is usually seen as a better test of the actual viability of candidates because its secret ballot process better mirrors the general election. And reporters, campaign consultants, and many of the candidates see New Hampshire as an important test for another reason—New Hampshire voters expect to see and meet most of the candidates running. The fairly small and low-population state has held the first-in-the-nation primary for so long many of its residents have come to approach their role in the process with great seriousness; they expect a lot out of the candidates who trek to the state. As one Democratic organizer and New Hampshire gubernatorial candidate explained the role of the Granite State is particularly important because it is "a state that demands one-on-one campaigning of its candidates. A state that a candidate of modest resources can actually go into and state his case, whether it be door to door, whether it be coffee klatches throughout the state" (Foley, Britton, and Everett 1980). This is one of the defining characteristics of New Hampshire and the media focuses on these elements when covering the state. Coverage of the New Hampshire primary follows candidates to these often very small rallies and assesses the candidate's ability to connect with voters one on one.

These two contests often winnow the field considerably as candidates who underperform or fail to catch fire (and the needed windfall of money to continue) bow out of the contests and often endorse one of the remaining candidates. Generally after the first two states, the contest moves to larger states, typically South Carolina. The campaign, which has often taken years to reach these first two contests, suddenly speeds up enormously. Media coverage moves away from the tight picture of candidates interacting with individual voters, to much more general coverage of how campaigns are performing, debate performances, or outside news influencing candidate positions. Many people argue this is a hugely problematic way to cover the primary campaign since fewer than a million people will have cast a ballot by the end of the South Carolina primary, but it reflects a couple of realities of the media's ability to cover the campaign. First, financial, as political writer John Ellis said, "The media (broadly speaking) blow through their pre-primary budgets quickly, overspend on early caucus and primary coverage, and then cut back sharply to conserve funds for convention and general election coverage. The net result is that the early state caucuses and primaries are disproportionately important to determining the eventual nominee and that anyone who does not finish first or second in the Iowa caucuses and/or the New Hampshire primary is probably not going to command media coverage thereafter" (Ellis 2011). Although just one writer's take on what happens, the budget process is certainly built on what has happened in the past. Rarely do newsrooms budget for the kind of war of attrition that was the Democratic primary fight in 2008.

The traditional primary campaign cycle focuses on the early contests as a test of electoral viability and, as was mentioned, winnows the field headed into larger primary contests. States and parties have sought to increase their role in the selection of candidates, often trying to move their primary contest earlier in the calendar. Sometimes states have banded together to increase a regional voice in party politics. This notably happened in the Democratic Party and the development of a heavily southern "Super Tuesday" in 1988. That year, moderate Democrats wanted to exert more influence in the nomination fight and organized nine states all in the South to hold a primary on that date, often a Tuesday early in March. These contests cannot be waged in the way New Hampshire voters demand. Few voters will ever see a candidate in person and much more of the campaign is waged via mass media—from advertising to online communication and news reporting.

Experts who have studied this period report there can be massive swings in party member preferences between the Iowa Caucuses and these more regional, multistate contests. One examination of those 1988 Democratic contests found that "only 29 percent of those interviewed before Iowa held their same preference by the time Super Tuesday arrives" (Norrander 2015). The political scientists found that much of the change that occurred among voters happened because of perceived momentum the candidate developed by winning early contests, like Iowa or New

Hampshire. This momentum, especially in contests where there are limited resources and primaries occurring in quick succession, can be the critical element of the campaign and is often the focus of media coverage from one contest to another. Some factors can alter this, with 2008 being the outlier. When two candidates possess enough resources to mount fights in state after state, the momentum question can be less decisive. So, for example, when Barack Obama went on a streak winning 10 contests in a row over nearly a month, it came down to a major stand by Senator Hillary Clinton to win the critical states of Texas and Ohio to end the increasing drumbeat of Obama momentum. Even though she managed to win those contests and later large states like Pennsylvania and Indiana, the sense of the campaign had already shifted to whether she would concede he had won or not. Even in this case of two very competitive candidates with enough money to run a campaign in all 56 contests—including votes in territories and D.C.—the idea of momentum was a critical one in helping propel Obama to the nomination.

In all of these areas—from scrutinizing debates for gaffes to monitoring candidates' effectiveness in wintry New Hampshire to the quest for momentum from the early contests—the media, fueled by polls and perception, help shape many voters' impressions of the candidates, their electoral viability, and the sense of inevitability.

See also: Invisible Primary; Presidential Nominating Conventions

Further Reading

Banville, Lee. 2013. *Debating Our Destiny: Presidential Debate Moments That Shaped History.* Arlington, VA: MacNeil/Lehrer Productions.

Barbaro, Michael. 2016. "Once Impervious, Marco Rubio Is Diminished by a Caustic Chris Christie." *New York Times*. February 7. Accessed June 14, 2016. http://www.nytimes.com/2016/02/07/us/politics/chris-christie-marco-rubio-gop-debate.html?_r=0.

Ellis, John. 2011. "Here's How The Presidential Primary Process Actually Works." *Business Insider.* February 3. Accessed July 6, 2015. http://www.businessinsider.com/how-the-presidential-primary-process-works-2011-1#ixzz3f8Pkm34Q.

Foley, John, Dennis Britton, and Eugene Everett. 1980. *Nominating a President: The Process and the Press*. New York: Praeger.

Healy, Patrick, and Maggie Haberman. 2015. "Martin O'Malley Rails at Democrats for Debate Schedule 'Rigged' to Aid Hillary Clinton." *New York Times*. August 28. Accessed August 31, 2015. http://www.nytimes.com/politics/first-draft/2015/08/28/martin-omalley-rails-at-democrats-for-debate-schedule-rigged-to-aid-hillary-clinton.

Lanoue, David, and Peter Schrott. 1989. "The Effects of Primary Season Debates on Public Opinion." *Political Behavior* 11, no. 3 (September).

McKinnon, Mark. 2012. "Gone Rogue: Time to Reform the Presidential Primary Debates." Joan Shorenstein Center on the Press, Politics and Public Policy. January. Accessed July 5, 2015. http://shorensteincenter.org/wp-content/uploads/2012/03/d67_mckinnon.pdf.

Norrander, Barbara. 2015. *Super Tuesday: Regional Politics and Presidential Primaries*. Lexington: University Press of Kentucky.

Siddiqui, Sabrina. 2016. "Marco Rubio: 'It's not that we lost, it's that Donald Trump won.'" *Guardian*. May 24. Accessed June 14, 2016. http://www.theguardian.com/us-news/2016/may/24/marco-rubio-interview-presidential-nomination-donald-trump.

PROPUBLICA

If one concept drives digital-first publications, it is finding a niche to serve. Although that is often topical, for ProPublica it is about a niche type of reporting: Investigative journalism.

Launched in 2008, the nonprofit news organization based in New York City has made developing in-depth investigations its sole purpose. What makes the project unique was the service from its outset sought to partner with traditional news outlets such as the *New York Times* or *60 Minutes* to ensure the work reached a wide audience. The service has also broken new ground in terms of honors for online reporting, garnering the first Pulitzer Prize for an online publication in history.

The effort was conceived by Herb and Marion Sandler, who made their fortune running the savings and loan firm Golden West Financial Corporation. The Sandlers had helped fund other efforts, such as the Center for Responsible Lending, when in 2007 they announced they would support ProPublica to the tune of $10 million.

At the time, many worried that this form of journalism—funded by wealthy patrons—may be inherently flawed because of the power of the funders. Jack Shafer at Slate demanded of any partner of the new news organization, "If I were a newspaper editor considering ProPublica copy for a future issue, the first thing I'd want is proof of a firewall preventing the Sandlers and other funders from picking—or nixing—the targets of its probes" (Shafer 2007). Shafer and others worried that the Sandlers, who had donated hundreds of thousands of dollars to Democrats and liberal groups like the Center for American Progress, were building a news organization to attack conservatives and not just investigate newsworthy topics.

The Shafers responded by hiring Paul Steiger, the former managing editor of the *Wall Street Journal*, to run the new project. Steiger admitted he had questions about the independence of the new group and said he pressed the funders to be clear that there would be no political influence over their work. He later told the *PBS NewsHour* that together they built an organization where "the board of directors, on which I sit and which Herb is the chairman, does not know in advance what we're going to report on. I think that's a very important consideration, and it gives me essentially the same freedom I had when I was running the *Wall Street Journal*" (*PBS NewsHour* 2008). The new structure did have clear benefits. Without printing and distribution to pay for, ProPublica is able to devote more of its budget to actual reporting. "About two-thirds of ProPublica's funds are devoted to news, according to the organization. To put that into context: Many major newspapers spend a mere 15 to 20 percent of their budgets on news" (Kaye and Quinn 2010, p. 54).

With the organization structure apparently in place, ProPublica launched with an urgent call to reinvigorate the investigative side of journalism. On its site it warns, "Investigative journalism is at risk. Many news organizations have increasingly come to see it as a luxury . . . New models are, therefore, necessary to carry forward some of the great work of journalism in the public interest that is such an integral part of self-government, and thus an important bulwark of our democracy" (ProPublica 2015). The site was soon publishing investigations on a variety of topics—from hydraulic fracking to dark money to Wall Street corruption. The organization pursued its reporting as an independent group, but also often partnered with traditional media to publish the resulting stories. In 2009 one such partnership led to the *New York Times* publishing a ProPublica investigation centered around one hospital flooded during Hurricane Katrina. The reporting garnered the 2010 Pulitzer Prize for investigative reporting. The next year the organization scored another Pulitzer, this time for a series that ran only on ProPublica on Wall Street bankers who made themselves rich often at their clients' expense, the first time the Pulitzer went to stories not published in traditional print.

The news organization has spent countless hours reporting on dark money organizations that have cropped up in the wake of the *Citizens United v. Federal Election Commission* decision. Its coverage has included obtaining the pending applications for federal nonprofit status by groups like Karl Rove's Crossroads GPS. The organization has published more than 120 stories on dark money and campaigns, making it one of the most covered topics ProPublica highlights in its ongoing investigations site.

Although the site continues to rack up journalism awards and has had little problem finding partners to publish and co-produce their reporting, some conservative critics have continued to argue there is a liberal bias in the site's reporting. Cheryl Chumley, a reporter for the *Washington Times*, wrote a critical examination of the site: "ProPublica reporters should receive high praise for their stories on Obama's stimulus package and banking bailouts, on recent business and financial scandals, and on other issues related to open records and open government. But on embarrassments closer to the liberal policy agenda the group tends to link its website to outside media reports rather than conduct independent investigations" (Chumley 2009).

Nevertheless, the site has seen success and receives far more praise than criticism. It has drawn support from readers who can donate to the reporting and has successfully navigated the retirement of Steiger and transition to a new management team under Stephen Engleberg, former managing editor of the *Oregonian* and investigative reporter and editor at the *New York Times*. Perhaps the most fulsome praise for the organization comes from the fact that the site has lasted and, in fact, grown from 25 to 34 reporters and editors. One glowing tribute to the success of the service hailed that "ProPublica has shown conclusively that it is possible to build a major news gatherer that the public will reward with donations, recognizing that the return on that support will only be in the amazing array of stories that profoundly affect how our institutions of government and private enterprise function" (Osnos 2012).

See also: Center for Public Integrity (CPI); Nonprofit Journalism

Further Reading

Chumley, Cheryl. 2009. "ProPublica: Investigative Journalism or Liberal Spin?" Phoenix University. Accessed February 15, 2015. http://www.phoenix.edu/about_us/media-center/fact-checker/2009/12/propublica-investigative-journalism-or-liberal-spin.html.

Kaye, Jeff, and Steven Quinn. 2010. *Funding Journalism in the Digital Age: Business Models, Strategies, Issues and Trends*. New York: Peter Lang Publishing Inc.

Osnos, Peter. 2012. "In Praise of ProPublica." The Atlantic. May 22. Accessed February 15, 2015. http://www.theatlantic.com/national/archive/2012/05/in-praise-of-propublica/257514.

PBS NewsHour. 2008. "Non-profit Groups Financing Independent Journalism." June 24. Accessed February 16, 2015. http://www.pbs.org/newshour/bb/media-jan-june08-mediamodel_06-24.

ProPublica. 2015. "About Us." Accessed February 15, 2015. http://www.propublica.org/about.

Shafer, Jack. 2007. "What Do Herbert and Marion Sandler Want?" Slate. October 15. Accessed February 14, 2015. http://www.slate.com/articles/news_and_politics/press_box/2007/10/what_do_herbert_and_marion_sandler_want.html.

PUBLIC INTEREST OBLIGATION

Unlike its print brethren, radio and television broadcasters have a government requirement that they operate in the "public interest, convenience and necessity" to qualify for a broadcast license from the Federal Communication Commission. This responsibility—often known by its acronym PICON—requires that broadcasters fulfill certain civic duties or risk losing the government-sanctioned monopoly the broadcaster enjoys over a specific frequency. It's a concept that helped build news divisions within large broadcast networks, especially in the early days of television. News coverage helped make the case that stations were fulfilling their duty by keeping the public informed, so the early development of news on radio and television can often be traced to this government mandate more than it was a quest for advertising revenue.

Almost from the inception of radio, government regulators felt uneasy giving the new media the same hands-off approach that the Constitution had ensured for the printed press. As early as 1924—only four years after the first radio station went on the air, U.S. Secretary of Commerce Herbert Hoover argued the technology "is not to be considered as merely a business carried on for private gain. . . . It is a public concern impressed with the public trust and is to be considered primarily from the standpoint of public interest to the same extent and upon the basis of the same general principles as our public utilities" (Bensman 2000). Hoover sought to have his government agency reallocate the airwaves to address this concern but found his way blocked by court decisions that found he lacked the authority.

By the early Roosevelt administration almost a decade later, the government crafted a new law to give the government the power Hoover had sought. The governing laws that built federal government agencies and rules connected to broadcasting carry this odd phrase that outlines why the government will give a company monopolistic control over a finite public asset—or put in broadcast parlance, an FCC license to broadcast on a specific channel of the public airwaves. The rationale appears in the Communications Act of 1934 and says those broadcasters licensed by the government must operate in the "public interest, convenience and necessity" to merit continued access to the spectrum. The phrase itself was not new to government regulations. It was first used in the 1920 Transportation Act to explain why the government needed to have a role in deciding where railroads and other infrastructure projects would be located. Historians have said much of the same thinking went into its use in regulating broadcasting. "[T]he public interest was understood in strictly practical, technical terms; transferred to communications regulation, this conception of the public interest would be interpreted to mean that overlapping radio signals did not serve the public interest. Therefore, the government needed to license individual broadcasters so that such technical problems could be eliminated" (Hendershot 2011). But unlike the more clear-cut rules governing transportation infrastructure, the new broadcast regulations were quickly interpreted to mean more than just technical issues. The commission was not going to use its authority simply to ensure that stations operated on the same frequency and at the same power day after day. Implied in the statute was what Hoover discussed years earlier—an obligation to serve the public with this new technology.

By the mid-1940s the FCC had more formalized its vision of what the "public interest, necessity and convenience" really meant and published a guide, commonly referred to as the Blue Book, to help stations. The new *Public Service Responsibility of Broadcast Licensees* urged stations to offer a variety of services to the public, but put special emphasis on news, stating, "American broadcasters have always recognized that broadcasting is not merely a means of entertainment, but also an unequaled medium for the dissemination of news, information, and opinion, and for the discussion of public issues. . . . Especially in recent years, such information programs and news and news commentaries have achieved a popularity exceeding the popularity of any other single type of program. The war, of course, tremendously increased listener interest in such programs; but if broadcasters face the crucial problems of the post-war era with skill, fairness, and courage, there is no reason why broadcasting cannot play as important a role in our democracy hereafter as it has achieved during the war years" (Waldman 2011).

This focus on news as one of the most concrete—and expected—ways that a broadcaster would demonstrate the public interest obligation of holding an FCC license translated into a specific vision for network news: their job was to justify the license application and demonstrate the civic responsibility of the station. As ABC's Ted Koppel recalled fondly, "In the old days, the FCC still had teeth and still used them every once in a while. And there was that little paragraph, Section 315 of the FCC code, that said, 'You shall operate in the public interest, convenience and necessity.' What that meant was, you had to have a news division that told people what was important out there. And I just don't necessarily believe that showing me what my pets are doing when I'm not at home to see them falls under that category"

(*Frontline* 2004). News organizations were seen not as profit centers, but more as the broadcasters' investment for being granted government sanction to make money off of a public asset like the broadcast spectrum.

The reality was always a bit murkier than what Koppel and even the Blue Book sought to outline. First, the *Public Service Responsibility of Broadcast Licensees* was never formally adopted as a policy. Not doing what the FCC outlined did not threaten a station's license and so it was seen more as aspirational rather than a specific rule. And second, the definition of what fulfilled the public interest remained politically connected to the public's perception of television. Following a series of scandals in the 1950s connected to rigged quiz shows, the FCC decided it should try to better define a public mission for broadcasters in part to counter the damage done in the eyes of the public. So in 1960 the commission held 19 days of hearings, taking testimony from 90 witnesses about what the public interest obligation ought to look like. In the end, the commission generated a list of 14 criteria that it saw as fulfilling the PICON requirements. The FCC did not mandate a certain number of these programs, but instead used them as evidence stations could submit as proof they were operating in good faith. These included the following:

1. Opportunity for local self-expression.
2. The development and use of local talent.
3. Programs for children.
4. Religious programs.
5. Educational programs.
6. Public affairs programs.
7. Editorialization by licensees.
8. Political broadcasts.
9. Agricultural programs.
10. News programs.
11. Weather and market services.
12. Sports programs.
13. Service to minority groups.
14. Entertainment programming.

Even with these general criteria in place the larger question of how much the government could regulate broadcasters' content, or punish them, remained largely open and confusing. PICON has sometimes put the FCC in the difficult position of weighing the First Amendment rights of the broadcaster against the First Amendment rights of those seeking access to the public through those broadcasters. (One of the tools that sought to balance those two rights was the Fairness Doctrine, which gets its own heading in this text.) How much the government should work to provide access to the media remained a major question from the 1920s through the 1980s.

In perhaps its most striking argument that the government should guarantee access to the airwaves, the FCC ruled in 1967 that stations that ran cigarette ads must also run commercials about the dangers of smoking. It was a ruling unlike any other in FCC history and the commission struggled to explain why cigarettes were different than alcohol, politicians, or any other position or product that may have a counter-argument. The FCC argued this case was different. "It pointed to what it thought was a unique combination of the official health hazard status of cigarettes considering the Surgeon General's Report of 1964, the popularity of smoking, and the dangers of normal use" (Schmidt 1976, p. 167). But the commission had opened a Pandora's box of questions with that ruling. Did the station need to run the same number of anti-cigarette ads as it did pro? The FCC said no. But how many then? The commission struggled to find a rationale for the line it chose to draw, but advised stations that five-to-one during primetime viewing in the evening and a three-to-one ratio at other times seemed "reasonable." Two years later, the commission was let off the hook when Congress banned all tobacco ads on television and radio.

The cigarette debate perhaps marked the highpoint in government interference in the broadcaster's schedule. By the early 1980s the FCC began to shift its approach. Cable had begun to bring new stations to the television and the idea of scarcity—that public airwaves because of their limited bandwidth could only accommodate so many channels and so the public needed to ensure each channel lived up to its public interest obligation—began to fade. The FCC shifted its regulatory mindset away from a more government-centered approach to relying on the marketplace of stations and channels to fulfill the public's need for information and multiple viewpoints. A report from the Benton Foundation on the public interest obligations of broadcasters concluded, "In essence, the FCC held that competition would adequately serve public needs and that federally mandated obligations were both too vague to be enforced properly and too much of a threat to broadcasters' First Amendment rights. Many citizen groups argued that the new policy was tantamount to abandoning the public interest mandate entirely" (Benton Foundation 1999).

This FCC deregulatory move involved several critical changes that altered the commission's role in ensuring broadcasters abided by the public interest obligations. First, and perhaps most importantly, it changed the FCC license renewal process, ending the more in-depth examination of the station's performance and adherence to PICON requirements and creating an almost automatic renewal. Stations now simply send in a postcard to the FCC requesting a renewal and, unless the public raises significant issues that prompt a review, the station receives its new license. A copy of the station's full report is supposed to be kept on hand at the station for people to review, but the FCC itself only takes action to look into it if the station has prompted public outcry. Second, as mentioned the FCC reforms of the 1980s shifted the position of the government from one of active participation in the guidance of broadcasters to one of defaulting to station competition correcting any problems. Finally, the commission took several concrete steps to ease the burden of proof on broadcasters that they were operating responsibly by eliminating the rules that required stations to maintain program logs, air minimum amounts of public affairs programming, and formally ascertain community needs.

This is not to say that the government walked away from all regulations of broadcast material. The FCC continued to monitor and punish broadcasters for violating decency standards, such as broadcasting obscenities or nudity. There were also efforts by Congress to restore some of the government's old doctrines of enforcing the public interest. For example, the Children's Television Act of 1990 sought to make a deal with broadcasters—if stations guaranteed a certain minimum hours of children's programming each week, the government would continue its largely hands-off approach to licensing. It was a move conservatives, like Adam Thierer of the Heritage Foundation, derided as "regulatory extortion," adding, "The FCC still uses the public interest standard to restrict beneficial industry advances that, in turn, deny new services to the public. It also inhibits the free flow of information and free speech in general. How, then, can 'the public interest' be truly served? By encouraging vigorous market competition—and by rejecting misguided social compacts and vague regulatory standards flowing from Washington" (Thierer 1996).

And this vision has largely won out in regulatory questions outside of decency rulings by the commission.

That is, until net neutrality blew up in the 2010s.

The commission had taken what sounds like a hands-off approach to the Internet and the World Wide Web as it developed, but actually in the minds of those who provide access to the Internet, government moves in the early days of the web seemed to mirror radio and television. The commission ruled early on that all content moving across the Internet should be treated the same by service providers. Content from Netflix would travel the same as video provided for free from PBS. But cable companies and some phone companies wanted this changed so there could be deals between content providers and service providers to ensure certain content traveled faster. Verizon sued the FCC, seeking to have the courts throw out the government-mandated net neutrality.

The FCC took up the issue and proposed ending net neutrality, a move that prompted millions to flood the commission with comments about how this would ruin the Internet as a more equal playing field. In the end, the commission relented, citing, among other things, the public interest. The final vote by the commission to continue the policy of net neutrality was hailed as "the biggest victory for the public interest in the agency's history" by some, and also prompted lawsuits from telecom and cable companies deriding it as massive government interference in the private sector.

The net neutrality debate and the earlier clashes over PICON and radio and television broadcasting highlight the continued struggle by the government with how to regulate electronic media. Regulators have seen these tools as powerful media to impact public opinion as well as inform potential voters. However, they have created a system where electronic media has not enjoyed the same freedoms as newspapers and magazines. FCC involvement in both broadcast and Internet industries remains a politically divisive issue, one that has prompted major legal challenges as well as major support. The battles over defining and enforcing "public interest" will likely drag on for years.

See also: Broadcast Television Networks; Fairness Doctrine

Further Reading

Aaron, Craig. 2015. "Net Neutrality: Biggest Public Interest Victory in FCC History." *The Progressive*. February 26. Accessed June 16. http://www.progressive.org/news/2015/02/188021/net-neutrality-biggest-public-interest-victory-fcc-history.

Bensman, Marvin. 2000. *The Beginning of Broadcast Regulation in the Twentieth Century*. Jefferson, NC: McFarland & Company, Inc.

Benton Foundation. 1999. Charting the Digital Broadcasting Future. Accessed June 14, 2015. https://www.benton.org/initiatives/obligations/charting_the_digital_broadcasting_future.

Frontline. 2004. News War. Accessed June3, 2015. http://www.pbs.org/wgbh/pages/frontline/newswar/tags/entertainment.html.

Hendershot, Health. 2011. *What's Fair on the Air: Cold War Right-wing Broadcasting and the Public Interest*. Chicago: The University of Chicago Press.

Schmidt, Benno. 1976. *Freedom of the Press vs. Public Access*. New York: Praeger.

Thierer, Adam. 1996. "Is the Public Served by the Public Interest Standard?" *The Freeman*. September 1. Accessed June 5, 2015. http://fcc.org/freeman/detail/is-the-public-served-by-the-public-interest-standard.

Waldman, Steven. 2011. *Information Needs of Communities: The Changing Media Landscape in a Broadband Age*. Collingdale, PA: DiANE Publishing.

PUBLIC OPINION

The very nature of American politics sets up an uneasy relationship between the governed and those they claim to represent. The American system of representative democracy creates an arrangement that should have its congressmen and women working to represent the needs and reflecting the opinions of the people back in their district. The question, almost from the very inception of the republic, was how to do that and how to give the voice of the people some sort of shape and coherence. Initially this was through voting, but with the advent of public opinion surveys the media could, in 24 hours or less, obtain the "opinion" of the public on any given political issue. Still questions remain as to how to use this power and what, if any, role it ought to play in the running of the government.

The most obvious testament to the role of public opinion in the political system is an election. If a representative does not do his or her job in giving voice to the people who sent them to a city council, a state capital, or Washington, D.C., the assumption is that people will vote him or her out of office. This is the public's voice. But reality has never really measured up to these aspirations. First, not all the people can or do vote. In fact, as far back as 1925 political thinkers were bemoaning the paucity of voters who actually cast ballots in the election. Their concern essentially was in a day when only half of the people eligible to vote do so, there is no true public opinion. Despite this fact, politicians would still claim the mantle of a "mandate" from the people to execute a given policy, regardless of whether this policy had helped him or her win election. Could a popular vote of the people actually grant such a mandate or did it simply reflect the preferences of a small subset of the public who chose to cast a ballot in a given race?

These questions led to a growing movement in the early twentieth century to try to capture a more scientifically legitimate snapshot of the public's view of a given campaign or issue. Born somewhat of the Progressive Movement in the first decades of the 1900s, this new political science focused on using polling to better understand the will of the people. Polling pioneer George Gallup, along with Canadian Saul Rae, published their thoughts in a book entitled *The Pulse of Democracy*, and argued that the will of the public could now be accurately measured within 48 hours. The goal of studying public opinion was nothing less than a revitalization of democracy itself, with the two writing, "Shall the common people be free to express their basic needs and purposes, or shall they be dominated by a small ruling clique?" and adding that democracy itself should be "a process of constant thought and action on the part of the citizen" (Gallup and Rae 1940).

The goals of this work were being echoed by many at this time as scholars sought to use social science to understand the public's will and to inform public policy debates. To truly incorporate these polling results into the political process, social scientists undertook a series of studies and debates, looking to clearly define what exactly public opinion is and what role it should play in the functioning of democracy. This spawned an array of opinions. Should polling try to capture the views of all the voters in a geographic location? All of the people? Should it simply reflect these views, or should the work be used to inform policy and policy makers? One lengthy work on how government and the public should be connected concluded it was important to understand that public opinion "is not the sum total of the individual opinions of isolated men. It is made up of the opinions of men living an associated life and affected by the contacts with one another. Common interests, common elements of environment and inheritance, similar sources of information, and discussion among individuals give it unity of force. Public opinion is reflected not only in political matters, but also in matters of morals and art and in all the other common interests of human beings" (Smith 1939). Fueled by this progressive view of the public and the influence it should have over the political system, a battery of social scientists and journalists began advocating for a way to measure the views of the public and to convey those views to the voters and the elected. Their work spawned a new array of public opinion pollsters.

Polls were seen as more than just a snapshot of popular views, but as a form of public vote. Now, one did not have to decipher the message the electorate was trying to send by electing Congressman A or President B, one could ask the public directly. This was seen as a way to empower the general public as Gallup and Shae outlined in their battle against governing elites. A poll could, with impressive accuracy, select a representative sample of a state or the country and within two days—with 1940s technology—spit back an answer within a few percentage points about the public's feelings on the matter. And this is where the always-controversial relationship between polling and the press comes in, because simply knowing how the public felt only mattered if the public itself as well as the elected officials knew the results. If the elites knew the views of the public and could ignore them without fear of repercussion, then the empowering nature of the polling would be lost and so, from some of the earliest writings, journalists and pollsters knew public opinion needed to be used to apply pressure on the political process. As Walter Lippmann, the reporter and political commentator of the mid-twentieth century, reflected, "A public opinion is expressed by a vote, a demonstration of praise or blame, a following or a boycotting. But these manifestations are in themselves nothing. They count only if they influence the course of affairs. They influence it, however, only if they influence an actor in the affair. And it is, I believe, precisely in this secondary, indirect relationship between public opinion and public affairs that we have the clue to the limits and the possibilities of public opinion" (Lippmann 1925). Put more simply by political scientist V.O. Key, "Unless mass views have some place in the shaping of policy, all the talk about democracy is nonsense" (Key 1961). As expression of the voice of the public who were supposed to be the ultimate arbiters of politics in a democratic system, the use of polls quickly grew and their serious treatment by reporters expanded. Public opinion surveys also offered a new tool to evaluate how the public was changing over time. Representative samples over years and later decades were asked about issues like the role of government, the direction of the country, and their confidence in the political system. Their views became a sort-of touchstone for political reporters seeking to contextualize the current opinion polls or trends within the electorate.

But the public reporting of polls was only one way the emerging social science of survey research was affecting politics. For campaigns, the ability to assess public perceptions of candidates, issues, and messaging quickly took root. By the 1960s, campaigns were hiring private polling firms to conduct their own surveys of voters, to gauge what policies resonated with the public and how they may respond to a new initiative. A growing narrative soon emerged that politicians used these polls to drive their decision-making, basing their own proposals on the public's views, and banking on that public support to translate into support from other elected officials or popular support even if the proposal failed. Those who have studied the use of polls by campaigns and political operations noted the focus on the work quickly expanded beyond the basic "temperature taking" to something more aggressive. Political scientist Lawrence Jacobs contends, "Although polls are (mistakenly) equated with tailoring policy to majority opinion, private surveys are primarily geared today to manipulating public opinion—not responding to it . . . The particular words that prominent politicians use in high-profile and momentous settings are often researched and crafted to produce particular reactions" (Jacobs 2011). Polls, while not always used so nefariously, were certainly no longer simple bellwethers; they had become tools in crafting the messages of the campaign, and in tailoring them to different audiences. Modern polling firms can use public opinion techniques to gauge reactions to social issues that may come up, explore the responses to a breaking scandal, or shape micro-targeted messages to particular parts of the population.

An interesting aspect of the use of surveys is the degree to which they are treated as fact. Consider the Pew Research Center, widely respected as perhaps the most scientifically valid and thoroughly vetted surveys of opinions. Pew wanted to gauge the public's view of the Supreme Court, so they surveyed 2,002 Americans across a week in July 2015. That represents only 0.00063 percent of the nation's 319 million residents and yet the survey could conclude and was reported with assertiveness by Pew and others, "Currently, 48% of Americans have a favorable impression of the Supreme Court, while 43% view the court unfavorably. Unfavorable opinions of the court, while up only modestly since March (39%), are the highest recorded since 1985" (Pew 2015). Pew can make this claim, and it is repeated by the media, because it uses highly sophisticated algorithms to identify and reach out to representative samples.

Although there seems to be consensus on the science of sampling and polling, there remain many critiques of the use of public opinion and surveys in politics. The science of sampling and then extrapolating from the raw numbers a conclusion is often seen as a dark art. There runs through politics a skepticism about efforts to capture public opinion, and the actual value of poll numbers. Winston Churchill is said to have coined the later much-copied phrase, "There is no such thing as public opinion. There is only published opinion."

There is an important difference between public opinion and public opinion polls. Although increasingly sophisticated means are used to find a representative sample, to pose balanced questions, and to accurately project a general sense of the public, at the core a poll tends to ask: does a person favor or oppose a general proposition, like abortion rights or universal background checks for gun purchases? Many outside influences can affect the answer. If you ask the gun control question in the days following a school shooting, some people will respond in a way that seems to give the expected response, namely we should do something about gun control, rather than to seem unmoved by tragedy. Another issue is that often reporters will dismiss those who respond they don't know or have no opinion. One analysis of the use of polls by the media seemed to echo Churchill's concerns, concluding, "The news media stories about the polls usually report only the results, and by leaving out the questions and the don't knows, transform answers into opinions. When these opinions are shared by a majority, the news stories turn poll respondents into the public, thus giving birth to public opinion" (Gans 2013). There is real concern about what this reporting does to the underlying public opinion it seeks to understand. As reporters use survey results as a stand-in for the public, do the results actually affect, rather than just reflect, that opinion?

Researchers have found that as people read about public opinion polls, their opinions often change, usually drifting toward agreeing with the majority. One study by a pair of social scientists found specific evidence, writing, "In the political domain people learn about prevailing public opinion via ubiquitous polls, which may produce a bandwagon effect. Newer types of information—published probabilities derived from prediction market contract prices and aggregated polling summaries—may have similar effects. Consequently, polls can become self-fulfilling prophecies whereby majorities, whether in support of candidates or policies, grow in a cascading manner" (Rothschild and Malhotra 2014).

These two concerns about using polls to try and understand the underlying opinions of the public touch on critical issues reporters and pollsters must grapple with. Does their effort to assess how the public feels about an issue inherently affect their views of the issue itself? Can you break complicated questions into agree/disagree dichotomies? And then once you have this information, does reporting it as "the public's opinion" push people toward the views held by the majority or ostracize those who do not agree with most people?

The goals of understanding public opinion carry more weight in a democracy—or even a representative democracy—than in other forms of government. The American system is built on the idea that the governing are in their positions and make their decisions only with the consent of the governed, not from some divine or other authority. To understand what the public wants and how they feel about an issue is to try and add their voice to the political process without relying simply on the vote of half the eligible voters who cast ballots in the election every two, four, or six years. And so the quest to understand public sentiment means more in this type of system than in many others. To try and understand these views, journalists and social scientists have relied on pollsters to capture this information and synthesize it. This is a major responsibility, and so is the job of then reporting that information accurately and as completely as possible. To take short cuts in the reporting or in the polling is to create possible misperceptions of the public's view or, at a minimum, an overly simplistic take on what "the people" think. To capture and convey it accurately can offer real insights into how representative our government actually is.

See also: Pew Research Center; Public Policy Polling; Rasmussen Reports; Real Clear Politics; Zogby Analytics

Further Reading

Gans, Herbert. 2013. "Public Opinion Polls Do Not Always Report Public Opinion." Nieman Lab. April 29. Accessed August 28, 2015. http://www.niemanlab.org/2013/04/public-opinion-polls-do-not-always-report-public-opinion.

Jacobs, Lawrence. 2011. "What Do Political Polls Really Accomplish?" *American Prospect.* December 23. Accessed August 26, 2015. http://prospect.org/article/what-do-political-polls-really-accomplish.

Key, V. O. 1961. *Public Opinion and American Democracy*. New York: Alfred A. Knopf.

Lippmann, Walter. 1925. *The Phantom Public*. New York: Harcourt, Brace and Company.
"Negative Views of Supreme Court at Record High, Driven by Republican Dissatisfaction." 2015. Pew Research Center. July 29. Accessed August 27, 2015. http://www.people-press.org/2015/07/29/negative-views-of-supreme-court-at-record-high-driven-by-republican-dissatisfaction.
Rothschild, David, and Neil Malhotra. 2014. "Are Public Opinion Polls Self-Fulfilling Prophecies?" *Research and Politics*. July-September. Accessed August 25, 2015. http://rap.sagepub.com/content/sprap/1/2/2053168014547667.full.pdf.
Smith, Charles. 1939. *Public Opinion in a Democracy: A Study in American Politics*. New York: Prentice Hall.

PUBLIC POLICY POLLING

Public Policy Polling is a public opinion and political survey company based in North Carolina. The three-man firm works with Democratic candidates, often serving as the in-house polling firm of unions and liberal candidates, but its results are also widely distributed through polling aggregation services and media coverage.

The firm's approach to polling makes it controversial at times and has drawn fire for its techniques. This criticism mainly focuses on its use of interactive voice response (IRV) surveys, or what critics have dubbed "robo-polls." In these surveys, voters receive automated calls from computerized systems that allow them to simply press numbers to respond to the survey. This approach to polling has one huge upside—it's cheaper than hiring people to call individuals and therefore the polls can have larger sample sizes. But it also has some potential downsides. First, there is no indication of exactly who is answering the questions. Therefore, sample gender division, age ranges, and even income distribution cannot be guaranteed. Some pollsters argue it makes these polls difficult to extrapolate to larger populations. Secondly, Public Policy Polling is unable to call cell phones with most of its lists and therefore people without landlines will be completely left out of the sample.

The concerns have prompted some to err on the side of not using these IRV polls. The *New York Times* in its "Polling Standards" report in 2006 simply stated, "Anyone who can answer the phone and hit the buttons can be counted in the survey—regardless of age. Results of this type of poll are not reliable" (*New York Times* 2006). That said, throughout the time Nate Silver was working for the *Times*, PPP numbers would often appear in his posts, but always with the caveat that the firm was "Democratic-leaning."

Public Policy Polling is quick to counter these claims of problems with IVRs, arguing that automated polling allows for more accurate polling by eliminating potential interviewer bias. The firm proudly proclaims, "Every poll respondent hears the exact same questions read the exact same way. We also utilize the voter registration database for most of our surveys. Calling only registered or likely voters gives us a much more accurate sample of the target populations for most political and campaign based polling" (Public Policy Polling 2015). They also argue that automated polling may more accurately record people's opinions on sensitive or more controversial issues like sexual behavior or drug use because of the anonymity of the automated system. The firm is quick to point to its track record in campaigns, most notably in 2012 when its pro-Obama picks in nearly every battleground state played out on Election Day. One assessment of PPP's performance in 2012 stressed, "While more than a few firms picked the right winners, PPP also nailed the exact result—at the moment, at least—in Florida, 50-49. And in most cases it was never more than a point or two off each candidate's performance" (Mahtesian 2012).

Notably, the polling firm has done most of its work in non-federal campaigns. By 2015, some 14 years after the firm launched, it boasted about its work on only five U.S. House races and three for U.S. Senate. On the other hand it has worked on more than 40 state races and done work for dozens more organizations. Also all of this work has been for Democratic or progressive groups, which has drawn fire from conservatives who sometimes argue it is a partisan firm simply finding ways to promote good news for Democratic candidates and causes.

The polling firm has not just had critics on the right. Nate Silver, the data-modeling guru behind FiveThirtyEight.com, criticized the company in 2013 for its decision not to release data in a recall election in Colorado. At the time, PPP director Tom Jensen wrote, "We did a poll last weekend in Colorado Senate District 3 and found that voters intended to recall Angela Giron by a 12 point margin, 54/42. In a district that Barack Obama won by almost 20 points I figured there was no way that could be right and made a rare decision not to release the poll. It turns out we should have had more faith in our numbers because she was indeed recalled by 12 points" (Jensen 2013). The post angered some pollsters, like Silver, who said that PPP suppressed the data because they did not "like" the results. Silver went so far as to call the practice "totally indefensible" on Twitter. PPP responded that they were a private firm and it was up to them to decide what data should be released.

The result is that PPP has become one of the most controversial polling firms in the American political system. It continues to deliver results that aggregators and reporters use, but some polling experts worry the firm has become too focused on being "right," that is accurately predicting the outcome of a vote and not actually scientifically valid in the way they get there. A lengthy piece in the *New Republic* raised serious questions about the firm's approach, concluding, "No other pollster employs a truly ad hoc approach, with the flexibility to weight to whatever electorate it chooses, while allowing the composition of the electorate to fluctuate based on the inconsistent and subjective application of controversial or undisclosed metrics" (Cohn 2013). Still the firm continues to attract dozens of clients each cycle and its numbers are promoted on sites like Real Clear Politics and Politico.

Further Reading

Cohn, Nate. 2013. "There's Something Wrong with America's Premier Liberal Pollster." New Republic. September 12. Accessed February 10, 2015. http://www.newrepublic.com/article/114682/ppp-polling-methodology-opaque-flawed.

Jensen, Tom. 2013. "Reflecting on the Colorado Recalls." Public Policy Polling. September 11. Accessed February 10, 2015. http://www.publicpolicypolling.com/main/2013/09/reflecting-on-the-colorado-recalls.html.

Mahtesian, Charles. 2012. "PPP Nailed It." Politico. November 7. Accessed February 9, 2015. http://www.politico.com/blogs/charlie-mahtesian/2012/11/ppp-nailed-it-148911.html.

New York Times. 2006. "Polling Standards." June. Accessed February 9, 2015. http://www.nytimes.com/packages/pdf/politics/pollingstandards.pdf#search=%22site%3Anytimes.com%20%22polling%20standards%22%22.

Public Policy Polling. 2015. "About Us." Accessed February 10, 2015. http://www.publicpolicypolling.com/aboutPPP/about-us.html.

R

RAPID RESPONSE TEAMS

Rapid response teams are loosely organized campaign organizations that use research, communications, and social media teams to ensure that claims or attacks lobbed against their candidate are responded to as soon as—or sometimes even before—they are made. These groups supply journalists, social media, and the interested public with information defending their candidate and have become central parts of damage control strategies.

The term rapid response team was initially used to describe medical emergency response squads and those disaster management organizations sent to natural disasters and large-scale catastrophes. Like the political version that would emerge later, these groups were developed to gather in a time of crisis to perform a diverse array of tasks. The modern campaign version of the team now monitor media buys made by their opponent and the social media feeds of countless reporters, commentators and politicos seeking stories they should craft responses to. These teams often seek to use social media, in particular Twitter, to fire back immediate responses, usually while the speech or story they are responding to is still unfolding. The goal of this communication is two-fold: to minimize the political damage to the candidate or politician and to ensure that reporters covering the story have access to information and comments from their side of the political fight.

The art of response media is one that campaign professionals have become increasingly polished at executing. Now, a counter-ad that seeks to combat the negative message of a new ad can be up within hours. But simply responding to the attack is often not enough, as two campaign advisers wrote in a lengthy advice column in *Campaigns & Elections* magazine, "As in Judo, use the momentum of the attack itself to throw the opponent. One of our first rules in creating a response ad is to begin the response ad with the first opening seconds of the opponent's attack ad. The reason is simple but often overlooked: you don't want the audience to forget the ad you're responding to. You want to destroy their ad by actually making it work against the opponent and for your candidate" (Nuckels and White 2012). The two strategists and others also stress that campaigns should not get mired in details of the attack ad but rather should find a weak spot in the claims and attack that, meaning that rapid response media can be just as problematic when it comes to accuracy and context as the original attack and forces journalists and the public to dissect both the original claim and the response.

The role of these groups has become more critical as Super PACs and dark money groups have poured money into attack ads aimed at muddying candidates. These groups can, with unlimited donations and spending available to them, saturate markets with a negative ad or mailing, putting the candidate on the defensive. But rapid response teams increasingly do more than respond to attack ads. They often seek to create a more positive angle in the media about an evolving news story. Take, for example, the early efforts of the campaign of former secretary of state Hillary Clinton. Less than two weeks after she had unveiled her campaign for the 2016 Democratic presidential nomination, Clinton faced a public relations storm over accusations made in a book by Peter Schweizer that some of her decisions while at the State Department may have been influenced by people making large donations to the Clinton Foundation, headed by her husband and the former president. Clinton's press secretary went through one particularly damning story from the *New York Times* and wrote a point-by-point response to it, posting the entire thing on the free web publishing platform Medium. Political commentator Mark Halperin said that day, "Most valuable player for the Clinton campaign today is this guy Brian Fallon who put out a document in the middle of the day with some really strong rebuttal points. It doesn't defuse the thing completely, but if they can reply substantively, they can put this story away to a much greater degree than it was at 6 a.m." (Knowles 2015). Within hours of the story coming out, the Clinton campaign had outlined a detailed response that every cable talk show host and reporter covering the story could use to offer the other side of the story.

The other aspect of the rapid response that has changed, as social media has become such a major component of political communication, is that these teams often no longer disband after the election. Instead response teams are constantly working within political offices or in partisan think tanks to shape the debate over public policy and to influence the media's coverage of the president and Congress. One small case was captured by the *New York Times* in 2011 when they tailed the staff of then-U.S. Representative Eric Cantor, a conservative Republican leader. The reporters observed as Cantor's communication team watched President Barack Obama tell a crowd that he would consider "any serious idea" from Republicans when it came to jobs and the economy. What happened next?

> Within seconds, Brad Dayspring, Mr. Cantor's Rasputin of retort, was on the case, his fingers ripping across the keyboard as if individually caffeinated. "Obama says he's open to any 'serious #GOP idea,' typed Mr. Dayspring, the aggressive spokesman for Mr. Cantor, the Republican from Virginia who serves as House majority leader, in a message on Twitter. 'Here are 15 jobs bills stalled in the Senate to get him started.'" (Steinhauer 2011)

Dayspring's tweet helped spark conversation among conservatives and also was read by many political reporters covering the speech. This captures an important part of the rapid response aim. It is not simply to counter the argument put forward in the speech or attack ad, but to influence the coverage of the entire topic by the media. A quick response helps ensure news organizations looking for comment or rebuttal from the campaign have a clear and composed message to counter the other side. This actually allows rapid response teams to ride the media's interest in the attack and counter-attack to try and make a larger point about the campaign. Many rapid response messages mix an attack or clear repudiation of the other side and a positive message about what is good about their candidate.

As the political debate has moved from newspapers to the 24-hour news cycle of cable news and now to the instant conversations of Twitter, rapid response techniques have become increasingly sophisticated. Campaigns now are careful to have on-hand research and facts they need to counter potential attacks, often using detailed dossiers developed by their own opposition research teams to identify ahead of time possible weak points their candidate may be hit about and crafting ready-made response to send out at a moment's notice. This allows communications professionals within the campaign to already have on hand a crafted series of tweets, a press release, or a post to Medium within hours or even minutes of a story breaking. The key is to get the response of the campaign in the same news coverage as the initial reporting of the accusation, thus ensuring no attack is allowed to stand without some formal counter-attack from the campaign. In this modern era of politics and the political echo chamber, time is the enemy and the rapid response team is the candidate's best friend.

See also: Damage Control; Fact Checking; Opposition Research; Social Media and Politics; Spin

Further Reading

Knowles, David. 2015. "Clinton Camp Tries to Defuse Damning Report Point by Point." Bloomberg Politics. April 24. Accessed September 24, 2015. http://www.bloomberg.com/politics/articles/2015-04-24/clinton-camp-tries-to-defuse-damning-report-point-by-point.

Nuckels, Ben, and Joe Slade White. 2012. "The Art of Rapid Response." *Campaigns & Elections*. December 27. Accessed September 25, 2015. http://www.campaignsandelections.com/magazine/1777/the-art-of-rapid-response.

Steinhauer, Jennifer. 2011. "The G.O.P.'s Very Rapid Response Team." *New York Times*. October 24. Accessed September 24, 2015. http://www.nytimes.com/2011/10/25/us/politics/after-being-burned-in-08-republicans-embrace-twitter-hard-for-12.html?_r=0.

RASMUSSEN REPORTS

Rasmussen Reports is a political polling firm that has built a name for itself by providing extensive tracking of public opinion about the president's performance as well as public positions on hot button issues being debated in Congress.

The Asbury Park, New Jersey–based firm is not hired by candidates to conduct polling, instead it makes money through subscriptions to a stream of polling data and articles not available to the general public. The newsletter and articles also carry advertising, which is another revenue source for the firm. The firm also offers a "Platinum Service," which offers access to detailed demographics around its surveys, including its presidential performance tracking poll. The company was founded in 2003 by Scott Rasmussen, a former sports play-by-play announcer and co-founder of cable giant ESPN. Rasmussen left the business in 2013 and the firm is owned by the investment firm Noson Lawen Partners.

Rasmussen Reports has made its name by offering instant-polls and ongoing polls about an array of political news and other current events. The tagline on its site sums it up well claiming, "If it's in the news, it's in our polls." The reports sit aside a separate polling service, Pulse Opinion Research, that can be hired by clients and businesses and promises that it "licenses methodology developed by veteran pollster Scott Rasmussen, providing a survey platform for a host of clients, from individuals to special-interest groups. In fact, we provide the field work for all Rasmussen Reports surveys" (Pulse Opinion Research 2015).

Rasmussen's methodology has always used automated polling technology to conduct its polls. This technique uses computerized calling programs to contact voters and the person answering the phone indicates their preferences by selecting numbers. The firm claims this approach is "identical" to traditional pollster calls by people in its validity and even may be better because, "automated technology insures [sic] that every respondent hears exactly the same question, from the exact same voice, asked with the exact same inflection every single time" (Rasmussen Reports 2015). But others are skeptical of those claims. They point out that there is no way to know who is responding to the survey and therefore ensure their demographics are accurate and that federal law bans "robo-polls" from calling cell phones, meaning Rasmussen and others must account for those who do not own landlines. To account for these problems, firms like Rasmussen and Public Policy Polling create a system methodology that takes the automated survey responses and weighs them against their projected likely voter turnout and demographics to create their final numbers. Some have questioned this approach, warning that the automated systems "combine deficient sampling with baffling weighting practices" to generate more a guess than an accurate snapshot of the electorate (Cohn 2014).

Despite these concerns about their methodology and modeling, the firm and its numbers continue to be a major player in the coverage of campaigns and many of the reasons are financial more than political. As early as 2010, the *Washington Post* was reporting, "As cash-strapped newspapers and television networks struggle to meet the growing demand for polls, Rasmussen . . . is supplying reams of cheap, automated surveys that will measure—and maybe move—opinion" (Horowitz 2010). While that fact is undeniable—their polls are mainstays of political reporting and aggregators like Real Clear Politics—one of the nagging questions about Rasmussen Reports has centered on the question of possible partisan bias. With so much riding on its model of likely voters and weighting of its automated responses, some worry that it would be easy for those seeking specific slants to insert them into the weighting. Rasmussen is often a guest on Fox News and had been called the in-house pollster for the network. A 2010 analysis by polling whiz kid Nate Silver found that Rasmussen had overstated support for Republicans by an average of 4 points during that midterm. Silver dinged the firm not for political bias, but warned that "the methodological shortcuts that the firm takes may now be causing it to pay a price in terms of the reliability of its polling" (Silver 2010).

By 2013, Rasmussen had reached an impasse with his investors and left the company "in part because of disagreements over its business strategies" (Diamond 2013). He started a new media firm, Styrk, that aims to serve as a social media and news service. Rasmussen's new service doesn't have a specific polling component to it, but as he left the research firm and news service he founded a decade earlier, Rasmussen warned those in the survey business to brace themselves for a digital revolution, writing in his syndicated column, "New technology will fundamentally alter the ways that polls are conducted. Other online techniques will replace polling entirely in some situations. These shifts will be good for everyone except those who defend the status quo" (Rasmussen 2013). That revolution may still be coming for political polling, but for now the site that still bears his name continues to crank out a view of public opinion that is helping drive media coverage and, perhaps, public opinion as well.

See also: FiveThirtyEight (538); Gallup; Public Opinion; Public Policy Polling; Zogby Analytics

Further Reading

Cohn, Nate. 2014. "When Polling Is More Like Guessing." *New York Times*. May 28, 2014. Accessed February 11, 2015. http://www.nytimes.com/2014/05/29/upshot/when-polling-is-more-like-guessing.html?_r=0&abt=0002&abg=1.

Diamond, Michael. 2013. "Scott Rasmussen Leaves the Asbury Park Polling Company He Founded." *Asbury Park Press*. August 23. Accessed February 11, 2015. http://www.app.com/article/20130822/NJBIZ/308220082/Scott-Rasmussen-polling-company-Noson-Lawen.

Horowitz, Jason. 2010. "Pollster Scott Rasmussen's Numbers Are Firing Up Republicans and Democrats." *The Washington Post*. June 17. Accessed February 12, 2015. http://www.washingtonpost.com/wp-dyn/content/article/2010/06/16/AR2010061605090.html.

Pulse Opinion Research. 2015. "About Us." Accessed February 11, 2015. http://www.pulseopinionresearch.com/About-Us.

Rasmussen Reports. 2015. "Methodology." Accessed February 11, 2015. http://www.rasmussenreports.com/public_content/about_us/methodology.

Rasmussen, Scott. 2013. "The Digital Threat to the Political Class." Real Clear Politics. August 26. Accessed February 15, 2015. http://www.realclearpolitics.com/articles/2013/08/26/the_digital_threat_to_the_political_class_119700.html.

Silver, Nate. 2010. "Rasmussen Polls Were Biased and Inaccurate; Quinnipiac, SurveyUSA Performed Strongly." *New York Times*. November 4. Accessed February 10, 2015. http://fivethirtyeight.blogs.nytimes.com/2010/11/04/rasmussen-polls-were-biased-and-inaccurate-quinnipiac-surveyusa-performed-strongly.

REAL CLEAR POLITICS

If polling is the drug of modern political reporting, Real Clear Politics is a Colombian kingpin. The site, launched in 2000 by two Princeton graduates and at first all done by hand, focuses on aggregating local news content with the latest polls from a given state. The result is a site that allows readers to gather the most recent news from on the ground and the polling numbers to assess the state of the race.

A 2004 *Chicago Tribune* story let the public see behind the numbers to where founders Tom Bevan and John McIntyre were hidden away in a one-room office, culling through dozens of newspaper sites and other resources to pull together the latest round of polling and commentary from around the country. "Between them, they read the editorial and op-ed sites of more than 50 publications, Bevan said, looking for a mix of well-articulated views on the vital issues of the day and news of the latest opinion polls" (Zorn 2004). Published first at 6 a.m. and then updated throughout the day, the site culls scores of online publications, looking for commentary and analysis from both national and local news organizations.

The site was never intended to be for everyone. But for those in 2004 watching the race unfold between President George W. Bush and Senator John Kerry, the site offered a simple answer to the question political junkies always want to be able to answer—Who's winning? The site would answer it by averaging the latest polls to create the RCP Average. This Real Clear Politics average would then inform who was leading in a given state, and from there the editors could project election results and the Electoral College tally. All this without ever conducting a poll themselves.

The site has grown to attract nearly 6 million unique visitors a month and has spawned Real Clear divisions that replicate the model of aggregating links from a variety of sources and adding data whenever possible. Real Clear has sections covering sports, business, international, religion, history, and defense issues and the company has grown to more than two dozen staff. By 2007, the site had attracted a major media supporter when Forbes Media purchased a majority stake in the entire company. Former Republican presidential candidate and Forbes president and CEO Steve Forbes described what he saw as a key addition to the company's growing digital assets, saying, "Republicans, Democrats, Independents—anyone with an interest in politics and its impact on the economy—all find this site indispensable for staying on top of critical news and analysis. It will be even more critical as the election season heats up" (Business Wire 2007).

Supporters credit the resulting service with improving the knowledge of reporters and commentators discussing campaigns for federal office. *Reason Magazine* editor David Weigel said, "the site has already done a huge service by boosting the IQ of all political junkies. Between the polls and the local stories . . . the site is doing a lot to democratize punditry" (Gustafson 2008). But not everyone hails the site, and many liberal blogs have pointed to a conservative bent to the columns it chooses to highlight and the way it frames developments. During the 2012 campaign, writers at the Daily Kos and DemocraticUnderground argued Real Clear Politics was deliberately highlighting positive news on Republican candidate Mitt Romney in an effort to make the race appear closer. "Although RCP was founded by conservatives to combat the 'liberal' media, RCP became one of the web's go-to political websites with a reputation for nonpartisanship—aggregating articles and polls favorable to both right and left. No more. RCP lost its cool after Romney won the first debate, salivating over the prospect of booting Obama from office" (Defiant-One 2012). A look at the About Us page does carry a string of endorsements, including conservatives David Brooks, Brit Hume, Paul Gigot, and Michael Barone.

But perhaps the most damning indictment came from another political prognosticator, Nate Silver of FiveThirtyEight.com. Silver, in a 2008 column, blasted RCP for "cherry-picking" numbers to suit its interests. "I am a Democrat, and I see the world through a Democratic lens. But what I can promise you is that we'll keep the spin separate from our metrics . . . Unfortunately, that is not a choice you have at RCP. Their partisan leaning is infused into their numbers. If RCP disclosed their methodology—articulated their rationale for excluding or including certain polls—I would give them the benefit of the doubt. But they do not, so I do not" (Silver 2008). Silver later backed off some of this criticism, but maintained RCP should do more to be transparent about the way it generates numbers and selects polls to track.

This debate over the selection of polls and the transparency of methodology speaks to the degree to which the site has become a sort of barometer of the campaign. RCP itself highlights a quote from Ben Smith of Buzzfeed that calls the site "a huge force. Their polling average is the Dow Jones of campaign coverage" (RealClearPolitics 2015).

Further Reading

Business Wire. 2007. "Forbes Media Acquires Fifty-One Percent Stake in RealClearPolitics.com." November 7. Accessed January 22, 2015. http://www.businesswire.com/portal/site/google/?ndmViewId=news_view&newsId=20071107006128&newsLang=en.

DefiantOne. 2012. "As Obama Lead Solidifies, RealClearPolitics Shows Right Wing Bias." The Daily Kos. October 25. Accessed January 22, 2015. http://www.dailykos.com/story/2012/10/25/1150097/-As-Obama-lead-solidifies-RealClearPolitics-shows-right-wing-bias.

Gustafson, Colin. 2008. "On Web, Political Junkies Make a Real Clear Choice." *New York Sun*. March 10. Accessed January 22, 2015. http://www.nysun.com/business/on-web-political-junkies-make-a-real-clear-choice/72596.

Real Clear Politics. "Media Kit." Accessed January 22, 2015. http://dyn.realclearpolitics.com/media_kit.

Silver, Nate. 2008. "Real Credibility Problems." FiveThirtyEight.com. October 2. Accessed January 22, 2015. http://fivethirtyeight.com/features/real-credibility-problems.

Zorn, Eric. 2004. "Political Site Polls Well with Election Junkies." *Chicago Tribune*. October 26. Accessed on January 22, 2015. http://articles.chicagotribune.com/2004-10-26/news/0410260258_1_polls-projection-site.

RED STATE-BLUE STATE

Inspired by the Electoral College map used by television broadcasts on Election Night to report the winners of different states, red states and blue states have become a shorthand way to refer to political divisions between Republicans and Democrats, often serving as an editorial short-cut to explaining divisive issues and complex political beliefs in different parts of the country. Even as it is used to describe this separation, some argue it also exacerbates the perception of deep political and cultural divisions in the American political electorate. In fact, then aspiring national politician Barack Obama used the trope in his famous keynote address at the 2004 Democratic National Convention, arguing communities did not need to be separated into red America and blue America.

The terms red state and blue state originate from the display of returns on election night. As early as 1976, television networks used illuminated maps to indicate how each state had voted in the presidential election. Given the winner-take-all nature of presidential elections, no matter how close the vote was, the entire state would be declared for the party's camp that garnered the most votes. The result was when journalists projected the winner in a given state, that state would turn blue or red. Today we instinctively think of red as Republican and blue as Democratic. But this iconic, and sometimes overly simple, way of describing the politics of a state actually started out the exact opposite way.

In 1976 NBC used the colors to mark each victory by incumbent president Gerald Ford and challenger Democrat Jimmy Carter. At the time, red stood for Democrats and blue for Republicans! For the election team at NBC the colors were an easy decision. Roy Wetzel, who ran the team, said the decision was made "without giving it a second thought, we said blue for conservatives, because that's what the parliamentary system in London is, red for the more liberal party. And that settled it. We just did it" (Edna 2012). Wetzel had looked across the ocean to Europe, where the difference was connected to the historical colors connected with conservative and socialist parties. Since the French Revolution the color red had been associated with labor groups and socialist organizations—and later liberal political organizations in general. Blue, meanwhile, was the color of conservative groups and parties. By the late nineteenth century, the same color palette was in use in the United States where Republicans like Grover Cleveland and Benjamin Harrison used the color blue to signify the Republican Party.

Even as late as 1980, blue had been the color of Republicans for many in the media. As the results poured into NBC and the map behind John Chancellor, Tom Brokaw and David Brinkley filled in with Republican blue victories, Brinkley commenting that, "It's beginning to look like a suburban swimming pool." Over time different networks and news magazines tinkered with the colors. By 1984 the results were thoroughly mixed, with ABC using red for Republicans and NBC sticking with its blue for the same party. Why blue shifted from Republican to Democrat and red vice versa remains unclear. At the *New York Times*, which did not publish a color election map until 2000, Republicans became red because, according to their graphics editor, "Both Republican and red start with the letter R" (Zeller 2004).

By 2000, it had become the norm that Democrats were blue and Republicans red, and the tumultuous election cemented that dichotomy. That year, with Florida's recount halted by the Supreme Court thus ensuring the election of George

W. Bush, news outlets kept the election map in the minds of voters for weeks. In particular, the *Washington Post* credited NBC's Tim Russert for using the terms "red state" and "blue state" to explain the divide in the electorate and the Electoral College deadlock that night. Experts agree this was the year that blue became the color of Democrats and red that of Republicans. After that, the colors became a sort of shorthand for describing the politics of states and communities. Analysts and pundits would talk about just how blue a Democratic community truly was or whether a traditionally Republican state may see an increase in support for Democrats, thus turning a red state purple.

The dichotomy created by labeling entire states or regions blue or red also fed into a political narrative that took shape during the 2000s, that of political polarization. Democrats were seen as drawing support from the highly populated regions along the coasts and in a handful of urbanized states in the middle section of the country, while Republicans had a lock on Midwestern, southern, and Rocky Mountain states.

The concept has sparked countless columns, dozens of books, and hours of commentary. One example from the *American Prospect* captures how the red-blue divide is often used as a platform for understanding the political polarization in the United States. In a long, conceptual piece, author Paul Starr outlines how America has always been a place of fundamental political differences, starting with the conception and acceptance of slavery and the war that was waged to end it. Starr goes on to find the divide is now the red-blue divide and that "when politics become polarized between two alternatives, voters have clearer choices. They have more reason to pay attention and turn out. Each side may then mobilize, take power, and get its way in different jurisdictions or private institutions. That is what is happening now in state and local governments and civil society. Two ideologically based societies have developed within the United States, and the differences between them are growing. The question will ultimately be which America, red or blue, dominates the nation's future" (Starr 2014).

The concept has also influenced political science work, as researchers have used the Electoral College results to assess and analyze the competitiveness and voter demographics of different states. One 2008 academic work dived into religious behavior and red-blue states and found, "Compared with blue state voters, red state voters were much more likely to be Protestants, to consider themselves born-again or evangelical Christians, and to attend religious services at least once per week. They were also much more likely to have a gun owner in their household and much less likely to have a union member in their household. Red state voters were much more likely to take a pro-life position on abortion, to oppose marriage or civil unions for gay couples, to support the war in Iraq . . ." (Abramowitz and Saunders 2008).

But for every analysis that finds a useful context for understanding the state of politics there as many who find the red-blue dialectic misleading and damaging. Many contend that blocking huge swaths of the nation through the simplest color choice is too general to help someone understand the political situation in the country. Dante Chinni, a political reporter from the *Christian Science Monitor*, particularly found the dichotomy useless in its new role. He wrote in an introduction to his work *Our Patchwork Nation*, that "it's not that the red and blue map is itself misleading. It's useful as a political scorecard, especially on that one all-important evening every four years. The problem is what it has become. We have invested it with a power it doesn't deserve, as a quick identifier for places and people and what they think and do" (Chinni 2010). The problem, Chinni and others argue, is that a red state does not exist. Even in a safe "Republican" state like Texas there is a "blue" area like Austin. And when you compare two "blue" cities like Detroit and Ann Arbor, their similar Democratic voting pattern may be the only thing the communities truly have in common.

It even became part of the campaign rhetoric, with then-state Senator Barack Obama connecting with this frustration with a divided nation in his keynote speech at the 2004 Democratic Nation Convention. He mesmerized the crowd and was thrust instantly into the national spotlight as he rejected the concept of red-blue, telling thousands of delegates and millions of viewers, "There's not a liberal America and a conservative America; there's the United States of America . . . The pundits like to slice and dice our country into red states and blue states: red states for Republicans, blue states for Democrats. But I've got news for them, too. We worship an awesome God in the blue states, and we don't like federal agents poking around our libraries in the red states. We coach little league in the blue states and, yes, we've got some gay friends in the red states" (Obama 2004). Political scientists have also sought to fight the perception that certain states are destined to fall into one political column or the other. They argue that politics is more complicated than a population choosing one party or the other, or as one in-depth study of the so-called purple state of Virginia found, "Demography is not political destiny; it only helps to establish the field on which the major contenders must play. The economy, current events, and the candidates themselves have at least an equal role" (Cable and Claiborn 2012).

And that note may be the most important thing to consider when journalists, politicians, or analysts use the red/blue divide. There is nothing particularly predictive about how a county or state voted from one election to another, even if it does help decipher the political winners or losers on Election Day. Relying too much on a simple political binary—are you from red America or blue America—overlooks the more complicated picture of the American voter. And the broader the generalization—is your city red or blue? Your state? Your country?—the less insight it offers.

One more thing to throw into the effect of creating "red states" and "blue states" comes from research done to see whether such labels do more than simply reflect a political divide in our nation, but perhaps help create it. Researchers from Cal State, Michigan, and Syracuse tested people's perceptions of political division in the United States by showing them the Electoral College map, where states are a bright red or bright blue, and then showing them other maps with the actual voting results at a more local level, creating subtler color variations and much more purple. The results were clear. "Participants viewing the Electoral map saw the nation as more divided both in general and with respect to specific political issues. Exposure to Electoral maps thus polarized perceptions of political attitudes: residents of conservative states were seen as more conservative, and residents of liberal states were seen as more liberal, than when participants were exposed to Proportional maps" (Rutchick, Smyth, and Konrath 2009). Although just one study, it does raise an important question about whether portraying Electoral College maps is, in fact, increasing the perception of how deep the partisan divide is in the United States.

But as a political code that helps to inform the debate about the degree to which the United States has become politically polarized, the idea of "red" and "blue" has clearly captured some element of our understanding of politics. It will surely continue to be used by those seeking to explain politics and political behavior in the years to come.

See also: Political Polarization and the Media

Further Reading

Abramowitz, Alan, and Kyle Saunders. 2008. "Is Polarization a Myth?" *The Journal of Politics* 70, no. 2 (April).

Chinni, Dante. *Our Patchwork Nation: The Surprising Truth about the "Real" America*. 2010. New York: Gotham Books.

Enda, Jodie. 2012. "When Republicans Were Blue and Democrats Were Red." *Smithsonian Magazine*. October 31. Accessed May 19, 2015. http://www.smithsonianmag.com/history/when-republicans-were-blue-and-democrats-were-red-104176297/?all.

Obama, Barack. 2004. "Transcript: Illinois Senate Candidate Barack Obama." *Washington Post*. July 27. Accessed May 19, 2015. http://www.washingtonpost.com/wp-dyn/articles/A19751-2004Jul27.html.

Rutchick, Abraham, Joshua Smyth, and Sara Konrath. 2009. "Seeing Red (and Blue): Effects of Electoral College Depictions on Political Group Perception." *Analyses of Social Issues and Public Policy* 9, no. 1. Accessed May 19, 2015. http://www.ipearlab.org/media/publications/rutchick_smyth_konrath_asap_2009.pdf.

Starr, Paul. 2014. "Red State, Blue State: Polarization and the American Situation." *American Prospect*. November 3. Accessed May 19, 2015. http://prospect.org/article/red-state-blue-state-polarization-and-american-situation.

Zeller, Tom. 2004. "Ideas & Trends; One State, Two State, Red State, Blue State." *New York Times*. February 8. Accessed May 19, 2015. http://www.nytimes.com/2004/02/08/weekinreview/ideas-trends-one-state-two-state-red-state-blue-state.html.

REDSTATE

When Rick Perry decided to launch his late-in-the-game presidential campaign in 2011 he turned up not in Washington or Austin, but at a gathering of bloggers, a conference organized by the conservative blog RedState. RedState, and its editor Erick Erickson, spent much of 2011 in the GOP spotlight. In fact, that year one

Republican consultant said of the commentary site, "RedState has emerged as the most influential blog in the conservative movement" (Embry 2011).

Like other political blogs such as the liberal Daily Kos, RedState often focuses on the internal politics of the party it supports. For example, in late 2012 contributor Ned Ryun posted a provocative piece urging conservatives to depose Speaker of the House John Boehner for lacking the ideological purity and determination to lead the Republican caucus, writing, "If Speaker Boehner wants to purge independent, bold conservatives—I think it's time he gets fired as Speaker. Not only for the purge. He has failed to effectively win negotiations with President Obama and appointed moderate committee chairs. To the public, Boehner may appear radical but in reality he proposes milquetoast policies, like the tax-hikes he proposed this week" (Ryun 2012).

The site is owned by Salem Communications, a Christian radio broadcaster that in 2014 purchased Eagle Publishing, a company that ran a series of conservative blogs and publications. However, it is still most closely associated with the work and views of its editor-in-chief Erick Erickson.

Erickson has built a position of political importance through his site and his work as a political commentator on cable news. The *London Telegraph* ranked Erickson as the 65th most influential conservative in the United States, ahead of former U.S. House Majority Leader Dick Armey and former Florida governor Jeb Bush. The paper said Erickson's RedState "draws much of its strength from its image as a voice of the heartland, far outside the Washington Beltway" (Harnden 2010). Erickson has at times drawn public attention and scorn for his comments—especially on Twitter. One major episode developed in 2010 after he tweeted, "The nation loses the only goat f*$#*&^ child molester to ever serve on the Supreme Court in David Souter's retirement." He quickly expressed regret to media reporter Howard Kurtz, "Erickson made very clear in that interview that he plans to 'grow up,' as he put it, and refrain from the kind of inflammatory personal attacks he was known for. He described the Souter slam (involving a goat) as the dumbest thing he ever did" (Kurtz 2010).

Another potential scandal briefly erupted in 2011 when a sales account manager from RedState's publisher Eagle Communications circulated an email to conservatives that offered, "Erick Erickson's reputation along with his rising profile, combine to make RedState the most influential conservative blog on Capitol Hill and across America. Why not put Erick's influence to work for your organization?" This program offered Erickson's "endorsement" as part of a sponsorship package for the site. Erickson was quick to respond, writing, "Just to start it off, no, my endorsements are not for sale. I don't know who the guy is who sent the email, but he certainly did RedState no favors" (Erickson 2011). The controversy quickly blew over when Erickson clarified his role in the process and added that he would not endorse candidates who had appeared at RedState events.

Despite these and a few other controversial social media attacks on President Obama and feminists, Erickson was able to move from the blogosphere to television. In 2010, CNN hired the Georgian to serve as a political commentator on John King's program and in 2013 Erickson moved to Fox News. But RedState is more than just Erickson's personal platform. The site features multiple tiers of writers. Diarists can post stories that appear on the less trafficked parts of the site, but still are given a platform to comment on the day's news. Front page editors have more sway, posting more regularly and garnering more control of the overall site. The site also sponsors yearly RedState Gatherings where conservative activists gather to hear from rising GOP leaders and potential national candidates. One former front page editor described the power the blog gives to regular grassroots activists, writing, "Through RedState, I've met and interacted with some of the finest, most influential conservative minds in the country. I was an eyewitness to the political 'coming out parties' of Nikki Haley, Marco Rubio and Ted Cruz, among others" (Maley 2014).

In all of these comments and gatherings, RedState stresses that it represents a Republican and conservative vision that is not of the nation's capital, but rather small towns, and especially the South. It is a philosophy that Erickson and many other bloggers at the site adhere to and espouse on the site and in political appearances on television. It can be somewhat summed up by Erickson when, while discussing his book *RedState Uprising* at the conservative Heritage Foundation, he said, "The problem we have is when Republicans get to Washington, Republicans are more likely to compromise with the Democrats in favor of a government program than the Democrats are likely to compromise with the Republicans on a free market program . . . Republicans are always very bad at showing the impact of government on its citizens. We have to do a better job of that" (Erickson 2011).

See also: Conservative blogospere; Red State-Blue State

Further Reading

Embry, Jason. 2011. "Perry's Announcement Highlights RedState's Growing Influence." *Austin American-Statesman*. August 11. Accessed January 15, 2015. http://www.statesman.com/news/news/state-regional-govt-politics/perrys-announcement-highlights-red states-growing-i/nRdRj.

Erickson, Erick. 2011. "Erick Erickson: 'Red State Uprising: How to Take Back America'." CSPAN BookTV. February 11. Accessed January 13, 2016. https://www.youtube.com/watch?v=eq-Kd_1mIr4.

Erickson, Erick. 2011. "Selling Endorsements? [updated]." RedState. June 7. Accessed January 13, 2015. http://www.redstate.com/diary/Erick/2011/06/07/selling-endorsements.

Harnden, Toby. 2010. "The Most Influential US Conservatives: 80-61." *The Telegraph*. January 12. Accessed January 14, 2015. http://www.telegraph.co.uk/news/worldnews/northamerica/usa/6967325/The-most-influential-US-conservatives-80-61.html.

Kurtz, Howard. 2010. "Media Backtalk: Howard Kurtz on the Media." Washingtonpost.com. March 29. Accessed January 14, 2015. http://live.washingtonpost.com/media-backtalk-03-29-10.html.

Maley, Steve. 2014. "Ten Years at RedState." Maley's Energy Blog. September 21. Accessed January 13, 2015. http://stevemaley.com/2014/09/21/ten-years-at-redstate.
Ryun, Ned. 2012. "Fire Boehner: We Only Need 16 Votes to Depose Boehner." RedState. December 5. Accessed January 13, 2015. http://www.redstate.com/diary/nedryun/2012/12/05/fire-boehner-we-only-need-16-votes-to-depose-boehner.

ROLL CALL

The common perception of Capitol Hill is a place of heated rhetoric and political grandstanding. But Capitol Hill is also a unique community of some 25,000 staffers, Capitol Hill Police, and workers who keep the 535 members of Congress in touch with their constituents, safe, and fed.

This is the small town within Washington that *Roll Call* was developed to serve.

Launched in 1955 by a Hill staffer named Sid Yudain, the paper was part church newsletter, part yearbook, and part gossip sheet. Then-senator Lyndon B. Johnson wrote a first person account of his recovery from a heart attack in an early edition, and Yudain recalled later how some were offended by the paper's decision to run a weekly "pinup" girl photo of a Hill staffer. Fifty years later Yudain described the early days of *Roll Call* as a time when he and a handful of staff "had a little Remington portable typewriter—I guess it was one of the first ones that came out, and we all learned how to use it, even when we were really small—and we published these newspapers, writing editorials against each other instead of staging fists or rocks or something" (Weber 2013). Yudain remained the owner of what he described as his community newspaper until 1986 when he sold it to Arthur Levitt, who then ran the American Stock Exchange. When Levitt was nominated to the Securities and Exchange Commission he sold his majority shares to the Economist Group, the British publishers that already owned 40 percent of the paper.

The Economist later acquired another long-time Capitol Hill entity, *Congressional Quarterly*, in 2009 and created the CQ-Roll Call Group. With the shift in owners the newspaper also changed, growing to cover legislative news more while still offering that community paper function, where "*Roll Call* tracks staff members, who come and go with great regularity from Senate and House member and committee offices. In times of budget turmoil, it keeps staff and members informed about impending cuts and changes. For the administrative and other support staffs, including the Capitol Police, it is a source of often otherwise unavailable news" (Dennis and Snyder 1997, p. 63). The paper publishes twice a week and has a circulation of just over 20,000, almost all of it going to offices on Capitol Hill and to a handful of locations near the White House and lobbyist offices. But the paper has also added a significant web presence—keeping much of the tone and inside baseball-style interest of its print edition even as it attracts more than 900,000 unique visitors a month as of early 2015.

But just because it is the small town newspaper for Congress doesn't mean *Roll Call* doesn't sometimes break national political news. The fact that it is read by congressional staff and members so closely and that their reporters essentially live on the Hill means at times the paper receives tips and hears things before the big news organizations do. It happened notably in late 1998. The drama in the Capitol was intense as members considered the impeachment of President Bill Clinton for lying about an extramarital affair with a former White House intern. But that wasn't the scoop. Porn publisher Larry Flynt had published a full-page ad in the *Washington Post* offering big bucks for information on any affair involving other political leaders in Washington. And the reporters at *Roll Call* had learned he'd gotten a bite. "Bob Livingston, a Republican congressman from Louisiana and Speaker-designate of the House of Representatives, was confiding in his fellow congressional leaders that he had cheated on his wife" (Sabato, Lichter, and Stencel 2000, p. 33). The paper decided to break the news online, still something novel in 1998. Livingston admitted to the scandal and resigned.

With the purchase by the Economist, the paper has expanded its political coverage immensely, adding elements that make it more like Politico and other D.C.-based political news organizations, but there is something of the old Yudain philosophy here. The founder always argued, "It just seemed that this was the most important community in the world [and] the only news coming out of Congress was about legislation, which bored me, and I think bored most people, including some of the Congressmen" (Yachnin 2005).

That attitude, mellowed with time, still echoes in the words of the current editor as well, who seems to view the place she covers with a bit more empathy than many outside the beltway. Christina Bellantoni said, "In general, people in government have good intentions . . . That's something I always tell my reporters to remember, 'You have access to people and places and things that most of America will never see. Most of America will not tour that Capitol. Most of America will not have a conversation with John Boehner. That's an important responsibility: We can't forget it or take it for granted" (Sullivan 2014).

Further Reading

Dennis, Everette, and Robert Snyder. 1997. *Covering Congress: Media Studies Series*. Piscataway, NJ: Transaction Publishers.

Sabato, Larry, Mark Stencel, and Robert Lichter. 2000. *Peepshow: Media and Politics in an Age of Scandal*. Lanham, MD: Rowman & Littlefield Publishers.

Sullivan, Mark. 2014. "A Polarized Atmosphere." *Worcester Telegram & Gazette*. March 5. Accessed February 1, 2015. http://www.telegram.com/article/20140306/NEWS/303069810&Template=printart.

Weber, Bruce. 2013. "Sid Yudain, 90, Dies; Created Congress's Community Newspaper." *New York Times*. October 26. Accessed January 14, 2015. http://www.nytimes.com/2013/10/27/us/politics/sid-yudain-who-created-roll-call-dies-at-90.html?_r=0.

Yachnin, Jennifer. 2005. "Sid Yudain, the Man Who Started It All." *Roll Call*. June 9. Accessed February 2, 2015. http://www.rollcall.com/features/50th-Anniversary_2005/fifty_anniversary/-9594-1.html.

ROVE, KARL (1950–)

Karl Rove in many ways represents the modern political campaign. He has built a reputation of exploiting social issues for political gain, fueled controversy over his use of independent organizations to raise and spend huge sums of money with little oversight, and as a political commentator annoyed and challenged partisans on both sides of the political aisle. Rove served as the "architect" to President George W. Bush's political victories in Texas and helped him win the White House twice. He has been compared to a modern Machiavelli and dubbed "Bush's brain."

Karl Christian Rove was born in 1950 in Denver, Colorado, and experienced a turbulent upbringing, finding out later that the man his mother was married to was not his father and struggling academically in college. He attended four universities but never ended up earning the political science degree he sought. But what he didn't do in school he did for real, taking senior positions in the College Republicans and developing key skills that would inform his career. He would befriend fellow master strategist and hardball politico Lee Atwater in the College Republicans and later introduce Atwater to President George H. W. Bush. But more than simply make connections, Rove also understood the power of hitting certain voters with certain messages—the idea of microtargeting campaigns.

It began with direct mail, the art of sending out political letters and pamphlets to the right people to get the donations and votes needed. Rove was a natural at both the approach and the technology. He would later explain to Mark Halperin and John Harris how he used technology to build his political consulting business in the 1980s. They would write, "By using computer programs to organize his mailing lists . . . he might find that a planned mailing of 100,000 could be trimmed to 93,000 by identifying people who had moved out of a district or state . . . Additionally, overhauling the lists so that they included nine-digit zip codes was a worthwhile expense since it saved money later on postal rates. These were seemingly small things, hardly glamorous, but in Rove's line of work they were the difference between a profitable business and a struggling one (and often between winning an election and losing one)" (Halperin and Harris 2006). That interest in data and finding issues that will motivate voters or weaken opponents became his core skill. He worked for the Republican National Committee at the age of 23 for the elder Bush and did campaign work in Virginia. After moving to Texas he worked for Republican Governor Bill Clements, before opening his own political consulting business in Austin: Karl Rove & Co.

He ran that business from 1981–1991, helping Republican candidates win statewide and local elections, but decided to end the firm to work full-time for George W. Bush, becoming his political adviser and chief strategist for Bush's gubernatorial campaign. Those who sought to explain his innate ability often focused on his work in identifying voting blocs and finding ways to use them or combat them. A lengthy, and largely negative, *Vanity Fair* profile described it as, "For Rove, all politics is partitive, and there is almost nothing he can't explain by slicing up the electorate and slotting it into place. Divide and organize. Divide and categorize.

Divide and conquer" (Purdum 2006). This work of finding the right messages and the right voters helped Bush win the Texas governor's mansion and later fueled Bush's successful White House run.

Those for whom he worked often marveled at how he could find ways to attract voters that were not historically Republican, while also using red-meat social issues to fire up voters who would vote for the GOP when motivated. Ed Gillespie, who would chair the RNC during President Bush's tenure, recalled, "Karl conceived of an election that was designed to bring more people into our party, designed to increase our percentages in nontraditional Republican voting demographics, like Hispanic voters and women and African Americans, where we had a sizable gain, and at the same time enfranchise more naturally Republican voters and 'lazy Republicans,' as we call them in the parlance, into the process and get them out to vote, and do that with a bottom-up structure, a grassroots structure" (*Frontline* 2005).

But to those who saw the Bush presidency as a disturbing mix of political opportunism and troubling policy making, Rove became a lightning rod of criticism and speculation. Columnists, critics, and authors turned Rove from a consultant into a second president. He was compared to the Italian brutal political adviser Machiavelli and the crazed Russian mystic and royal adviser Rasputin. People labeled him "Bush's Brain" and a book of that name described his perceived effect on policy, writing: "The president may arrive at his own conclusions about politics and policy. But virtually all of the data, and its interpretation, are coming from Rove. And the material, undoubtedly, points the president where his expert wants him to go on matters of both politics and policy" (Moore and Slater 2003). Rove would serve in different roles through much of the Bush presidency and would leave still carrying the credentials of a skilled, if controversial, political operative.

In the wake of the Bush presidency, Rove has worked primarily with the American Crossroads Super PAC and its affiliate social welfare nonprofit Crossroads GPS. These organizations have used the post–*Citizens United* campaign finance rules to raise and spend hundreds of millions on behalf of Republican candidates. The organization has had a mixed track record delivering actual victories for Republicans but it has allowed Rove to deploy huge resources using his political strategies. That work has continued to make him a boogey man of the left, but he has also caught flak from the tea party-style Republicans who see him as lacking any true ideological conviction. Rove, who is said to prize strategy over partisanship, has criticized the tea party Republicans for damaging the electoral possibilities of moderate and more mainstream candidates, even helping launch a project called the Conservative Victory Project that raises money to protect so-called establishment Republicans. The moves have made him a controversial figure among Republicans but have also kept Rove a major player in the Republican Party as the GOP debates its political future.

See also: Microtargeting; Political Consultants

Further Reading

Alexander, Paul. 2008. *Machiavelli's Shadow: The Rise and Fall of Karl Rove*. New York: Modern Times/Macmillan.

"Ed Gillespie Interview." 2005. *Frontline*. Interviewed December 21. Accessed January 15, 2016. http://www.pbs.org/wgbh/pages/frontline/shows/architect/interviews/gillespie.html.

Halperin, Mark, and John Harris. 2006. *The Way to Win: Taking the White House in 2008*. New York: Random House.

Moore, James, and Wayne Slater. 2003. *Bush's Brain: How Karl Rove Made George W. Bush Presidential*. New York: Wiley & Sons.

Purdum, Todd. 2006. "Karl Rove's Split Personality." *Vanity Fair*. November 30. Accessed January 15, 2016. http://www.vanityfair.com/news/2006/12/rove200612.

Rove, Karl. 2010. *Courage and Consequence: My Life as a Conservative in the Fight*. New York: Threshold Editions.

RUSSERT, TIM (1950–2008)

No one who sat down with Tim Russert on the set of *Meet the Press* got an easy ride. Helped by a frightening memory and prodigious use of archival tape, politicians and commentators alike knew they would have to contend with Russert's prosecutorial style. "Because of Russert's preparation, appearing on *Meet the Press* was like a visit to the dentist," columnist Robert Novak wrote in the *Washington Post* (Novak 2008).

Over 18 years of going toe-to-toe with the political elite on the Sunday morning talk show, Tim Russert became a giant in American political journalism. Presidents, members of Congress, and even athletes sat down to talk with him, conversations that often produced information that drove the next week's news coverage. The man was so revered in D.C. circles that his unexpected death in 2008 dominated headlines and news broadcasts. But those who heaped praise upon the late Russert had a reason. David Carr of the *New York Times* wrote that for those who treated politics as something of a religion, who scheduled their Sundays around the airing of *Meet the Press*, Tim Russert was the "high priest" (Carr 2008).

Timothy Russert, Jr. was born May 7, 1950, in Buffalo, N.Y., where his father was a sanitation worker. Russert went to John Carroll University in Ohio and later earned a law degree from Cleveland State University. He began his career in politics as special counsel for Senator Daniel Patrick Moynihan, and later working for with New York governor Mario Cuomo. However, he wouldn't be a political flack for long. He joined NBC in 1984, making the transition from political aide to journalist at a time when such a shift was rare. He worked on special news projects, including getting Pope John Paul II to appear on one of the network's programs. He was eventually named Washington bureau chief for NBC News and, in 1991, was invited to take over the show that vaulted him to Beltway stardom.

Meet the Press had long been a D.C. institution before Russert took the helm, boasting decades of appearances by powerful figures and tough interviews. Despite having no previous on-camera experience, Russert took the job as the show's moderator. When he asked the show's founder, Lawrence Spivak, for advice, Spivak told Russert to study the positions of his guests and take the opposite side—a tactic Russert took to heart. He also used his connections and work ethic to be ultra-prepared for each show.

"He had a face that seemed to be carved out of potatoes, but he worked on television by working harder than your average talking head, making the calls and pulling the levers of power with an alacrity few possessed," Carr wrote (2008).

One famous interview took place with the former Ku Klux Klan grand wizard and Nazi sympathizer David Duke. Duke was running for governor of Louisiana against Democrat Edwin Edwards, who had been tried on federal racketeering charges. During the interview, Russert asked Duke what he found "so offensive and so objectionable about the United States of America that you found Nazi Germany to be preferable?" Later in the program, he pressed the candidate to name Louisiana's largest employers—something Duke was unable to do (Ball and NBC News, 1998).

With *Meet the Press*, a separate program he hosted on MSNBC, and moderating presidential debates, Russert became a major figure in the insular Beltway culture. But many who marveled at his work did so because Russert grounded so much of his approach in his Buffalo upbringing. "With his plain spoken explanations and hard-hitting questions, Mr. Russert played an outsize role in the coverage of politics," wrote Jacques Steinberg of the *New York Times* in a 2008 obituary for Russert (2008). His position inside that culture set up the media environment that mourned him so heavily when he died. His broadcast and cable competitors memorialized him, and politicians issued statements remarking on his influence in Washington.

The spectacle was lamented by some, like Slate's Jack Shafer, who wondered whether viewers and readers cared as much about Russert as the networks and newspapers thought. But it may have been because Russert had become such an enormous figure for those people. *New York Times Magazine* writer Mark Leibovich would use the funeral as the opening scene in his scathing rebuke of Washington, This Town, writing, "The showing today testifies to the man who died, Russert, the boldfaced impresario of the longest-running show on television and the most powerful unelected figure in the country's most powerful, prosperous, and disappointing city. A buoyant part of This Town was being put to rest today . . ." (2013).

Carr wrote that Russert's death came at a time when the landscape of political coverage was changing. Blogs and online-only news organizations were changing the way national politics were covered, political campaigns were changing. He posited that the loss of Russert inspired such widespread grief in D.C. because it further signaled to the elites that their idea of politics was on its way out. "Perhaps, in their bones, they are worried that if the king is gone, the kingdom will soon follow," he wrote (2008).

Michael Wright

See also: *Meet the Press;* NBC

Further Reading

Ball, Rick. 1998. *Meet The Press: 50 Years of History in the Making.* New York: McGraw-Hill.

Carr, David. 2008. "In Mourning for a Man, and His Era." *New York Times.* June 16. Accessed January 1, 2016. http://www.nytimes.com/2008/06/16/business/media/16carr.html.

Leibovich, Mark. 2013. *This Town: Two Parties and a Funeral—Plus Plenty of Valet Parking—in America's Gilded Capital.* New York: Blue Rider Press.

Novak, Robert D. 2008. "My Friend and My Source." *Washington Post.* June 19. Accessed January 1, 2016. http://www.washingtonpost.com/wp-dyn/content/article/2008/06/18/AR2008061802730.html.

Shafer, Jack. 2008. "The Canonization of Saint Russert: The Media Overdo the Death of a Journalist." Slate. June 16. Accessed January 1, 2016. http://www.slate.com/articles/news_and_politics/press_box/2008/06/the_canonization_of_saint_russert.html.

Steinberg, Jacques. 2008. "Tim Russert, 58, NBC's Face of Politics, Dies." *New York Times.* June 14. Accessed January 1, 2016. http://www.nytimes.com/2008/06/14/business/media/14russert.html?_r=0.

S

SALON

Salon is a digital magazine of politics and culture that has carved out a niche as a liberal journal that covers everything from trade agreements to the latest sex scandal. The site sometimes feels like a bizarre combination of high and low. One typical array of stories had "Donald Trump's xenophobic genius: The GOP frontrunner will never give up racist pandering—because it's working" sitting beside "13 of 'Girls' most cringe-worthy sex scenes."

The site was one of the earliest attempts at creating a unique online publication, launching in 1995. It was created by David Talbot and a handful of other reporters from the *San Francisco Examiner* who bolted the paper to embrace the Internet (and after a bitter newspaper strike in 1994). They sought to create an eclectic publication that was part alternative newsweekly and part journal of the culture of technology. The site at launch was unique to the Internet, with a visual layout reminiscent of a print magazine like the *New Yorker* and with lengthy interviews and feature stories. Throughout its early run, the site was often compared with Microsoft-backed Slate, which was run by more D.C.-centered Michael Kinsley. Talbot seemed to delight in the comparison, even while disparaging his competition. One article about the tiff reported, "Mr. Talbot enjoyed characterizing his publication as a kind of smokin'-in-the-boys-room renegade to Slate's trust-funded nerd, calling Salon 'sexier' and 'more fun' and deriding Mr. Kinsley's publication as an 'inside-the-Beltway read for an elite audience.' Mr. Kinsley often returned the volley, charging Salon with inflating its readership numbers, and challenging its decision to go public in 1999 (Salon's stock proved to be a flop)" (Pappu 2002).

In an ominously entitled *American Journalism Review* piece called "Can Salon Survive," from 2001, Talbot still expressed his underlying belief in the experiment. "'Where are the independent news voices on the Internet?' he asks. 'Where's the great, flourishing media democracy?' He clicks on his list of bookmarked sites, turning up, among others, CNN.com, Matt Drudge, Slate, NPR.org. 'Most of these are extensions of bigger media organizations,' he says somewhat dismissively, adding, 'There's got to be room for a few independent voices'" (Farhi 2001). From its inception, the site sought to defy the expectations of a digital publication. When most content was being shortened to work for readers with minute attention spans, Salon would craft long-form pieces on political issues. The site broke news on engaging stories like a secret deal between television producers and the White House to include anti-drug messages in their shows, and the site reaped attention for its investigations connected to the impeachment scandal of President Bill Clinton, including a story that outted a past affair by the Illinois congressman running Clinton's impeachment prosecution in the Senate. Throughout its history the publication has been home to provocative commentary about not just politics, but political coverage. It has blasted traditional political coverage, publishing a column from Jay Rosen that simply declared that campaign reporting "sucks." On social media, it has taken its political tilt to the left even more starkly, running, at least according to a group of researchers from Duke University, the third most liberal Twitter feed on the social media platform.

Although the site has carved out a somewhat unique space in the digital magazine world, it's a business that has struggled. The Salon Media Group public offering was, as Kinsey gleefully pointed out, a disaster. Financially, Salon has struggled since the day it launched. The company has tried several different pay models, including a premium service. Early on it came up with an innovative option, telling readers they could look at an advertisement before being allowed to read the story OR sign up for an ad-free premium service. At its peak, the site could boast 100,000 paying subscribers, but the number now hovers around 10,000. The company stock has not been north of $1 a share since 2008 and has sometimes plunged to 5 cents. Throughout its history, the site has experimented with business models. It purchased the online community "The WELL" in 1999 only to sell it to a group of long-time community members in 2012. It tried launching a blog platform called Open Salon in 2008, hoping to emulate the success of Huffington Post that launched as an aggregation of political blogs in 2005, only to watch the community slowly atrophy. It shuttered the entire thing in 2015.

The site continued to lose more than a million dollars a year and relies on occasional cash injections from wealthy patrons. Despite the hand wringing and continued economic struggles, the site continues to be a source for news, some 14 years after AJR warned the whole enterprise could collapse tomorrow. It has been an important platform for reporters and advocacy journalists like Glenn Greenwald. The reporter who would break the National Security Agency's widespread surveillance of Americans built a name for himself at Salon first. Other reporters like Andrew Leonard and Thomas Frank have carved out names for themselves, Leonard winning a 2012 Online Journalism Award for best explanatory journalism.

Although the site has offices in Washington, D.C., and New York City, the headquarters remain in San Francisco, where the site started 20 years ago. This left coast base has kept much of its political commentary even sharper than the east coast-based reporters. For example, the site maintains an entire section on Obamacare, the controversial health care legislation championed by President Barack Obama. One article mixes its criticism of Republican threats to revoke the legislation with the media's inability to accurately cover the story, writing, "The Affordable Care Act suffers from a condition that afflicts all controversial legislative achievements: its failures are closely scrutinized and widely covered, while its successes go largely unnoticed. This imbalance is understandable in some ways—'Law Functions as Planned' isn't as exciting a story as 'Law Flops in Embarrassing Faceplant Hah Hah Let's All Point and Laugh'" (Maloy 2015). With its unique west coast take on politics, ability to develop new voices of the left, and ability to defy the financial predictions of imminent collapse (at least for now), Salon remains a unique, left-leaning member of the digital media and an active contributor to the liberal wing of social media.

See also: Daily Kos; Huffington Post; Liberal Blogosphere; Slate

Further Reading

Farhi, Paul. 2001. "Can Salon Survive?" American Journalism Review. March. Accessed September 18, 2015. http://ajrarchive.org/article.asp?id=314.
Maloy, Simon. 2015. "Obamacare Is (Still) Working: California Puts the Lie to Right-Wing Horror Stories." Salon. July 31. Accessed September 19, 2015. http://www.salon.com/2015/07/31/obamacare_is_still_working_california_puts_the_lie_to_right_wing_horror_stories.
Pappu, Sridhar. 2002. "Slate is Becoming . . . Salon!" Observer. June 17. Accessed September 17, 2015. http://observer.com/2002/06/slate-is-becoming-salon.

SINGLE-ISSUE POLITICS

As political parties have receded in power, struggling to hold together electoral coalitions and to rein in their own members, a fragmented and controversial political system has grown to fill the power vacuum. This system is built less on broad coalitions of fairly like-minded voters and politically active groups and more on an uneasy agreement between narrowly interested, but often well-funded or highly motivated, groups that make a single issue their primary purpose. This system of politics imbues more power to highly organized and active groups like those that oppose or support abortion rights or gun control. Often these single-issue groups raise money and lobby on their one topic, casting aside other issues that may have more impact but attract less attention. These groups and the individuals who support them usually are taking their stand on the issue based on strong moral beliefs, making political compromise more difficult as such compromise is often viewed as political betrayal.

In American politics, single-issue movements began, for the most part, as startup political parties carved out an electoral foothold in a system dominated by two parties. These single-issue groups initially developed outside of the other parties, organizing start-up parties of their own. The Anti-Masonic Party and the Free Soil Party are two such groups that formed in the mid-nineteenth century. The anti-Masons made the influence of the secretive Freemasons' societies their core raison d'être. For the Free Soilers, it was an effort to develop a political party that neither endorsed the continued spread of slavery nor embraced the divisive politics of the abolitionist movement who wanted the slave system ended. In both cases, these parties were short lived, their political issues absorbed into the major parties, but they also indicate that even in the era of far stronger parties there was a tendency for political organizations to grow up around a specific issue. In the American system these groups rarely existed as standalone or permanent new parties, but rather a movement that caught fire and attracted one of the existing major parties to embrace their issue in hopes of attracting their supporters' electoral backing.

In recent years, fueled in part by the media and new technologies that allowed groups to organize without forming a formal political party, the stage was set to allow longer-lasting single-issue interest groups to form and thrive. Now able to attract supporters and financial backing, such groups are able to lobby candidates and elected officials to address the single issue that unifies them. These groups often rely on media attention and the emotional impact of their message to garner support and influence the political establishment. A straightforward example of this type of organization is MADD, Mothers Against Drunk Driving. The group grew out of one woman's tragedy and her determination that her daughter's death would not be in vain. On May 3, 1980, Clarence Busch struck and killed 13-year-old Carime Anne Lightner, or "Cari." Her mother Candy, enraged that Busch would serve a very light sentence and then be free again, joined by other mothers who had lost their children to drunk drivers, formed Mothers Against Drunk Driving. The group began as a way to shame public officials and the drivers themselves into addressing the issue. With attention and donations spurred by a made-for-television movie about the Lightners, MADD used its new strength to lobby for a 21-year-old drinking limit and a lower threshold for legally being considered intoxicated, advocating for strict federal and state policies and using the media to draw attention to the issue and the victims. Candy reflected later that Cari "was a remarkable child, and, thanks to the work of thousands of volunteers when MADD was grass roots, we saved thousands and now hundreds of thousands of lives. I know she would be proud" (We Save Lives).

MADD reflects many of the aspects that have marked the growth of single-issue advocacy groups: deeply held beliefs, deeply personal work, and a reliance on mass media to draw attention to the issue and pressure the political process to address it. What makes MADD unlike most other single-issue groups is the lack of an opposing point of view. There is no pro-drunk driving organization. Most single-issue groups have competing organizations seeking the exact opposite policies—a traditional example being the abortion debate.

The power of a single-issue group often comes down to whether the organization has the ability to rally enough support to help a candidate or whether the issue is so deeply felt that a sizable number of voters will cast their ballot based on the candidate's position. For these single-issue voters it does not matter what other issues the candidate may hold that the voter agrees with; it all comes down to that one topic and what the candidate says about it. In 2012, Gallup surveyed voters and found about 17 percent of voters would support candidates for major office who share their own views on abortion. "Gallup finds slightly more pro-life voters than pro-choice voters saying they will vote only for a candidate who shares their views, 21% vs. 15%. That represents 9% and 7%, respectively, of all voters—a slight pro-life tilt, albeit one that could potentially benefit pro-life Republican candidate Mitt Romney. Additionally, by 49% to 43%, pro-life voters are a bit more likely than pro-choice voters to say they will consider a candidate's position on abortion as one of many important factors in arriving at their vote choice. That means pro-choice voters are more likely than pro-life voters to say abortion is not a major issue to them" (Saad 2012). Although pro-life voters are more likely to rigidly demand their candidate agree with their position on abortion, the survey indicated that voters on both sides make the political litmus test an important consideration in whether to back a candidate—regardless of party or other issue positions. The fear is that these deeply held beliefs and the political ramifications of being seen as soft in your support for the single-issue group's positions could reach the point that political debates grind to a halt, crippled by the inability of interest-group-driven politicians to compromise on the issue.

Although many would argue this is more a hypothetical concern than a real one, others said the near-government shut down at the end of September 2015 was the result of single-issue politics run amok. That year, the continued function of the federal government was thrown into question after conservatives, headed by Texas senator and Republican presidential candidate Ted Cruz, threatened to block any continued funding of the federal government that included any support for Planned Parenthood. Planned Parenthood had become a hotspot in the abortion debate after anti-abortion activists recorded officials discussing the potential sale of aborted fetus tissue for research. The video fueled outrage at the organization and prompted pro-life politicians to argue that they would oppose any budget that included money for the group. Planned Parenthood, which has reported that about 3 percent of its services are actually abortions, receives some $350 million a year from government contracts and grants. None of that money is used for abortions—that is banned by federal law—but it does go to support women's health care and most of that money comes from Medicaid to help lower income women. Following the release of the video, conservatives rallied against the group, with Congress holding hearings and Cruz pledging to fight any budget that included funding.

The question of whether this debate should lead to a closure of the federal government highlighted how one subsector of a party—the pro-life Republicans who believe that a government shutdown was better than any money going to Planned Parenthood—could dictate what Congress does. David Harsanyi of the conservative website the Federalist said, "Conservatives will start to question whether this iteration of the Republican Party is worth even having it if they can't fight on an issue like this even with the threat of a shutdown . . . That's basically the only leverage they have and so I think they would blame the party. If it is worth it in the long run, I don't know" (To the Point 2015). But the idea was that for voters who believe strongly in limiting or banning abortions taking a stand for this issue, even if it threatened the government itself, would be worth it to prove the seriousness of their beliefs. This form of politics, while troubling to many, also reflects what some would say is a success of the grassroots activists who make up the party over the professional politicians who hold positions of authority in the government or the partisan apparatus.

In the end, the Republicans backed away from the threatened government shutdown. But the incident and the ensuing political turmoil within the Republican Party about whether and how far it was willing to fight on principles has caused many to worry that single-issue politics could threaten the political stability of the American system. They worry that if compromise is made impossible by interest groups whose legitimacy and fundraising support is based on standing up unswervingly for a single issue, then the political system may be held hostage repeatedly by politicians beholden to those groups for financial and electoral support. Even back in 1978 members had worried that this special interest funding and lobbying was skewing the political process. That year Massachusetts senator Edward Kennedy said during a campaign finance debate, "Representative government on Capitol Hill is in the worst shape I have seen it," adding, "The heart of the problem is that the Senate and the House are awash in a sea of special interest campaign contributions and special interest lobbying."

And this is the other element of single-issue politics that worries observers inside and outside the Beltway. If politics becomes a battle of who feels more strongly about one divisive issue, then a vocal and organized minority may outweigh the beliefs of large swaths of the population. According to President Barack Obama, this is what has plagued the issue of gun control in the United States for decades. Obama sought to pass new gun control legislation following the murder of 20 young children and six adults at a Connecticut elementary school in 2012. Despite the national horror that followed the shooting, no bill was passed by Congress. As additional mass shootings unfolded around the country, Obama would appear, call for people to help one another, and express increasing frustration at the political process that stymied any response. Following another shooting at an Oregon community college the president explained what the public needed to do if anything was going to change, telling people:

> You have to make sure that anybody who you are voting for is on the right side of this issue. And if they're not, even if they're great on other stuff, for a couple of election cycles you've got to vote against them, and let them know precisely why you're voting against them. And you just have to, for a while, be a single-issue voter because that's what is happening on the other side. And that's going to take some time. I mean, the NRA has had a good start. They've been at this a long time, they've perfected what they do. You've got to give them credit—they're very effective, because they don't represent the majority of the American people but they know how to stir up fear; they know how to stir up their base; they know how to raise money; they know how to scare politicians; they know how to organize campaigns. And the American people are going to have to match them in their sense of urgency if we're actually going to stop this. (Theen 2015)

Obama repeatedly cited surveys that noted that upwards of 93 percent of the American public supported the idea of background checks on all people attempting to purchase guns, but that did not seem to be enough to convince Congress. That reality is one of the difficult aspects of single-issue politics. As blogger Kevin Drum noted at *Mother Jones*, the political debate about guns hinges often on not what people believe but how important they think it is, noting, "Most polls don't tell us how deeply people feel. Sure, lots of Americans think that universal background checks are a good idea, but they don't really care that much. In a recent Gallup poll of most important problems, gun control ranked 22nd, with only 2 percent rating it their most important issue. Needless to say, though, gun owners are opposed to background checks, and they care a lot" (Drum 2015). Not only do these voters care a lot, but as Obama noted, they are supported by one of the most influential and controversial single-issue groups in the United States: the National Rifle Association. The NRA, which boasts 5 million members, has itself evolved to meet the needs of its members. For many years the organization focused on gun safety and marksmanship training at a time when the vast majority of its members owned guns for hunting. As gun ownership shifted away from hunters and to those who own guns for protection, the organization also shifted to focusing on questions of gun control and limiting legislation on private gun ownership. The organization spent, according to the Center for Responsive Politics, some $6.8 million in lobbying during 2013–2014 and another $28 million in outside spending on political contests. Gun control advocates have only been able to deploy a fraction of those totals and have never really approached the NRA in terms of active members.

This is the conundrum of single-issue groups: at what point does the interest of a minority of voters who believe strongly in one issue override the feelings of the majority of Americans who disagree, but do feel less passionately? The gun control debate, for most observers, is an example where a single-issue group has come to so dominate one policy question that even though the Pew Research Center reports 73 percent of the NRA's own members would support background checks for gun purchases, the organization's effective lobbying has thus far made it impossible for Congress to act. President Obama, frustrated by the what he saw as the inability of Congress to stand up to the pressure of this one single-issue group, finally proposed an executive order from the White House that required universal background checks for all gun purchases.

It is perhaps not surprising then that this fear, that politics would no longer represent the amorphous "people" but the more tangible and organized special interests, has been a refrain in political reform fights going back as far as the founding of the republic. Still there are those political scientists who argue the single-issue politics critique is off point and misses what these groups bring to the process. For example, MADD helped redefine the acceptance of drinking and driving, turning it from something generally tolerated and rarely punished severely to a major crime that can lead to lengthy prison sentences. Experts argue that groups like MADD and even the more controversial National Rifle Association play an important part to the political process, giving active individuals an avenue to effect policy and shape public debate. As one researcher put it, "While it would be foolish to understate the dilemmas policymakers face when the nation, as represented by issue groups, is divided on questions such as the place of women, the control of violence, or the proliferation of nuclear armaments, it is a mistake to malign citizen organizations. Their goal is to make the nation more democratic, to entice more people into responsible citizenship, to foster public discussion about the principles that guide us, and to ensure that the compromises that necessarily occur are based on broad understandings of the common good" (Tesh 1984).

This reality of single-issue groups should not be overlooked. In a political system often focused on maintaining the status quo and protecting the electoral interests of those already in office, single-issue groups are sometimes agents of political change that come from the ground up. They are less beholden to political parties and individuals and can advocate for change using mass media as well as political lobbying. In an era where political parties lack the ideological strength to maintain political discipline, these groups, for good or ill, sometimes wield it from the outside.

See also: Grassroots Campaigns; Political Parties

Further Reading

"Cari's Story." We Save Lives: Highway Safety Advocates. Accessed November 2, 2015. http://wesavelives.org/caris-story.

Drum, Kevin. 2015. "Gun Control's Biggest Problem: Most People Just Don't Care Very Much." *Mother Jones*. October 3. Accessed November 2, 2015. http://www.motherjones.com/kevin-drum/2015/10/gun-controls-biggest-problem-most-people-just-dont-care-very-much.

Saad, Lydia. 2012. "Abortion Is Threshold Issue for One in Six U.S. Voters." Gallup. October 2. Accessed November 2, 2015. http://www.gallup.com/poll/157886/abortion-threshold-issue-one-six-voters.aspx.

Tesh, Sylvia. 1984. "In Support of 'Single-Issue' Politics." *Political Science Quarterly* 99, no. 1 (Spring).

Theen, Andrew. 2015. "Obama Talks about Umpqua Shooting for Second Time (full transcript)." *The Oregonian/OregonLive*. Accessed October 2, 2015. http://www.oregonlive.com/pacific-northwest-news/index.ssf/2015/10/obama_talks_umpqua_shooting_fo.html.

"Will Single-Issue Politics Lead to a Government Shutdown?" 2015. To the Point. September 10. Accessed October 30, 2015. http://www.kcrw.com/news-culture/shows/to-the-point/will-single-issue-politics-lead-to-a-government-shutdown.

60 MINUTES

60 Minutes is CBS's premier newsmagazine show. With its scheduled broadcast following football on Sundays, the program for decades was one of the most popular shows on television. Its popularity spawned dozens of imitators on CBS and other networks, and its hard-hitting style and wild profitability helped shift the expectation of how news programs should look like on TV. Also, with a viewership unlike any other news venue, the program has been the go-to outlet for politicians looking to deal with scandal or raise their profile.

The program premiered on September 24, 1968, with what would become a familiar sound, the ticking of a stopwatch. On its debut program, co-host Harry Reasoner, who had held many positions within CBS, declared it a "kind of a magazine for television." The program mixed taped segments, commentaries, and erudite discussions, hosted by Reasoner and fiery correspondent Mike Wallace. Initially *60 Minutes* drew a modest audience as it bounced around time slots. Finally in 1971 it found its home at 6 p.m. on Sundays and moved to an hour later in 1975, where it still sits. That Sunday evening slot helped propel the program to the top five by the next year and by 1978, *60 Minutes* was the most popular program on television. Around the same time as the program first moved to Sunday, Reasoner left CBS and "the complexion of the broadcast soon changed as it began to reflect Wallace's more muscular style. It became harder in tone, more investigative in subject matter" (Gates 1978).

The program, created by longtime CBS News producer Don Hewitt, would become part current events variety show and part hard-hitting investigative series. It created a new style of television news journalism where the correspondent and their search for the truth became the storytelling technique. Fronted by original co-host Mike Wallace, these pieces often featured *60 Minutes* reporters chasing reluctant interviewees from their workplace, camera blazing and Wallace demanding answers. The audience loved the technique, but some of those who helped found CBS News were worried about what the program was becoming. By 1983, former CBS News president and fabled Edward R. Murrow producer Fred Friendly worried publically, "You can't think of audience first and substance second. *60 Minutes* has become a caricature of itself, the avenging angels who swoop in wherever there is trouble, wave their mighty electronic cape, slay the dragon, and leave in time for the next commercial. They're trapped in that form" (Schwartz 1983). Others worried the new form of journalism that the program encouraged focused on making the reporter, rather than the story, the star. The correspondents for the show would become some of the best paid and most praised reporters in the business and the celebrity correspondent became more a fixture of television news.

Despite the concerns that Friendly and others have expressed over the style of the newsmagazine, Hewitt and others always had a good response. But it works on TV. More than that, it works for advertisers on TV. The economic force of *60 Minutes* was hard to overstate. In 2001, Hewitt said the program made CBS a profit of $1 million an episode. And that fact was critical to the program that showed up on the air each week, he said, telling C-SPAN, "It was the most profitable broadcast in the history of television . . . And so the luxury—what you get from that is they leave you alone, and nobody messes with you. And you become a 900-pound gorilla because you make a lot of money. And I must say, they do leave us alone" (Lamb 2001).

But the profitability also provoked another understandable reaction. CBS executives sought to recreate the magic of the program and network competitors ABC and NBC tried to copy the program's success, giving birth to a series of newsmagazines, from *Dateline* on NBC, to *20/20* and *Primetime Live* on ABC, to *48 Hours* and *60 Minutes II* on CBS. Many of these programs returned a sizable profit but none could ever eclipse the original in terms of audience and profitability. Hewitt himself answered his critics like Friendly and others by telling them they needed to face the reality of television—"It was never entirely about journalism even in the good old days. William S. Paley of CBS, David Sarnoff of NBC, and Leonard Goldenson of ABC were businessmen, and the companies they headed were then and are today profit-making enterprises. The difference between then and now is that they were obliged to give something back in exchange for their use of the public airwaves. That was what the Federal Communications Commission demanded. So if news was a loss leader, that was the price of doing business. *60 Minutes* ended that" (Hewitt 2002). Hewitt's ability to embrace the entertainment and business sides of the business in a much more aggressive way than Murrow and Friendly had in the 1950s helped cement the program's success within the network.

This economic strength was built on the size of the *60 Minutes* audience, which was unparalleled in television news. The program topped the ratings chart for years, drawing 20 million or more viewers in its treasured Sunday night slot. This audience made the program a powerful force in campaign news coverage. The outlet became a primary venue for politicians seeking to reach the largest possible audience. Even though the show was known for its combative investigations, the program also would do lengthy, although edited, interviews where the correspondent sat down only with the politician. This created a safer environment since the program would not then interview other sources for the piece. One example of this role came in 1992 when Bill Clinton, battling a potentially fatal flurry of stories about a possible affair with former Arkansas model and actress Gennifer Flowers, appeared one Sunday with his wife to answer questions, offering this famous exchange with *60 Minutes* correspondent Steve Kroft:

> *Kroft:* You've been saying all week that you've got to put this issue behind you. Are you prepared tonight to say that you've never had an extramarital affair?
>
> *Bill Clinton:* I'm not prepared tonight to say that any married couple should ever discuss that with anyone but themselves. I'm not prepared to say that about anybody. I think that the . . . .
>
> *Kroft:* . . . That's what you've been saying essentially for the last couple of months.
>
> *Bill Clinton:* . . . You go back and listen to what I've said. You know, I have acknowledged wrongdoing. I have acknowledged causing pain in my marriage. I have said things to you tonight and to the American people from the beginning that no American politician ever has.

Clinton is but one of the many politicians who have appeared on the program, and the correspondents' reports have fueled political debate on issues both foreign and domestic. Although the program no longer draws the numbers it did as viewership of news continues to fragment across cable channels and the Internet, the program remains the top-rated news show on television, bringing in an average 12.2 million viewers a week, more than double the next newsmagazine and 3 million more than the nightly network news.

See also: Broadcast Television News; CBS News; *Face the Nation*; Murrow, Edward

Further Reading

Gates, Gary Paul. 1978. *Air Time: The Inside Story of CBS News*. New York: Harper & Row, Publishers.

Hewitt, Don. 2002. *Tell Me a Story: 50 Years and 60 Minutes in Television*. New York: Public Affairs Publishers.

Lamb, Brian. 2001. "Booknotes." C-SPAN. April 1. Accessed July 20, 2015. http://www.booknotes.org/Watch/163061-1/Don+Hewitt.aspx.

Schwartz, Tony. 1983. "The Lessons of the '60 Minutes' Case." *New York Magazine*. June 20.

SLATE

Michael Kinsley was a journalist at the top of his game. As editor of the *New Republic* starting in 1979, he had guided the magazine to be one of the most respected left-leaning periodicals in the country. His column, TRB, had also established him as one of the most reputable liberal thinkers on politics. By 1989 he had joined the popular CNN political talk show *Crossfire*.

Then he did something in 1995 no one would have expected. He quit all of it to start a new online publication funded by Microsoft called "Slate."

The new magazine, based in Seattle, would offer online readers an original publication that would mirror some of the liberal-leanings and contrarian attitude that Kinsley brought to the *New Republic*. It was a unorthodox approach to bring to the web, at this point so focused on snark and brevity, a more linear and traditional voice. But as Ken Auletta described in 1996, "Kinsley is an unabashed elitist, dismissive of the tell-me-what-you-think Zeitgeist of the Web. He does not apologize: 'I'm too old to go whoring after twenty-somethings.' Later, he adds, 'I'm operating on the assumption that you can give people a meal'" (Auletta 1996).

To hear journalists and even Kinsley discuss the online magazine, the focus was as much on the finances of online-only publication as creating a new voice or platform for political and other forms of reporting. But this experiment was important in testing whether independent journalism could sustain itself in this new medium. Looking back a decade later it was this conceptual test that Kinsley said drove much of his work. Despite having the backing of technology giant Microsoft, Kinsley stressed that "for a publication, like an individual, financial independence brings intellectual independence. The technical term for this, I believe, is "f***youability" (FUA) . . . The theory that Slate set out to prove was that the Internet made FUA more widely available. From the beginning, the economics of publishing on the Internet—no paper, no printing, no postage—were more important to us than the hyperlinks and the multimedia. In a way, though, we got this point wrong. Slate is sleek compared with equivalent paper magazines, but we are a galumphing contraption compared with blogs and wikis and instant messaging and other Internet innovations" (Kinsley 2006).

But many of those innovations have created a new wave of political reporting and commentary that has been a hallmark of Slate. Perhaps none were more important than the "Gabfest" podcasts. The initial podcast, launched in 2003, was focused on politics. To hear one of the producers describe its development, it was really about creating a political talkshow that felt more genuine. NPR veteran and new podcast producer Andy Bowers remembers, "I would listen to our Slate editorial conference calls, where people just love to throw out ideas and debate them and argue about them, and they were really funny and fun and insightful . . . I thought, you know, if I could just capture this in a podcast, I think people would [find it] really interesting. It would be like the discussion the political reporters have at the bar" (Phelps 2012). That podcast, coupled with others on books, culture, and sports, attracts some 2 million downloads a month, creating another major way in which the magazine both attracts revenue and affects the dialogue.

The Slate model has been successful enough for its producers, the Slate Media Group, to launch a companion service in France in 2009. The producers argued, "If it works in France, it will absolutely be a very powerful argument to try in other international territories . . . if it becomes financially self-supporting and sustainable and supports high-quality web journalism" (Andrews 2009). It is currently a model that has gone through several iterations, and weathered the departure of Kinsley and many of the other founding editors, and still survives.

Underlying its political reporting and business model is a focus on analytics, that is the measuring of what people read or download. The corporate hierarchy of Slate has, at times, relied on Microsoft's support to get it through difficult years and so Kinsley's FUA remains an elusive beast, but its publishers feel its latest focus on what it calls "evidence"-based editorial decisions will help ensure its economic independence. To do that, "Slate's latest incarnation is as a data-driven social-media beast. The site thinks it can use viral wizardry to spray smart writing around the internet and, at the same time, finally earn a profit from being perspicuous. The money question has become pressing because Slate, despite its years as a high-brow conversation starter, has yet to show it can survive without the largesse of a corporate mothership" (Roberts 2013). This focus on data-driven decisions has worried some that see it as a ticket to creating low-news features that aim to garner social media traffic, but Slate argues it doesn't have to be that.

The site aims to attract an educated, usually liberal elite—the kind Kinsley himself sought to draw some 20 years ago—and that has led to the creation of features that draw repeated visitors. With special features on science and a still-heavy focus on political debates playing out in Washington and in state capitals around the country, the site works to attract continued sponsorship even as it delivers far more readers than most other high-brow media outlets online.

Further Reading

Andrews, Robert. 2009. "Interview: Jacob Weisberg, Chairman, Slate Group: Breaking Out of the Beltway." CBS News. February 15. Accessed January 16, 2015. http://www.cbsnews.com/news/interview-jacob-weisberg-chairman-slate-group-breaking-out-of-the-beltway.

Auletta, Ken. 1996. "The Re-education of Michael Kinsley." *New Yorker*. May 13. Accessed January 17, 2015. http://www.kenauletta.com/reeducationofmichaelk.html.

Kinsley, Michael. 2006. "My History of Slate." Slate. June 18. Accessed January 17, 2015. http://www.slate.com/articles/news_and_politics/slates_10th_anniversary/2006/06/my_history_of_slate.html.

Phelps, Andrew. 2012. "Slate Doubles Down on Podcasts, Courting Niche Audiences and Happy Advertisers." Nieman Labs. June 4. Accessed January 15, 2015. http://www.niemanlab.org/2012/06/slate-doubles-down-on-podcasts-courting-niche-audiences-and-happy-advertisers.

Roberts, John Jeffery. 2013. "The Brain of the New York Times, the Body of BuzzFeed—Slate's Third Act." Gigaom. February 5. Accessed January 16, 2015. https://gigaom.com/2013/02/05/the-brain-of-the-new-york-times-the-body-of-buzzfeed-slates-third-act.

SOCIAL MEDIA AND POLITICS

Social media, with its easy content creation and distribution and ability to catch viral fire, has had a profound impact on almost every aspect of modern politics. As a source of information (and misinformation), a tool to rally support, and a dangerously decentralized medium, social media and especially social networks like Facebook and Twitter have become major platforms for those seeking political support and governmental change. The tools themselves, while largely apolitical, are used both by activists outside the political mainstream and by the institutions that make up the mainstream and empower those with political authority. The tools have also made it easier for individuals to express their opinions on political issues, but have created a public space where some feel inhibited from posting their views for fear of online or real world backlash.

It is important to understand what social media is, to fully comprehend the breadth of the changes this form of media has had on politics and journalism. Social media should be understood as any media built to be shared across the Internet. This includes blogging as well as the social networking tools like Facebook, LinkedIn, and Twitter. Often social media is used as shorthand for the social networks, but is actually a broader form of communication and also a bit older. Blogs date back to the late 1990s and served as the first major disruptor of the Internet age. Up until the time that publishing platforms became easier to use, producing content for the World Wide Web, while cheaper than any other form of production, still required a level of technical understanding and competency to achieve. Blogging simplified the production of web content and allowed anyone able to order a book from Amazon to become a publisher. This reality represented the most significant shift in the power to publish information since the creation of the printing press. Although blogging required Internet connectivity, a fact that limited the number of people who could participate, it allowed hundreds of thousands of people to begin publishing information that others could consume, comment on, and later share with the social networks.

With the advent of social networks like MySpace and later Facebook and Twitter in the mid-2000s, the publishing power of blogging became more connected with people's networks of friends, colleagues, and families, allowing people to easily share snippets of thoughts, photos, links to web content, and other material.

The result was a new networked media that people not only consumed, but produced content for. Experts and social scientists struggle to find analogies to convey how profound a shift from the mass media world this truly represented, but one analysis described the new social media platform as "not only instant and transspatial but multilateral, including many participants and connecting many different activist groups. Not since the institutionalization of the U.S. Postal Service have we seen a communication development in society that can give power to individuals like this" (McCaughey and Ayers 2003).

This decentralization of both content production and information distribution has affected both campaigns and the news media from the earliest incarnations of social content. Many early blogs focused on political issues, often giving voice to partisan views not fully embraced by the editorial gatekeepers of traditional media outlets. As social networks evolved, people often shared political content across their networks, posting articles, commenting on political figures, and liking candidate pages on Facebook or following campaigns on Twitter. The effect social media had on all of this communication can be broken down into essentially three core changes: It allowed campaigns and political figures to push communications directly to the public and supporters without the media. It also allowed the candidates, policy makers and the media to gather input and garner nearly instant reactions from the connected public. Finally, it empowered interested members of the public to share their own views with one another directly.

Blogs began affecting politics from a very early age. By 2001 Josh Marshall had launched Talking Points Memo. The next year, when former senate Majority Leader Trent Lott spoke at the 100th birthday party of South Carolina senator Strom Thurmond and appeared to endorse his segregationist policies of the 1940s, Marshall had a platform to speak out on an issue he felt the mainstream press was missing. He later told PBS's *Frontline*, "When you unpacked what Trent Lott said, it was really egregious. It was terrible . . . In the way that the news media works, a story really has a 24-hour audition, that it makes its case whether it's going to catch fire and whether it's going to become a real story. And that story failed its 24-hour audition . . . I think in a pre-blog world that would have been the end of it. But my blog and others picked up the story and basically started making the case for it, that it was a lot more important than the rest of the news media had thought" (*Frontline* 2007). Liberal blogs lit up, citing Marshall's posts and keeping the story alive. The mainstream press soon picked up the story and Lott was forced to resign over the comments. The incident highlighted the new role that individual writers could play in driving the political narrative and in questioning the decisions by the mainstream media.

But social media also became a tool for more than just political commentators. The ability to easily gather and publish information without having to go through the traditional media created a new avenue for political organizations and campaigns to target their opponents. By 2004 and 2006, campaigns began sending out volunteers and hiring young people to serve as trackers. These campaign workers would document everything an opponent said or did, snapping photos, capturing videos, and sending the material back to campaign HQs. This may seem inconsequential, but in 2006 the power of full time tracking blew up in the hotly contested U.S. Senate race in Virginia. That year Republican senator George Allen pointed to a volunteer for Democrat Jim Webb, telling a crowd, "This fellow here, over here with the yellow shirt, Macaca, or whatever his name is. He's with my opponent. He's following us around everywhere. And it's just great," later adding, "Let's give a welcome to Macaca, here. Welcome to America and the real world of Virginia" (Craig and Shear 2006). Macaca is a derisive term for African immigrants and the volunteer was an Indian American. He was also armed with a camera, capturing Allen's comments and propelling the story onto social media. The video, uploaded to YouTube, soon was airing on cable channels and fueled a public outcry over the candidate's comments. Allen later apologized, but the incident forced the campaign off message and onto the defensive for weeks. Webb would end up beating Allen in a close contest, and trackers became a permanent fixture of major campaigns. Every public moment of a candidate's life is now likely captured and can be turned into social media or traditional advertising within hours.

New media like Facebook and Twitter also empower the individual to participate in politics as never before. Individuals can produce and share political commentary, share links to articles about current public issues, and affiliate with causes and candidates publically. Social media has become a new sort of yard sign, a public way to express support for an idea or individual. Much like the commercial world, this publicity from an individual has become a sort of Holy Grail for political marketers who know having a friend or respected colleague express support for something has much more power than a commercial. The concept is sometimes called "citizen advertising" and, according to marketing experts who have studied it:

> [Citizen advertising] can appear on video-sharing sites like YouTube, and links to them may be embedded in blogs or on social-networking sites. Their distribution grows virally . . . Consumers of organic citizen ads are influenced by the credibility and authenticity that accompanies communication that is not sponsored by a commercial entity but is offered for consideration from one consumer to another. (Tuten 2008)

This concept has bled into modern campaigns, who now aim to craft messages that don't just resonate with individuals, but spur them to share those ideas with their network of friends. Even beyond campaigns, elected officials have embraced the idea to build and maintain the public's opinion of the political figure. Minnesota's governor, for example, has taken to creating entries on Buzzfeed, the popular website known for its listicles (articles that are essentially just one person's opinion) and their social media share-ability. Governor Mark Dayton has made these lists a part-humorous, part-Minnesota pride, part-political communication platform, producing a list of "26 More Reasons to Love Minnesota" that included the governor signing the bill to legalize same-sex marriage in 2013, and "9 Thoughts That Go through Your Mind at the Minnesota State Fair" that ended with a call for volunteers for the governor's re-election campaign. The Dayton campaign used these posts to reach not only supporters but those who would not traditionally follow the Democratic governor of Minnesota.

For all the power of social media to help politicians shape their connection with the public and make direct appeals for support and donations, social media has also been a perilous platform that has helped ruin several high profile politicians who were caught because of their use of social media. Candidates like Donald Trump, who made a media career by being abrasive and outlandish, could face intense questioning over what they had tweeted out or posted to Facebook. And other times politicians have been caught using social media for sexually inappropriate behavior, like former congressman Anthony Weiner who was forced to resign his leadership position and seat because of sexually graphic tweets that became public.

Underlying all of these stories and trends is a fundamental shift in politics from a more controlled top-down domination of public discussion by campaigns, to a more decentralized reality where individuals in the public can operate, organize, and communicate independently. Many early advocates for the Internet hoped to see social media become a sort of electronic town hall where issues could be publically debated and consensus found between those who govern and the governed. The hope was that this digital meeting house could help shape policy at the local, state, and national level. Many candidates have espoused belief in this idea of a more participatory system, but as the technology has changed and more and more people have come to use the system to try and shape public opinion, the potential of social media to be a place of political discussion and consensus-finding has remained unfulfilled. One examination of the proclamations of then-candidate Barack Obama and the actions of President Obama found that the actions of leaders rarely live up to the empowered individuals candidates claim to want. They wrote, "[W]e continue to see social media as a mirage insofar as they can be used to have the wishes and ideas of the general public play into the macro-level decisions and choices of policy-makers. The mirage has an appealing, refreshing, even energizing image; hovering as it does on the horizon, it seems real and reachable. But even as we press our way toward it . . . it eludes us, and remains as far away as when we started" (Katz, Barris, and Jain 2013).

This illusion of the power social media could possess has been undercut, oftentimes, by its very decentralized nature. Social media does little to bring those of differing views together, but rather allows them often talk only with one another. By reducing the role of gatekeepers and allowing individuals to filter their own sources of information through choosing whom to follow or friend, political partisanship has actually been partially fueled by this technology. Now groups can self-segregate around ideas, developing blogs and Twitter feeds that support certain views on controversial issues. This makes the establishing of basic facts even more difficult. For example, for years a group of conspiracy theorists have contended that

President Barack Obama was not born in the United States and should, therefore, be disqualified to serve as commander-in-chief. Any factual examination of the record has found that Obama was born in Hawaii, as he claims, but still a solid social media-driven campaign rejects these facts and continues to fuel the myth. In a traditional mass media world, very few news outlets would report such a claim and the solid drumbeat of reporting would make it a rumor that only existed on the very fringes of society. In a social media age, this fringe can organize around the idea, build supporters, and communicate with them directly. As one liberal activist concluded, "[S]ocial media, like all media before them, can be used by institutions as well as individuals, and either for good or for ill, to transmit lies or truth and to promote or constrain liberty" (O'Connor 2012). These tools are powerful, but are also open to the manipulation and misinformation that any media can create and those potentials for misuse increase as the ease of using them improves.

And the other fact is that they are now firmly engrained in the political process for many people. A survey in 2012 found that some 66 percent of those people who used social networking sites participated in civic activities through those accounts. The survey from the Pew Research Center found that "younger users are more likely to post their own thoughts about issues, post links to political material, encourage others to take political action, belong to a political group on a social networking site, follow elected officials on social media, and like or promote political material others have posted" (Raine 2012). This means that younger Americans are more likely to be the citizen advertisers mentioned early and means as this group becomes older, their perception of political involvement and their willingness to express their political views online could continue to shape campaigns.

This reality worries some who say that it is important to remember that the tools that drive social media are themselves not devoid of politics. These thinkers worry that as the push to decentralize politics picks up more steam, the potential for abuse increases as well. Social media received much of the credit for helping fuel a series of uprisings against authoritarian regimes in the Middle East in 2010 and 2011, but others argue that it is as much a tool of repression as it is a weapon of freedom. Those uprisings led in some cases to political reforms, but in others to now-endemic violence in much of the region, fueled by the rise of groups like ISIS that use social media to communicate and coordinate. Evgeny Morozov is a Belarusian who wonders if people who see these tools as great emancipators are putting too much faith in a flawed instrument, writing, "Internet-centrists like to answer every question about democratic change by first reframing it in terms of the Internet rather than the context in which that change is to occur. They are often completely oblivious to the highly political nature of technology, especially the Internet, and like to come up with strategies that assume that the logic of the Internet . . . will shape every environment that it penetrates rather than vice versa" (Morozov 2011).

But as much as Morozov and others worry about the agenda of the tools themselves and others worry about the polarization the tools may enable, the tenor and volume of the debate itself is perhaps the best indicator of the degree to which these tools are now shaping the discussion and much of people's understanding of modern politics in the United States.

See also: Internet Advertising; Political Polarization and the Media; Post-Truth Politics

Further Reading

Craig, Tim, and Michael Shear. 2006. "Allen Quip Provokes Outrage, Apology." *Washington Post*. August 15. Accessed August 11, 2015. http://www.washingtonpost.com/wp-dyn/content/article/2006/08/14/AR2006081400589.html.

Frontline. 2007. "News War Transcript." PBS. Accessed February 15, 2015. http://www.pbs.org/wgbh/pages/frontline/newswar/etc/script3.html.

Katz, James, Michael Barris, and Anshul Jain. 2013. *The Social Media President*. New York: Palgrave Macmillan.

McCaughey, Martha, and Michael Ayers. 2003. *Cyberactivism*. New York: Routledge.

Morozov, Evgeny. 2011. *The Net Delusion*. New York: Public Affairs Books.

O'Connor, Rory. 2012. *Friends, Followers and the Future*. San Francisco: City Light Books.

Raine, Lee. 2012. "Social Media and Political Engagement." Pew Research Center. October 19. Accessed August 11, 2015. http://www.pewinternet.org/2012/10/19/social-media-and-political-engagement.

Tuten, Tracy. 2008. *Advertising 2.0: Social Media Marketing in a Web 2.0 World*. Westport, CT: Praeger.

SOUND-BITE POLITICS

As television, particularly commercial television, came to dominate how people were exposed to politics, political thinkers and some within the media grew concerned that television's tendency to simplify complex debates into two-sided arguments could be damaging to the American system. Experts worried that television's need to focus on the personal story and its increasingly brief storytelling format would make it harder for the public to find a middle ground on multifaceted issues. This concern came to be symbolized by the debate over the dreaded sound bite.

Sound bites, as a term, emerged in the 1980s as a way to describe that perfect quote that was short, pithy, or provocative and summed up one side of an argument. The single line that would capture the point of a speech or the key elements of the argument became the focus of politicians and speechwriters. These professionals knew that television networks would often grab the same quote because it was, in many ways, served up with them in mind, accompanied with the appropriate backdrop during a speech or delivered by a surrogate or adviser in a series of interviews. The phrase would be repeated over and over again in different interviews to ensure the consistency of the message. The result was stories that often echoed the core argument that the campaign aimed to make. But experts argue that the television media's inability to embrace complex discussion allows politicians to oversimplify political debates into yes/no questions. Is abortion murder? Should we militarize the border? Is the war on terrorism being fought correctly? Writing about her frustration of the tone and tenor of the 2012 election, the first in which she would be able to vote, Danielle Fong vented in the *Columbia Review of Politics*, "Politics always has had mudslinging and distracting sound bites, but in this election we are faced with two competing visions for the American government to bring the country out of its economic recession. We know the choices boil down to allocation of taxes and spending, but how either side wants to tackle these and actually achieve the bipartisan goal of deficit reduction is a mystery and certainly not one solved by 'gotcha' sound bites" (Fong 2012). Fong's critique is the common refrain of frustration that candidates have overly simplified the issues at stake in the election and that this simplification is a product of the focus on making a political argument that will resonate on television.

Television swept past other media as the primary way in which people receive their news in the post–World War II period, quickly consolidating its importance as the premier medium for politics. By the 1960s, it was assumed that campaigns would begin factoring into their operations television advertising. This pushed campaigns to adopt television friendly slogans and jingles, replacing the campaign buttons that for decades had captured the slogan of the campaign. TV advertising quickly became the largest line-item in most candidate budgets. And even in the Internet age television still retains much of its power. A summer 2015 assessment from the Pew Research Center found that 60 percent of baby boomers still rely on local television for their election news. The number slips to about 50 percent for Generation X and down to 37 percent for so-called Millennials. Still, with the baby boomers making the largest voting group, the role of television remains fairly entrenched in the political process.

It is important to note that when people discuss television and its power in the political process, they usually mean local broadcast television. Cable news networks make a mark, true, but the structure of local television news contributes enormously to the power of the sound bite. Another Pew report noted that as of 2012 the average length of a local television news report sat at 41 seconds. At that length, there is little room for lengthy discussion, so the importance of *the* quote increased. It became a quest for a single bit of audio that captured not just the policy but the drama of the story. It is that quest for a source to supply both that also fuels problems with local news coverage. As one political scientist noted, "Often, the sound bite which makes it to the air is not the comment that best summarizes the speaker's position, but the one which captures the most emotional, dramatic, or controversial remarks . . . as a result of such tendencies, colorful and charismatic politicians often come to be covered more extensively—and taken more seriously by the public—than their election chances warrant" (Kaniss 1991).

Nearly all academics who have studied the media and politics will at some point take a shot at television as one of the things wrong with the American system. In their analyses, television does not operate by appealing to the intellect, but by banking on emotion. One lengthy examination of what the sound bite-obsession had done to the American political mind noted, "Television, in nearly all its forms and functions, and for both economic and structural reasons, acts as a simplifying lens, filtering out complex ideas in favor of blunt emotional messages that appeal to the self and to narrower moral-political impulses" (Scheuer 1999). Jeffrey Scheuer goes on to argue that this narrowing of the political world to more basic dichotomies is, itself, biased towards political conservativism, which he says is a politically less complex philosophy. While not tackling the validity of the simplicity of conservative ideas compared to liberalism, the underlying reality that television simplifies the political debate is one scholars across the spectrum generally adhere to.

As negative as those assessments are of the sound bite trend, the news gets only worse when one considers how the quote itself has changed. According to research—basically political scientists clocking with a stop watch how long television news programs allow a politician to talk—news organizations have contracted from lengthy, uninterrupted quotes to dizzyingly quick bursts of sound bites. One piece of research found in 1968 CBS News produced a segment on Vice President Hubert Humphrey and Republican Richard Nixon that used five quotations from the candidates with an average length of 60 seconds each. The same researcher found that in 1992 a segment on the presidential campaign included 10 sound bites of the candidates that averaged 8.5 seconds.

But it is also something that television producers have experimented with ways to combat. Criticism of the shallowness of political reporting has caused reporters to periodically reconsider the way they do their jobs. For example, in 1992 CBS News, the home of Edward R. Murrow and Walter Cronkite, took a stand. That year CBS said it would not use any sound bite that was less than 30 seconds. It failed and nine years later a columnist would write in the *Boston Globe*, "Whether running for president of the United States or for city council, politicians can count on seeing their words broken into ever smaller and more fragmentary bits. You might debate whom to blame—asked about nine-second sound bites, one TV executive replied, 'the politicians started it'—but you can't dispute the trend. In recent presidential elections, the average TV sound bite has dropped to a tick under eight seconds. A shorter, dumber, and shriller political discourse, it seems, has become another hazard of modern life" (Fehrman 2011).

But more than just a hazard of political life, the reducing of political issues to nine-second chunks is partly a result of careful planning by campaigns to take advantage of television journalists' need to find the sound bite that captures the story. Candidates and consultants quickly came to understand that developing the perfect sound bite and placing it in the right setting could almost guarantee media coverage. Any assessment of the sound bite cannot solely blame the press, as the development of sound bites and the strategy of who will deliver them to the media is a significant part of the daily political communications strategy. Campaigns will develop provocative, funny, and very much canned one-liners they feel will earn them media coverage. Some candidates who lack significant resources may rely on extremely provocative quotes in the hope of winning "free media"—the campaign term for news coverage or television appearances they do not have to pay for.

But it is not just broke candidates who can use the sound bite focus to win a lot of media attention. The king of this in recent elections may be real estate mogul and reality television star Donald Trump who every couple days during the 2016 campaign would end up in the nightly news with quotes like his description of former GOP nominee and Vietnam War hero John McCain—"He's not a war hero. He was a war hero because he was captured. I like people who weren't captured." Or his description of the immigration crisis—"When Mexico sends its people, they're not sending the best. They're sending people that have lots of problems and they're bringing those problems. They're bringing drugs, they're bringing crime. They're rapists and some, I assume, are good people, but I speak to border guards and they're telling us what we're getting." Those outspoken comments garnered enormous media attention and were played again and again by local, national, and cable television. Despite the anger they provoked from many, the attention and the publicity helped keep Trump atop polls and aided in his capturing the Republican nomination.

But even a candidate's ability to get their sound bite picked up by the press is only a partial success. Candidates and political consultants have often groused about the story the journalists construct around the campaign's canned sound bite, with one campaign handbook complaining, "In addition to shortening the time for a candidate to speak, the news media also focus little of their coverage on real or substantive public issues, preferring instead to fill news time with discussions of campaign strategy, analyzing the campaign as a 'horserace.' Breaking through the wall of journalistic narcissism that focuses more on what journalists think than on what the candidates say and casting campaign news in a continuously negative light presents modern campaigns with difficult challenges" (Johnson 2010). Of course, it probably goes without saying that should the media cover substantive issues of the campaign in a way that does not align with the campaign's interest, they would probably express frustration with that as well.

The power of the sound bite is directly related to the power of television as the dominant political medium and as was noted earlier, a change appears in the works. Millennials—those born in the 1980s and 1990s—increasingly turn to Facebook and Twitter for their political news and with that shift to a new medium there could be a shift in the depth and complexity of news. The Internet is now the home of sites like the *New York Times*' Upshot and Vox that market themselves as explaining the context of the "bigger story." This medium can allow voters to explore lengthy white papers, watch full-length issue documentaries, and seek independent sources. All of this is true, just like television is home to hour-long documentaries about presidential candidates and lengthy policy discussions on the *PBS NewsHour*. But like the sound bite of television, the current currency of political communication is the tweet. Twitter, with its 140-character burst of communication, takes almost all of the concepts and problems of the sound bite and updates them for the twenty-first century by moving them from the TV to the iPhone or Android. Consider this online piece of advice about how to think about a tweet:

> Let's dissect a tweet.
> It's a very short statement.
> It takes less than five seconds to read.
> It's authenticated, so it's likely to come directly from the source.
>
> Sounds a little like a sound bite, doesn't it? Sure, that last one could be faked or given by an intern or PR person, but that's the same as a lot of public statements. They're written by publicists and access is carefully planned. (Moneta 2010)

Like the much-maligned sound bite, tweets from candidates are often heavily strategized and coordinated by the campaign communications team. These professionals will consider everything from how best to phrase a tweet to what hashtags to use. In fact, politicians who do not embrace the heavily structured and vetted use of Twitter become news unto themselves. For example, Republican senator Chuck Grassley became a sort of cult figure for his clearly uncoordinated tweets that ranged from: "Fred and I hit a deer on hiway 136 south of Dyersville. After I pulled fender rubbing on tire we continued to farm. Assume deer dead" to "Just turned to history channel. No history. I used to get history. Why do we h v such a channel when it doesnt do history." Grassley said he took to the social media as a way to bypass the media which he accuses of being liberal. But those who following his wandering Twitter feed found his use something to marvel at. Yahoo News's Virginia Heffernan described it as, "Grassley has been zealously tweeting for a full four and a half years, employing a reckless but not uncongenial style, like a competent fiddler who late in life takes up the hurdy-gurdy . . . Twitter just speaks to some people. They get religion and learn it as they go" (Heffernan 2012). What makes Grassley's feed so unique is it does not read like a series of carefully planned sound bites, which is how the vast majority of politicians and campaigns approach social media; instead it sounds like the senator talking off the cuff.

Twitter and other social media have added a new tension to the old sound bite argument. In particular, Twitter still limits the depth of content that can be conveyed in any single tweet, but the social media outlet also presents political actors with the ability to break out of the highly scripted world of television-driven sound bite campaigning. But for all that freedom, few candidates choose to embrace it as such. To move beyond the carefully vetted and considered quip or one-liner is to risk making a damaging and continuously retweeted mistake.

But when candidates or politicos express frustration with the need to speak in sound bites, their usual target is obvious—the media. Howard Dean, the former presidential candidate and head of the Democratic Party, said politicians are now too trained to supply anything more than the series of 10-second sound bites given their fear of how the press will use anything other than the most basic unit of political speech. Dean told a conference of the Mortgage Bankers Association that the only way to get the candidates to open up is to bar the press, saying, "Politicians are incredibly careful not to say anything if they can possibly help it, except if it is exactly scripted. And if you want to hear anybody's true views, you cannot do it in the same room as the press. If you want to hear the truth from them, you have to exclude the press" (Farrington 2007).

Dean's admonition seems especially prescient in the wake of the secretly recorded comments of GOP nominee Mitt Romney talking about the 47 percent of the American public he will never get to vote for him and don't pay taxes, or then-senator Obama's comments about some voters clinging to God and guns. In a world where anything can and often is recorded and posted, the sound bite politics that have frustrated decades of political observers have become even more entrenched given the always-on nature of the modern campaign. The result is, regardless of the rise of the Internet as a source for political news, campaigns are carefully scripting communication via Twitter and other media to ensure pick-up and retweets. Sound bites are still heard, but often now are never spoken and typically carry hashtags.

See also: Broadcast Television News; Social Media and Politics; Spin; Television Advertising

Further Reading

Farrington, Brendan. 2007. "Dean: Bar Media and Candidates Will Talk." *Washington Post*. April 27. Accessed November 20, 2015. http://www.washingtonpost.com/wp-dyn/content/article/2007/04/25/AR2007042500476.html.

Fehrman, Craig. 2011. "The Incredible Shrinking Sound Bite." *Boston Globe*. January 2. Accessed November 20, 2015. http://www.boston.com/bostonglobe/ideas/articles/2011/01/02/the_incredible_shrinking_sound_bite/?page=full.

Fong, Danielle. 2012. "Sound Bite Politics." *Columbia Review of Politics*. September 23. Accessed November 20, 2015. http://cpreview.org/2012/09/sound-bite-politics.

Heffernan, Virginia. 2012. "Leaves of Grassley: A Song of Chuck, the Senator from Twitter." Yahoo! News. April 12. Accessed November 20, 2015. http://news.yahoo.com/leaves-of-grassley—a-song-of-chuck—the-senator-from-twitter.html.

Johnson, Dennis. 2010. *Routledge Handbook of Political Management*. London: Routledge.

Kaniss, Phyllis. 1991. *Making Local News*. Chicago: University of Chicago Press.

Moneta, Brett. 2010. "Twitter Is the New Sound Bite." Digital Pivot. Accessed November 20, 2015. http://www.talentzoo.com/digital-pivot/blog_news.php?articleID=12272.

Scheuer, Jeffrey. 1999. *Sound Bite Society: Television and the American Mind*. New York: Four Walls Eight Windows.

SPIN

Modern political campaigns try to shape, regulate, and manage the news about their candidate. But sometimes things are outside of their control. A new piece of data causes trouble, an unscripted comment by a candidate or surrogate sparks outcry, or the campaign must respond to a news event while it is happening. During these scenarios, the idea of spin and the role of the so-called spin doctor has become a regular, if controversial, feature of political reporting.

Spin, at its core, was born in a desire by campaigns to manage the news that was generated about their candidate and the election. These management efforts emerged as campaigns moved from the sphere of political parties and into a profession where men and women prided themselves on running coherent and efficient campaigns. This included feeding the press, literally and metaphorically. Timothy Crouse in his Gonzo-style take on the 1972 campaign, *The Boys on the Bus*, wrote of this process, "While reporters still snored like Hessians in a hundred beds throughout the hotel, the McGovern munchkins were at work, plying the halls, slipping the long legal-sized handouts through the cracks under the door of each room. According to one of these handouts, the Baptist Ministers' Union of Oakland has decided after 'prayerful and careful deliberations' to endorse Senator McGovern. And there was a detailed profile of Alameda County ('. . . agricultural products include sweet corn, cucumbers, and lettuce'), across which the press would be dragged today—or was it tomorrow? Finally, there was the mimeographed schedule, the orders of the day" (Crouse 1973). Crouse's McGovern munchkins were some of the first, most passive, manifestations of news management, supplying helpful information and detailed schedules that the campaign expected would make their way into news articles, radio reports, and television segments. As campaigns became more aggressive about supplying specific arguments to the press, the role of spin became more central. With the advent of cable news and the emergence of the 24-hour news cycle, these communication experts moved more and more to the fore, becoming the official source for the quotes to contextualize the candidate's speech or campaign stop, offering a response to the accusation from the other campaign. These sources became more personalities unto themselves and consultants and spokespeople became political celebrities.

The idea of spin comes from sports like pool, tennis, and curling where putting a spin on the ball can allow the player to hit the desired target even if blocked. In political parlance it has become the term used to try and reframe a political development in a way that favors the campaign. By "framing" or describing an issue, candidate, or policy a certain way it creates an impression in the mind of a voter. Sometimes framing is far from subtle. For example, opponents of abortion do not use the medical term for a specific late-term abortion procedure known as "dilation and extraction." They framed it in the public debate by naming it "partial-birth abortion," an act that sounds inherently violent and by including the word birth in the name, very close to killing a child after it has been born. All of those words used to describe the same act but portray it in very different ways. Spin in the political context is slightly different, seeking to alter the reality of a story to serve the narrative or issues of a given candidate. The wordsmith William Safire once used another sport—baseball—to capture the essence of spin, saying that the English the pitcher put on the "ball causes it to appear to be going in a slightly different direction than it actually is." A column a few weeks later carried a lengthy clarification from the chief spinner of the recently reelected President Bill Clinton Mike McCurry. In the column, McCurry clarified that, "The spinner's 'English' on a story is designed to move the story in a more favorable direction. That said, the pitch had better cross the plate. Too many wild spins, and someone sooner or later sends you to the showers" (Safire 1996). McCurry and the Clinton team should know, as their work in 1992 and 1996 are often seen as prime examples of spin. McCurry had been working for Clinton opponent Bob Kerrey in 1992 as the well-oiled Clinton machine began its work. Battered by a possible sex scandal, Clinton had dropped in the polls. Following a critical debate ahead of the New Hampshire primary, Clinton's operatives sought to convince reporters how a second place finish would be a political resurrection. The *New York Times* described the scene, writing, "For the voters of New Hampshire, the Democratic debate on Sunday offered a final chance to watch five solemn men engage in an intellectual Olympiad, a dense burst of meaning in the waning moments of the primary contest here. But for the principal architects of campaigns—the political henchmen, the minders and puppeteers who make their living by calling the Titanic the Love Boat—the evening offered something better: an opportunity to hype, twist, contort, convulse and, if talent failed, bludgeon a punch-drunk press corps into understanding how only their candidate could possibly have been the winner" (Specter 1992). The room in which the operatives launched their campaigns, just off the stage from the actual debate, would become known as the "spin room" and the idea of spin as a regular part of the campaign was firmly set. The Clinton team would win the nomination and only up its game. At the first debate between Clinton, President George H. W. Bush, and independent businessman H. Ross Perot, the Clinton team had more than 200 files of articles, datasets, and white papers that could be used to send out blast communications (and fuel the spinners in the room) that could document and combat any attack lines launched against their candidate.

Even as the Clinton campaign and presidency proved adept at the art of spin, the act itself was getting wider and more negative attention. Spin was nothing new in a political campaign but by the early 1990s, the political process was becoming a more transparent one, with the entirety of the campaign drawing more attention. Cable news operations started setting up cameras in the spin room and the continued focus on campaign strategy coverage would fuel behind-the-scenes articles like the one from the 1992 primary mentioned earlier. These stories, though, only made up a portion of the coverage. Many of the articles and television interviews still incorporated the spin, rather than singling it out for its own scrutiny. If a Clinton campaign staffer was able to factually combat a claim made by President Bush, that would merit inclusion in the story about the debate.

But the coverage of the spinners themselves was somewhat rare. The spinner, in these days, was still just a source for the story the journalist was going to write or produce. This relationship of spin-doctor as source, according to the social scientists who have studied the idea of news management, was always difficult for the journalist. One survey noted, "Political actors can influence the news by supplying particular types of information and denying access to others. Journalists might have information about a particular event but in the absence of sources are limited in how they can use this information. Secondly, the rules of the game prohibit lying but accept that it is legitimate for politicians and their spin doctors to present information in a partial and misleading way" (Brown 2011).

This uneven relationship between the press and spinner has helped fuel the antagonism that is even present in the term spin. Spin has become something of a dirty word, taking on the connotation of lying or at least deliberately misleading the press and therefore the public. Although the idea of spin can be connected to sports, it derivation is actually connected to spinning a yarn, the idea that someone is telling you a story that may or may not be true. By the mid-1980s the term began to be used by the highly trained and well spoken sources who could supply broadcast journalists with the perfect sound bite, the one or two sentence synopsis of an issue that both conveyed the information and offered a pithy take on it that aligned with the interests of the official or campaign position. As campaigns' spokespeople became increasingly smooth at turning a bad story into something less bad—if not outright good—they became known as "spin doctors" who could respond to any question in a way that seemed polished, earnest, and still got their take on the news out.

This skill becomes more important when things go wrong. Spin, or at least efforts at spin, are a central tactic in times of crisis and scandal, with spokespeople using selective information and attempts to refocus the story on other matters, but spin is actually a basic function of all public relations and can be loosely grouped into several different types. First is to cherry pick facts that support the candidate's position. This form of spin has become so prevalent that often the factual basis of a story can become almost indecipherable. Take the debate over the Affordable Care Act, or as some spin doctors have called it "Obamacare." The Department of Health and Human Services released a report that found that for those people who shopped for their insurance in states with marketplaces, they could save hundreds of dollars. The very same week saw reports that the cost of health insurance plans had skyrocketed. Which was true? Both, depending on what facts and which people were examined. Cherry picking facts does little to help people understand what is probably a complex story and instead seeks to influence the discussion to support one side of the political debate.

Another form of spin relies on the speaker neither confirming nor denying a specific fact. President Clinton declared in 1998, "I want to say one thing to the American people. I want you to listen to me. I'm going to say this again: I did not have sexual relations with that woman, Miss Lewinsky. I never told anybody to lie, not a single time; never. These allegations are false." Later that claim would come down to whether oral sex constituted "sexual relations." This form of spin is often called the non-denial denial where the speaker through verbal loophole or careful statement creates a misleading impression of denying a fact when, once the words are parsed, they may not have denied anything.

Often there is no way to avoid the bad news and so some forms of spin have to do with how to place the news or release it. A basic technique is to release bad news late in the day on Friday. That way many people may not be paying attention since they are off for the weekend, and Saturday in particular is a bad day for news. This approach relies on the speed of the news cycle to make it so fewer people see the bad news. Another approach that has grown in popularity in recent years has been to turn hostile toward the media for disclosing the information. When the press raised questions about the background of Dr. Ben Carson, a Republican running for the 2016 presidential nomination, the stories ran into this form of spin. There were a series of pieces, some focusing on claims that he, as a troubled youngster, had tried to stab a friend, and that he had received a full scholarship to West Point, that came from Carson's memoir. Another used a 1998 video of Carson positing that the biblical figure Joseph built the pyramids of Egypt to store grain. The stories erupted into social media-fueled scuffles, but central to the Carson response was an accusation that the media is liberal and unfair to conservatives. In exploring the reaction to the stories, which did little to dampen enthusiasm for Carson at the time, the *Atlantic*'s David Graham noted, "These stories seem to have run into three problems. First, the outlets that pursued them seem not to have understood how they might be received. Second, the abiding distrust of the media on the right ensured they would be met with a degree of skepticism by Republican voters. And third—and relatedly—the sloppy presentation of some scoops served to undermine the better-documented allegations of other stories" (Graham 2015).

The era of spin has also intersected with another trend of modern politics, complicating the situation for those voters who simply want to know what the "truth" is in a given situation. As audiences have fragmented and the mass media's ability to dictate the truth eroded, the era of post-truth politics has emerged in recent years. In this political environment, facts are malleable and can be bent to the political will and interests of both the communicator and the recipient of that communication. In this world, spin is no longer simply a sound bite that makes the case of one side or the other of a political debate. It has the power to become the reality for that side of the argument. It is no longer a question whether Carson fabricated claims in his autobiography. For many of his supporters, the source of the information makes the information tainted and therefore it can be dismissed. In this era, noted Grist's David Roberts, "There are no referees any more, no members of the elite who transcend the partisan war and are respected by both sides. Or at least very few. There are only the sides and their respective worlds. Conservative credibility can only come from the conservative side, and if conservatives refuse to grant it, it doesn't exist, any more than a rainbow exists when no one's looking at it" (Roberts 2012). Spin in this environment takes on more weight when it can be tweeted out and shared on Facebook and the core story that the initial spin was aimed at addressing no longer enters the equation. The role of spin doctor is shifting as political reporting becomes only one of the audiences they seek to influence. Now, these communications specialists may be communicating with supporters on social media, emailing the same talking points to potential financial backers, and also using the political press to combat a story that they seek to knock down.

Some, like former Democratic operative Joe Trippi, disagree, arguing that these tools of the Internet actually could spell an end to spin. Trippi argues that the evolution of the media to a constantly on 24/7 media environment where every public statement (and many private comments) is being recorded will make spin fall away, telling the British *Guardian* newspaper, "Before TV, what mattered was how your voice sounded. Then with TV it matters what your candidate looks like . . . Anybody can fake it on TV: all the Joe Trippis and Alastair Campbells get really good at making sure our guy looks great for the eight seconds that are actually going on the news . . . We are now moving to a medium where authenticity is king, from what things look like to what's real . . . You have to be 'on' 24 hours a day, seven days a week" (Branigan 2007). Whether the Internet will turn political spin into the partisan truths of a fragmented media world or a relic of campaigns past like the campaign song or button remains to be seen.

See also: Access to Candidates; Damage Control; News Conferences; Post-Truth Politics; Sound-Bite Politics

Further Reading

Branigan, Tania. 2007. "Internet Spells End for Political Spin, Says US Web Guru." *Guardian*. June 13. Accessed November 9, 2015. http://www.theguardian.com/media/2007/jun/13/newmedia.egovernment.

Brown, Robin. 2011. "Mediatization and News Management in Comparative Institutional Perspective." In *Political Communication in Postmodern Democracy*. Edited by Kees Brants and Katrin Voltmer. London: Palgrave Macmillan.

Crouse, Timothy. 1973. *Boys on the Bus*. New York: Random House.

Graham, David. 2015. "How Ben Carson and Marco Rubio Outfoxed the Media." *The Atlantic*. November 9.

Roberts, David. 2012. "In an Era of Post-Truth Politics, Credibility Is Like a Rainbow." Grist. September 27. Accessed November 9, 2015. http://grist.org/politics/in-an-era-of-post-truth-politics-credibility-is-like-a-rainbow.

Safire, William. 1996. "The Spinner Spun." *New York Times*. December 22. Accessed November 9, 2015. http://www.nytimes.com/1996/12/22/magazine/the-spinner-spun.html.

Specter, Michael. 1992. "The Media; After Debate, the Masters of 'Spin' Take the Floor." *New York Times*. February 18. Accessed November 9, 2015. http://www.nytimes.com/1992/02/18/us/the-1992-campaign-the-media-after-debate-the-masters-of-spin-take-the-floor.html.

STAGING

The idea of candidates and politicians being performers is a modern trope of political communication. Campaign consultants carefully choreograph speeches, do dozens of run-throughs of key stump speeches, and dissect candidate performances for style as much as substance. The use of artfully organized public events has created both a need for candidates to have media advisers to help craft the moment and a cynicism by some in the media about simply being trucked around the country to record a one-person show rather than a campaign about real issues and featuring real people.

The idea of carefully considering the location and look of a given moment has been a concern of candidates and campaign staff since the growth of television as the primary media for political news in the 1960s and 1970s. By the 1980s, the campaign team of former California governor and actor Ronald Reagan moved staging from a goal to a profession. Michael Deaver, who worked for the campaign and then became a White House deputy chief of staff, was widely praised for his ability to carefully craft a moment for television. One incident that highlighted this awareness of the visual above all else was Reagan's visit to Germany to mark the 40th anniversary of the end of World War II. Reagan's advance team had visited a cemetery near the town of Bitburg. The advisers had set up a planned visit with the West German chancellor and had even planned the media position to show Reagan moving through the graveyard on the evening news. The problem was the initial research that noted both German and American soldiers were buried there was wrong. American remains had been removed years before and some 49 of the graves were those of the dreaded German SS, a division of the Germany military that had carried out the bulk of the Holocaust against Jews.

What should have been a made-for-TV moment was suddenly thrown into chaos and the well-oiled Reagan public relations machine kicked into gear. Deaver soon added a visit to the Nazi death camp at Bergen-Belsen to the itinerary and the media were positioned in the cemetery in such a way to ensure that the television cameras shooting the president would film the back of the gravestones so as to not see the swastika on the front. The visit received mixed coverage in the nation's newspapers, but on television, the footage of Reagan at the cemetery in the snow was striking and the speech he delivered at the camp widely aired.

Liberal writer Mark Hertsgaard used the incident in Germany in his book *On Bended Knee*, which accused the press of being willing pawns in the Reagan campaign and White House. He argued that the press used the footage that Deaver and his team set them up to use and rarely challenged the messaging from the White House. At Reagan's death, Hertsgaard would say the former president had benefited from a keenly run PR team, writing, "The apparatus understood the value of repetition—in an information-saturated society, only messages that get repeated can pierce the static and register on the public consciousness—and they pursued it with discipline and skill. Reagan's PR was planned months in advance and fine-tuned every morning in meetings that set the line of the day that the administration's spokesman would duly repeat to reporters. The settings of the president's public appearances were carefully controlled so he stood before flattering backdrops and too far away for reporters to ask questions" (Hertsgaard 2004).

Election scholars claim that now almost every campaign appearance by a candidate running for president is staged to convey specific elements of the campaign's message. Professor William Adams has noted that campaigns have always used carefully staged events to connect with voters in a way a policy white paper or stump speech cannot. He has said, "The old cliché of politicians kissing babies is there for a reason. It symbolizes a politician that's human, that cares, that's loving, that's nurturing. And having a family seems emblematic of that nurturing kind of politician" (Siegelbaum 2011). Candidates can do this a variety of ways, attending the Iowa State Fair or hitting a small diner in New Hampshire. But as Adams and others note, the backdrop is only part of the staging. Campaigns consider what the message is they hope to convey—that the candidate is one of you or he or she is the person to help get America working again—and then build the made-for-TV moment from there. Specific people who are meant to represent a target audience may be contacted to appear at the event. A specific location may serve as a backdrop. Even the candidate's clothing and the time of day will be selected with the hopes of getting the right mix of visual and content.

Of course, all this planning can go horribly awry. Take long-shot Republican candidate Gary Bauer. Bauer had run the Family Research Council and so his credentials as a social conservative were airtight, but he was also a Washington insider in a campaign where conservatives wanted someone from outside D.C. To help bolster his every-man street cred, Bauer agreed to participate in a completely staged event—"The Bisquick Pancake Presidential Primary Flip-Off." When Bauer went to flip his pancake he backed up to catch it and fell off the stage. The video of him falling quickly became the footage of the day, running again and again on cable television and late night comedy shows. Bauer's campaign quickly went from long shot to punch line and he would soon drop out.

Other staging moments have also come back to haunt the stager, notably the famous footage of Democratic presidential candidate Michael Dukakis riding in a tank, but more often than not the staging is accepted by the press as the price of covering the candidate, allowing them to gather footage they need for the night's news, and offering them a readily made story with visuals, context, and the candidate. This thinking permeates all of the campaign but reaches its apex during the nominating conventions every four years. All aspects of the event are carefully coordinated, with some crafted message behind every sign and each speech. A 2012 story by NPR ahead of the nominating convention for Mitt Romney noted that "staging matters. That's why campaigns seek picture-perfect backdrops for speeches—natural vistas when the subject is the environment, shuttered factories when talking unemployment . . . To counter perceptions that Romney is aloof and distant, for instance, Republican strategists are designing their stage in Tampa to have the warmth of a living room, with stairs running from the podium into the audience to convey the candidate's approachability" (Mondello 2012). This attention to detail is deliberately subtle, but still the product of a carefully molded strategy. Even as television has begun to lose some of its power as the primary medium through which people receive the political news, the idea of carefully crafting public appearances remains a central idea of campaign strategists.

See also: Advance Teams; Photo Ops and Optics

Further Reading

Hertsgaard, Mark. 2004. "Ronald Reagan: Beloved by the Media." *The Nation*. June 28. Accessed December 16, 2015. http://markhertsgaard.com/ronald-reagan-beloved-by-the-media.

Mondello, Bob. 2012. "In the Theater of Politics, Staging Is Everything." NPR. August 23. Accessed December 16, 2015. http://www.npr.org/2012/08/23/159915199/in-the-theater-of-politics-staging-is-everything.

Siegelbaum, Deborah. 2011. "Campaign 2012: Staging the Unexpected." *The Hill*. October 18. Accessed December 15, 2015. http://thehill.com/capital-living/cover-stories/188065-campaign-2012-staging-the-unexpected.

STEFFENS, LINCOLN (1866–1936)

Lincoln Steffens found corruption in nearly every city he went in the early 1900s. Political machines and powerful bosses ran the show in St. Louis, in Minneapolis, in Philadelphia, and he decided the American people were to blame. "We cheat our government and we let our leaders loot it, and we let them wheedle and bribe our sovereignty from us," he wrote in the introduction of *The Shame of the Cities*, a collection of articles he originally wrote for *McClure's* in the early 1900s. "We break our own laws and rob our own government . . . The spirit of graft and of lawlessness is the American spirit" (Steffens 1904). Steffens was one of the original muckrakers, early investigative journalists who refused to turn a blind eye to corruption and instead wrote articles to expose the dark underbelly of power, helping to fuel the Progressive Movement of the early 1900s. Steffens used his work in newspapers and later magazines to crusade for reforms of government, demanding the public take a stand against the widespread malfeasance he found.

Lincoln Joseph Steffens was born in 1866 in San Francisco to a fairly wealthy family. His father, Joseph, was a banker and a prominent figure in California. He moved the family to Sacramento when Lincoln was young and served as vice president of the California National Bank and president of the Board of Trade. The family was so well off, in fact, that their home would later become the California governor's mansion.

Lincoln's curiosity about the world was evident from childhood, Doris Kearns Goodwin writes in *The Bully Pulpit*. His parents gave him a pony when he was young. He took long rides after school and on days off from school, trying to see as much of the world as he could and talking to people from all corners of the world. He befriended a jockey at a racetrack, bridge tenders at the railroad, and convinced a page at the capitol to sneak him into committee rooms and hotel apartments where lawmakers and lobbyists crafted legislation (Goodwin 2013).

Despite his natural curiosity, he was a less-than-stellar student. He got into the University of California–Berkeley only after a year of intense work with a tutor. His time there made him a more focused student, and after graduation he continued his studies in Europe. He spent time in Germany, France, and England. Philosophy was a passion of his, though he also dabbled in art history and psychology. His time traipsing about Europe ended when his father wrote him a letter imploring him to return to the states to learn the "practical side" of life. Lincoln moved to New York and landed a job reporting for the *New York Evening Post*.

Starting in 1892, he covered Wall Street and the police beat at the *Post* before departing in 1897 for the *Commercial Advertiser*, where he became the city editor. But after a few years there, *McClure's* came calling. The magazine's founder, S.S. McClure, was impressed by his work as a police reporter and his ability to run a news desk, and he tapped Steffens to join the venerable Ida Tarbell and Ray Stannard Baker. Steffens flourished, producing the work that would cement his legacy as a muckraker; some even refer to him as the first muckraker.

One day while in the *McClure's* office, he told a colleague he was going to do a series for the magazine about city government. The colleague asked him what he knew about city government, and he replied, "Nothing. That's why I'm going to write about it" (Hartshorn 2011). A contact in Chicago pointed Steffens toward St. Louis, the city that would be the subject of the first in his extensive series. There he found a city lousy with corruption, led by the town's boss Colonel Edward Butler. On the other side was a young district attorney named Joe Folk, who eventually did convict Butler of corruption. The tale would become "Tweed Days in St. Louis," one of the groundbreaking municipal corruption pieces in a seminal issue of *McClure's*. He would move on to Minneapolis, where his exposé vaulted him to a new level of fame. "Citizens across the country invited him to their localities, promising scandals more sordid than those described in Minneapolis and St. Louis," Goodwin wrote (2013).

Steffens's reporting established several critical elements of modern political reporting. First, it was built on a deep skepticism of power, seeking to find examples of government that has ceased to function or is corrupted by money. Second, the public's culpability in the dysfunction of politics was a central part of his argument. Finally, it created a desire for change. His pieces fueled the Progressives, who wanted to stomp out corruption in government, and Steffens—along with the other muckrakers—was a voice encouraging their outrage.

Michael Wright

See also: *McClure's Magazine*; Muckraking; Tarbell, Ida

Further Reading

Baker, Kevin. 2011. "Lincoln Steffens: Muckraker's Progress." *New York Times*. May 13. Accessed September 20, 2015. http://www.nytimes.com/2011/05/15/books/review/lincoln-steffens-muckrakers-progress.html?_r=2.

Hartshorn, Peter. 2011. *I Have Seen the Future: A Life of Lincoln Steffens*. Berkeley, CA: Counterpoint Press.

Kearns Goodwin, Doris. 2013. *The Bully Pulpit: Theodore Roosevelt, William Howard Taft and the Golden Age of Journalism*. New York: Simon & Schuster.

Steffens, Lincoln. 1904. *The Shame of the Cities*. New York: McClure, Phillips, and Co.

STEWART, JON (1962–)

Over a 16-year run as the anchor of the nightly news-parodying the *Daily Show*, Jon Stewart became one of the most prolific commentators about the state of the nation's politics and media. The program, through a mix of taped reports and Stewart-led interviews, became a ratings hit and an influential voice for a generation of Americans not drawn to the serious, he-said/she-said approach of the nightly news and cable programs.

Much of that program's success can be connected not just to the smart writing that helped earn the show 22 primetime Emmy awards, but the unique style of the *Daily Show*'s host. As one scholar who has studied the program and its approach, Stewart carved out a unique persona, writing, "Through Stewart's body language—the intonations, gestures, and facial expressions that mark him as a clown—and his self-deprecating humor that deflates any sense of self-importance, he disavows his own seriousness and suggests that he, too, might be thought silly . . ." (Morreale 2009). Part aww-shucks joker and part angry intellectual, Stewart created a persona that was both likable and scathing.

It's perhaps testament to his unlikely rise to celebrity. Born Jonathan Stuart Leibowitz in New York City to a teacher and professor, he stopped using his last name after his parents divorced when he was 11. He and his brother grew up with his mother in New Jersey. He headed south to attend college, graduating in 1984 from the College of William and Mary. After he graduated he headed back to the New York area, holding an array of jobs from high school soccer coach to bartender. He finally performed his first stand-up act in 1987 in the city. He started writing and performing on cable programs on Comedy Central and MTV and was considered as a replacement for David Letterman when Letterman left NBC in 1993.

In 1999 he was selected to replace the original host of the *Daily Show* and soon began to alter the style of the program. Under his leadership, the show shifted from a mix of entertainment and some politics to a comedy show that focused heavily on politics and the media. The program grew in popularity and audience.

Then came *Crossfire*.

To promote his 2004 book *America (The Book): A Citizen's Guide to Democracy Inaction*, Stewart appeared on the CNN political debate show and he came loaded to bear. In a segment in front of a live audience at George Washington University, Stewart confronted hosts Tucker Carlson and Paul Begala over the fiery debate show. He told the two, "I'm here to confront you, because we need help from the media and they're hurting us." Later he and Carlson clashed:

Jon Stewart: You have a responsibility to the public discourse, and you fail miserably.

Tucker Carlson: You need to get a job at a journalism school, I think.

Stewart: You need to go to one. The thing that I want to say is, when you have people on for just knee-jerk, reactionary talk . . .

Carlson: Wait. I thought you were going to be funny. Come on. Be funny.

Stewart: No. No. I'm not going to be your monkey.

The debate electrified the audience and, as researchers of the intersection of pop culture and politics noted, it was a seminal moment for Stewart and his show. One wrote, "The importance of *The Daily Show* and its host became undeniable in early January 2005. It was then that new CNN president Jonathan Klein announced that the 'head-butting debate show' *Crossfire* would be canceled. In his reasons for the cancellation of the show, Klein cited the criticisms articulated by Jon Stewart in his infamous appearance as a guest on *Crossfire* in October 2004" (Young 2008). Stewart and his program would help spur a series of other comedy programs that furthered the media and politics commentary, including the *Colbert Report*, which was a parody of Fox News's the *O'Reilly Factor*, and John Oliver's *Last Week Tonight* on HBO.

Although he always stressed he was not a journalist, Stewart would often emerge in discussions about the future of journalism, a fact that would visibly irritate him. Still, when NBC decided its venerable program *Meet the Press* needed a new host in 2014, the network approached Stewart. Rumors swirled that he was offered a huge contract to consider the position, but he later told *Rolling Stone*, "I felt like that was one of those situations where someone says, 'We really like what you do. Why don't you come over here and do something different, maybe something you don't do as well, for us?' I can understand notionally where it comes from. News and entertainment have melded in a way. But they would be overcompensating on the entertainment side. That's certainly not an outlandish decision, although I don't necessarily think that's the best direction for it" (Greene 2014). Stewart passed on NBC and the next year announced his retirement from the *Daily Show*.

In describing Stewart and his odd mix of characteristics, his biographer Lisa Rogak admitted, "Jon Stewart is a bundle of walking contradictions. On the one hand, he makes no bones about exactly how he feels about things at any given moment, delivering his opinions and thoughts to his audience seriously—usually with an eye toward making them laugh—while also hopefully making them question the way the world works. On the other hand, he is a man who hides in plain sight. Stewart is an enigma who shuns the spotlight, and his contempt for certain people and philosophies sometimes make him so enraged on the show that he starts to shake and spit" (Rogak 2014).

In the wake of his departure as host of the *Daily Show*, he has largely dropped out of the public eye, except for a very public battle with Senator Mitch McConnell in 2015 to keep funding for a program that ensures health coverage for those firefighters and workers who worked at Ground Zero in the wake of the September 11 terror attacks. Stewart used his celebrity to pressure members of Congress to back the bill and then went back on the *Daily Show* to pressure McConnell to pass the bill, which he agreed to do.

See also: Comedy, Satire, and Politics; Oliver, John

Further Reading

Greene, Andy. 2014. "Jon Stewart on 'Meet The Press' Offer: 'They Were Casting a Wide and Weird Net.'" *Rolling Stone*. October 30. Accessed January 14, 2016. http://www.rollingstone.com/tv/news/jon-stewart-on-meet-the-press-offer-they-were-casting-a-wide-and-weird-net-20141030.

Morreale, Joanne. 2009. "Jon Stewart and The Daily Show: I Thought You Were Going to Be Funny." In *Satire TV*. Edited by Jonathan Gray, Jeffrey Jones and Ethan Thompson. New York: NYU Press.

Rogak, Lisa. 2014. *Angry Optimist: The Life and Times of Jon Stewart*. New York: St. Martin's Griffin.

Young, Dannagal Goldthwaite. 2008. "The Daily Show as the New Journalism." In *Laughing Matters: Humor and American Politics in the Media Age*. Edited by Jody Baumgartner and Jonathan Morris. New York: Routledge.

STONE, I.F. (1907–1989)

If you wanted to boil down some 70 years of investigative work by Isidor Feinstein Stone you could probably use the words he himself coined: "All governments lie."

Stone was a pioneering journalist and gadfly, who worked as an outspoken reporter and Washington chief for the liberal magazine the *Nation* and the leftist New York newspaper *PM*. His work and his political beliefs led to his blacklisting in the 1950s, but rather than be silent, Stone developed his own newsletter he would write, edit, and send to subscribers. Glenn Greenwald, the muckraking journalist who broke the story of National Security Agency monitoring of Americans' phone calls and emails, credits Stone for serving as a trailblazer for others who would follow, saying in a film about the journalist, "I often think of I.F. Stone as the nation's first blogger. He really embodied this cantankerous, disruptive, insurgent energy that I think has come to be the defining attribute of political blogging at its best" (White Pine Films 2015).

Growing up in New Jersey, Stone demonstrated his journalistic drive even as he failed to apply himself to school. He would graduate 49th in his class of 52, but had already launched his first newspaper, the *Progress*, before he got to his junior year. Early on, he was an activist on political issues, volunteering for the Popular Front, a Communist organization, and later joined the Socialist Party of America. He landed a job at the *New York Post*, but he soon found it hard to pursue his career and his strongly held political beliefs. The owner of the *Post* fired Stone because of his pro-Soviet views. He landed at the more liberal-friendly *Nation* magazine, publishing a damning account of J. Edgar Hoover's FBI. He later moved to the leftist newspaper *PM* where he worked until it failed in 1948. It was then that his outspoken political beliefs came back to haunt him. By 1950, Stone, who had admitted his interest and support for leftist causes, found himself blacklisted from working at mainstream media organizations. In the McCarthy era of red-baiting and anti-Communist rallies, Stone found himself cast to the outer edges of the media.

To respond, he launched his own outlet, *I.F. Stone's Weekly*. The newsletter cost 15 cents an issue to subscribe to and allowed Stone to continue his investigative work. That newsletter attracted a small, but influential readership. Albert Einstein shelled out a subscription and Marilyn Monroe actually paid for subscriptions for every member of Congress. It would reach some 70,000 subscribers by the time he retired in 1971.

The newsletter took on difficult and controversial issues, including race relations and the deepening crisis in Vietnam. His newsletter famously questioned in 1964 the Gulf of Tonkin incident, where North Vietnamese forces reportedly fired upon an American warship. The attack was used as justification to ramp up the American involvement in Vietnam, and President Lyndon Johnson stressed the clash as his rationale. Stone went to New York to sit in on the United Nations discussions, and wrote in his newsletter that the official reports led him to believe the incident was in response to American provocation, writing to his readers, "Our warships, according to the official account, just happened to be hanging around. The only rational explanation for their presence at the time was that the Navy was looking for trouble, daring the North Vietnamese to do something about it" (Stone 1964). Stone would maintain his outspoken opposition to the Vietnam War and would press the mainstream media to do a better job in documenting what was really happening.

Stone, for all his skepticism, remained confident in the liberal idea that so long as the public could find out the information it needed to choose who should govern, the American experiment would be fine. Still he worried, "If something goes wrong in the United States, a free press can uncover it and the problem can be solved. But if something goes wrong with the free press, the country will go straight to hell" (MacDonell 2015). In marking his death in 1989, his old magazine the *Nation* would memorialize Stone and his style of reporting, noting, "One reason the establishment had so much trouble classifying Izzy was his attitude toward it: 'All idols must be overthrown; all sacred dogmas exposed to criticism; the windows thrown open; the cobwebs swept away!' As editor and publisher of the world's most famous newsletter, *I.F. Stone's Weekly*, as a reporter and columnist for *PM* and its successor papers, as Washington editor of *The Nation*, as a frequent contributor to *The New York Review of Books*, Izzy was a quadruple threat. He combined the meat-and-potatoes moxie of a police reporter, the instinct for precision of a scholar, the question-phrasing skill of a Socrates . . . and the political philosophy of an anarchist" (*Nation* 1989).

That approach to reporting has spawned countless bomb-throwing journalists who seek to ferret out the truth from institutions that inherently obscure the truth to protect their own interests. The investigative work of Seymour Hersh and the crusading work of Glenn Greenwald and his team at the Intercept can both trace their lineage to the thick glasses and battered typewriter of I.F. Stone.

See also: Advocacy Journalism; Muckraking

Further Reading

Editorial. 1989 "I.F. Stone 1907-1989." *Nation*. July 10.

"*The Legacy of I.F. Stone: Part One.*" White Pine Pictures. Accessed November 15, 2015. https://vimeo.com/123974841.

MacDonell, Allan. 2015. "I.F. Stone's Legacy: A Fulcrum for Journalistic Independence?" Knight Foundation. May 6. Accessed November 16, 2015. http://www.knightfoundation.org/blogs/knightblog/2015/5/6/if-stones-legacy-fulcrum-journalistic-independence.

Stone, I. F. 1964. "What Few Know about the Tonkin Bay Incident." *I.F. Stone's Weekly*. August 24. Accessed November 16, 2015. http://www.ifstone.org/weekly8-24-64.pdf.

SULLIVAN, ANDREW (1963–)

Often it is the intellectual liberals and conservatives who most aggravate those who claim the same political moniker. William F. Buckley riled Republicans by attacking the hard-line John Birch Society. Liberal Noam Chomsky has for years criticized Democrats, as well as Republicans, for their foreign policy. In a similar, but far more new media way, Andrew Sullivan has established himself as a leading political thinker and blogger, irritating other media figures while also inventing the power of popular blogging.

Sullivan, who served as an editor of the liberal *New Republic*, launched his own blog, the Daily Dish, in 2000 as a sort of archive of his magazine articles and columns. The blog, like Sullivan himself, is hard to nail down. Part musings on his own life and beliefs, part aggregation on news and opinion from around the Internet, and part exploration of political matters from a PhD, the blog was soon a must-read in Washington circles. Part of this interest was a reflection of the topics Sullivan and his team were writing about, and part was a fascination with a writer who does not fall into easy categorization. As writer and feminist Naomi Wolf described Sullivan, "He's Catholic and gay and an exile. That's all very helpful—his background forces him not to be confined in any single identity" (Kornbluth 2011).

Andrew Sullivan was born into a Roman Catholic family in Surrey, England. A gifted student, Sullivan had a difficult time in his teenage years after realizing he was homosexual and struggling with the ramifications of this on his life and beliefs. Despite feeling isolated due to his sexuality, Sullivan was widely respected as a student and was elected president of the Oxford Union by his university classmates. Sullivan came to the United States to pursue his graduate degree at Harvard and began writing for several top-tier magazines. He joined the *New Republic* in 1986 and became an editor in 1991. During his tenure there, he pushed the magazine to take risks, including his decision to publish an extended excerpt of the controversial book *The Bell Curve*, which explored the different abilities and capacities of ethnicities and gender. Sullivan would later write of the controversy that, "One of my proudest moments in journalism was publishing an expanded extract of a chapter from *The Bell Curve* in the *New Republic* before anyone else dared touch it. I published it along with multiple critiques (hey, I believed magazines were supposed to open rather than close debates)—but the book held up, and still holds up as one of the most insightful and careful of the last decade. The fact of human inequality and the subtle and complex differences between various manifestations of being human—gay, straight, male, female, black, Asian—is a subject worth exploring, period" (Metcalf 2005). It was the kind of decisiveness and intellectual provocation that would become his hallmark in years to come.

When he started the Daily Dish he launched himself into the world of self-publishing. Unconstrained by editors and production schedules, Sullivan produced content at a frenetic rate. He would write about everything from the war on terror to the latest *South Park* episode. His style was at once breezy and philosophical, and it tended to echo his political beliefs in limited government and libertarian views on social issues. He was soon attracting readers and mainstream media interest. He moved his blog to *Time* magazine for a while before taking it to the *Atlantic* and later the Daily Beast. In 2013, he decided to go independent, launching the Daily Dish as a standalone media company and charging a subscription of $20 a year. Sullivan noted that his site was often more popular than the legacy magazines he was writing for and so he wanted to have a go alone.

Throughout his run at the Daily Dish, Sullivan made himself a regular on television, appearing on the *Colbert Report* and *Real Time with Bill Maher* on television. His quick wit and willingness to provoke played well on those programs, and his unique mix of views offered viewers an unusual conservative voice. He still claims the mantle of a conservative, but as he told the Harvard Graduate School of Government in 2011, "I do not recognize the current Republican Party as in any way a conservative force in this society . . . For me conservatism is fundamentally and deeply about the limits of human beings. It's about the tragedy of the human condition. It is about the paradox of progress. It is about questioning the liberal assumption that we have a solution to the problems of mankind" (Sullivan 2011).

Throughout his life he has faced numerous health issues, having had asthma since a young age and after a 1991 diagnosis of HIV, and by 2015 Sullivan knew he had to step back from the site. The site, with nearly a dozen staff, was publishing some 40 posts a day, seven days a week. He would later say in a speech the pace "was killing me" and so he decided to suspend his blog in January of that year. In saying goodbye, Sullivan struck the same irreverent tone and personal connection with his readers. He told the Colorado governor, "f—you, Hickenlooper" and praised those who had been with him when all he had was a blog and a tip jar. He ended his post, "When I write again, it will be for you, I hope—just in a different form. I need to decompress and get healthy for a while; but I won't disappear as a writer. But this much I know: nothing will ever be like this again, which is why it has been so precious; and why it will always be a part of me, wherever I go; and why it is so hard to finish this sentence and publish this post" (Sullivan 2015).

He still occasionally writes on the Daily Dish and has remained vocal on Twitter. He has also begun writing for the *Sunday Times of London*, but the site that made him a cerebral celebrity and moved political blogging forward as a profession has largely gone dark.

See also: The *Atlantic*; The Daily Beast; *Time* Magazine

Further Reading

Kornbluth, Jesse. 2011. "World's Best Blogger?" *Harvard* Magazine. May/June. Accessed December 17, 2015. http://harvardmagazine.com/2011/05/worlds-best-blogger.

Metcalf, Stephen. 2005. "Moral Courage: Is Defending The Bell Curve an Example of Intellectual Honesty?" Slate. October 17. Accessed December 17, 2015. http://primary.slate.com/articles/arts/culturebox/2005/10/moral_courage.html.

Sullivan, Andrew. 2011. "Conservatism and Its Discontents." T.H. White Lecture at Harvard University. November 28. Accessed December 15, 2015. https://www.youtube.com/watch?v=SjE49UnJiwE&feature=plcp.

Sullivan, Andrew. 2015. "A Note to My Readers." Daily Dish. January 25. Accessed December 15, 2015. http://dish.andrewsullivan.com/2015/01/28/a-note-to-my-readers.

SUPER PACs

If nonprofit, "dark money" groups are one end of the campaign funding spectrum and direct donations to candidates are the other, Super PACs have carved a major space out between the two. These groups can raised unlimited donations from individuals, corporations, or unions and can spend unlimited amounts of that money advocating for or against candidates, although there are two caveats. First, Super PACs are expressly prohibited from coordinating their spending or messaging with the campaign they seek to aid. Second, Super PACs must report their donations to the Federal Election Commission.

Those who have studied the role Super PACs have come to hold in the process note that these groups often target the candidates opponent for attack. "For super PACs, which are still operating in uncharted and untested legal waters, it's safer to bash a candidate than it is to back one, lest the independent groups come in for charges of coordination with candidates, which is illegal" (Graham 2012). And so Super PACs have focused on areas where they can more clearly argue they are not directly working with the campaign they seek to help. These include, most visibly, running ads often attacking the opponent of their candidate as well as other vital roles like canvassing door-to-door for support and conducting opposition research and tracking of opponents.

But the question of coordination has dogged these organizations since they radically expanded their work at the federal and state levels. The federal government declares independent expenditures as, "An expenditure by a person for a communication expressly advocating the election or defeat of a clearly identified candidate that is not made in cooperation, consultation, or concert with, or at the request or suggestion of, a candidate, a candidate's authorized committee, or their agents, or a political party committee or its agents" (Federal Register 100.16, 2 U.S.C. 431 (17)). But beyond this limitation, Super PACs are allowed to raise and spend as much money as they like seeking to influence elections.

The results have been dramatic.

Consider the difference in spending by the largest traditional PACs compared to Super PACs in 2014. The largest Super PAC in 2014 was the pro-Democrat Senate Majority PAC that aimed to help Democrats in close-fought elections to help the party maintain its majority. That one Super PAC raised nearly $67 million and spent some $46.7 million in their unsuccessful attempt to defend the Senate. That total equaled the donations made by the top 19 traditional PACs combined, according to the Center for Responsive Politics. In fact, there were 19 Super PACs that spent more money on the 2014 elections than the largest traditional PAC, pouring more than a quarter billion dollars into the off-year election.

But it is not just traditional PACs that these new organs have diminished, according to one of the most authoritative assessments to date. Melissa Smith and Larry Powell studied the role of these groups in 2012, the first real election cycle in which they could operate at full steam, and concluded, "Super PACs have taken over some of the areas that were traditionally covered by political parties, including voter identification drives and get-out-the-vote campaigns, thereby leaving both political parties with less power" (Smith and Powell 2013, p. 109).

This reality, coupled with the enormous amount of money flowing through registered Super PACs and the even more murky "dark money" groups registered as social welfare organizations, has created a largely negative impression of these organizations in the public's and journalists' views. Even those who support the right to spend, like Robert Samuelson, admit, "The perception that political operatives and wealthy donors are skirting contribution limits—as they are—creates the aura of corruption and even criminality. Super PACs also seem to make candidates' campaigns less accountable" (Samuelson 2012).

These organizations and their large bankrolls are doing more than just alter the pattern of giving in campaigns; they are also beginning to alter the dynamics of presidential campaigns and the politics of governance according to experts. On the presidential front, 2012 ushered in a new era of Super PAC politics when a single donor was able to direct $10 million into the sagging campaign of Republican Newt Gingrich. Las Vegas businessman Sheldon Adelson and his wife each cut major checks to the Gingrich-connected Super PAC Winning Our Future, allowing the former House Speaker's supporters to air a barrage of negative attacks on frontrunner Mitt Romney. The infusion of cash, while it did not propel Gingrich to the nomination, still breathed new life into his campaign and kept the primary fight going longer than it would have otherwise. At the time, some expressed real concern about the idea of individuals having so much sway in a campaign, with the head of the Sunlight Foundation telling the *New York Times*, "To me, the amounts of money and the directness with which wealthy individuals give it is even more excessive than it was in the days of Watergate . . . What we are seeing now is a systematic breaking of the floodgates, effectively eliminating any firewalls between candidates and unlimited political giving" (Confessore 2012). But despite those concerns, some pointed out that the amount and source of the money was known at the time it occurred, unlike the nonprofit "dark money" groups.

The other impact of these large, often hardline partisan, groups has been a growing concern by some in Congress that they will be targeted for defeat in the primary if they do not support the Super PAC's ideological position. In fact, the 2012 analysis of the groups and their impact found, "The potential damage from these organizations has created a fear among moderates of both parties that could lead to further governance issues and to reluctance on the part of House and Senate members to take controversial stands on issues" (Smith and Powell 2013, p. 110).

See also: Campaign Finance Reform; Dark Money Organizations; Political Action Committees (PACs)

Further Reading

Confessore, Nicholas. 2012. "'Super PAC' for Gingrich to Get $5 Million Infusion." *New York Times*. January 23. Accessed December 31, 2014. http://www.nytimes.com/2012/01/24/us/politics/super-pac-for-gingrich-to-get-5-million-infusion.html?_r=0.

Graham, David. 2012. "The Incredible Negative Spending of Super PACs—in 1 Chart." *Atlantic*. October 15. Accessed December 30, 2014. http://www.theatlantic.com/politics/archive/2012/10/the-incredible-negative-spending-of-super-pacs-in-1-chart/263643.

Samuelson, Robert. 2012. "The Super PAC Confusion." *Washington Post*. February 19. Accessed December 31, 2014. http://www.realclearpolitics.com/articles/2012/02/20/the_super_pac_confusion__113178.html.

Smith, Melissa, and Larry Powell. 2013. *Dark Money, Super PACs, and the 2012 Election*. Lanham, MD Lexington Books.

SURROGATES

Campaign surrogates are well-known politicians and celebrities who speak on behalf or at the behest of candidates. These big names are used to draw crowds to events and garner media attention at the national and local levels. Surrogates have become increasingly important as more and more parts of the campaign become funded and run by independent groups associated with the same interest groups as the candidate, but not run by the candidate. Some analysts have noted these independent groups and fellow politicians are often only partial surrogates, de-emphasizing, but not eliminating their own self-interest when speaking on behalf of a campaign.

Surrogates can play several critical roles on the campaign trail and in media interviews. First, they may be well-respected thought leaders in a given field. Having a Nobel Prize–winning economist endorse a candidate's economic policy on the face of it carries more weight than having the candidate themselves discuss the benefits. These speakers may also have more credibility with a given audience and so having a popular governor speak on behalf of a candidate that is seen with more skepticism in that governor's state may have more influence than the candidate. For decades, campaigns have tapped the expertise of former senior officials and well-established congressional leaders to help presidential candidates bolster areas of their resume that may be lacking and to help craft thorough policy positions on key issues of the day they may not have had to deal with in the past.

This process often remained behind the scenes with experts contributing to white papers or perhaps briefing the candidate on key issues. But as campaigns ratcheted up to respond to the increasing demands of the 24-hour news cycle and the constant media requests, campaigns began using these same experts to help craft the public message. These former government officials took on increasing numbers of interviews and stump speeches, often standing in for the candidate in an effort to address any questions with the weight of experience and legitimacy. For example, the campaign of President Bill Clinton was famous for deploying former Cabinet members, veteran elected officials, and big-city mayors in its efforts to shape the interpretation of speeches and debates during the 1996 campaign. A *New York Times* article at one of the debates between President Clinton and former Senate Majority Leader Bob Dole described the use of experts and senior elected officials as a use of overwhelming force against the Republicans, writing, "At times there seemed to be more Clinton spinners than spinnees. Some less-prominent governors and mayors were left standing alone, but for aides bobbing their signs in hopes of luring any reporter—like the hapless squires who ran behind horseless knights in the movie *Monty Python and the Holy Grail*, banging coconuts together to simulate the clopping of hooves" (Bennet 1996). But campaigns hardly limit themselves to using stand-ins at debates and Clinton is not the last to deploy them. By 2012, both Republicans and Democrats deployed scores of officially dubbed surrogates into the field to make their cases. The day before the election, the campaign of Barack Obama sent out 181 designated surrogates, some policy experts and many celebrities, to headline rallies calling for the president's reelection. Mitt Romney's side sent out 100 of their own, including former officials from President George W. Bush's administration and Romney's five adult sons. Many of these same surrogates were included in appeals to supporters to volunteer to the campaign or to donate money to the effort.

But surrogates are not always employed solely because of their policy prowess and local political success. Some of these speakers also have the benefit of being seen as non-political, and so increasingly candidates have used family members and celebrities that may attract an audience and appear less self-motivated in their address. As Robert Thompson, a Syracuse professor and expert in the use of television, described it, these types of surrogates can possess "that gotta-have but hard-to-get element of candor and sincerity. At least the illusion that they're actually telling the truth and that they're speaking from their heart" (Moore 2012). Ann Romney, wife of former Massachusetts governor Mitt Romney, was tapped throughout the Republican's 2008 and 2012 campaigns for president to play this personal and candid surrogate. Throughout the 2012 Republican primary that featured some 10 candidates and dragged on for months of debates and public appearances, Romney was the only candidate's wife to take to the trail alone, drawing large crowds and stressing her personal health story of struggling against cancer and multiple sclerosis in discussing her husband's political credentials. She reprised this role at the Republican National Convention, rallying supporters with a personal and impassioned speech, saying, "I read somewhere that Mitt and I have a 'storybook marriage.' Well, in the storybooks I read, there were never long, long, rainy winter afternoons in a house with five boys screaming at once. And those storybooks never seemed to have chapters called MS or Breast Cancer. A storybook marriage? No, not at all. What Mitt Romney and I have is a real marriage . . . He has tried to live his life with a set of values centered on family, faith, and love of one's fellow man" (Romney 2015). Romney played one of the most classic roles of a surrogate, that of an apolitical voice who could talk about the intangible character traits that many people seek to understand about the candidate.

But as personal and warm and fuzzy as some surrogates can be, others are brought into the campaign media strategy to go on the attack. This role has two benefits for the candidate, allowing them to take a punch at the opponent, but also keeping the candidate out of the fight. There are a couple of reasons campaigns typical deploy an outsider to combat an accuser. In some cases the campaign itself may not want to give the claim added legitimacy by having the candidate directly address it. This may show the campaign is deeply concerned about the accusation and could be seen as forcing the candidate "off message." Deploying a surrogate to counterattack allows the campaign to respond without turning it into a debate with the candidate him- or herself. The use of surrogates also insulates the candidate from the muddying up of opponents. For example, former secretary of state Hillary Clinton has stressed that she wanted to focus her criticism on Republicans versus engaging in attacks on the Democrats that were running against her for the 2016 Democratic presidential nomination. But that is not to say the campaign did not have plenty to say about her opponents. The campaign carefully briefed its supporters—elected officials, strategists, and donors—each week by phone to ensure certain messages were hammered home when talking with the media. So, when Senator Claire McCaskill in June of 2015 raised the question of whether Vermont senator Bernie Sanders was too liberal to win, she said, "I very rarely read in any coverage of Bernie that he's a socialist." And months later she continued to raise the questions of electability, telling CNN, "I think the question that some of us have is can someone who has said, 'I'm not a Democrat,' has chosen the title of socialist, is that person really electable?" (Karni 2015). McCaskill's comments are part of the Clinton campaign strategy of raising the question of whether one of her chief competitors stands a chance of winning in the general election. All the while, Clinton can stress she is not attacking her opponents and can focus her comments on Republican opponents without ostracizing Democrats who may like Sanders.

Another, less controversial role for surrogates is to help feed the media's interest in the internal strategy and planning of the competing campaigns. These surrogates tend not to be the elected officials or family members but rather the campaign consultants, pollsters, and senior managers. These veteran political operatives, like Democrat James Carville or Republican Karl Rove, become expert sources for journalists looking to explain the strategy of one campaign or to critique the decisions of another campaign. The media use these types of surrogates to try and dissect policy arguments and public performances by the candidate. The campaign can use them to frame media coverage by putting out a series of talking points or attack arguments ahead of the speech or debate, and then following up after the event to put out the campaign's case for why they won the confrontation or raised real questions about the candidates. This type of surrogate often is familiar to the television audience as many of them are professional commentators when not directly involved in a campaign. So their use has the added benefit of being connected in the minds of viewers with regular political commentary and not specific campaign spin.

While using surrogates has clear advantages and may be able to help a candidate in ways other forms of communication cannot, the technique is not without risks. Many surrogates are themselves professional politicians with their own electoral interests. For example, Republican Mitt Romney deployed many Republicans like Senators Marco Rubio and Lindsey Graham and Governor Bobby Jindal, who would themselves run for president four years later. Many of those advocates would also be the first to question the decisions and tactics of Romney in the aftermath of his defeat, seeking to define how they could have done it differently. It got so bad that one Romney adviser went on television and criticized his former supporters, telling MSNBC, "some of them were already talking to our transition to position themselves for a Romney cabinet," adding that after the former governor lost, "It was unbelievable. It was five, six days later, (they were) absolutely eviscerating him" (Killough 2012).

This is an important thing to understand about how surrogates think of their own role. For many who are fellow politicians, being a surrogate can be about supporting a fellow Republican or Democrat you honestly believe in, but it can also be a way of building up your own national presence or earning a credit you may seek to turn into a position in a new administration. Most politicians see this as a mutually beneficial relationship and so if a candidate loses or even stumbles badly, some surrogates may be less inclined to stay on the message the campaign wants them to promote. Others, like family members and paid campaign staff, are more easily kept in line due to the relationship with the candidate, but independent politicians and outside organizations and advocates are often less likely to stick to the rhetoric of the campaign. In fact, some research has shown that these outside politicians and organizations often compete to shape the campaign narrative rather than bolster the one put forward by the campaign. A study of the 2012 campaign found that often the surrogates who worked with the losing campaign quickly blamed the campaign for the loss, seeking to distance themselves from a failed candidate. The authors found that "the postelection narratives proffered by independent sources on the conservative side appear to have been designed to serve the agenda of the media organizations and interest groups in question, rather than the electoral interests of the Republican Party. In sum, conservative groups appear to have used social media to act as competitors more often than their liberal counterparts" (Azari and Stewart 2015).

The other danger of surrogates is that they can sometimes become a lightning rod for criticism when they anger a specific constituency or through their comments create new problems for the campaign they are supposed to aid. Back in 1989, former prosecutor Rudolph Giuliani was running for mayor of New York City against African American incumbent David Dinkins. Giuliani had tapped famed Jewish comedian Jackie Mason to be his point person with other Jewish voters, but when Mason said that Jews vote for blacks only because they "are sick with complexes" the ensuing debate about racism and anti-Semitism threw the Giuliani campaign off the tracks for weeks as they sought to repair the damage done by the comedian.

Often celebrities are used in very controlled ways to ensure they don't say such ill-considered things that could cause trouble for the campaign. But it is not always celebrities or newbies to the political world who can cause heartburn for the campaign. In 2008, one of the most successful politicians of the modern Democratic Party triggered weeks of stories when former President Bill Clinton's efforts to defend his wife and attack then-opponent Barack Obama created an array of problems for Senator Clinton's presidential campaign. The former president declared Obama's claim that he had always been opposed to the Iraq War—a regular topic he used to criticize Hillary Clinton—a "fairy tale" and later said "the idea that one of these campaigns is positive and the other is negative when I know the reverse is true and I have seen it and I have been blistered by it for months is a little tough to take. Just because of the sanitizing coverage that's in the media doesn't mean the facts aren't out there." Clinton's outburst triggered a wave of stories about the former president's frustration at both the claims made by Obama and what he saw as the dereliction of the political press to test those claims.

Looking back at the 2008 campaign, the *New York Times* would write that much of the problem was tied to the former president's tendency to lecture about the politics of a campaign in the moment. "That tendency to analyze out loud turned into a liability when he saw his wife's shot at the presidency in 2008 begin to slip away. After it became apparent Mr. Obama won the South Carolina primary that year, Mr. Clinton memorably compared the victory to Rev. Jesse L. Jackson's two victories in the state, seeming to marginalize the achievement. He also called Mr. Obama's antiwar position 'the biggest fairy tale I've ever seen,' a comment that enraged some African-Americans who interpreted the comment to mean that Mr. Obama's candidacy was a fantasy" (Healy and Chozick 2015). Clinton's comments turned the president from one of the most effective surrogates to more of a political liability, and soon his wife's campaign was using Clinton in a much more low profile sort of way.

Despite their clear liabilities, the use of surrogates has become an accepted practice of the modern campaign, allowing candidates to use others to attack opponents and raise questions that may make the candidate appear negative and also drawing in large crowds to campaign events and fundraisers. Some veteran politicians have expressed concerns that the use of surrogates allows campaigns to take cheap shots at one another—former president George W. Bush has said, "I think the discourse generally is lowered by surrogates" (Zeeble 2015). Still, campaigns stand by the strategy of using surrogates. Their communication staffers have even made the use of and selection of surrogates a sort of pseudo-science. The Obama campaign famously used big data analysts to help decide which celebrities might help spark the most interest from certain types of voters, and most Senate and gubernatorial candidates will use fellow politicians to help draw audience and donations. The use of these non-candidates to influence voters has changed the way campaigns go on the attack and seek to appeal to voters, and that change is here to stay.

See also: Damage Control; Political Consultants; Spin

Further Reading

Azari, Julia, and Benjamin Stewart. 2015. "Surrogates or Competitors?" In *Controlling the Message: New Media in American Political Campaigns*. Edited by Victoria A. Farrar-Myers and Justin S. Vaughn. New York: New York University Press.

Bennet, James. 1996. "In Spin Wars after the Debate, Clinton Campaign Takes Lead." *New York Times*. October 8. Accessed October 12, 2015. http://www.nytimes.com/1996/10/08/us/in-spin-wars-after-the-debate-clinton-campaign-takes-lead.html.

Healy, Patrick, and Amy Chozick. 2015. "To Avert Repeat of 2008, Clinton Team Hopes to Keep Bill at His Best." *New York Times*. March 28. Accessed October 14, 2015. http://www.nytimes.com/2015/03/29/us/politics/to-avert-repeat-of-2008-clinton-team-hopes-to-keep-bill-at-his-best.html.

Karni, Annie. 2015. "Hillary Clinton's Proxies Ramp Up Attacks against Sanders." Politico. September 4. Accessed October 12, 2015. http://www.politico.com/story/2015/09/hillary-clinton-2016-proxies-attack-bernie-sanders-213359.

Killough, Ashley. 2012. "Former Romney Adviser Blasts Top Surrogates for Now 'Eviscerating' Romney." CNN. November 21. Accessed October 14, 2015. http://politicalticker.blogs.cnn.com/2012/11/21/former-romney-adviser-blasts-top-surrogates-for-now-eviscerating-romney.

Moore, Martha. 2012. "'Surrogates' Do Heavy Lifting on Interview Circuit." *USA Today*. September 5. Accessed October 12, 2015. http://usatoday30.usatoday.com/news/politics/story/2012-09-05/surrogates-convention-Salinas-candidates/57615674/1.

Romney, Ann. 2015. *In This Together: My Story*. New York: Macmillan.

Zeeble, Bill. 2015. "Two Presidents and a Maverick: At SMU, a Night with Bush, Clinton and Cuban." KERA News. July 10. Accessed May 31, 2016. http://keranews.org/post/two-presidents-and-maverick-smu-night-bush-clinton-and-cuban.

SURVEYUSA

SurveyUSA is one of the new brand of polling firms, noted for its wide-ranging political polling and its use of automated calling of potential voters. Its polls often project bold results, but its methodology at times draws criticism for allowing whomever answers a call to punch in their answers.

The firm has built its business by conducting quick and fairly inexpensive polls for local television outlets—some 50 stations across the country—and a handful of newspapers. The company also conducts viewer surveys for the stations, often gauging the effectiveness and popularity of programs and anchors for news directors planning their coverage. Additionally, the firm, which is run by a privately held company, conducts research for greeting card companies, food producers, and publishers of everything from books to software. In the political world, the company is known for its prolific polling of national and statewide contests, creating a regular feed of results that gets aggregated into sites like Real Clear Politics and used by media companies.

One poll highlights the controversial role SurveyUSA now plays in reporting on the horse race of politics. Just after Labor Day 2015, the firm dropped a bombshell on the still emerging campaign for the Republican and Democratic nominations in the 2016 contest. The company reported real estate mogul and reality television star Donald Trump would defeat any likely Democratic nominee—including former secretary of state Hillary Clinton, Vice President Joe Biden, and Vermont senator Bernie Sanders. What's more, Trump was attracting support from 25 percent of black voters and 31 percent of Hispanic voters. Both those numbers are more than double any Republican nominee's success with those two large voting blocs in recent history. The poll made headlines all over the Internet and prompted analysis from many about why Trump was surging in the polls.

But for many political experts the survey results were "absurd" on the face of them, and a closer look at the survey raised major questions about the findings. People pointed out the survey only polled 38 percent of its respondents on cell; 62 percent were people contacted on a traditional landline phone. SurveyUSA admitted that among the people surveyed on cell phones Trump lost by double digits, but cell phone users tend to be Democratic voters and so they sought to limit the influence of this bias in the final survey results by capping the number of respondents accessed that way. This sent one analyst over the edge. He wrote on his blog, "Corporate media is running with this survey to show that Donald Trump is the real deal, America's next President. The Republican Party is dancing in the streets. The problem is the results of the survey are absurd, and yet no one in corporate media is questioning it. What is the problem with the survey? The most obvious is that it doesn't pass the smell test when you look at the results" (Ring of Fire 2015). While this critic worked for a liberal talk radio program, the underlying question of how this survey is conducted and how accurately it reflects the feelings of voters is an open question that sparks heated debates within the polling world and among some political commentators.

SurveyUSA uses a controversial technique when conducting its polls, relying on automated systems to pose the questions to callers and then allowing the person answering to choose their responses by pressing a button on their phone. By not hiring human pollsters the company keeps the price of its surveys down, but some question whether this approach can skew the results in dangerous ways. The surveys are sometimes called interactive voice response (IVR) polls and are built in such a way that the polling firm can create different surveys based on what people say or what they select on their phone. SurveyUSA also begins with a huge database of questions it has asked in the past, which allows the firm to field surveys quickly and cheaply. But many worried that this quest to cut costs would lead to problems in the results. For example, IVR surveys cannot confirm the person answering is the person initially targeted in the survey since it will survey (or at least try to survey) whomever answers the phone. Secondly, people worry that IVR surveys allow people to simply press buttons in hopes of ending the call sooner without considering the responses.

These concerns first came to a head in 2004 when many Democrats expressed real doubt over the accuracy of polls showing President Bush headed toward reelection. The two major IVR firms—SurveyUSA and Rasmussen Reports—showed a fairly solid lead compared to some of the traditional polling firms. In the end, the two IVR firms did either the same or slightly better than their human-interview counterparts, prompting Slate to conclude, "We won't settle the relative merits of the two approaches in this article or this election. But . . . it's time to broaden the experiment in automated polling and compare results to see what's working and why. Clearly, the automated pollsters are onto something, and the human pollsters who have fallen behind will have to figure out how to beat it—or join it" (Kenner and Saletan 2004). In the wake of the 2004 successes, the political press accepted these polls as equal to, or sometimes more accurate than, traditional human polling and so a survey like the Trump poll of September 2015 is picked up by media and reported as an accurate snapshot of the electorate.

SurveyUSA defends its techniques, its editor Jay Leve saying, "Professionally-voiced polls are not inherently superior to headset-operator polls, and I do not make that claim. I just rebut the assertion that professionally-voiced polls are inherently inferior. Used properly, SurveyUSA methodology can have advantages" (Blumenthal 2005). Leve and others with the firm contend that having professionals create one recording of the survey has clear advantages. First, it ensures the queries made of each person are identical, with the same intonation, pronunciation, and delivery. IVR advocates also point out that people are less likely to give a response that they think is what the interviewer wants to hear, which can lead to unintended biases in the results. Finally, the IVR proponents point out that their track record is not substantially different than traditional pollsters in key election contests. But the use of these polls continues to draw fire, especially from the side doing poorly in the results. And the use of complicated methodologies and weighting strategies—like the use of 62 percent landlines and 38 mobile phones in the Trump survey—makes it more important for political reporters as well as consumers of news to pay attention to methodologies and margins of error as they read the latest breathless survey results in the heat of a campaign.

See also: Gallup; Horse-Race Journalism; Public Opinion; Public Policy Polling; Rasmussen Reports; Real Clear Politics

Further Reading

Blumenthal, Mark. 2005. "The Hotline's SurveyUSA Interview." Mystery Pollster. February 9. Accessed September 8, 2015. http://www.mysterypollster.com/main/2005/02/the_hotlines_su.html.

Kenner, David, and William Saletan. 2004. "Let's Go to the Audiotape: Who Nailed the Election Results? Automated Pollsters." Slate. December 9. Accessed September 8, 2015. http://www.slate.com/articles/health_and_science/human_nature/2004/12/lets_go_to_the_audiotape.single.html.

Ring of Fire Staff. 2015. "SurveyUSA Shows Trump Winning the Presidency: ROF Explains Why This and All Polling Is Now Hogwash." Ring of Fire. September 8. Accessed September 9, 2015. http://ringoffireradio.com/2015/09/surveyusa-shows-trump-winning-the-presidency-rof-explains-why-this-and-all-other-corp-media-polling-is-hogwash.

T

TALK RADIO

Perhaps more than any other media, radio has provided political conservatives with a potent platform for mobilizing its supporters and pressing Republican leaders to adhere to a conservative dogma or face real opposition from within their own party. Although the audience numbers have fluctuated over the years, conservatives like Rush Limbaugh and Sean Hannity boast more than 12 million listeners each and others like Glenn Beck, Laura Ingraham, and Mark Levin can claim millions of their own.

It would actually take an act of deregulation, championed by a Republican administration, to allow this explosion of political talk on the radio to take place. Up until the mid-1980s, the Federal Communications Commission had maintained a policy called the Fairness Doctrine that required the radio stations to cover political issues of the day, but it also stated that those same stations had to offer differing viewpoints on those matters. So, if a station offered four hours of conservative political talk, the FCC could force it to offer four hours of liberal talk. But the Reagan administration included broadcasters in a wave of deregulations during the 1980s and in 1987 the FCC voted to end enforcement of the policy. Commission chairman Dennis Patrick said after the 4-1 vote, "We seek to extend to the electronic press the same First Amendment guarantees that the print media have enjoyed since our country's inception." Now free from possible government sanction for airing politically biased talk, radio networks began experimenting with format, airing conservatives and liberals on different channels.

Then came Rush Limbaugh.

Limbaugh, a college drop-out but radio junkie, had bounced from deejay job to deejay job and had landed a job in Sacramento. As the Fairness Doctrine ended, Limbaugh pushed the limits of what was now allowed, finding a mix of political commentary and humor that soon drew listeners and advertisers, and a syndication deal followed. Limbaugh was but the first of many who would follow, almost all of them conservative. A handful of liberal talkers exist, but draw far smaller audiences than their colleagues on the right. Limbaugh and his growing number of colleagues took aim at Democrats in Congress and, later, President Bill Clinton, attracting millions of listeners by launching broadsides against Democrats. What *The Daily Show* did for liberals, mixing humor with biting political commentary, had already been tried successfully on talk radio for Republicans. By the early 1990s, Limbaugh was advocating on behalf of House Republicans who hoped to take their hardline criticism of Democrats to the voters in 1994. That year, with frustration mounting with Clinton and congressional Democrats, Limbaugh encouraged listeners to rally around Republican leader Newt Gingrich, hoping to spur a stunning GOP landslide in the off-year election that handed the Republicans control of the U.S. House for the first time in 40 years. It was a heady time in the relationship between the party and talk radio, notes the *Wall Street Journal*'s Patrick O'Connor, who wrote, "Republicans touted conservative talk radio as a foolproof medium to communicate directly with their most ardent supporters. Democrats and liberal groups tried to replicate that success by building their own left-leaning television and radio stations, with far less success" (O'Connor 2015). These talk show hosts, especially Hannity and Glenn Beck, were able to translate their radio popularity into cable news success, hosting programs on Fox News and CNN. The audience often followed them and many of them found that the sharper their criticism became, the bigger audiences and more ardent fans they gained.

As talk radio became more competitive with itself and the audience more self-selected, talk show hosts found themselves pushing the envelope of what is acceptable commentary on the day's news. Glenn Beck said there were members of the Obama administration who are "Marxist revolutionaries who have dedicated themselves to principles that will destroy our nation as we know it." Michael Savage has said, "Every stinking, rotten left winger in this country poses a far greater threat to your freedom than does al-Qaida." Many who analyze political speech began to question whether the talk had gone too far. Kathleen Hall Jamieson told the *PBS NewsHour* in 2009, "The downside occurs when this type of insulating discourse is used to tag the other side, the opposition, as more different than it actually is from the listener. It polarizes. So, the audience becomes locked up in its own little ideological world. The rhetoric becomes more shrill, more strident. It becomes hysterical and hyperbolic. And then one's sense of that as appropriate discourse is something that one begins to feel. One thinks that it's appropriate to ridicule the other side, to demonize the other side. One stops calling it ridicule and demonization. One starts to think that that's how we talk politics" (Brown 2009).

But it was more than just a coarsening of the rhetoric. The economics of talk radio have also evolved as money has poured in from conservative think tanks, advocacy groups, and tea party-aligned organizations to work with these radio hosts. A 2014 investigation from Politico found that "conservative groups spent nearly $22 million to broker and pay for involved advertising relationships known as sponsorships with a handful of influential talkers including Beck, Sean Hannity, Laura Ingraham, Mark Levin, and Rush Limbaugh between the first talk radio deals in 2008 and the end of 2012. Since then, the sponsorship deals have grown more lucrative and tea party-oriented, with legacy groups like The Heritage Foundation ending their sponsorships and groups like the Tea Party Patriots placing big ad buys" (Vogel and Weinger 2014). The Politico investigation, which included examining FCC reports and filings with Federal Election Commission, found that as talk radio hosts ramped up their criticism of President Obama and any Republican working with the Obama administration, tea party groups and other hardline conservative organizations were sponsoring more and more radio programs and hiring those talk show hosts to speak on behalf of their organizations.

The connection is not just economic; these vocal radio critics of both Democrats and Republicans found deeper partnerships with organizations aimed at rejecting political compromises. This has helped lead to talk radio hosts becoming increasingly active within the Republican Party, offering support and an audience for outsider candidates who may challenge more moderate members of their own party. Although part of this influence can be found simply through their harsh critiques of party leadership, this effort took on a more concrete reality in 2014. Tension between conservative activists aligned with the Tea Party and the more mainstream Republican Party had been brewing for years as leaders in Congress, at times, sought to strike agreements with Democrats in the White House and Congress to move compromise agreements forward. Some within the party base saw these moves as selling conservative principles out for political benefit. One of their first targets was House whip Eric Cantor. Cantor, a conservative from Virginia, seemed a shoe-in for the GOP nomination for his seat he had held since 2001. But then talk radio hosts Ingraham and Levin got involved. Ingraham endorsed Cantor's conservative rival Dave Brat. She appeared at Brat's rallies and electrified crowds in the central Virginia district. Soon, money and volunteers swelled Brat's ranks and he was able to eke out a victory over his vastly better funded opponent. Ingraham would later say, "I helped shine a light on a race where the establishment was vulnerable. I helped give Brat a platform that he was not getting through any other media outlet. The national media wasn't giving him his due and national tea party groups weren't lifting a finger to help him. . . . I knew that if he had a little bit of a boost, he would make a really good run at this" (Byers 2014).

This connection between conservative activism and talk radio continues to evolve, but it also comes as talk radio listenership has begun to sink. The format still attracts 50 million listeners a week, putting it behind only country music for popularity on commercial radio, but advertisers have grown wary of the backlash their sponsorship may provoke. Advertising on talk radio stations now on average costs half as much as advertising on music channels. How this economic crunch and political activism may affect its future business remains uncertain, but talk radio remains a potent and combustible force among conservatives.

See also: Beck, Glenn; Conservative Blogosphere; Fairness Doctrine; Hannity, Sean; Limbaugh, Rush

Further Reading

Brown, Jeffrey. 2009. "TV, Radio Talkers Shaping Political Discourse in U.S." PBS NewsHour. November 5. Accessed December 16, 2015. http://crooksandliars.com:8080/heather/pbs-newshour-tv-radio-talkers-shaping-poli.

Byers, Dylan. 2014. "Right-Wing Radio's Win." Politico. June 11. Accessed December 16, 2015. http://www.politico.com/story/2014/06/eric-cantor-laura-ingraham-107743.

O'Connor, Patrick. 2015. "How Talk Radio Is Informing the GOP's Presidential Race." *Wall Street Journal*. November 23. Accessed December 16, 2015. http://blogs.wsj.com/washwire/2015/11/23/conservative-talk-radio-informs-gop-presidential-race-in-new-way.

Vogel, Kenneth, and Mackenzie Weinger. 2014. "The Tea Party Radio Network." Politico. April 17. Accessed December 15, 2015. http://www.politico.com/story/2014/04/tea-party-radio-network-105774#ixzz2zLJnotjJ.

TALKING POINTS MEMO

Talking Points Memo is a left-leaning political reporting website that mixes its blogging roots with an increasingly journalistic approach to covering news of the day. The site boasts 3 million unique visitors a month and claims to reach well-educated and wealthy viewers with more than half reporting an income of more than $100,000 a year (TPM 2015).

Launched in 2000 as the more politically opinionated (and a bit hot-headed) version of *Washington Monthly* reporter and *Hill* columnist Joshua Micah Marshall, TPM was a platform that allowed Marshall to start writing a more informal blog that aimed to articulate the critical political debates of the day. At the time of its creation there was plenty of political fodder for Marshall to dig in to. He launched TPM during the Florida recount controversy that ended the 2000 presidential election and with sharp and intelligent criticism of the right, TPM quickly developed a sizeable D.C.-area following.

By 2001 Marshall was writing full time at TPM (while contributing to other sites and news organizations). So the next year when former Senate Majority Leader Trent Lott spoke at the 100th birthday party of South Carolina senator Strom Thurmond and appeared to endorse his segregationist policies of the 1940s, Marshall had a platform to speak out on an issue he felt the mainstream press was missing. He later told PBS's *Frontline*, "When you unpacked what Trent Lott said, it was really egregious. It was terrible . . . In the way that the news media works, a story really has a 24-hour audition, that it makes its case whether it's going to catch fire and whether it's going to become a real story. And that story failed its 24-hour audition . . . I think in a pre-blog world that would have been the end of it. But my blog and others picked up the story and basically started making the case for it, that it was a lot more important than the rest of the news media had thought" (*Frontline* 2007). TPM and other blogs helped keep the story alive, and when the mainstream did pick it up, Lott was forced to resign over the comments.

With the role TPM had played in the Lott story, Marshall had established himself as one of the growing legion of political bloggers that demanded attention. By 2004 Marshall was described by the *New York Times Magazine* as "an irate spitter of well-crafted vitriol aimed at the president, whom he compared, one day, to Tony Soprano torching his friend's sporting-goods store for the sake of a little extra cash" (Klam 2004). With a mix of clear opinion and strong reporting, TPM was beginning to transform into something more than just a blog.

Soon the site was applying the same approach it has taken with politics to other areas, creating spinoffs that focus on culture and society (TPM Café), investigative reporting (TPM Muckraker), and election-year politics (TPM Election Central). But running through all of these efforts is an approach that TPM veterans say is ingrained in the news organization—a two-way relationship with its readers. As a profile in the *Columbia Journalism Review* put it, "From the very early days of Talking Points Memo, [Marshall] has (by accident or design) cultivated an intense relationship with a well-connected set of readers—lawyers, activists, policy wonks, and veterans of intelligence agencies. Those readers have offered an endless stream of tips, and they have occasionally been deployed en masse to plow through document dumps from the Department of Justice or to ask members of Congress to publicly clarify their positions on Social Security" (Glenn 2007).

It was because of the strong network he had built and the reporting abilities the TPM staff had grown that they were able to respond to the biggest story they had ever had in early 2007. TPM Muckraker had caught whiff of a series of firings and reappointments within the ranks of federal prosecutors. Some readers of TPM saw a political motivation for the moves, accusing the Justice Department of a political purge of its ranks. The team at TPM ran with the story and became the first to report that the Bush administration was cleaning house of anyone deemed not politically supportive of White House policies. The reaction by the mainstream press was skeptical. At *Time* magazine, Washington bureau chief Jay Carney dismissed the report as partisan paranoia.

TPM reporter Paul Kiel later explained, "TPM's reporters were surveying media around the country and following up links to local papers sent in by readers, 'so it was kind of a mix of what you might call blog reporting and traditional reporting,' or what might be termed a kind of 'wisdom of crowds' method of reporting, combined with some good old-fashioned banging of the phones" (McLeary 2007). What emerged was a widespread perception that the Bush White House was seeking to politicize the U.S. attorney system and anyone who did not support their efforts was subject to dismissal. Carney would take to his blog at *Time* again in March of 2007. This time, though, instead of dismissing Marshall, he praised him, writing, "The blogosphere was the engine on this story, pulling the Hill and the MSM along. As the document dump proves, what happened was much worse than I'd first thought. I was wrong. Very nice work, and thanks for holding my feet to the fire" (Carney 2007).

The story would earn TPM a George Polk award and lead to the resignation of the U.S. attorney general and eight other high-ranking Department of Justice personnel. It also help spark a major overhaul of TPM, completing its shift from politically engaged blog to news organization with an intense and effective relationship with its readers.

See also: Daily Kos; Huffington Post; Liberal Blogosphere

Further Reading

Carney, Jay. 2007. "Where Credit Is Due." *Time*. March 27. Accessed February 16, 2015. http://swampland.time.com/2007/03/13/where_credit_is_due.

Frontline. 2007. "News War Transcript." Accessed February 15, 2015. http://www.pbs.org/wgbh/pages/frontline/newswar/etc/script3.html.

Glenn, David. 2007. "The (Josh) Marshall Plan." *Columbia Journalism Review*. September 5. Accessed February 16, 2015. http://www.cjr.org/feature/the_josh_marshall_plan.php.
Klam, Mathew. 2004. "Fear and Laptops on the Campaign Trail." *New York Times Magazine*. September 26. Accessed February 15, 2015. http://www.nytimes.com/2004/09/26/magazine/26BLOGS.html?_r=0.
McLeary, Paul. 2007. "How TalkingPointsMemo Beat the Big Boys on the U.S. Attorney Story." *Columbia Journalism Review*. March 15. Accessed February 16, 2015. http://www.cjr.org/behind_the_news/how_talkingpointsmemo_beat_the.php.
Talking Points Memo. 2015. "Advertise." Accessed February 15, 2015. http://advertising.talkingpointsmemo.com.

TARBELL, IDA (1857–1944)

Special deals with railroaders, shrewd business tactics, and a desire to stamp out his competition helped John D. Rockefeller shape Standard Oil into the biggest company in the business. One crusading female journalist helped bring it to its knees.

Ida Tarbell had watched the toll Standard Oil took on its competitors firsthand. The daughter of a small-time oil man, she was 14 when the so-called Cleveland Massacre happened. Rockefeller worked out a deal through something called the South Improvement Company where a railroad would charge small producers more to ship their oil while giving Standard a price break. The scheme kept Standard and railroad companies in the green while driving many competitors out of business (King 2012). Tarbell would recall the incident 30 years later as part of her devastating profile of Rockefeller and his empire. "Under the combined threat and persuasion of the Standard, armed with the South Improvement Company scheme, almost the entire independent oil interest of Cleveland collapsed in three months' time," Tarbell wrote in *The History of Standard Oil*, a book that grew out of a series of investigatory articles that appeared in *McClure's* in 1902 and 1903 (Tarbell 1904). Her work—which targeted the company's wrongdoing, not its size or stingy business practices—led to the breakup of the company's monopoly and helped usher in the era of the muckraker, a time when investigative journalism thrived.

Ida Minerva Tarbell was born November 5, 1857, in Pennsylvania where her father built and sold oil tanks. In 1876, she went to Allegheny College in Meadville, Pennsylvania, as the only woman in her class. She decided to be a writer, after concluding "that no woman could be both a wife and pursue a career outside the home" (Starkman 2014).

Her first journalism job came at a paper in Meadville, the *Chautauquan*, where she spent eight years and became managing editor. But the newspaper life wouldn't be hers forever. She moved to Paris in 1891 to study and write freelance. That's where Sam McClure found her and convinced her to come work for him.

At *McClure's Magazine*, Tarbell, alongside the likes of Lincoln Steffens and Ray Stannard Baker, would become a top-tier investigative journalist of the time. Her style was to dive into the documents of history, and her early works included lengthy pieces on Napoleon Bonaparte and President Abraham Lincoln.

By the turn of the century, Tarbell used the same extensive investigation technique to go after John D. Rockefeller, Sr., and the Standard Oil Company. Tarbell crafted the 19-part series using internal company memos, public records from government investigations into the company, and detailed interviews. What resulted became one of the seminal works of investigative journalism. In his book *The Watchdog That Didn't Bark*, Dean Starkman called it "the greatest business story ever written." It provoked public uproar and helped inspire reform movements that would demand the government take action to protect consumers and competition. In 1911, the U.S. Supreme Court found that Standard had violated the Sherman Antitrust Act. Standard was broken up into several smaller companies. As it turns out, Rockefeller would only get richer. Stock shares of the companies that came from the breakup soared, and he went "from a mere millionaire into nearly a billionaire" (Starkman 2014).

Despite that, Tarbell's legacy was secure. She was an early example of a journalist that challenged the powerful and exposed malpractice, and an inspiration for investigative reporters to come.

Michael Wright

See also: *McClure's Magazine*; Muckraking

Further Reading

"Ida M. Tarbell, 86, Dies in Bridgeport." *New York Times*. 1944. Obituaries sec.

King, Gilbert. 2012. "The Woman Who Took on the Tycoon." Smithsonian.com. July 5. Accessed August 31, 2015. http://www.smithsonianmag.com/history/the-woman-who-took-on-the-tycoon-651396/?no-ist.

Starkman, Dean. 2014. *The Watchdog That Didn't Bark: The Financial Crisis and the Disappearance of Investigative Journalism*. New York: Columbia University Press.

Tarbell, Ida. 1904. *The History of the Standard Oil Company*. New York: McClure, Phillips, and Co.

TEA PARTY MOVEMENT

Unlike a centrally organized political party or campaign, movements are a complicated concept for journalists to cover and accurately contextualize. The coverage of the tea parties by the political media highlight the struggle of journalists to frame and explain an odd mix of organizations and individuals that includes established libertarian organizations, grassroots activists, cultural conservatives, and constitutionalists. The media has portrayed these groups as the dawn of a third party, an ideological civil war within the Republican Party, a manufactured front for wealthy political donors, and a genuine outpouring of public frustration with the current state of public affairs and the role of government in their lives. All of these descriptions are to some extent correct and dead wrong. Exploring the roots of the tea parties also help cast a light on how the media seeks to label and group organizations in way that serves as a sort of journalistic short-hand when covering the multidimensional realities of politics and political movements.

Even finding an origin to the tea parties movement highlights how difficult it is to cover a fairly new and decentralized movement. The name "tea party" had been in use by a variety of conservative and libertarian groups that were protesting government policies throughout the 1980s, 1990s, and early 2000s. These groups were often unaffiliated and were only connected by the name "tea party," a reference to the 1773 protests in Boston where the Sons of Liberty anti-British group boarded three ships in Boston Harbor and dumped some 342 chests of tea overboard to protest British tax policies. The name took on more national attention as activists inspired by the candidacy of former libertarian presidential candidate Ron Paul launched an online fundraising plan, dubbed "the moneybomb," to raise money for the 2008 GOP candidate. The group rallied around the anniversary of the Boston Tea Party and used that date, December 16, to focus its fundraising effort. The campaign netted $6 million in one day—the largest single-day donation total up until that point—and for those backers the idea of the "tea party" was born. A few weeks later, Paul supporters would still be basking in the glow of the concerted, but decentralized effort, telling the Online NewsHour, "What's really special about the Ron Paul campaign is so many of these different initiatives, whether you're talking about the Ron Paul blimp or you're talking about the Tea Party that just occurred—the Moneybomb—all of that is not affiliated with the campaign. The campaign is made up of many different organizations" (Bowman 2008).

Some see this campaign as the real roots of the tea party movement that would take off in 2009. Commentator Juan Williams would write on Fox News, the movement rose out of the "ashes" of the Paul campaign, claiming, "Since then, the Tea Party has bullied the Republican leadership in the House to force budget cuts at the risk of shutting down the government and collectively become the most persistent critic of the Obama presidency on financial regulatory reform and health care. The roots of all of this are in the libertarian mind of Congressman Paul" (Williams 2011). But like so many of the media narratives about the tea party movement, the idea that there is one set of roots and one organization is often misguided. While true that many activists embraced the power of collective action that the "moneybomb" represented and saw this power as a way to stand up to the party elites, there were other organizations critical to the tea parties' growth that existed long before the 2008 campaign.

At least one branch of tea party efforts can be traced back to one critical organization, FreedomWorks. This group is the latest incarnation of a political organization organized and funded by the Charles and David Koch's foundations. The organization was incorporated in 1984 as Citizens for a Sound Economy, a think tank dedicated to smaller government, lower taxes, and limited regulations. The organization developed policy papers on everything from global warming to health policy and accepted donations from the Koch brothers as well as corporations like Exxon, Philip Morris, and Microsoft. When flat tax-advocate and House Majority

Leader Dick Armey retired from Congress in 2003, he took the helm of CSE. It was also at this time that CSE was going through a fundamental transformation. In 2002 it had designed and launched its first "tea party" organization website, usteaparty.com, to foster anti-tax efforts, claiming, "our U.S. Tea Party is a national event, hosted continuously online and open to all Americans who feel our taxes are too high and the tax code is too complicated" (Jarvis 2013).

By 2004, CSE divided itself into FreedomWorks, headed by Armey, and Americans for Prosperity, under David Koch. Americans for Prosperity became the primary political advocacy group for the Koch brothers and FreedomWorks served as a critical group to organizing the early protests against President Obama's policies. But how much of FreedomWorks remains under the influence of the Koch brothers is debatable. The organization claims it is fueled primarily by small-dollar donors and activists—in short, tea party members—while many liberal activists see the organization as a faux grassroots group run by the Koch brothers. Former House Speaker Nancy Pelosi and other Democrats have accused the tea parties of being "Astroturf"—fake grassroots that work for big money donors. But the organization has brought in tens of thousands of members and donations that total millions of dollars. One expert concluded, "The complexity of the brothers' relationship to the Tea Party derives from many of the same ambiguities that define American politics in the 21st century. Paths of influence are obscured behind organizations with ambiguous names and few obligations to explain who funds operations" (Brown 2015).

Like the remnants of the Paul campaign in 2008 and the Koch-funded efforts of FreedomWorks, other organizations with diverse interests and agendas also grew up under the tea party umbrella, and it would take a spark to turn these disparate actions into an actual movement. That moment came in 2009 and was the creation of mass media.

The year 2009 saw a series of protests erupt around the country in response to the government moves to stave off an economic crisis. President Barack Obama proposed a major economic stimulus bill that planned to pour money into projects to bring down unemployment and ease the credit crisis. Many saw it as simply a government hand-out, including a blogger and math teacher in Seattle named Keli Carender, who organized a protest of some 150 people opposed to the stimulus bill and would go on to work with the Tea Party Patriots group. But at least one tea party advocate and conservative figure, Glenn Beck, attributes much of the national tea party effort to CNBC commentator Rick Santelli. On February 19 he took to the floor of the Chicago Mercantile Exchange to blast the government moves to help homeowners who were defaulting on their home payments—a reality that threatened to snowball into a major economic collapse. Santelli, clearly agitated, turned to the traders and declared, "This is America. How many of you people want to pay for your neighbor's mortgage and has an extra bathroom and can't pay their bills? Raise your hands. (Boos) President Obama are you listening? . . . We're thinking of having a Chicago Tea Party in July. All you capitalists that want to show up to Lake Michigan, I'm going to start organizing" (Meckler and Martin 2012). The moment, captured and broadcast on cable news, helped give voice to a growing frustration among a whole different set of people who had not been engaged in the Koch brothers' CSE or the Ron Paul campaign. As Beck later told *Business Insider*, "A lot of people have been credited with starting the modern-day tea party but make no mistake, it was Rick Santelli. His off the cuff monologue spoke the words that millions of Americans felt but could not nor dare not speak" (Perlberg 2014).

A national rally was quickly held on February 27 and a larger one was planned for April 15. FreedomWorks quickly became a major backer and organizer of the events and conservative commentators like Michelle Malkin, Beck, and Sean Hannity soon began promoting the April event. Even at this point, it was unclear how much of the tea party effort was to protest government action and how much was to promote Republican politics. As the *New York Times* noted in its story, "The events were meant to protest government spending, particularly the Obama administration's $787 billion stimulus package and its $3.5 trillion budget. Although organizers insisted they had created a nonpartisan grass-roots movement, others argued that these parties were more of the Astroturf variety: an occasion largely created by the clamor of cable news and fueled by the financial and political support of current and former Republican leaders" (Robbins 2009). The article went on to play the role of FreedomWorks and Armey heavily in its story about the protest, but it also laid out some of the key elements that would mark media coverage of the tea party for months to come. Outlets like the *Times* and the *Washington Post* often reported on the protests as Republican rallying efforts, seeking to draw political authority and later electoral success from people's frustrations.

The protests only grew in intensity as President Obama's health care reform law caught political fire. Tea party groups are credited with organizing widespread protests that greeted lawmakers who returned home for the August recess in 2009, and a September rally in Washington also drew hundreds of thousands. The protests were covered in the media, but the force of the tea party within conservative ranks was still under-reported in these early efforts. Despite these disparate groups, different sources of funding, and varied agendas, the tea party movement, loosely described as a conservative, populist effort to rein in the size of government, had energized a new wave of political activists. One historian of the groups argued that the most important element of the movement happened in the sudden sense of collective action, writing, "For many activists immersion in the Tea Party has represented a political awakening as well as a sense of fulfillment. Their voices were being heard; their actions, they now believed, were making a difference. Participation submerged their feelings of powerlessness and gave them what political scientists call a 'sense of efficacy,' a healthy mentality in a democratic republic" (Formisano 2012). But this newfound "healthy mentality" also came with a set of expectations that these rallies would lead to immediate change.

In an odd way, the tea parties' growth and message of change echoed the promise of the 2008 Obama campaign, a connection neither side would agree with nor welcome. But the fact remains, the "Change we can believe in" crowds that sought a post-partisan Washington created by Obama and the small-government activists rallying in Washington in September 2009 both wanted a different political system, and they wanted it now. And both found themselves stymied by the current political system. For the tea party those roadblocks came from within the Republican Party and from the government.

The government reaction could be most damningly found in the Cincinnati offices of the Internal Revenue Service. The organization was tracking a surge in applications for nonprofit status by tea party-aligned organizations and began flagging those groups for further scrutiny. When news came out at the IRS was targeting tea party groups for investigation, the conservative media exploded in criticism. Within a week of the news, the head of the IRS was out, and the conservative narrative that the Obama administration was after them had taken hold. Just as telling was the uneasy response of Republican leaders to the tea parties. These activists represented a double-edged sword for the GOP. On the one hand, they represented a new jolt of energy and voters for a party flagging in the wake of devastating electoral losses in 2006 and 2008. But with this newly energized bloc of voters came a profoundly difficult set of demands to fulfill. The head of one group, the American Majority, that helped foment the tea party grassroots groups and inspire new candidates to run, put the goals of their group in these terms, "The Tea Party needs to realize is that its objective is not about shifting paradigms or having a short-term impact. It's about crushing paradigms and creating a new set of rules that dictate how the game is played decades from now . . . The Tea Party, if it is to be remembered a hundred years from now, must shrink the bureaucratic state, returning government to its proper role. It must also fundamentally change the process of electoral politics, whether it's a return to a caucus and convention nomination process or even repealing the 17th Amendment and the direct election of Senators" (Ryun 2012). But not all Republicans agreed with this position, and many of the elected officials who hoped to leverage these voters to secure re-election soon faced opposition in their own primaries from candidates who saw their role as to blow the whole system up rather than discuss evolutionary tweaks to Washington.

This internal discontent, intraparty electoral fights, and ongoing clash with the president's governing efforts all created rich fodder for political reporting and campaign coverage in particular. But how the media chose to portray the tea party groups varied widely from story to story and news outlet to news outlet. Often news organizations sought comments from tea party figures to serve as a balance to establishment figures on the right and left. But the question remained: who do you quote in a system as decentralized as the tea party? Sometimes, the media simply botched it. One organization, which almost no tea party activist endorses, is teaparty.org, and yet several news organizations, including the *Washington Post*, quoted the head of the site as a reputable spokesperson for the movement. This partly speaks to the lack of awareness by the reporter but also the difficulty of news reporters seeking "a" comment from a series of amorphous groups that specifically reject the idea of a single organizer.

Still, the media, whether through the partisan hyping of the tax day protests in 2009 or their portrayal of the movement in other reporting, usually organize their coverage in a way that is sympathetic to the movement. One analysis of the way the media frame their coverage of the tea party movement, or what they call the TPM, found that, "Overall, the U.S. media depicted the TPM with supportive frames (Everyday American, Grassroots, Fiscal Federal Frustrations, and Election Impact) more than twice as often as the deprecatory characterizations the activists opposed (Non-Mainstream, Establishment-Affiliated, Amalgam of Grievances, and Flash-in-the-Pan). Usually, media portrayed the TPM as an electorally influential grassroots movement—albeit sometimes depicted with a non-mainstream fringe—primarily concerned with an overreaching, fiscally irresponsible federal government" (Boykoff and Laschever 2011).

This coverage often faltered when the campaign season kicked in as the tea party then moved from a coalition of activists seeking policy change to a part of campaign strategy and efforts to get out the vote. This often showed up by labeling one candidate the "tea party-favorite" or "tea party-backed," although this was more a simple way to categorize the candidate rather than an effective explanation of the candidate or his or her policies. Meanwhile, in the increasingly heated blogosphere and among left-leaning and right-leaning news outlets, the tea party became a far more controversial movement. Some liberals and supporters of President Obama soon began dismissing critics as "tea baggers" and radicals bent on derailing the orderly function of government. Conservative outlets split; some aligned with the movement while others argued that its supporters were unrealistic and misguided. One conservative thinker who argues the tea party defies any of these simple descriptions, declared, "A more apt characterization of the Tea Party would be that of an antiparty, a close conglomeration of individuals coalescing around certain principles, challenging the existing political parties to embrace them. The movement has no formal, centralized decision-making authority that dictates talking points or policy positions to its members" (Foley 2012).

And perhaps that is why the tea party movement remains less a cohesive entity, and more a label that conveys a set of pre-existing ideas to the reader—often views the reader or viewer themselves possess. Some see the tea party as a source of collective power for those frustrated by government's role in the modern American life; others see a source of disorder and political chaos.

See also: Grassroots Campaigns; Koch Brothers: Koch, Charles and Koch, David; Political Polarization and the Media; Political Parties; Single-Issue Politics

Further Reading

Bowman, Quinn. 2008. "Paul Campaign Attracts Array of Supporters." Online NewsHour. January 19. Accessed January 12, 2016. https://www.youtube.com/watch?v=65FGzf8wctI.

Boykoff, Jules, and Eulalie Laschever. 2011. "The Tea Party Movement, Framing, and the US Media." *Social Movement Studies* 10, no. 4 (November). Accessed January 19, 2016. http://courses.arch.vt.edu/courses/wdunaway/gia5274/TeaParty.pdf.

Brown, Heath. 2015. *The Tea Party Divided: The Hidden Diversity of a Maturing Movement*. Santa Barbara, CA: ABC-CLIO.

Foley, Elizabeth Price. 2012. *The Tea Party: Three Principles*. New York: Cambridge University Press.

Formisano, Ronald. 2012. *The Tea Party: A Brief History*. Baltimore, MD: The Johns Hopkins University Press.

Jarvis, Brooke. 2013. "Big Tobacco's Tea Party Ties Exposed." *Rolling Stone*. February 13. Accessed May 31, 2016. http://www.rollingstone.com/politics/news/big-tobaccos-tea-party-ties-exposed-20130213.

Meckler, Mark, and Jenny Beth Martin. 2012. *Tea Party Patriots: The Second American Revolution*. New York: Macmillan.

Perlberg, Steven. 2014. "Rick Santelli Started the Tea Party with a Rant Exactly 5 Years Ago Today—Here's How He Feels about It Now." *Business Insider*. February 19. Accessed January 19, 2016. http://www.businessinsider.com/rick-santelli-tea-party-rant-2014-2.

Robbins, Liz. 2009. "Tax Day Is Met with Tea Parties." *New York Times*. April 15. Accessed January 16, 2016. http://www.nytimes.com/2009/04/16/us/politics/16taxday.html?_r=0.

Ryun, Ned. 2012. "A Tale of Two Movements." *American Spectator*. March. Accessed January 19, 2016. http://spectator.org/articles/36085/tale-two-movements.

Williams, Juan. 2011. "The Surprising Rise of Rep. Ron Paul." Fox News. May 10. Accessed January 19, 2016. http://www.foxnews.com/opinion/2011/05/10/juan-williams-surprising-rise-rep-ron-paul.html.

TELEVISION ADVERTISING

Although much has been made of the revolution the Internet has brought to media and campaigning, the largest portion of any campaign's budget is still devoted to a tried-and-true form of political electioneering: the 30- or 60-second campaign ad. Since their use first in the 1950s, television ads have become a primary way in which campaigns shape and deliver their message. This message can include paid media, where the campaign purchases airtime, and free media where provocative ads get picked up and repeated by the news media. As the financial power of elections has shifted from individuals running for office and established political parties to those groups seeking to influence the race, television ads purchased by outside groups have also exploded. The result is that in 2012 the total bill for political ads purchased topped $1.92 billion.

The 2012 campaign saw an unprecedented amount of money flood the political process. The campaign of President Barack Obama raised some $1.1 billion for its re-election effort and outside groups poured another $550 million into the campaign. Much of this spending in the presidential race, along with congressional and statewide contests, ended up on television. Nearly 3 million television ads were purchased during the 2012 election campaign, but few played nationally. Instead, television advertising was a highly targeted affair according to the Wesleyan Media

Project, which tracked broadcast and cable ads. The project's co-director Erika Franklin Fowler said later, "Not only did we see record, pulverizing amounts of advertising on the air, but we saw it concentrated, so heavily concentrated, into just a small number of markets . . . [The ads] were crammed into just a few key battleground markets. If you were in one of those markets, you were getting inundated from May right up through election day, whereas if you were outside of those markets, you didn't really see very many presidential ads, if [any] at all" (Overby 2013). The cycle highlighted that even in the era of social media and micro-targeted mailings, television advertising remains a powerful tool and the most expensive line item in most campaign budgets.

The purpose of ads is fairly straightforward and boils down to two simple goals: outline who your candidate is and why they are ideal for the office they seek and secondly, define your opponent in a way to emphasize the personal or political positions that make him or her not a good fit. Early advertising focused heavily on the idea of self-identification and explanation. These ads sought to introduce the electorate to the candidate and offer a political biography or outline of issues they may support if elected. As television became a more dominant form of media and advertising specialists honed their craft, advertising came to involve more attacks on opponents and less biography of the candidate. Within 20 years of the first television campaign ad, there were as many attack ads, or so-called negative ads, as there were more positive messages.

The form has clear advantages to other modes of political communication. Unlike a stump speech or press release that must get through the filter of a reporter or editor before it is broadcast to a mass media audience, television ads allow the campaign to control the message and the visual accompaniment. Ads also allow a campaign to target specific communities through the selection of different broadcast markets and channels. As the television audience began to fragment over multiple channels, campaigns began to target not just geography, but certain types of voters—for example, those who watching daytime cooking shows on cable could be counted on to be more likely female, and therefore a campaign could tailor its ad to be seen on that cable channel in a critical battleground community. Finally, their effect can be monitored to see whether they are working. A top scholar of president debates and campaign commercials in America wrote, "Ads are increasingly used in conjunction with tracking polling, so that the effectiveness or ineffectiveness of an ad can be measured and monitored. In the old days an ad played at the intuitive instinct of the ad maker. Now pollsters and focus groups test ads, and now the ads are often pulled or played more heavily as a result of tracking polls or focus group performance" (Devlin 1995).

These ads, while heavily vetted and tested for their effectiveness, can be broken into playing four distinct roles in campaigns and often can be plotted out over the timeline of the race. Early in the race, as mentioned earlier, ads focus on increasing the name recognition of the candidate. Social science literature shows that one of the most critical elements that can predict the success or failure of an ad campaign involves the degree to which a voter recognizes the name of the candidate on the ballot. So early ads focus on this issue and creating a general knowledge about the candidate's qualifications and personal history. Once that is established, often ads shift emphasis onto the critical issues the candidate is focusing their campaign on. These issues tend to connect clearly to the candidate's ideology and to the core issues that will motivate his or her party's voters to get out on Election Day and cast their ballot. With their name and core issues out, media strategists tend to turn negative later in the campaign, using ads to highlight issues or personal facts that may cause voters to view an opposing candidate more negatively, seeking to soften their support among voters who are not as committed to the opponent. Finally, in the closing days of the campaign, ads often turn more positive as candidates look to "close the deal" with voters, stressing their vision for the future and seeking to cast themselves more as leader and less as a politician. The rise of early voting, where many people cast their ballots weeks ahead of the election, has altered this strategy somewhat, forcing candidates to air whatever their core argument is sometimes up to a month before the actual Election Day to ensure that voters see their messages before marking their ballots.

Advertising as a force in political campaigns began in the presidential race and emerged in the post-war period as television itself became a major force in mass media. Unlike other mass media, television seemed to have a special power in politics and by 1952 Republican strategists working with Madison Avenue ad men were crafting the first political advertisements. President Harry Truman had decided not to run as his popularity plummeted and after he lost the New Hampshire primary. He then threw his weight behind Illinois governor Adlai Stevenson. Although not on the ticket, Truman continued to make the argument to keep the Democrats in power after 20 years in the White House. He famously declared, "You never had it so good!"

The exclamation became a sort-of unofficial slogan of the Democrats' campaign and the supporters of Republican candidate and former U.S. General Dwight Eisenhower wanted to counter the argument. Instead of developing a slogan of their own, the Republicans decided to launch a targeted ad buy, the first of any political campaign. Despite the assumption of experts now that ad men created ads on their instincts, the response was carefully planned and executed. The team first shot Eisenhower offering his responses to a series of questions. The ad team then went out and found different voters who represented key demographic targets of the campaign and filmed them asking each question. The result ran something like this: a young black man says to camera: "General, the Democrats are telling me I never had it so good." Eisenhower, dressed in a suit and looking stern answers, appeared to face the young man: "Can that be true when America is billions in debt? When prices have doubled? When taxes break our backs and we are still fighting in Korea? It's tragic." Eisenhower then turns to face the camera, ending with, "and it is time for a change." The spots, dubbed "Eisenhower Answers America," were then planned to air for maximum impact on the Electoral College, targeting 62 counties in 12 states.

According to one study of the campaign, none of the decisions about the campaign were accidental. "In order to gain 249 electoral votes only 844,320 voters needed to be influenced by the campaign. So, the . . . plan isolated 844,320 voters in sixty-two counties in twelve states. The plan evolved over time as political constraints caused a realignment in strategy. Massachusetts, for example, was not in the original twelve states but was added to the priority list because of unspecified 'political developments in the past four weeks'" (Wood 1990). The success of the campaign firmly established the campaign ad spot as a part of the modern political campaign.

As the value of advertising became apparent to political strategists and candidates, the form quickly developed an aesthetic and common elements. The visual aspects of ads soon took on real importance. Warmly lit video of smiling candidates with their families became a staple of campaign ads. Also, candidates often sought to surround themselves with people who would resonate with important voting demographics including union members, teachers, mothers, and owners of small businesses. The use of the American flag and video of the candidate with sleeves rolled up all became elements of many ads that sought to introduce the candidate and their key issues. Similarly, ads that aimed to raise questions or fears about the competing candidate became stylized in their own way. For these ads, the use of black and white photographs and low, menacing music were regular attributes.

These tropes developed less because of clear evidence of their effectiveness than from a perceived impact. Social science evidence into whether these ads convince people to change their mind about a candidate seems slim, but it is clear that ads can increase people's negative feelings toward a candidate. Still, one exhaustive study of the role of campaign ads declared the techniques of campaign ad makers can only be so effective in an age where the media consumers are such grizzled veterans of television ads, writing, "The typical thirty-five-year-old American has been watching television for three decades and has been through more than a dozen political campaigns as a television consumer. The majority of the audience belongs to the party of skeptics, and not just about political promises . . ." (Diamond and Bates 1984). Despite this now-inherent skepticism and the high price of ads, no campaign is willing to forego the ad buys. Whether it is based on a direct effect ads played on the campaign or simply the mounting list of memorable ads, they quickly came to be a source for discussion by the political reporting corps, which created a new way for the ad itself to affect the campaign.

This relationship between the press and ads has been around since at least 1964, the year an ad that ran only once. "Daisy," became one of the most memorable in American politics. In the ad a two-year-old girl is shown sitting in a field pulling petals from a daisy—actually a black-eyed susan—as she counts, or at least tries to count, from one to nine. When she reaches nine the screen freezes and slowly zooms in on the girl's eye as an official-sounding man counts down from 10 to zero. At zero, as the screen fills with the girl's pupil and a series of devastating nuclear explosions fill the screen. President Lyndon Johnson is then heard saying, "These are the stakes. To make a world in which all of God's children can live, or to go into the dark. We must either love each other, or we must die." Another voiceover then adds, "Vote for President Johnson on November 3rd. The stakes are too high for you to stay home." The ad sought to raise concerns about conservative Senator Barry Goldwater and whether the Republican would be more likely to lead America into a nuclear Armageddon.

The ad ran on NBC once, and the campaign never played it again after some raised questions about how appropriate it was to scare voters with such an emotional spot. Still, the ad ran again and again in news reports and conversations about the controversy. The coverage, more than the one time it ran, helped spread the underlying message of Goldwater's radicalism. This free media repeating of the original ad also connects to a larger reality that ads help shape the coverage of campaigns and not just the voters' information about the candidates. Although the media's fact checking or conversation about ads are usually aimed at testing the ads' accuracy or exploring the political strategy behind the message, it often serves the purpose of repeating the message to a new group of potential voters.

This coverage of ads and the controversial strategies behind them remains a major element of how ads are covered in modern political campaigns. Experts analyze the visual and auditory elements for insight into what the campaign is trying to get at, and this focus on advertising as a strategy fuels expanded coverage of ads in other media. According to some experts, this leads to a blurring in the minds of many voters what the difference is between the original ad and the reporting about it.

Willie Horton speaks to this blended reality. Willie Horton was a convicted murderer who received a weekend furlough from a Massachusetts prison. While out, Horton took off and later raped a Maryland woman and assaulted her boyfriend. The case became a major milestone in the 1988 presidential campaign when two ads and a lot of media discussion of those ads made the front-page news for weeks. Then-vice president George H. W. Bush had made reference to the case while on the campaign trail, seeking to connect the horrible incident to a theme that his rival, Massachusetts governor Michael Dukakis, was soft on crime. The story had not drawn much attention, but then a Republican-connected political action committee launched an ad that told the story again. The reaction was intense as many questioned whether the ad aimed to talk about crime or to raise racial fears of a Horton, a black felon, raping a white woman because of Dukakis's policies. The ad was soon pulled, but then the Bush campaign launched a second ad that showed the front gate of a prison having a revolving door and felons—both black and white—walking into prison and then leaving again. The Bush ad noted that 268 prisoners had escaped during the furlough program, although most were not series criminals like Horton. Bush and his campaign officials insisted they had not made their point about race, but those who have studied the incident noted that voters connected the original ad, the Bush campaign ad, and the ongoing media discussions and so the Horton incident became one of the major themes of the entire campaign. Later, Bush strategist Lee Atwater would admit that the campaign wanted voters to connect the candidate and the issue, saying, "By the time we're finished, they're going to wonder whether Willie Horton is Dukakis' running mate" (Simon 1990).

But even those in the media admit that ads and their coverage tend to blur together in the minds of most voters. One former NBC president told political communications expert Kathleen Hall Jamieson, "Some of the ads start to look like news stories, they're the same length, 30 seconds . . . Television is not just separated in the minds of the viewers between this is news, this is commercial, and this is entertainment. Sometimes it all gets fuzzed up because it all comes into the house through the same little piece of glass" (Jamieson 1992).

Although political ads hold an especially controversial role in the political process, they have become a major staple of the business of local television. In an era where polarization has swept cable news outlets—few swing voters are watching Fox or MSNBC—and digital ads have focused on connecting campaigns to their base of support, local television channels remain one of the few media outlets that can attract a broad spectrum of viewers. The result has meant that local broadcast stations have become the main organizations to profit from campaign spending by candidates and outside organizations. One Pew Research Center report from 2014 found, "Local TV has been receiving the largest portion of political media spending for at least a decade, but the share it consumes and the total dollars reaped continue to grow. Through mid-October, local TV stations have captured 95% of the television political ad spending, which includes spot, national cable, and national network broadcast (local cable political ad spending is not part of this analysis). In 2012, during the last presidential elections, local TV stations captured 92% of total political TV ad spending, based on the same analysis" (Matsa 2014). Although stations are required to charge only the normal rate for political ads, the reality is that campaign fundraising and spending on advertising has emerged as a critical part of the economics of local broadcast television, a fact that many media companies seem oddly mum about when reporting on the spiraling costs of politics in the United States.

See also: Campaign Strategy Coverage; Fact Checking; Issue-Advocacy Advertising; Microtargeting; Negative Advertising

Further Reading

Devlin, L. Patrick, 1995. "Political Commercials in American Presidential Elections." In *Political Advertising in Western Democracies*. Edited by Lynda Lee Kaid and Christina Holtz-Backa. Thousand Oaks, CA: Sage Publications.

Diamond, Edwin, and Stephen Bates. 1984. *The Spot: The Rise of Political Advertising on Television*. Cambridge, MA: The MIT Press.

Jamieson, Kathleen Hall. 1992. *Dirty Politics: Deception, Distraction, and Democracy*. New York: Oxford University Press.

Matsa, Katerina Eva. 2014. "Interest in Midterms May Be Low, but Local TV Awash in Political Ad Spending." Pew Research Center. October 31. Accessed September 14, 2015.

http://www.pewresearch.org/fact-tank/2014/10/31/interest-in-midterms-may-be-low-but-local-tv-awash-in-political-ad-spending.
Overby, Peter. 2013. "A Review of 2012 Confirms A 'Pulverizing' Level of Political Ads." NPR. February 14. Accessed September 14, 2015. http://www.npr.org/sections/itsallpolitics/2013/02/14/172044192/a-review-of-2012-campaign-confirms-a-pulverizing-level-of-political-ads.
Simon, Roger. 1990. "How a Murderer and Rapist Became the Bush Campaign's Most Valuable Player." *Baltimore Sun*. November 11. Accessed September 14, 2015. http://articles.baltimoresun.com/1990-11-11/features/1990315149_1_willie-horton-fournier-michael-dukakis.
Wood, Stephen. 1990. "Television's First Political Spot Ad Campaign: Eisenhower Answers America." *Presidential Studies Quarterly* (Spring).

THEBLAZE

TheBlaze is a news and entertainment website launched in 2010 to counter what its founder, conservative radio host and former Fox News contributor Glenn Beck, sees as a pervasive liberal bent found in almost all mainstream media.

Beck was riding high when he launched the site in 2010, just as his "Restoring Honor" rally attracted a reported 100,000 to Washington, D.C. He would write as one of the first stories on the site a sort of manifesto of what Beck saw as missing from the array of websites out there, saying, "Too many important stories are overlooked. And too many times, we see mainstream media outlets distorting facts to fit rigid agendas . . . TheBlaze will be about current news—and more. It's not just politics and policy. It's looking for insight wherever we find it. We'll examine our culture, deal with matters of faith and family, and we won't be afraid of a history lesson" (Beck 2010). Assembled and developed within seven weeks, the site serves as a sort of platform for Beck and affiliated talk show hosts and writers. The site has hired away several editors from other conservative sites, including editor Scott Baker, who worked for Breitbart TV, and folks from Townhall and *American Spectator*. The site became more important in 2011 when Beck left his spot on Fox News, focusing on building TheBlaze and its video companion, TheBlaze TV.

With an array of content, including a kids program called *Liberty's Treehouse*, the network-in-training has worked to build an audience, focusing especially on building the subscription streaming service into a full-fledged cable channel. The growth on that side has reportedly been slow. CNN media reporter Brian Stelter explored the issue in 2014 and wrote, "I told Beck about an exchange I had with an executive at one big distributor—almost as big as Comcast. There's a simple reason why the distributor hasn't picked up TheBlaze yet, the executive said: 'What happens if Beck gets hit by a bus tomorrow?' In other words, what makes the channel worth carrying, besides Beck's own daily talk show?" (Stelter 2014). Beck has invested heavily in answering that question, adding programs that mix political talk with current events and history and science programming. The 24/7 stream of content, that promises 170 new hours each month, can be purchased and reports have circulated that it has as many as 400,000 paying viewers right now, but the TheBlaze has refused to confirm any number.

Still, in October 2015, TheBlaze finally broke through, signing a multi-year deal with Dish Network to be regularly available on the satellite network. Regular cable has been a tougher hill to climb, since many see TheBlaze as direct competition to Fox News. TheBlaze's digital radio channel, which launched in 2012, has faced an easier go, being picked up by Sirius/XM and made available to millions of subscribers each day. Baker, talking about the growth of the overall service, stressed that "broadcasting was in TheBlaze DNA from the start. Much more so than many other media companies. Glenn could see the multi-media horizon in ways most others could not. He knew that radio was the core part of his relationship with his audience. But the spokes went out from there. TV. Books. Web. Live events. TheBlaze grew up with that oxygen in the atmosphere" (Holliday 2015).

As the network seeks to build its carriage on television, it has focused on developing a complete website that appears to be based on the model first developed by liberal blogging queen Arianna Huffington, who uses a mix of aggregated news with original reporting and hosted blogs to attract millions to the site. TheBlaze website relies heavily of aggregation of other reporting to fill its daily quota of stories. The homepage makes special notice of TheBlaze original stories, but, much like Huffington Post, these stories make up a small fraction of the stories featured on the homepage. The site also hosts "sponsored content" from advertisers in a model that emulates Buzzfeed's highly lucrative style of allowing so-called native advertising. The site reports it has some 25–30 million monthly visitors and boasts 1.6 million followers on Facebook.

The site has carved out a somewhat softer tone than the one Glenn Beck became famous for. Beck, whose work on CNN and later Fox mixed incendiary commentary against Democrats and President Barack Obama, in particular, with a folksy, sometimes tear-filled earnestness, has created a platform that offers a broader array of voices. Following a deadly mass shooting in South Carolina, one writer praised a liberal activist for offering words of praise about the black and white communities both coming together to work together. A video promoting TheBlaze TV has Beck perched on a desk telling the television audience, "Tonight's show is not to finger-point and mock and show how wrong people are. The point I want to stress tonight is people are actually coming together. We agree more than we disagree" (TheBlaze 2015). Despite the less confrontational approach, the site still has a clear conservative bent, featuring exclusive interviews with Republican presidential candidates and targeting issues that fire up conservative voters like immigration and federal money going to family planning organization Planned Parenthood. Perhaps not surprisingly, a Pew Research Center profile of the typical TheBlaze viewer or reader found, "Just 5% of respondents get news from TheBlaze in a typical week, and fully 85% of its audience is right-of-center (by comparison, 26% of all panelists are right-of-center). About half of its audience (51%) is consistently conservative in their political views (compared with just 9% of all respondents)" (Pew Research Center 2014).

As the site continues to expand and the accompanying television service expands to more cable and satellite offerings, the ability of TheBlaze to attract a conservative audience will play out as it battles its own ideological kin online and on-air for viewers. The site has stressed that its coverage of politics and presidential elections in particular will be a major part of its own campaign to attract more viewers, but with Beck's continued presence on the commentary stage, TheBlaze starts the battle from a place of impressive strength for such a young network.

See also: Beck, Glenn; Conservative Blogosphere; Fox News; Huffington Post; Townhall.com

Further Reading

Beck, Glenn. 2010. "A Message from Glenn." TheBlaze. August 30. Accessed October 4, 2015. http://www.theblaze.com/stories/2010/08/30/a-message-from-glenn.

The Blaze TV. 2015. "The Blaze TV in 2014: Dream Big." Accessed May 31, 2016. http://www.theblaze.com/tv/.

Holliday, Ryan. 2015. "The Quiet Co-Founder of the Media Juggernaut No One Writes About." *The Observer*. September 30. Accessed October 5, 2015. http://observer.com/2015/09/the-quiet-co-founder-of-the-media-juggernaut-no-one-writes-about.

Stelter, Brian. 2014. "Glenn Beck's Challenge: Getting onto Your TV." CNN. August 10. Accessed October 4, 2015. http://money.cnn.com/2014/08/10/media/glenn-beck-cable.

"Where News Audiences Fit on the Political Spectrum." 2014. Pew Research Center. October 21. Accessed October 5, 2015. http://www.journalism.org/interactives/media-polarization/outlet/theblaze.

THIRD-PARTY MARGINALIZATION

Since the dawn of the American system, American politics has been built around a two-party divide. There were the Federalists and the Anti-Federalists, the Democratic-Republicans and the Whigs, and the Democrats and Republicans. The history of American politics is littered with grassroots, often well-funded political startups that failed to gain enough traction to become a significant political force. Teddy Roosevelt formed the Bull Moose Party, political reformers built the Progressive Party, environmentalists have championed the Green Party, and billionaire Ross Perot launched his Reform Party in the mid-1990s. None of them have lasted. Only the anti-slavery Republican Party in the mid-nineteenth century was able to break through, and that only happened because of the collapse of the Whig Party over the very same issue. The media has faced repeated accusations of promoting the two-party system and suppressing the potential development of third-party movements. While it is true that media almost exclusively focus on the two leading party candidates, the reasons for doing so and the impact of those decisions are far less planned than many may assume.

The first third party was the Anti-Masonic Party that organized in 1832. The party actually garnered 100,000 votes that year and won Vermont's seven Electoral

College votes, but like the history of many independent party movements, the anti-Freemasons were soon swallowed up in the larger Whig Party, which tweaked its position to appeal to those who backed the new party. Since then more than 100 third parties have formed and fielded some 300 nominees for president. However, only about a dozen of those parties are truly significant in U.S. political history. The question of why is complex and has as more to do with the structural nature of the American political system, but has been aided by a media that seeks to focus on the candidates that "matter" and will likely affect the outcome of the race. Perhaps the greatest challenge to third parties came with something as simple as the advent of the ballot. One political historian noted, "Ballot access was a problem after 1888 when official ballots replaced a freewheeling system where parties printed and distributed their own 'tickets.' In the new system, each state made its own rules about who would be listed on the new, so-called, Australian ballots. As if the influence of two main parties hadn't made the rules difficult enough, now there would be 50 rule books to decipher and master" (Green 2010). This question of simply navigating the state laws to ensure that the party even appears on the ballot became a major challenge to these emerging parties, which suddenly needed enough money and organization to either gather the signatures or navigate the different state regulations to qualify.

From the outset and throughout history, many have argued the two-party system in the United States was too limiting to the political aspirations of the public. Even Chief Justice Earl Warren argued in a 1957 Supreme Court ruling that "all political ideas cannot and should not be channeled into the programs of our two major parties. History has amply proved the virtue of political activity by minority, dissident groups, who innumerable times have been in the vanguard of democratic thought and whose programs were ultimately accepted." Also, the Founding Fathers, while expressing concern over the development of too much factionalism, built no part of the American system to specifically require a duality of American political parties. The Constitution does have two key elements that ended up being tools that helped marginalize new parties—the single-member district and the Electoral College. The single-member district ensured that each congressional district would select one representative to send to Congress. This meant the winner needed to garner the most votes and would control the single seat, meaning candidates or factions getting even a sizeable minority would still have no power in the resulting Congress.

On top of that, the Electoral College system applied this thinking to the entire state, awarding all the delegates to the presidential candidate who won the most votes. This winner-take-all approach meant that even though independent Ross Perot won 19 percent of the popular vote, he garnered no Electoral College votes because he did not receive the most votes in any state. These two decisions in the Constitution did not force third parties from the stage (for example regional parties like the Dixiecrats did win electors in their presidential campaigns), but made it difficult for general political movements to win the presidency or even many seats in Congress.

Rather by chance than design, the American system has the oldest and strongest two-party system in the world. Despite countless books, polls, and analyses of the two-party system, there is no clear reason why. One argument, put forward by many, has to do with the beliefs of the American public. Even in a society with enormous ethnic, religious, and economic diversity, there is a general lack of group identity that cannot be incorporated into one of the general, largely centrist parties. The country lacks voting blocs that think of themselves as unique—there are no regional parties that represent "the West." No religious groups feel separate or punished enough to form a political faction. And outside political movements like socialism or environmentalism have not developed a strong enough following to sustain themselves as more than a wing within one of the major parties.

In fact, twentieth-century third parties that garnered the most votes and most media attention revolved around individuals rather than movements. Roosevelt's Bull Moose Party was a tool used for him to run against the Republican he had tapped to replace him. George Wallace's American Independence Party was a platform for his segregationist beliefs. The Reform Party was a creature of Ross Perot that descended into irrelevance after its originator stepped aside. Perot won 19 percent of the vote in 1992 and 8 percent in 1996. In both cases the party qualified to receive millions from the Federal Election Commission, but the $12 million in campaign funds it got from the FEC triggered a wave of fights within the nascent party and in 2000 Patrick Buchanan, the party's nominee that year, garnered only 1 percent.

Structural challenges have made third-party efforts even more difficult. Congress, which itself is controlled by members of the Democratic and Republican Parties, has implemented a series of laws that, perhaps not surprisingly, have made it more difficult for those activists not affiliated with either of those parties. The reforms of the 1970s that created the Federal Election Commission and helped increase the flow of federal funds to parties did nothing to help third parties. First, the new FEC would be governed by six people, divided equally between the GOP and Democrats, which ensured little love for third parties. Second, the Federal Election Campaign Act created a pool of money that would go to the parties' presidential nominees, but was based on how they performed in the most recent election. For new parties seeking to build excitement around an outsider candidate this can be particularly problematic, as money is released only *after* the election, making the funds more useful for building the future party than for financing the current campaign.

Key court decisions have also stifled efforts to grow new parties. In 1997 the Supreme Court ruled that states could ban candidates from being listed under the banner of more than one party. For example, in New York, which still allows this practice, a candidate could and often is listed under the banner of the Republican Party and the Conservative Party. This allows voters to become more familiar with the other party and often garner the necessary support to qualify to run their own candidates in other elections. In the 1997 decision Chief Justice William Rehnquist ruled, "States may, and inevitably must, enact reasonable regulations of parties, elections and ballots to reduce election and campaign-related disorder" even when they "favor the traditional two-party system."

But these structural challenges to the electoral legitimacy of third parties does not exonerate the media for eliminating them from their political coverage, say many critics who see the media as more than just reflecting the political reality, but rather playing gatekeeper to the political information the public has to consider. The press often bases its decision to limit or simply not cover third-party candidates on a central argument—the third-party candidates, due to the structural difficulties of gaining access to ballots and running significant campaigns, will not win. At best, third-party candidates can play the role of spoiler, peeling off enough voters who might otherwise vote for the Republican or Democrat to swing the decision from one candidate to the other. Some political observers see this rationale as fundamentally flawed. Political scientist Ernest Evans succinctly criticized the media's position in a column in the *Christian Science Monitor*, arguing that the role of elections is a place to discuss the important issues confronting the nation; the rationale that third-party candidates can't win and don't deserve coverage is dangerously self-fulfilling; and it is antidemocratic to allow the media to decide who is going to win—or at least who isn't (Evans 1988).

The first of Evans's arguments is perhaps the most important to consider, as media coverage of the election is supposed to be more than the story of whom is going to win. The coverage of campaigns, most feel, should also be a discussion of critical issues facing the country and the potential solutions. In this area, third parties have often been a source of policies that would later become mainstream and incorporated into the platforms of the major parties. Perot, for example, championed deficit reduction in his 1992 run and Democrat Bill Clinton embraced that issue, making it one of his signatures of his presidency. Other issues like an end to child labor, the forty-hour workweek, and minimum wage started as the campaign promises of third parties, but eventually became absorbed into one or both of the major parties. Sean Wilentz, director of the American Studies program at Princeton University, says this is one of the core realities of third parties in the political process, arguing, "Third parties act as a gadfly. There'll be an issue that's being neglected or that is being purposely excluded from national debate because neither party wants to face the political criticism that it would bring . . . It's a kind of bitter sweetness. [Third parties] are the ones that raise the issues that no one wants to raise and in the process they change the political debate and even policy, but they themselves as a political force, they disappear" (Nwazota 2004).

Much of the influence comes from how the much the media embraces and amplifies the topic and how much the public responds to it. This reality has fueled perhaps the most heated and regular debate in how the media handles third party candidates—debates. Whether it is the presidential debates or a local congressional race, the question of what candidates should or should not appear has sparked lawsuits and countless op-eds. Debates are built to inform the public as to the positions and differences between candidates, so participation in them can be a critical step for both established candidates but especially third party candidates that usually lack the financial resources and party infrastructure that Democrats and Republicans enjoy. The Commission on Presidential Debates, which has run all debates since 1988, has only allowed one third party candidate—Ross Perot in 1992—to participate. By 1996, the commission decided he didn't qualify to participate again. He filed suit but lost and the debates went on. The argument that the commission and other debate sponsors make is that they need some baseline rationale to say no to marginal candidates. For example, in 2012 there were 417 presidential candidates registered running for president in the United States, according the FEC (FEC 2013). The argument is that the debates should only include those who have some chance of winning so that the precious little time debates have to explore the issues actually gives the public the most information possible about the possible winners that fall. Any standard about whom to include will leave many people out, but organizers argue they need such rules. This debate has been echoed at state and local levels, even though third-party candidates often appear in these debates.

Much about the political and media business has changed since these critics of the mass media first charged them with mistreating third parties. The technological revolution that swept through both since the advent of the commercial Internet and World Wide Web have disrupted both the political world and the media environment. Social media and direct communication have allowed politically interested groups to self-organize online, and the number of media outlets that cover politics has exploded even as the once powerful local newspapers and television outlets have lost readers and influence. One analysis of this period noted that third parties have historically taken advantage of new technologies and that "in the current hyperpartisan atmosphere, voters may be poised for new choices and may find outlets in minor party candidates. Information technology has afforded minor parties a greater opportunity than ever before to communicate with a large pool of voters at minimal cost" (White and Kerbel 2012).

Still, third parties have yet to reap the real benefits of this shift, which may raise the question of whether the traditional mass media was as much of a barrier to the potential power of third parties. Only a couple of governors and senators have been independent or third-party members and even at the state legislature level, fewer than 30 state representatives and senators are not Democrats or Republicans—most of them are from New England states. For example, in 2012, third-party candidates took to social media and built their websites to solicit supports for financial donations and help organizing their efforts. One analysis of the 2012 third-party candidates' use of Twitter to engage potential supporters and participate in the discussion of issues found, "As smaller political parties in the U.S. struggle to garner even minimal mainstream media coverage, the well-documented flood of tweets surrounding the third presidential election debate . . . provided an excellent opportunity for minority party candidates to jump on top of that tweet wave, and to weave their respective political messages into the broader political discourse" (Christiansen 2013).

But unlike the millions of followers the major candidates could boast, these third-party candidates could only count support in the thousands. The audience fragmentation the Internet has wrought across media and politics has not equaled more opportunities for third-party candidates as of yet. Perhaps this is connected to the increasing cost of campaigns and the interest of outside groups pouring money into campaigns to affect the outcome for one party or the other. The new media environment has not leveled the playing field for politics. And third parties, although they have new opportunities to organize and to try and affect the public dialogue, remain as marginalized in this era of politics as they did when the major parties and the dominant mass media created barriers in the past.

See also: Political Parties; Political Polarization and the Media; Presidential Debates

Further Reading

Christiansen, Christian. 2013. "Wave-Riding and Hashtag-Jumping: Twitter, Minority 'Third Parties' and the 2012 US Elections." *Information, Communication & Society*. April 3. Accessed October 19, 2015. http://www.tandfonline.com/doi/full/10.1080/1369118X.2013.783609

Evans, Ernest. 1988. "Covering Third Parties." *Christian Science Monitor*. October 20.

Federal Election Commission. 2013. "2012 Presidential Form 2 Filers." March 15. Accessed May 31, 2016. http://www.fec.gov/press/press2011/presidential_form2nm.shtml.

Green, Donald. 2010. *Third-Party Matters*. Santa Barbara, CA: Praeger.

Nwazota, Kristina. 2004. "Third Parties in the U.S. Political Process." *PBS NewsHour*. July 26. Accessed October 19, 2015. http://www.pbs.org/newshour/updates/politics-july-dec04-third_parties.

White, John Kenneth, and Matthew Kerbel. 2012. *Party On! Political Parties from Hamilton and Jefferson to Today's Networked Age*. Boulder, CO: Paradigm Publishers.

THIS WEEK

ABC's Sunday morning news program was born in a period of rapid expansion of the news division of the famously third network but has survived to become a solid member of the network club. The program soared in viewership due to its format and the popularity of its acerbic host for many years, former NBC News anchor David Brinkley. Although the program has waned in influence due in part to the growing competition and audience fragmentation of the cable news and Internet age, it remains an important venue for politicians seeking to shape their public image and the political debate. It's also worth noting that even though the program often comes in third in terms of viewership with about 2.75 million viewers, the program ranks tops in terms of viewers 25 to 54, an influential advertising sector.

The program grew out of ABC's well-financed bet on news in the 1980s. The brainchild of television executive Roone Arledge, ABC News's rebirth that decade included the launch of a nightly new magazine *Nightline*, a huge investment in their nightly news program with then-anchor Peter Jennings, and then the creation of a new Sunday morning talk show like CBS's *Face the Nation* and NBC's *Meet the Press*.

Arledge, who had made a name for himself by creating some of the most popular shows on broadcast television like *Wide World of Sports* and *Monday Night Football*, was brought in to run the news side of ABC. While viewed skeptically by the journalists within ABC, Arledge threw his energy behind the creation of an array of top-tier television journalists and top-rated news programs. The launch of *This Week* was a central part of that work. Arledge hired David Brinkley to be the first host of *This Week*, which was seen as a major coup for the network. Brinkley had suddenly quit after 38 years at NBC News, 14 of them as co-anchor of the nightly news, and his hiring by ABC gave the network a veteran anchor to build the new program around.

The program replaced a less-weighty show *Animals, Animals, Animals*, in which children answered questions about, well, animals, and an ancient, largely unwatched news program *Issues and Answers*. But the new program took time to catch on and find its footing. Brinkley, with his distinct voice and at-times sharp wit, initially struggled to create a show that had the energy of the other morning shows. After the first couple of shows, the *New York Times*' television critic warned, "The idea behind 'This Week' is basically sound, even promising . . . Despite a serviceable format, despite the injection of enough 'visuals' to satisfy even the voracious appetite of Roone Arledge, president of both ABC News and ABC Sports, despite the recruitment of some established news-business names, 'This Week' remains distressingly dull" (O'Connor 1981). The idea that John O'Connor found promising was a structure that made the program unique, a group interview of a newsmaker, anchored by Brinkley but featuring other correspondents who could pose questions. The show also featured a roundtable of columnists who would reflect on the interview and other matters of the week. It made household names of some of ABC News's talent like Sam Donaldson and Cokie Roberts as well as commentators like conservative George Will. As the show settled into this format, it became more freewheeling, with conversations and debates sometimes heated and often humorous. Donaldson would say at Brinkley's death in 2003, "I think he had the combination of substance and style. I know a lot of my colleagues who are very deep and substantive but they're dull and David was never dull. You wanted to watch him. You liked him and when you did watch him you got a lot of substance from a story" (Grace 2003).

Brinkley's style drew solid ratings, making it a competitor for Sunday morning guests and viewers. By 1996, Brinkley hung up the reins, and the program entered a period of struggle, burning through anchors and becoming mired in a distant third in terms of ratings. By 2002, ABC needed to make a new move and went outside the normal arena to find a new host, selecting longtime Democratic campaign aide George Stephanopoulos to take the chair. His clearly partisan history—having been a major player in the White House of Bill Clinton—angered many conservatives who saw the move as an overt expression of the program's liberal bias. But George Will and other noted conservatives stayed in place and the program seemed little different than under Brinkley. Still, Stephanopoulos was keenly aware of the criticism and he said it affected his early style, saying in 2007, "I think I was generally too tightly wound, a little too determined to show I had done my homework and knew what I was talking about, as opposed to finding the best way to ask a question and get the most information" (Steinberg 2007). Stephanopoulos began to create a more conversational air and his ratings began to climb. As his program improved, he also became a more important feature of ABC News and in 2009 took on anchoring the network's morning program *Good Morning America*. He left his spot on *This Week* a month later and the program again slid in the ratings.

ABC brought Stephanopoulos back in 2012 after the program foundered in the ratings while anchored by foreign correspondent Christiane Amanpour. Under Stephanopoulos, the program added some features that became regular elements, especially the "Sunday Funnies," a compilation of late night, politically oriented jokes, and the ratings began to improve. Stephanopoulos, now firmly established as one of ABC News's key political reporters, moderated a GOP debate in 2012 and appeared to have put his partisan past behind him in terms of being seen as an objective reporter until a controversy erupted in 2015 over donations the anchor had made to the Clinton Foundation. He admitted to donating $75,000 over three years to the foundation to help support the Clinton Foundation's work combating AIDS, but did not disclose this fact when he interviewed Peter Schweizer about his investigation into the possibility of donors to the foundation influencing Hillary Clinton's work as secretary of state. Stephanopoulos said Schweizer offered no evidence of misbehavior, but was blasted by conservatives and some media critics for not disclosing his relationship with the foundation.

Amid the furor, Stephanopoulos dropped out of moderating a GOP primary debate and apologized on air for not bring forthright with his involvement with the foundation. Republicans complained about the decision, but many of the candidates for the GOP nomination appeared on Stephanopoulos's show in the weeks that followed the disclosure. Some conservative writers said this speaks to the fragmented nature of the audience that tunes in Sunday morning to hear political talk. Matthew Continetti, editor in chief of the *Washington Free Beacon*, who first raised the questions about the donations, said, "Most of the people who would be upset about this don't watch 'Good Morning America' or ABC in the first place. They've given up on most establishment media anchors" (Farhi 2015). ABC has also forgiven the former Clinton adviser, continuing to promote him and his show as it battles each week for a share of the 10 million viewers who tune into Sunday talk shows.

See also: ABC News; *Face the Nation*; *Fox News Sunday; Meet the Press*

Further Reading

Farhi, Paul. 2015. "Republicans Seem to Have Forgiven ABC's George Stephanopoulos." *Chicago Tribune*. July 27. Accessed August 11, 2015. http://www.chicagotribune.com/news/nationworld/politics/ct-republicans-george-stephanopoulos-20150722-story.html.

Grace, Francie. 2003. "David Brinkley Dead at 82." CBS News. June 12. Accessed August 11, 2015. http://www.cbsnews.com/news/david-brinkley-dead-at-82.

O'Connor, John. 1981. "Brinkley's Show Has Yet to Find Itself." *New York Times*. November 29.

Steinberg, Jacques. 2007. "Not a Front-Runner, but Moving Ahead in Polls." *New York Times*. January 18. Accessed August 11, 2015. http://www.nytimes.com/2007/01/18/arts/television/18abc.html?_r=0.

TIME

Time magazine was launched in 1923 by two visionary publishers—Britton Hadden and Henry Luce—and became the first modern general newsweekly magazine published in the United States. For decades it was one of the most powerful voices in American media, delivering news to all corners of the country at a time when most news was more localized through newspapers or local broadcasts. As the news cycle sped up with the advent of broadcast television and later cable and the Internet, newsmagazines like *Time* struggled to find a new identity. Still, with its potent covers and seminal issues like person of the year, the magazine has survived as its general news brethren like *Newsweek* and *U.S. News and World Report* have plummeted in circulation. The magazine has also added new digital content, including blogs and video, much of it focused on political news and campaigns.

From its beginning *Time* began with a concept: to tell the news of the world through people and compelling storytelling. This focus on individuals versus esoteric policy helped pioneer a more personality- and character-driven form of journalism that would become commonplace in decades to follow, but was revolutionary when the first edition hit the newsstands on March 3, 1923. That first edition also declared its interest in politics and the institutions of government in no uncertain way by putting the 86-year-old retiring Speaker of the House, Joe Cannon, on the first cover. The story pulled no punches, declaring, "Never did a man employ the office of Speaker with less regard for its theoretical impartiality. To Uncle Joe the Speakership was a gift from heaven, immaculately born into the constitution by the will of the fathers for the divine purpose of perpetuating the dictatorship of the standpatters in the Republican Party. And he followed the divine call with a resolute evangelism that was no mere voice crying in the wilderness, but a voice that forbade anybody else to cry out—out of turn" (GPO 2004). The magazine also introduced one of its other hallmarks in that first edition, breaking the news down into clear sections, with separate areas to cover international news, the nation, business, education, law, and entertainment. This idea of sections of a magazine was another of the innovations created by Luce, the magazine's founder and the man who would come to stand as a goliath in magazine publishing.

Luce fueled the magazine with almost a missionary zeal to change the state of the country. The prospectus for the original *Time* declared simply, "People in America are, for the most part, poorly informed" and Luce's magazine set out to change that. Luce himself was often accused of being imperious and too rigid. He was an avowed anti-communist and saw organized labor as real threat to the nation. He was also a divisive figure, unafraid of alienating many. The *New York Times* obituary of Luce would report, "Virtually no one viewed him temperately, yet admirer and critic respected his business accomplishments, his ingenious brain, his insatiable curiosity, his editorial prescience. For example, he anticipated an American appetite for tersely packaged news, for the photojournalism of Life magazine and for the easy-to-grasp pictorial essay on such topics as 'The World We Live In,' 'The World's Great Religions' and 'The Human Body'" (Whitman 1967). And this may have been his most significant accomplishment, understanding the changing information diet of the American public. When the stock market crashed in 1929 Luce launched a new magazine boldly named *Fortune*. When the technology to capture and print photographs improved, he launched *Life* magazine that featured scant words and relied on glossy photographs to tell the story. In the post–World War II years, he would launch a magazine devoted just to sports, *Sports Illustrated*. All of them succeeded for a time and all were based on the creativity Luce first brought to *Time*.

Luce and Hadden were also behind one of the continued symbols of the magazine's success—its "Person of the Year" honor. Although the cover and lengthy story initially went to an individual man (in fact it was called the "Man of the Year" until 1999), the magazine has also selected groups, ideas, and even objects that its editors decide, "for better or for worse . . . has done the most to influence the events of the year." This selection was seen as an honor, but also was a way for the magazine to make up for a perceived editorial gaffe when it was first unveiled in 1927. That year, the magazine had failed to put Charles Lindbergh on its cover in May when he completed his nonstop transatlantic flight. So, in December that year Lindbergh graced the cover as the magazine's inaugural Man of the Year. But the magazine has also drawn criticism for choosing declared enemies of the United States including Adolf Hitler in 1938, Nikita Khrushchev in 1957, and the Ayatollah Khomeini in 1979. The magazine has also made many political figures their person of the year, naming almost every sitting president and many influential leaders to its coveted position.

From its first editions, the magazine has always taken a keen interest in politics, covering domestic and international affairs with an array of well-known reporters and columnists. Margaret Carlson and Joe Klein have covered politics for years and are regular commentators on cable news and political talk shows. The magazine has also tried to innovate on its political coverage, partnering with CNN to create a single political site AllPolitics in 1996 to cover the presidential campaign, creating a vibrant election site that drew more readers than any other site that year. The site would earn a Webby Award in 1998 as the best political site on the Internet, but like other endeavors, it faced growing challenges in the 2000s.

Despite the success of the magazine's covers and its influential political coverage, *Time* struggled with the digital transition as the Internet challenged the basic structure of a general news publication that only came out once a week. The idea of a digest of the week seems inherently dated in an era of 24-hour news and instant social media commentary. If the dated nature of the news wasn't enough of a challenge, *Time* also suffered from a wave of audience fragmentation as people who were interested in politics moved to more specialized journals like Politico, and international magazines like the *Economist* picked up those who wanted foreign news. Mass media magazines that aimed to appeal to the widest possible audience struggled in this new environment and *Time* was somewhat the poster child of this fight. For example, *Time* saw a nearly 35 percent drop in circulation in the second half of 2009 and continued to hemorrhage readers in 2010. By 2014 circulation hovered around 3.3 million. Although diminished from its heights of years earlier, *Time* remains the second widest circulated weekly magazine in the country, trailing only *People*. Today the magazine remains relevant in political coverage, but it lacks the staff size and audience reach that made the magazine such a force from its launch through the 1990s.

See also: Newsmagazines

Further Reading

Brinkley, Alan. 2010. *The Publisher: Henry Luce and the American Century*. New York: Knopf.

Cannon Centenary Conference: The Changing Nature of the Speakership. Washington, D.C.: Government Printing Office.

Whitman, Alden. 1967. "Henry R. Luce, Creator of Time-Life Magazine Empire, Dies in Phoenix at 68." *New York Times*. March 1. Accessed October 29, 2015. http://www.nytimes.com/learning/general/onthisday/bday/0403.html.

TOWNHALL.COM

If there is a father of the conservative political blogosphere it is probably Townhall.com. Launched in 1995 as a site that hosted opinion columns—blogs were still four years in the future—the site continues to be a voice in the established conservative wings of the Internet while it has shifted more toward political activism and not just commentary in recent years. Although it remains a vibrant source of commentary and columns from some of the bigger names of the conservative movement, it competes with more and more sites that aim to emulate its role and often have harsh criticism of the left and a more action-oriented approach.

The idea of a central source for conservative commentary actually pre-dates the official website. Townhall began as a bulletin board site from the pre–World Wide Web days. Begun by Heritage Foundation's Ed Feulner, the board was a place where staffers and others from Heritage and the *National Review* magazine could post articles and comments. By 1995, Heritage established Townhall.com as a standalone website that would play the same kind of role but would be open to the public. For much of the next decade the site served as a sort of reading room of the political right, hosting columns from Dinesh D'Souza and Patrick Buchanan as well as newcomers like Michelle Malkin and Jonah Goldberg. But throughout this period, the site did not call its readers to action, in part because it could not as a nonprofit wing of the Heritage Foundation.

Finally, by 2005, the site had appeared to outgrow its original home. Drawing some 1.5 million monthly visitors and boasting an email list of some 300,000 conservative activists, the foundation's nonprofit tax status had become a barrier to what the editors hoped would be a more activist platform. The site spun off of Heritage and formed a new company headed by a former chief of staff of Heritage named Drew Bond. At the time, Bond said, "For years our readers have asked us what they can do, and we haven't been able to tell them . . . In fact, we received a lot of frustration among the groups because they wanted more direction from us. Now we can let them know what they can do to make a difference" (Bluey 2005). The site remained an independent business for only a short time before being purchased in 2006 by Salem Media Group. Salem had started as a syndicate of Christian talk radio stations in California and North Carolina, but soon amassed more stations featuring more formats. The company added Townhall.com and later purchased Eagle Communications, which publishes another leading conservative site, RedState. Since the purchase by Salem, the site has become more integrated with other media properties controlled by the corporate owner, adding many of the conservative and Christian talk channels to the site and cross-promoting with RedState and other conservative blogs owned by the parent company.

Since leaving Heritage, though, the site has moved more decidedly to the right and added a strong activist edge to its message, describing its goal as bringing the conservative talk radio world together with the digital netroots idea. The site claims, "By uniting the nation's top conservative radio hosts with their millions of listeners, Townhall.com breaks down the barriers between news and opinion, journalism and political participation—and enables conservatives to participate in the political process with unprecedented ease" (Townhall.com 2015). This idea of activism can, in many ways, be traced back to the unsuccessful campaign of former Vermont governor (and Democrat) Howard Dean. Jonathan Garthwaite, then still at the Heritage Foundation but already director of Townhall.com, watched the campaign with real interest. He saw how the campaign rallied people online to both give money and meet in person. He later reflected that it was then he saw that the web could be much more than a place for commentary, but could change the relationship between politicians and activists, saying, "If you give your supporters a sense of ownership and the ability to give feedback, they will be your best salesmen" (Wallace 2004). That's what the mission of Townhall.com appears to be for the conservative movement.

The site continues to be a platform for established voices, especially those connected to the radio networks also owned by Salem, but it also serves as a springboard for some younger conservatives looking to build a reputation and audience. One of those is Katie Pavlich, who graduated from the University of Arizona in 2010 and quickly became the news editor at Townhall.com at age 22. Pavlich turned her gig at Townhall.com into a regular spot on Fox News Channel's *The Five*, soon becoming a substitute anchor of the show. She has continued to work at Townhall.com, even as she appeared on CNN, MSNBC, CNBC, and Fox Business, and has turned some of her reporting for the site into books on scandals within the Obama administration and combatting the narrative of the so-called Republican "War on Women." Pavlich has also lashed out at leading media personalities, accusing the press of a double standard in dealing with scandals within their own ranks. She expressed her frustration with ABC's decision not to remove former Bill Clinton staffer George Stephanopoulos from his position hosting their weekly political talk show *This Week*, despite his not disclosing donations he had made to the Clinton Foundation. She took to the pages of *The Hill* to take aim at many in the D.C. media, writing, "Any other anchor, even on the same network, would have certainly been punished if not fired immediately for this severe breach of journalistic ethics. This problem isn't about the donations being made in the first place, it's the fact that he hid them from viewers while covering, and defending, the Clinton Foundation . . . Special treatment isn't just reserved for Washington's politicians, it's for the most liberal, elite anchors as well. As for the rest of us, there are consequences for breaking the law and for conflict of interest nondisclosure" (Pavlich 2015). Pavlich and Garthwaite are two products of the modern conservative blogosphere that Townhall.com has come to represent. Articulate, activist-oriented, and as interested in the internal politics of their own party as they are in the governing decisions made in Washington, these political commentators and journalists blend their opinion into the reporting. They have, in many ways, made a career out of it, moving from editing a conservative website to appearing regularly on cable talk shows and on speaking circuits.

In 2010, the site added Michelle Malkin's outspoken commentary site HotAir.com to the fold, creating one of the largest conservative commentary sites online. At the time of the announcement, Garthwaite said the combination of the two sites would create one brand that had some 3 million readers a month. A Salem executive hailed the move, saying, "The addition of Hot Air doubles the size of Salem's expanding footprint in online conservative commentary. It's a perfect fit for us, since we can leverage talk radio, print, and other online assets to aggressively grow the site, while offering political organizations and advertisers an even more effective way to reach and engage the conservative audience" (Garthwaite 2010). The site continues to produce regular commentary and calls to action to conservative voters, but also seems to have lost some of its steam. In 2011, the site aimed to host an online national Republican primary ahead of the Iowa Caucuses, saying it hoped to influence the direction of the primaries that year, but the event drew little attention and there has been little effort to replicate the project. Still, as it continues to build audience and create conservative pundits for television and other media, Townhall.com marked its 20th year as a website service with continued outspoken posts about the media, Democrats, and the internal debates within the Republican Party.

See also: Conservative Blogosphere; Fox News; Heritage Foundation; RedState

Further Reading

Bluey, Robert. 2005. "Conservative Spotlight: Townhall.com." *Human Events*. April 5. Accessed July 31, 2015. http://humanevents.com/2005/04/05/conservative-spotlight-Townhall.comcom.

Garthwaite, Jonathan. 2010. "It's Official." Townhall.com. February 18. Accessed July 30, 2015. http://Townhall.com/tipsheet/jonathangarthwaite/2010/02/18/its_official.

Pavlich, Katie. 2015. "Katie Pavlich: The Protected, Connected Liberal Media Elite." *Hill*. May 18. Accessed August 3, 2015. http://thehill.com/opinion/katie-pavlich/242442-katie-pavlich-the-protected-connected-liberal-media-elite.

Townhall.com. About Us. Accessed July 31, 2015. http://Townhall.com/aboutus.

Wallace, Nicole. 2004. "The Mice That Roared." *Chronicle of Philanthropy*. July 22. Accessed August 3, 2015. https://philanthropy.com/article/The-Mice-That-Roared/164075.

TRACKERS

Trackers, sometimes called the strangest campaign job there is, are individuals who make it their work to capture every public moment of a candidate on the campaign trail. They are hired by campaigns or opposition groups to document every statement, every hand shaken, and every baby kissed with the hopes of capturing a misstep, an inaccurate statement, or a public faux pas that can then be used against the candidate in an ad or statement.

As the technology of filming and storing vast amounts of footage has become easier, trackers have become a staple of presidential campaigns as well as competitive Senate and statewide races. Often young and new to politics, these political operatives can find themselves in intense positions where those attending a rally or the candidate they are following can turn on them. One organization that employs trackers is the Democratic Super PAC American Bridge 21st Century. The Super PAC, which can take in large donations, but must report how they are spent and who gave them, employed 43 full-time trackers during the off-year election in 2014. Those staffers recorded 9,000 events and traveled some 693,000 miles collectively. According to American Bridge, the goal of this tracking is straightforward: "We monitor public appearances to prevent the cynical pandering that results in a candidate taking different positions depending on the audience they are in front of. And we work to get this information to you through mainstream and social media, grassroots activism, and our website" (American Bridge 2015). This puts them at every event filming the candidate's every move and statement.

Although trackers have been used by campaigns and parties for years, it remained a largely unheralded and quiet facet of campaigns until the "Macaca" incident in 2006 Virginia U.S. Senate race. That year an Indian American tracker named S.R. Sidarth was working for the campaign of Democrat Jim Webb and was deployed to film several events of then-senator George Allen. During one of these events Allen was filmed pointing out Sidarth and saying, "This fellow here, over here with the yellow shirt, Macaca, or whatever his name is. He's with my opponent. He's following us around everywhere. And it's just great," and then adding, "Let's give a welcome to Macaca, here. Welcome to America and the real world of Virginia." The comments were filmed by Sidarth and uploaded to YouTube. Soon news organizations were reporting that "Macaca" "could mean either a monkey that inhabits the Eastern Hemisphere or a town in South Africa. In some European cultures, macaca is also considered a racial slur against African immigrants, according to several Web sites that track ethnic slurs" (Craig and Shear 2006). The video was soon being used by local television and running on cable news channels. Allen later apologized, but the incident threw the campaign off message and forced them to deal with accusations of racism. Allen would go on to lose to Webb.

Since the "Macaca" moment, trackers have become far more visible and far more controversial. Trackers have been thrown out of many campaign events and some have been accused of using technology to surreptitiously record moments. In 2014 a Republican Super PAC—America Rising—caught Iowa Senate candidate Bruce Braley deriding the experience of his opponent, U.S. senator Chuck Grassley. In the video posted on the America Rising YouTube account, Braley can be seen at a private event in someone's home discussing his qualifications and comparing himself to "a farmer from Iowa who never went to law school, never practiced law" who if the Republicans took control of the Senate would be "serving as the next chair of the Senate Judiciary Committee." The Braley campaign, which had sought to portray the Democrat as a Washington outsider and man of the people, struggled to respond to the video.

Often the supporters at rallies now turn against these gadflies when they're spotted, booing them and sometimes physically accosting the workers. And the job itself is pretty tedious, following candidates to every campaign event of the day, listening to the same speech, and making sure the camera is on in case something unusual happens. One *Washington Post* reporter tracked down a tracker who was assigned to follow Republican gubernatorial candidate Ed Gillespie in Virginia.

> I ask one of the trackers how often he has heard this speech.
>
> "Probably about 150 times," he says, keeping his Flip cam focused on Gillespie and clutching a banh mi sandwich in his other hand. "I could recite it to you if you'd like."
>
> I ask if he likes his job.
>
> "Not especially," he says, his face quickly going red. "This is off the record." (I didn't agree to this, but I said I wouldn't use his name.) (Terris 2014)

Still, trackers often know more about the candidate they are following than the press does and their videos can serve an important journalistic function. If the tracker simply wrote down what a candidate said and repeated it, the campaign using the material could be accused of taking the comment out of context. The tracker's record is literally captured on video and is usually indisputable. The other thing about tracker footage is the degree to which it helps fuel television coverage of the incident. George Allen's "Macaca" moment or Braley's slight against Chuck Grassley has exponentially more impact because the media can run the video over and over again every time that the issue is discussed. And this ability to feed not only a

YouTube attack or a web ad from the campaign, but the free media campaigns can get from airing the gaffe, has turned tracking into a full-time job. One tracker who spent 2008 following Republican vice presidential candidate Sarah Palin, and recounted being chased out of a corn field by angry Palin supporters, said, "A lot of people think it's just an intern sent out with their iPhone. These kids have to know everything about that race. They follow these people three years at a time and become experts of everything they've ever said" (Roller 2014).

Although their importance in the modern campaign operation has been demonstrated by the impact they have had on races, the technique and the ethics remain hotly debated. Some campaigns have sought to stop people from recording at events for fear that the video will leak out into the public. Others have sought to ban trackers from events held in private homes—trackers following Bruce Braley were thrown out of at least two dozen campaign events—and more than a few have been accused of invading the privacy of candidates or badgering them. The camera in the face has become a new reality for candidates for any major office and the trend is likely only to continue and expand as more money and technology pours into political campaigns.

See also: Advance Teams; Social Media and Politics; Super PACs

Further Reading

Craig, Tim, and Michael Shear. 2006. "Allen Quip Provokes Outrage, Apology." *Washington Post*. August 15. Accessed September 11, 2015. http://www.washingtonpost.com/wp-dyn/content/article/2006/08/14/AR2006081400589.html.

Roller, Emily. 2014. "Inside the Strangest Job on the Campaign Trail." *National Journal*. September 3. Accessed September 11, 2015. http://www.nationaljournal.com/politics/2014/09/03/Inside-Strangest-Job-Campaign-Trail.

Terris, Ben. 2014. "Tracking the Trackers: What It's Like to Have the Most Mind-Numbing Job in a Campaign." *Washington Post*. October 14. Accessed September 11, 2015. https://www.washingtonpost.com/lifestyle/style/tracking-the-trackers-what-its-like-to-have-the-most-mind-numbing-job-in-a-campaign/2014/10/14/a2ed9d46-50a0-11e4-8c24-487e92bc997b_story.html.

"Who We Are." American Bridge 21st Century. Accessed September 11, 2015. http://americanbridgepac.org/about.

TRUST IN JOURNALISM

Journalism relies on trust. Its currency, relevance, and importance in the conversation relies on some portion of the public investing their belief in what the publication has put forward. Some readers value the information put out by the *New York Times*. Listeners believe Rush Limbaugh. Viewers welcome the investigations of *Frontline*. Without the support of those who seek out information from these sources, none of them would be able to attract advertisers or supporters and their audience and importance would be diminished. While some outlets can attract viewers or readers through the sheer weight of personality or the entertaining way they tell a story, most journalism banks primarily on being seen as a trusted outlet for information and opinion.

That said, trust in journalism has been eroding for decades as some outlets pursue audience and content strategies that emphasize partisan programming and others have weathered plagiarism and reporting scandals. Trust has also waned as many individuals, increasingly polarized in their personal beliefs, come to see media outlets that do not adhere to their view as inaccurate or biased. In fact, a 2014 Pew Research Center survey of public trust in different news organizations found that across the political spectrum CNN ranked as the most trusted, but it was trusted by only 54 percent of people. Among those who labeled themselves "consistently liberal," the most trusted outlet was NPR at 72 percent, and 88 percent of conservatives believed Fox News. In studies Pew has conducted it has found that faith in a given network or source is often affected by one's political beliefs. This connection between trust and partisanship has raised concerns that believing a given reported fact may be increasingly contingent on whether the news organization reporting it aligns with the individual's political beliefs.

Those who have studied these trends worry that if public trust falls too low, journalism itself may no longer be able to play the role of public skeptic. One report on the state of the media concluded that journalism "contributes to the development of trust in several societal parts, for example through journalism's capacity to distrust other social systems. But journalism is not only a trust provider; the media system itself relies on public trust. Changes in the environment of journalism challenge its ability to remain a trustworthy institution in contemporary society" (Blöbaum 2014). This erosion of trust has two significant implications. First, it weakens the trust in journalism itself, undercutting the ability of reporters and news outlets to position themselves as a surrogate for the public. If at best, as the Pew report notes, only half the public will put its trust in any one outlet, how can the news organization press for more access to public records or demand answers from a politician or public figure? These legal concepts as well as the popular pressure are built upon the idea that reporters often are asking on behalf of the public for information; without trust, that relationship falters. Add to this that reporters and news organizations play a second role in public trust, either building up or undermining the public trust in other institutions. Reporting will highlight whether a given candidate seems trustworthy and, if elected, whether he or she is fulfilling promises made on the campaign trail. Views of Congress or of the effectiveness of the president are deeply influenced by press coverage of those institutions. Without public trust, reporting will struggle to build support for these institutions or pose hard questions about how these organizations work.

To understand the current state of trust in the journalism, though, it is important to understand that the increasingly polarized use of media is only one of many factors that have changed. One must consider the change in the amount of information available to the public and the increased ability for the audience to make a counter argument to what the press has reported. Both of these are connected to the rise of digital publishing, and the shift of mass media from being in the hands of a few specialized publishers to something anyone with a phone can do from anywhere at any time. As technology expert Clay Shirky has observed, "There's no way to get Cronkite-like consensus without someone like Cronkite, and there's no way to get someone like Cronkite in a world with an Internet; there will be no more men like him, because there will be no more jobs like his. To assume that this situation can be reversed, and everyone else will voluntarily sign on to the beliefs of some culturally dominant group, is a fantasy" (Shirky 2012).

Shirky's point is based upon a fundamental shift in the media environment. Much of the early trust in journalism was, at least in part, based on the scarcity of information available to the public and their limited ability to question those few sources. When newspapers or television controlled the majority of an individual's information diet, they carried with them a sort of de facto consensus about news and information. Newspapers may make a mistake, but the assumption was that they were pursuing a consensus vision of the truth. But that may have always been an illusion since there was no way for those who disagreed with the journalist to be able to communicate with the same audience. A person may vehemently reject a newspaper's reporting, but he or she was left to simply write an angry letter to the editor, which may be published in the paper, or potentially sue a paper for libel, but only in certain situations. Add to this that if a person merely questioned the accuracy of a report they would have to go about verifying those doubts through an arduous research process. In the pre-Internet days there would be no Google, no instant archive of papers, or access to foreign or even other national news sources. Information was hard to come by, and therefore those who had information in the pre-Web days earned a level of near-automatic trust.

As the Internet exploded the old analog world of information scarcity, people began to question the level of trust news organizations had been granted in the past. New critics emerged who could, with the click of a mouse or tap of a finger on a smartphone, publish their own take or their own facts about a story. Journalists in this new model became a source of information, but not the only source and now a far more fallible one. Critics of reporting techniques and specific stories now had their own outlets, taking to the comment sections of the story, publishing their own blogs, and demanding accountability from reporters. One digital news editor at the site Fusion offered the kind of criticism that helps explain the slow eroding of public trust by comparing journalists to scientists. The commentary, provocatively entitled "Why You Can't Trust Journalism," argues that few journalists offer the empirical approach of a scientist, instead relying on narrative and story to capture the interest of the reader. This, he argues, is a fundamental fault in reporting that will inevitably lead to incorrect reporting and the continued loss of trust. As he put it, "Big journalistic stories always have many layers of editors and lawyers involved. And while at some level, in principle, those people are interested in telling the truth about the world, in practice, they are much more interested in making sure that any given statement is factually and legally watertight. Beyond that, they want something big, something punchy, something powerful. They want a narrative, with good guys and bad guys. And, of course, they want their story to be shared, and to elicit government investigations, and to win awards" (Salmon 2015).

And this may be the core of the argument, that journalists want to be trusted and most aim to do a good job, but they are also not academic researchers studying a historical moment, they are reporting in the here and now and doing as good a job as they can to be right and to be interesting. The result is almost destined to capture some of the truth and misinterpret other elements of the story, and unlike the days of yore where that story existed for a couple of days before being relegated to the microfiche archives of a local library it is now available for years online. Journalism has struggled with that transition. And during that transition the field has also been rocked by scandals like Jayson Blair's fabrication of dozens of stories for the *New York Times*, or CBS's Dan Rather being duped by fabricated documents about President George W. Bush's service in the National Guard, or NBC's *Dateline* program staging explosions in a report about the safety of General Motors's trucks. All of these stories damaged the reputation of the individuals involved in the story, but also raised questions about how the media does its job and empowered those inclined not to trust the press to have solid reasons for their skepticism.

One of the other components of the modern media ecosystem that contributes to the erosion of public trust in journalism is the speed with which news is spread, often with little or no confirmation. It may seem unfair to place this level of responsibility on something as simple as a retweet or loaded headline, but as experts in different fields witness the way information, or more often interpretation of information, can catch fire in the aggregation world, leading from a tweet to a brief story to an aggregated news piece to a cable discussion segment that then begins this news cycle again, it can be a point of frustration. This tendency to repeat news reported elsewhere as fact with little independent confirmation or reporting plagues most fields of reporting, including technology, celebrity, business, and politics. One example that erupted in 2014 highlights this trend. A piece of research from tech firms Google and Vodaphone concluded that some teens see little difference between their virtual lives and their real ones. The story was soon being reported that young people could not tell the difference between the digital and real worlds. This story, although not particularly connected to the study, spread across the Internet, appearing in shallowly sourced (or completely unsourced) stories. Danah Boyd, a researcher from Microsoft who had just published a book about the subject of young people's social media lives, found herself inundated with requests to comment on the story. She pressed the journalists who called her to send her the research, and she found no one had actually read the research. Frustrated, she took to her blog and the site Medium to declare, "Even though I had told the production team that this headline made no sense and there was no evidence to even support it, they continued to run with the story because the producer had decided that it was an important study. And yet, the best they could tell me is that they had reached out to the original journalist who said that he had interviewed the people who ran the study . . . [S]ince when did the practice of journalism allow for uncritically making s**t up?::shaking head:: Where's the fine line between poor journalism and fabrication?" (Boyd 2014).

Boyd's frustration has been echoed across thousands of experts, sources, and readers. One incident like the teenage digital survey deepens those experts' cynicism about the work of journalists, increasing the assumption that journalists are lazy or prone to sensationalism. Their tendency to seek out and amplify the voice of the most outspoken of sources on political stories further increases this frustration by missing, at times, the views of the vast majority of voters or members of a political party.

Some of these technologists and futurists have begun to advocate for a new form of journalism to combat what they see as a troubling lack of credibility in the media of the digital age. In the era of traditional mass media, the publication or broadcast of news and information was an expensive and involved process. It took capital to own a printing press, a government permit to broadcast on radio or television. These impediments to new outlets made journalism a profession that not everyone could do, and distribution of that journalism was no small task. This process meant that not only did the news organization that you read in the morning paper or listened to during your commute represent a far larger publication business, but it also came with a certain amount of credibility since their business required the most number of readers. Now, with a simple blog platform and a free web template almost anyone can create a website that appears as legitimate as most newspapers or television outlets. The look or even the name of a news outlet now does not convey legitimacy.

This reality has prompted the head of Google News and an independent journalist to pen a manifesto for a new form of journalism that would focus on building and maintaining trust. The two authors argue that journalism outlets ought to publish a statement on their ethics, cite sources for their information, and provide more information about the individual reporters writing the story to give a sense of expertise. They argue a more transparent news outlet will actually equate to more digital credibility and that credibility could then be turned into financial advantage, writing, "We believe that a new framework of journalistic trust would harvest great value. First, it would grow the respect and loyalty of the audience—the people that journalists strive to inform, that help spread the word via social networks, that support the news business through subscriptions and ad revenue. Second, it would create valuable signals for algorithmically driven search engines and recommendation systems—the ever more important tools to push news out to audiences. And third, it would increase ad revenue by luring commercial advertisers and sponsors that also value trustworthiness" (Gingras and Lehrman 2014). The proposal was an initial offering from the Trust Project, an ethics project from Santa Clara University. They have begun working with Vox Media, the ill-fated Al Jazeera America, and a handful of other news outlets to work on citations and ways in which to correct and document those corrections for news videos. Still, these efforts remain a tiny fraction of the media generated on a given day.

It would seem that trust in journalism is a problem for journalists and has little to do with the business of governing or the work of political operatives. They may publicly bemoan journalists who lack credibility or, as has become more and more common, attack the media as biased and unfair for how it chooses to do its work, but many see that the problems that plague the media in terms of trust have also swept through the worlds of politics and business. Trust in the media is not an end to itself, but rather allows those journalists with trust to hold powerful individuals and institutions to account. These same journalists have the power to build public trust in a politician or a policy working together to allow representative democratic systems to function. The former director of BBC News and Current Affairs has warned that there cannot be real separation of journalism and politics in this system, writing in 2005, "It is this erosion of trust that has spread rot through politics and business. Deterioration in standards of professional behavior by journalists, public relations people, and politicians have all contributed to this state of affairs . . . But without trust between them, politicians, business people, journalists, and public relations practitioners will not be trusted by the public, which means that none of them can do their jobs effectively. These people all depend upon trust in public communications. They are in the same boat and they would row to better effect if they acknowledged the fact, before then doing battle" (Hargreaves 2005).

This mutual dependence on being able to communicate with the public and the public's willingness to imbue those messages with a certain level of trust and belief are critical to the functioning of the American system of governance. A collapse in trust has helped spur the growth of so-called post-truth politics where politicians can deny basic facts and still find a sizable portion of the public willing to support their version of reality. The media's ability to hold politicians accountable for falsehoods or misleading claims is dependent on the public seeing those journalists as somehow separate from the political back-and-forth, he-said, she-said style of politics. Without public trust, journalism becomes simply an extension of the political debate and not an outside arbiter of the debate that helps the public weigh the two arguments, aided by the facts supplied by uninterested reporters. Without it, all political reporting is reduced to being equivalent to another version of the party email soliciting funds or the stump speech repeating disproved claims.

See also: Advocacy Journalism; Political Bias and the Media; Political Polarization and the Media; Post-Truth Politics

Further Reading

Blöbaum, Bernd. 2014. "Trust and Journalism in a Digital Environment." Reuters Institute for the Study of Journalism. University of Oxford.

Boyd, Danah. 2014. "Rule #1: Do No Harm." Apophenia. April 29. Accessed December 7, 2015. http://www.zephoria.org/thoughts/archives/2014/04/29/do-no-harm.html.

Gingras, Richard, and Sally Lehrman. 2014. "Online Chaos Demands Radical Action by Journalism to Earn Trust." Medium. October 17. Accessed December 7, 2105. https://

medium.com/@GingrasLehrman/online-chaos-demands-radical-action-by-journalism-to-earn-trust-ea94b06cbccb#.k6z8smo3n.

Hargreaves, Ian. 2005. *Journalism: A Very Short Introduction*. London: Oxford University Press.

Salmon, Felix. 2015. "Why You Can't Trust Journalism." Fusion. July 27. Accessed December 7, 2015. http://fusion.net/story/173383/science-cant-trust-journalism.

Shirky, Clay. 2012. "Shirky: 'We Are Indeed Less Willing to Agree on What Constitutes Truth.'" Poynter Institute. October 17. http://www.poynter.org/2012/shirky-we-are-indeed-less-willing-to-agree-on-what-constitutes-truth/191757/.

24-HOUR NEWS CYCLE

News has always been a 24-hour entity, with foreign coups and political debates occurring at any time all over the globe. Although the information being generated by the world was constant, media for much of its history was more like a photograph of the world than a constant video feed. Newspapers captured an individual day and told you what had happened yesterday. Evening news grappled with the technological feat of telling the viewer what had happened in their world that very day, but rarely did it have the capacity to capture the world live, as it happened. The advent of cable news networks and later the explosion of web and social media news shifted the news from being something prepared for delivery at a specific moment to something consumed by the public while it was happening. This change to a 24-hour model of news and reporting has shaped political news by leading to more reliance on commentary and punditry while also fueling an increasingly partisan media as these news feeds try to maintain and build audience.

The truly 24-hour news cycle is barely three decades old. Its origins can be traced back to the launch of the Cable News Network (CNN) in 1980. Ted Turner, the eccentric media mogul who had used broadcast towers to transmit his WTBS channel around the country, launched CNN to feed the growing cable audience. Turner pledged at the launch of the channel, "We won't be signing off until the world ends. We'll be on, and we will cover the end of the world, live, and that will be our last event" (CNN Observations 2007). His channel slowly grew for the next decade, until the 1991 Persian Gulf War served as a major catalyst for the cable news channel's influence in reporting. Breathless scenes of U.S. missiles landing in Saddam Hussein's Baghdad were broadcast live to a waiting world as CNN anchors huddled in a hotel room in the besieged city. The new model put forward by CNN was to cover breaking news as it was happening, allowing the audience to see the drama unfolding without a sense of what might happen next. These live news events drove huge ratings for the channel as people tuned in to track hurricanes approaching the coast or presidential election returns throughout the night.

Reflecting on the role that CNN and its later cable news brethren MSNBC and Fox News played in covering the world, NPR's media critic would say they amounted to a wire service, saying, "They give you brief bursts of updates. In fact, MSNBC now every 15 minutes gives you an update of the news. And in between they're trying to figure out ways to keep you watching. So they'll do reported pieces. They'll do a lot of interviews. There are a lot of talk shows. And to be honest, there's a lot of things that we would classify as kind of pulpy, quasi-tabloid, quasi-celebrity news; anything that's sort of waiting for the next great crisis. And when crisis hits, people turn to cable, they particularly turn to CNN. And when crisis abates, they kind of tune it out" (NPR 2005). Despite this rollercoaster audience cycle, the news channel was able to stitch together breaking news events to feed the daily beast of 24 hours. It tracked regional trials that drew large audiences. It paid serious attention to politics, hiring leading political reporters like Judy Woodruff and Candy Crowley. It worked as a business and eventually drew competition.

In the evolution of 24-hour news, 1996 played a seminal year. That year NBC joined forces with technology giant Microsoft to launch MSNBC and Rupert Murdoch announced the creation of Fox News. Also in the late 1990s, the World Wide Web created a multimedia outlet that could transmit information all of the time. By the end of the twentieth century all media were expected to be supplying news and information throughout the day and not simply when the evening news came on or the morning paper hit the doorstep.

This reality of news as a constant flow of information has been a source of major concern for years among journalists who said the model gave them neither the time nor the incentive to investigate, to build a story slowly and through careful reporting. Or as one critic wrote in a scathing take on the new speed of news, "Why should anyone bloody well care? For one thing, 'it is absolutely true, and anybody who says otherwise is slinging bulls—, that every mistake that's made in the news business is made because of speed,' says Keith McAllister, former executive vice president and managing editor for CNN's national newsgathering" (Rosenberg and Feldman 2008). The need to report for a live news station or tweet events as they occur creates a situation where the media has no time to always get it right and forces new reporters to file stories as they're finding out what those stories even are. There is no room for error, but errors are unavoidable. Many journalists have come to fear that the need 24-hour news creates to instantly report may actually lessen people's faith in that reporting. After all, if they get it wrong once, twice, what is to say they don't get it wrong most of the time.

The need to feed political stories with minute-by-minute updates creates challenges for campaigns seeking to unveil information on their schedule, rather than losing the news to a careless tweet or a sudden change of plans by a politician that can be breathlessly reported on a cable news outlet. Take, for example, the challenge of keeping vice presidential nominees a secret. The announcement of a nominee is one of the defining moments of a presidential campaign, usually coming just before or actually at the party's nominating convention. The man or woman selected for the job becomes both a source of interest unto themselves, and a sort of litmus test of the kind of presidency the candidate sees themselves running. Because so much can be read into these selections, the announcement of the vice presidential pick is usually a carefully orchestrated affair. The 2008 selection of Sarah

Palin hit the political world like a bombshell, catching reporters who had been hovering outside the houses of expected nominees completely flatfooted and re-energizing the sagging campaign of Republican senator John McCain.

Four years later, Republican nominee Mitt Romney wanted the same sort of moment, but he was set to tap one of the people reporters and pundits had been discussing for weeks, Wisconsin congressman Paul Ryan. Driven by a need to report things as they happen, members of the press were camped out at airports and even outside likely candidates' houses, looking for signals that one was getting the nod. According to the *New York Times*, Ryan had to slip out of his house through the back door and walk through the woods to reach an unwatched car that would drive him to the airport (Barbaro 2012).

But the 24-hour news cycle has had far more profound impacts on the world of politics than simply making it harder to make a surprise announcement. It has created more pressure to generate content and attract audience in an ever-increasingly competitive world of news providers. This competition for viewers has manifested itself in several ways within the political news media. First, there has been an increasingly partisan tone to certain outlets. When Fox News launched in 1996 to provide a counterpoint to the cable news dominance of CNN, one of the elements the channel banked on was its appeal to conservatives. The channel, over time, hired many influential talk radio stars, hoping to absorb the popularity of these established political talkers. MSNBC had been created to compete with CNN head-on in the coverage of more so-called hard news, putting more reporters in the field and seeking to combat CNN's website through its partnership with Microsoft. But soon the advantages of Fox's model began to become apparent. Viewers tuned to Fox in much the same way they tuned to Rush Limbaugh or Glenn Beck in their cars, for political entertainment.

This had a couple of major advantages over MSNBC's and CNN's model of more field reporting. First, it was cheaper. Reporters did not have to travel as much and more air time was devoted to punditry—that is, talking about the news—than to uncovering original reporting. Another clear benefit was in audience. People would tune to provocative political talk regardless of whether there was major news in the world that required 24-hour vigilance by reporters on the scene. This meant Fox's model established a more regular viewership that did not fluctuate based on the news of the day. CNN had always feasted or starved for viewers depending on the newsiness of the moment. This created other pressures on that network, but MSNBC soon saw that perhaps the Fox model could better serve the corporate bottom-line. Just a few years into the network's existence, it hired Keith Olbermann away from ESPN. Although a sports anchor, Olbermann had been known for saying provocative political things and his new program, "The Big Show with Keith Olbermann," was a short-lived success. He left in 1998 to return to sports, but came back to 2003, starting an eight-year run at the network. Olbermann quickly became a liberal talker in the model of conservatives Bill O'Reilly or Sean Hannity at Fox News. Olbermann saw his viewership grow and the program helped spawn a series of increasingly liberal hosts like Rachel Maddow, Lawrence O'Donnell, and Chris Hayes. With Fox News locked in with conservative viewers and liberals leaning toward MSNBC, that left CNN to try and find its way in between, a position that has left the network trailing in viewers and revenues.

Across all three cable networks and later across the web and Twittersphere, the shift from reporting to commentary cemented a new class of journalist and politico who existed somewhat in both worlds at the same time—the pundit. Pundits are usually experienced journalists or campaign consultants who are brought on cable programs or Sunday talk shows to discuss political strategy, fallout, and tactics. They are seen as experts in all things political and are tapped to serve as expert sources who can contextualize the day's news and provide insight and analysis to viewers and readers. They help decipher the political headlines and explain the political implications of news and developments in almost every branch of news—from the potential secretiveness of former secretary of state Hillary Clinton about her email as part of the Obama administration to the internal dynamics of a given campaign manager's decision to quit. These pundits provide several services to the 24-hour news cycle, offering a stream of analysis and opinion that cannot really be fact-checked or disproven, but still offer the viewer and reader more commentary on a given news item. And this can all be done with someone who either serves as regular guest on a program or can even be under contract to only provide their punditry to a given outlet.

The other thing this professional class of political commentator can deliver is viewers. Especially in the competitive world of cable news, pundits can deliver the sort of fireworks that enthrall viewers, but rarely do the actual newsmakers provide. As one political scientist who has studied the relationship between partisanship and the media observed, "Cable punditry, and the shouting that occurs when ideological opposites are pitted against one another, is theater. As noted by Fox News host Bill O'Reilly himself, 'If a producer can find someone who eggs on conservative listeners to spout off and prods liberals into shouting back, he's got a hit show. The best host is the guy or gal who can get the most listeners extremely annoyed over and over again'" (Dagnes 2010). This quest to find guests that can offer instant analysis on almost any given political story, coupled with the ability of pundits to play to the drama by provoking the other side, have been two enduring elements of the 24-hour news cycle.

Pundits have become a critical component of all three cable networks and have come to mark the coverage of breaking political news. As the digital revolution swept the media world, this idea of responding to news and commenting on it, rather than reporting it, has only expanded. The vast majority of politically oriented news outlets online, whether conservative or liberal, rely more on the idea of commenting and analyzing the news to develop and audience. Bloggers on both the right and left have taken to offering their own version of punditry, often even more heated and more partisan than the cable programs, daily fodder for political junkies.

The effects of this news ecosystem with partisan cable news and even more sharply political blogs is to create an environment where people may seek information from only those partisan outlets that either entertain or affirm the views already held by the potential voter. This has been a concern that has permeated politicians' views of the media since the earliest days, informing the decision by Congress to enforce the Fairness Doctrine on broadcasters to ensure coverage of multiple sides of political issues and fueling endless commentary about the dangers of personalized news filters on news websites like Yahoo. The reasoning goes that if people do not have their views challenged by facts and counter-arguments, then the partisan nature of the media may only sharpen the divide. Experts have sought to draw parallels between the increasingly partisan makeup of Congress and the polarization of media consumption in the United States. Others have worried that the excessively partisan nature of cable commentary and online blogging could further split an already fractured electorate. One study of how partisan media consumption affected voters found that choosing partisan news outlets did not really affect a person's tendency to vote, but did find evidence for "the proposition that exposure to partisan news affects political participation, particularly behavior during the campaign. Exposure to likeminded partisan news significantly increased campaign activity over time and encouraged an earlier decision time, while exposure to conflicting news had exactly the opposite effects" (Dilliplane 2011). That is, partisan media coverage inspired like-minded voters to make their decision about who to vote for earlier and often got those same voters to become more active in the campaign. The research demonstrates that these partisan outlets serve as a sort of giant soapbox for partisans to fire up their supporters and get them involved in the campaign.

The 24-hour news cycle does not dictate the growth of partisan press, but the business of it has certainly fueled the growth in the use of punditry and focus on politics as a multi-month drama. The need to offer new takes on the handfuls of reported information developed each day by reporters all over the globe put those reporters and editors seeking to fill Tweets, articles, and airtime under enormous pressure to generate copy all of the time. This has led to the development of regular sources who can comment and reflect on the news and an explosion in the discussion of news online and on air. The business of 24-hour news also forces the use of more and more commentary, as the idea of having reporters contributing enough content to fill three cable channels and a bottomless Internet with news outpaces the sources of that news. Therefore the 24-hour news cycle, while both affecting the way politicians think about and execute their own attempts to message a campaign or issue and the manner in which the media will portray and discuss that news, has made the work of political reporting more difficult. It demands more content and more live reporting without giving much time for the reporter's own process of gathering the news. News is instead gathered in front of the audience. Reporters live-tweet news conferences, cable news dips into each reporter's interview with a possible expert, and all of that content flows onto platforms that are increasingly partisan.

See also: CNN; Fox News; MSNBC; Political Polarization and the Media; Social Media and Politics

Further Reading

Barbaro, Michael. 2012. "How Campaign Outwitted the 24-Hour News Cycle." *New York Times*. August 12. Accessed August 25, 2015 http://www.nytimes.com/2012/08/12/us/politics/how-romney-and-ryan-outwitted-24-hour-news-cycle.html.

CNN. 2007. "CNN Launch." CNN Observations. November 7. Accessed May 31, 2016. https://www.youtube.com/watch?v=K2OafHhD17E.

Dagnes, Alison. 2010. *Politics on Demand: The Effects of 24-Hour News on American Politics*. Santa Barbara, CA: Praeger.

Dilliplane, Susanna. 2011. "All the News You Want to Hear: The Impact of Partisan News Exposure on Political Participation." *Public Opinion Quarterly* 75.

NPR. 2005. "The Power of the 24-Hour News Cycle." May 25. Accessed August 25, 2015. http://www.npr.org/templates/story/story.php?storyId=4671485.

Rosenberg, Howard, and Charles Feldman. 2008. *No Time to Think: The Menace of Media Speed and the 24-hour News Cycle*. New York: Continuum Press.

U

USA TODAY

Initially viewed with derision by many within the traditional newspaper industry, *USA Today* pioneered many of the trends of news reporting that would become a staple of the digital world, including concise storytelling and heavy use of photos and infographics. Although the paper and its digital ancillary led the way in many important ways, its structure and distribution system suffered as more news consumers sought the same kinds of information on-demand on the web.

The newspaper was seen as a gigantic gamble when it launched in 1982 in the Washington, D.C., area. The new paper, in full color and designed to be read quickly, was modeled after a similar effort the Gannett Company had run in Florida. There, under the guidance of newspaperman Al Neuharth, the company had created a morning paper called *Florida Today*. With a slick and innovative design and built with the journalism of several Gannett newsrooms in the Florida region, the paper soon was a circulation and business success. Neuharth then proposed a massive bet on a national version of *Today*. *USA Today* lost an enormous amount of money in the early years. With a cost of 25 cents and expensive color printing and design, the paper lost as much as $10 million a month. But Neuharth and his board at Gannett seemed unworried. Looking back, he would say, "See, we knew when we hit the magic number of 1,000,000 in circulation, which happened in seven months, we knew that was the end of the ball game, that then it was just a matter of time until those geniuses on Madison Avenue, the advertising geniuses who claim that they are the most creative people in the world but who are really the most conservative on earth and who do not want to invest their clients' money in a new publication or a new idea because they are afraid if it goes belly-up that they will be blamed for it. We knew that the 1,000,000 would get to them and that it would just be a matter of time" (Neuharth 1999).

The paper's approach to news reporting broke new ground in its storytelling technique, design, and organization. The paper was organized into color-coded sections, making it easier for people to find its reporting on business, sports, and entertainment, in addition to a splashy, full-color front page. The paper's editorial approach was to synthesize the news of the day into an easily digested single story, allowing a reader to catch up on a story quickly and rarely having to follow a story off of one page and onto another. The paper was built for a faster world where people read on the train or subway and less for the leisurely reader over breakfast. It was clearly aimed at the business professional, publishing Monday through Friday and relying heavily on distribution deals with hotels across the country. This also led to innovations in format that *USA Today* helped to make the norm for the news industry. For example, its Snapshot feature in the bottom left-hand corner of each section front page was soon changing the way journalists thought about data and graphics. But it was more than just some eye-catcher in the corner of the paper, according to those who have studied the way the paper thought about the use of graphics. "Editors at the newspaper considered the use of infographics a primary form of information presentation and required discussions of graphic potential for nearly every story assigned. Infographics were often used daily as the lead visual elements, with no story text beyond what was found within the infographic itself" (Williams 2013). These graphics were a hallmark of the paper and helped fuel a look that, while criticized by many when it was first introduced, would soon be emulated by regional and later national newspapers.

Even as the paper was soaring to one of the largest circulation newspapers in the country, *USA Today* was also leveraging its unique business model to cover politics in new ways. *USA Today* was the national newspaper that sat atop a massive chain, Gannett, that owned some 90 daily and 1,000 weekly papers in 41 states and six countries. With all of these newsrooms, the national reporters based at the suburban Virginia headquarters of *USA Today* represented a tiny fraction of the reporters employed by Gannett. The company was soon using its reporters from regional papers to cover the campaign and candidates, adding local, on-the-ground knowledge to the paper's national reporting.

Despite this unique local-national reporting structure, reporters who covered politics for the paper often found themselves making the same objections other political reporters make about modern campaign coverage. Former reporter Richard Benedetto, for example, complained that "reporters and editors need to remember that they're in the information business. Their job is to give readers and viewers information about the candidates so that they can figure out what it means and what matters to them. 'Instead, we overemphasize the conflicts and we overemphasize the strategy, and we don't tell them enough about where the candidates stand and why' " (Skewes 2007). And despite these concerns, as the paper beefed up its digital wing, usatoday.com, the coverage of politics seemed to emphasize these trends more and more. Its blog, onPolitics, blends horse race coverage of polls with occasional tidbits of policy. But the paper's political reporters are still seen as some of the best in the country and often appear on Sunday talk shows and other analysis programs to offer their take on what is happening on the campaign trail.

Perhaps more than most other newspapers, *USA Today* has keenly felt the economic pressures that have so damaged other newspapers in the last decade. As Neuharth noted, the paper aimed at circulation first in the tradition newspaper model and then planned on making its money from advertisers, but as the economics of print advertising began to grow shakier with the emergence of the Internet, *USA Today* struggled to find a viable business model. It aggressively pushed its content online, but it was unable or unwilling to implement a paywall around its content. Even as it was feeling this pressure on the advertising side, the circulation that the paper had banked on began to dry up. As late as 2011, the paper could boast a paid circulation of some 1.8 million copies, but as the economic slowdown made itself felt throughout the hotel industry, many chains stopped subscribing to *USA Today* and by 2014 the paper could only claim a print circulation of 1.08 million. The paper still claims an additional 1.6 million circulating editions of its so-called branded editions, mainly inserts that the paper includes in local Gannett papers to beef up the local papers and add circulation to the national edition. The paper remains one of the largest circulation print papers in the United States, trailing the *Wall Street Journal* and in a heated competition for second with the *New York Times*. Despite its economic troubles and reduced authority and readership, the paper remains a major force in political coverage.

See also: Daily Newspapers; Data Journalism; *New York Times,* Newspaper Industry; *Wall Street Journal*

Further Reading

Neuharth, Al. 1999. "Al Neuharth Oral History Interview." Samuel Proctor Oral History Program at the University of Florida. July 23. Accessed September 8, 2015. http://ufdc.ufl.edu/UF00005522/00001/pdf.

Skewes, Elizabeth. 2007. *Message Control: How News Is Made on the Presidential Campaign Trail*. Lanham, MD: Rowman & Littlefield.

Williams, Michael. 2013. "Informational Graphics." In *History of the Mass Media in the United States: An Encyclopedia*. Edited by Margaret Blanchard. New York: Routledge.

V

VOX

It should surprise no one that on the inaugural day of the new news and commentary site Vox, its editor, wonky policy blogger Ezra Klein, posted a 3,700-word opus about the lack of actual facts in the modern political debate.

The provocatively named "How Politics Makes Us Stupid" warned that American politics had come to be controlled by political viewpoints that were not informed by information, but rather operate in an effort to mislead or obscure facts. Klein wrote that the underlying thesis of American politics was that with more information the American political system would find a consensus from which to govern. He also wrote that that thesis is wrong. Instead he argued, "Washington is a bitter war between two well-funded, sharply-defined tribes that have their own machines for generating evidence and their own enforcers of orthodoxy. It's a perfect storm for making smart people very stupid" (Klein 2014).

Vox was founded to try and fix that.

Vox.com is operated by Vox Media, a company that initially built a sophisticated publishing system and then turned to launching niche sites aimed at specific topics. The company runs the popular sports site SBNation and the tech and gaming news sites The Verge and Polygon. Vox.com, initially known as "Project X," raised more than $24 million in startup capital, has attracted corporate sponsorship from General Motors and boasts more than 22 million unique visitors a month.

The site is driven editorially by a vision developed by Klein. Klein had made a name for himself while working at the *Washington Post*. There he launched the Wonkblog, a site that sought to explain the policy context of Washington, D.C., stories and grew to be a must-read for many inside the Beltway. Despite its popularity, Klein felt the paper was technologically and philosophically trapped. As the *New York Times* explained when Klein left the paper for Vox, "While the Post is an excellent publication, he said, he felt that the conventions of newspaper print journalism in general, with its commitment to incremental daily coverage, were reflected in publishing systems, which need first and foremost to meet the needs of printing a daily paper" (Kaufman 2014). Vox would be more than that. It would seek to add context and the larger story to news, especially around politics.

Its approach and claim to be rolling out a truly new form of political reporting created a couple of issues for the new organization. First, some journalists argued, it created an audience problem. As Bill Keller, the former *New York Times* executive editor, said four months into the site's existence, "I know why I pay attention to NYTimes.com (for news and opinion) or SB Nation (sports) or Politico (politics). Vox and 538 and the Upshot are not about subjects, they're about ways of looking at subjects. The nature of their appeal is not so obvious. So they have to figure out the right combination of social-media lures and brand appeal to grow an audience" (Byers 2014). Still, the site boasted a solid performance and markets itself to advertisers as a way to reach wealthy, younger news consumers.

The other problem the hype connected to Vox created was a frustration from journalists who saw the site as holier-than-thou in its approach while still creating a mix of intellectual news and so-called click bait. Forbes's Jeff Bercovici said the site's claim to focus on journalism that "explains" the news means some of what Vox does "sincerely attempts to put complicated matters of politics or policy or science into terms that readers who aren't that smart or haven't been paying much attention can understand. Some explanatory journalism is just an excuse to put words and names that get people's attention into headlines people will click on" (Bercovici 2014). It's a criticism that even one look at the site's homepage can confirm. One day in January 2015 found the site offering thoroughly nerdy entries like "9 things only neoclassical economists will understand" to the unexpectedly scientific "How America became addicted to road salt—and why it's a problem" to the traditional political analysis of "The new Democratic attack ad against Chris Christie is misleading" to the pop culture silly of "50 years of David Bowie's hair and makeup, in one gif" (Vox 2015).

Despite the criticism, the site's vision of breaking out of the daily grind of political coverage, the focus on the sound bite and the latest snippet from the campaign trail, coupled with the effort to create a compelling mix of policy and political coverage continues to hold a powerful interest for many within the field of political coverage. In late 2014, the site wooed one of Politico's top editors away to run its politics coverage who said that the site's presidential campaign coverage would seek "to explain to the reader what is significant about these candidates' policy perspectives [and] why they should be paying attention to specific candidates" (Calderone 2014).

It's the kind of aspirations that gel with the initial goals that Klein wrote on that first day, when he opined that coverage of politics is also coverage of policy and that no matter how much political communication seeks to obscure it, people understand a policy, a tax bill, a pollution threat. Although it is early in the site's run—too early to see if it can convince others of its view that "ultimately, there's no spin effective enough to persuade Americans to ignore a cratering economy, or skyrocketing health-care costs, or a failing war"—Vox is working hard to hammer home the idea that "a political movement that fools itself into crafting national policy based on bad evidence is a political movement that will, sooner or later, face a reckoning at the polls" (Klein 2014).

Further Reading

Bercovici, Jeff. 2014. "Why Do So Many Journalists Hate Vox?" Forbes.com. May 12. Accessed January 13, 2015. http://www.forbes.com/sites/jeffbercovici/2014/05/12/why-do-so-many-journalists-hate-vox.

Byers, Dylan. 2014. "Vox Not Living Up to the Hype, Explained." *Politico*. August 23. Accessed January 13, 2015. http://www.politico.com/story/2014/08/vox-ezra-klein-110276.html.

Calderone, Michael. 2014 "Politico's Laura McGann Joins Vox to Lead Political Coverage." Huffington Post. December 21. Accessed January 13, 2015. http://www.huffingtonpost.com/2014/12/21/laura-mcgann-vox-politics_n_6362452.html.

Kaufman, Leslie. 2014. "Vox Takes Melding of Journalism and Technology to a New Level." *New York Times*. April 6. Accessed on January 13, 2015. http://www.nytimes.com/2014/04/07/business/media/voxcom-takes-melding-of-journalism-and-technology-to-next-level.html?_r=0.

Klein, Ezra. 2014. "How Politics Makes Us Stupid." Vox. April 6. Accessed January 13, 2015. http://www.vox.com/2014/4/6/5556462/brain-dead-how-politics-makes-us-stupid.

Vox Homepage. Accessed January 13, 2015. http://vox.com.

W

WALL STREET JOURNAL

The fact that the *Wall Street Journal* is now one of the nation's few national newspapers and that it has become a major news source for developments domestically and internationally would probably come as a great shock to its founders, who sought to create a suite of information products, including the paper, that helped those working on the stock market have better information to make their business decisions.

Most papers that began in the mid- to late-nineteenth century aimed to reach the widest possible audience. Their business model was built around increasing the circulation of the paper and then turning that circulation into money through advertising. The *Wall Street Journal* had different roots and a different business model, and that shaped much of what would happen more than a century later when the digital revolution swept the industry. The *Journal* grew out of the work of three men—Charles Dow, Edward Jones, and Charles Bergstresser—who sought to build a business to serve the stock traders and financial professionals who worked in New York City. Dow, Jones & Company began in 1882 by printing and distributing newsletters that aggregated the business and political news of the day. The publication, called "Customer's Afternoon Letter," was hand-delivered to the floor of the stock exchanges and served as a sort of afternoon briefing for traders. By 1889 they formalized it into an afternoon paper—the *Wall Street Journal*—and began selling it for 2 cents a copy. This may not sound like much money, but it was double the price of most newspapers at the time and represented the fact that they did not seek a huge audience, just the right one. It was all part of Dow, Jones & Company's plan to create products that helped bankers and financial workers. The company went on in 1896 to create the Dow Jones Industrial Average to serve as a sort of benchmark for key stocks and the overall health of the stock market, and a year later developed the Ticker, the real-time newswire, to relay stock prices and news.

When Charles Dow, who had started writing the "Review & Outlook" column that still runs in the paper today, died in 1902, the company was sold to one of the nation's leading financial journalists of the day, Clarence Barron. Barron would guide much of the paper's growth over the next 30 years, ending the afternoon paper and shifting it to the morning and building up an array of talented writers and reporters. The paper offered concise columns that quickly told the businessmen of the day what the news of the world was and what it meant to them. This approach foreshadowed much of the digital news aggregation of the twenty-first century and served the *Journal* readers well. The paper focused heavily on the market and the news likely to affect business. This included a keen interest in politics, but the politics of the *Wall Street Journal* always leaned decidedly to the right. Although the reporting, especially in the modern era, was well respected for its craft and sourcing, the editorial page of the paper remained staunchly conservative. The paper's editorials traditionally endorsed free market solutions and argued against most government policies that involved regulations. One writer in the liberal *New Republic* would sum up the editorial page, writing in 2008 that editorials could be counted on for "the undying faith in voodoo economics, the staunch defense of executive privilege and disdain for independent counsels during Republican presidencies alternating with disdain for executive privilege and staunch defense of independent counsels during Democratic presidencies" (Chait 2008).

Despite this editorial propensity to maintain a healthy tilt to the right, the reporting of the *Journal* remained a major source of news for those seeking to understand the behavior of the market and the key issues facing American business. The model worked so well, the paper launched an Asian edition in 1976 and a European edition in 1983. The subscription cost remained far higher than most other newspapers and yet the paper was able to maintain readership because of its specialized focus on business. That model served it well in the early days of the Internet. As many papers embraced free distribution of their papers' content in hopes of increasing audience and making more money with ads, the *Wall Street Journal* quickly put their content behind a paywall, forcing people to subscribe to see the bulk of the content. While it kept the paper from becoming a force in the early web, it reinforced the idea that its content was worth paying for.

The paper was still starting to lose money in the early to mid-2000s because of the drying up of advertising dollars, but subscriptions remained solid and the *Journal* seemed to be slowly expanding its digital efforts. All of this changed in 2007. Dow Jones, with its array of market-friendly products, became the target of a takeover bid by Rupert Murdoch and his multinational News Corp. Although the company had publicly traded stock, some 60 percent was still owned by the Bancroft family, a relationship that dated back to the 1902 purchase of Dow Jones by Clarence Barron in 1903. The Bancrofts initially fought the bid, trying to rally other stockholders to reject the $60 per share offer—at the time the company stock was worth $33 a share. But Murdoch's team was able to persuade enough of the family and other shareholders to back the offer, and the paper and the rest of Dow Jones was purchased by December of that year. Sarah Ellison, a business reporter at the *Journal*, would later document the bid in a book entitled *War at the Wall Street Journal: Inside the Struggle to Control an American Business Empire*. She later considered why Murdoch had gone to such lengths to purchase the company and the paper, saying, "He loves newspapers. He covets the influence and power that come with owning the *Journal*. It is the most powerful business paper in the most powerful city in the most powerful country in the world. He wants to knock the *New York Times* off its perch as the paper that influences the cultural and political conversation in this country. The *Journal* is his weapon for doing that" (Ellison 2011).

Murdoch's purchase of the *Journal* in 2007 sent shockwaves through the news industry and worried many who thought Murdoch's News Corp. would soon seek to make the historically conservative, but not particularly ideological, paper more like Murdoch's other major American news outlet, Fox News. In fact, inside the *Journal*, reporters and editors offered varying takes on the impact of the News Corp. takeover. While some reporters quietly left or anonymously questioned the editorial policies of their corporate owners, publicly, senior editors said the initial fears of the Fox-ization of the *Wall Street Journal* were misplaced. Deputy managing editor Alan Murray told NPR in 2011 that instead the new ownership came with an expanded ambition to make the paper more a national newspaper that served those suffering from the collapse or shrinking of regional daily papers. He said, "when News Corp. came in, they made a conscious decision to say, 'Look—a lot of these papers are declining rapidly; they've become shadows of what they were in many of these urban markets. And yet there are people who still want to get a print newspaper delivered on their driveway every day and if we expand our general news coverage, we can be that paper'" (Folkenflik 2011). But the takeover did flare up in public at least once in 2008 when managing editor Marcus Brauchli resigned under pressure. Brauchli stated that he had come to see the need for a new managing editor who better adhered to where News Corp. wanted to take the paper, but denied that he was ousted for political reasons.

The Pew Research Center analyzed the Murdoch-owned *Journal* to compare its content to that of the Dow Jones-run paper and the results were clear. "The clearest change in the *Journal*'s editorial direction in the past three and a-half years has been a reduction in front-page business coverage . . . At the same time, front-page coverage of the U.S. government has steadily increased, starting in 2009. Government accounted for 3% of the space that began on the front page under the old ownership in 2007 (and fell slightly to 2% in the 2008 election year). But it has more than doubled since, jumping to 7% in 2009 and 2010 and to 8% in 2011 to date" (Pew Research Center 2011). The paper was turning away, at least in part, from it business-centered reporting world, adding coverage of national policy and international affairs—and becoming more a competing national entity to the *New York Times*.

To further its goal of becoming more of a national news organization, the paper reorganized its newsroom in 2015, adding more resources to its core topic areas and beefing up staff in new areas it aims to improve, including mobile content, interactive graphics, and data-driven journalism. The *Journal* reported on its own changes, noting, "Gerard Baker, editor in chief of Dow Jones and the *Wall Street Journal*, said the purpose of the moves was a 'full transformation of our newsroom with a bold but simple aim: to become the premier digital news organization in the world.' He added, 'This process will require us to discontinue some of our activities while investing more in others'" (Alpert 2015). Some of this work included expanding its digital coverage of politics. The paper added a series of D.C. and politics blogs and news feeds to its roster, including "The Washington Wire" and a partnership with the American Communities Project to inject more data-informed reporting about politics into its array of offerings. The paper has also expanded coverage of key issues like immigration, national security, and presidential politics in hopes of widening its audience and further competing with the *New York Times*.

The new *Wall Street Journal* jettisoned several of its market-oriented blogs and moved its economics coverage from New York to D.C. It also shuttered a couple of European bureaus as it sought to reduce costs. Still the paper remains a major source of news and reporting and as it continues to transition from a paper aimed at business people to a paper aimed at a wider swath of opinion leaders, its editorial efforts are worth monitoring and its election coverage is apt to look very different in 2020 than it did in 2008.

See also: American Communities Project; Daily Newspapers; *New York Times*

Further Reading

Alpert, Lukas. 2015. "News Corp to Cut Jobs, Shift Resources to Digital Media." *Wall Street Journal*. June 18. Accessed January 7, 2016. http://www.wsj.com/articles/news-corp-to-cut-jobs-shift-resources-to-digital-media-1434645075.

Chait, Jonathan. 2008. "Scared Yet?" *New Republic*. December 30. Accessed January 7, 2016. https://newrepublic.com/article/64702/scared-yet.

Ellison, Sarah. 2011. *War at the Wall Street Journal: Inside the Struggle to Control an American Business Empire*. New York: Houghton Mifflin Harcourt.

Folkenflik, David. 2011. "How Has 'Wall Street Journal' Fared Under Murdoch?" NPR. July 22. Accessed January 7, 2016. http://www.npr.org/2011/07/22/138588497/how-has-wall-street-journal-fared-under-murdoch.

"The Wall Street Journal under Rupert Murdoch." 2011. Pew Research Center. July 20. Accessed January 7, 2016. http://www.journalism.org/2011/07/20/wall-street-journal-under-rupert-murdoch.

WASHINGTON POST

Widely regarded as one of the leading daily newspapers in the nation, the *Washington Post* rode its dogged coverage of the Watergate scandal to a national reputation for political coverage and investigations. The paper suffered with other dailies during a troubled period of adjustment to the Internet age and was eventually purchased from its longtime owners by Amazon.com founder Jeff Bezos in 2013. In recent years the paper has seen a resurgence of strength, driven by its aggressive web operation, and remains a major source for news about national politics and the nation's capital.

The paper has always had a strong base in its political reporting, devoting much of its resources to covering Congress, the federal government, and the White House. Locals often complained that the paper was far more interested in national politics than what was happening in the city, but that reputation helped make it one of the nation's premier papers. The paper was founded in 1877 by Stilson Hutchins, who had launched a successful newspaper in St. Louis before heading to Washington, D.C. Hutchins had served as a state representative in Missouri and the new

Washington Post was intended to be an organ of the Democratic Party. The paper found a strong readership, though, and by 1888 Hutchins ended his connection with the party, purchased the competing the *Republican National*, and shuttered it. Hutchins sold the paper the next year to a former congressman and postmaster general and the paper enjoyed an era as a major player during the yellow journalism period. The *Post* often published the work of illustrator Clifford Berryman, running one famous piece that declared, "Remember the Maine" to rally support for the Spanish-American War. But within a generation the paper was floundering.

It went up for auction in 1933, and was bought by former chairman of the Federal Reserve Eugene Meyer, who would hand it to his son-in-law Philip Graham in 1946. Philip struggled with mental illness and often Katharine, Meyer's daughter, stepped in to help run the paper. In many ways, the rise of the *Post* would be connected to the daughter of Eugene Meyer. As one biographer noted, "Washington is in many ways Katharine Graham's town . . . When her husband committed suicide in 1963, Katharine inherited the Post and by harsh, efficient management built it into a news vehicle that is both economically and journalistically dominant in the capital of the United States. This means she has close social and political relationships with many of the city's, that is, the nation's, most important political actors, and that they influence her newspaper, just as her newspaper influences them" (Davis 1979). Under the Grahams, the paper merged with its last morning rival—the *Washington Times-Herald*—in 1954 and throughout the 1950s and 1960s established itself as the leading journal about the nation's capital.

The paper was often seen as a liberal outlet, with executive editor Ben Bradlee and Graham both holding close ties to President John F. Kennedy. FBI Director J. Edgar Hoover was recorded telling President Lyndon Johnson, "I don't have much influence with the *Post* because I frankly don't read it. I view it like the *Daily Worker*" (Beschloss 1998). But still, under Bradlee, the paper expanded its political reporting and often kept the pressure on the more nationally recognized *New York Times*. When the *Times* began publishing the so-called Pentagon Papers that documented American involvement in Vietnam, the *Post* was not far behind, picking up publishing after a court stopped the *Times*. It even kept with another 1970s story that other news organizations covered, but also viewed skeptically—the break-in at the Democratic National Committee's headquarters at the Watergate building in D.C. Five men wearing suits and surgical gloves were arrested trying to place listening devices in the DNC's offices. The *Post* jumped on the story and soon one of its Metro reporters, Bob Woodward, was documenting that the men claimed to be patriots, at least one of whom had worked for the Central Intelligence Agency. The burglars, it turned out, were part of a wide-ranging effort by President Richard Nixon's re-election campaign to sabotage his opponents and when they were caught, Nixon and his key aides worked to block the investigation. The *Post* stayed with the story, devoting more resources and column inches to the investigation than other news outlets, connecting the money for the break-in to the re-election effort and helping push the White House to cover up the incident.

The scandal would trigger an impeachment investigation about widespread abuse of power and force President Nixon to resign in 1974. The story made Woodward and his reporting partner Carl Bernstein household names and the film *All the President's Men* helped create, according to sociologist Michael Schudson, a mythology around journalism and the *Post*. Schudson wrote, "At its broadest, the myth of journalism in Watergate asserts that two young Washington Post reporters brought down the president of the United States. This is a myth of David and Goliath, of powerless individuals overturning an institution of overwhelming might. It is high noon in Washington, with two white-hatted young reporters at one end of the street and the black-hatted president at the other, protected by his minions. And the good guys win. The press, truth its only weapon, saves the day" (Schudson 1993).

That mythology informed much of the *Post's* history in the next 30 years, making the paper a force within American journalism. But even as it basked in the glow of its accomplishments, it struggled to maintain its position in the media. A 1980 fabrication scandal involving reporter Janet Cooke forced the paper to return a national Pulitzer Prize for reporting and stained the paper's reputation. In 1984 Graham organized the purchase of the educational company Kaplan, the testing and test-prep giant. That purchase would become critical as the company struggled in the Internet age. In 1996 the newspaper launched a website, making it a separate company based in Virginia, miles away from the downtown paper. Kaplan, by 2010, accounted for 60 percent of the company's revenue, and the separate web operation had not turned into a money-maker as hoped. When federal rules undercut the profitability of the Kaplan business, the paper was forced to make cuts, closing foreign and domestic bureaus and reducing the size of the staff.

A vaguely dire 2012 report in the *New York Times* summed up the troubles the D.C. paper was facing, writing, "The newsroom, once with more than 1,000 employees, now stands at less than 640 people, depleted by buyouts and staff defections. The newspaper's Style section, once one of the most coveted assignments in American journalism, has shrunk from nearly 100 people to a quarter of that size. Bureaus in New York, Los Angeles and Chicago are gone. There were so many Friday afternoon cake-cutting send-offs for departing employees last summer that editors had to coordinate them so they didn't overlap" (Peters 2012). Still, many of those "Posties" who remained were committed to the paper surviving. It added new political blogs like Chris Cillizza's "The Fix," and undertook aggressive fact checking and D.C.-area digital publications aimed at lobbyists and interest groups. Journalist Dave Kindred summed up the reality of the paper in his 2010 book *Morning Miracle*, writing, "Only a dreamer believes the Washington Post can ever again be the Post of the late twentieth century. Because those money machine days will not return, the newspaper will never again produce the cash necessary to put together a nine-hundred-person newsroom. Yet only a fool says the Post's days as a major player are over" (Kindred 2010).

In 2013, after an 80-year run in the Meyer-Graham family, the paper was sold to Amazon founder Jeff Bezos, who shelled out $250 million for the entire company.

Bezos said he was committed to expanding, reinvigorating, and turning the *Post* into "the paper of record," taking a swipe at long-time competitor the *New York Times*. As Bezos put it in November 2015, "Some of the things that have happened in the past, we wish we had known more about our political leaders and our other powerful institutions in this country, and that's been the role of the Post for a long time. And we're just gonna keep doing that. We're doing it now with more resources and we have a lot of patience for that job. We're just gonna keep working at it and make sure that that institution stays strong, so that it can shine a light on all of these important players especially in Washington" (Owen 2015).

That same month, the *Post* had surpassed the *New York Times* in web traffic—and went on to do the same in December of 2015—using social media, apps, and an aggressive website strategy to attract audience. The paper known for breaking Watergate appeared headed toward a bright future.

See also: Newspaper Industry; Woodward and Bernstein: Woodward, Bob and Bernstein, Carl

Further Reading

Beschloss, Michael. 1998. *Taking Charge: The Johnson White House Tapes 1963–1964*. New York: Simon and Schuster.

Davis, Deborah. 1979. *Katharine the Great: Katharine Graham and the Washington Post*. Bethesda, MD: National Press, Inc.

Himmelman, Jeff. 2012. *Yours in Truth: A Personal Portrait of Ben Bradlee*. New York: Random House.

Kindred, Dave. 2010. *Morning Miracle: Inside the Washington Post*. New York: Doubleday.

Owen, Laura Hazard. 2015. "Jeff Bezos Says *The Washington Post*'s Goal Is to Become the 'New Paper of Record.'" Nieman Lab. November 24. Accessed January 15, 2016. http://www.niemanlab.org/2015/11/spacesuit-wearing-jeff-bezos-says-the-washington-posts-goal-is-to-become-the-new-paper-of-record.

Peters, Jeremy. 2012. "A Newspaper, and a Legacy, Reordered." *New York Times*. February 11. Accessed January 15, 2016. http://www.nytimes.com/2012/02/12/business/media/the-washington-post-recast-for-a-digital-future.html?_r=0.

Schudson, Michael. 1993. *Watergate in American Memory: How We Remember, Forget, and Reconstruct the Past*. New York: Basic Books.

WATCHDOG JOURNALISM

One of the core principles that undergird the media's relationship with the public and the government is that of serving as a watchdog on the actions of the state. The concept, born of core classically liberal ideals, is that the press is essentially a surrogate for the public, monitoring the behavior of the state and guarding the public against abuses large and small. The concept of the press as watchdog has always garnered the support of the majority of Americans and even as trust in journalism has lagged, events like disclosure of widespread monitoring of the Internet and phone communications of Americans by the National Security Agency has further deepened the sense that the government needs to be kept in check and the media helps the public do this.

The idea that the media should play a semi-official role in the monitoring of the government has been built into the American system since its founding. From the very outset the ability of the press to inform and therefore influence public opinion was seen as essential to how the American experiment in self-governance would function. Unlike other systems where governmental authority flowed from a king or even a divine provenance, the American system vested authority in the voting public, even if it was often indirect. This meant those who helped inform and, to the degree possible, shape public opinion could affect the direction of government. Those advocates who had wanted to spur revolution against British rule, like Samuel Adams, had used the press to foment discontent and encourage increasingly brazen opposition to the king's authority. Voices like those who advocated rebellion would, only a decade later, use the post-revolutionary press to spread their argument for the new Constitution to replace the tottering Articles of Confederation. George Washington, in a letter to a confidante, argued these journals would decide the fate of the new governing document and those who backed the Constitution would depend heavily "on literary abilities, & the recommendation of it by good pens" (Washington 1997). Other advocates used the press to publish a series of articles, later dubbed the "Federalist Papers," to make their case to the public, but the idea that this persuasion was necessary and that a system of government could work that was held in check by the public created a system where the press, while not an official part of the government, would play a critical role in the ability for the American system to work.

This concept of the free press as a separate, and almost official, check on the governmental system is a profoundly liberal idea in the classical sense. The idea is simple: the government rests on its authority it receives from the public through their votes and so how well the voting public is informed and so the press is tasked with the idea of ensuring that any wrongdoing or abuse of that authority is exposed to the public is the cornerstone of watchdog journalism. Scottish social commentator Thomas Carlyle would credit philosopher Edmund Burke with coining a term for this semi-official role of the press, writing, "Burke said there were Three Estates in Parliament; but, in the Reporters' Gallery yonder, there sat a *Fourth Estate* more important far than they all. It is not a figure of speech, or a witty saying; it is a literal fact,—very momentous to us in these times. Literature is our Parliament too . . . Whoever can speak, speaking now to the whole nation, becomes a power, a branch of government, with inalienable weight in law-making, in all acts of authority" (Carlyle 1948). This idea that the press would serve as the people's platform for discussing issues and holding accountable those in power would come to be one of the core concepts of an independent press, and so the role of the media in reporting on those in power has become a central tenet of a professional press corps.

The importance of the independence of the media to play this role has also been central to many of the structural developments that would unfold in the American system. The philosophy behind it has had a huge effect in shaping modern libel law in America. It is far harder for a public figure (or celebrity, or anyone considered in the public eye) to win a libel case against the press. This stems from a crucial case in the 1960s where southern defendants sued the *New York Times* for running what they considered a libelous ad. In a decision that seemed to declare its intentions to protect the watchdog, Justice William Brennan boldly declared: "[W]e consider this case against the background of a profound national commitment to the principle that debate on public issues should be uninhibited, robust, and wide-open, and that it may well include vehement, caustic, and sometimes unpleasantly sharp attacks on government and public officials." The result was a libel law that factored in the First Amendment freedom of the press, ensuring that the press could not face lawsuits in areas where they exposed public officials to public scrutiny even if they had enormous authority in that area.

Federal judge Alex Kozinski, when discussing the implications of that 1964 decision in *New York Times Co.* v. *Sullivan*, actually even referred to the concept of the watchdog, saying without it "the media in the country would become as effective as a toothless guard dog." Other decisions like the 1971 Pentagon Papers case would empower editors and reporters to decide what information should be published, banishing the idea of prior restraint on the press, even when the information to be published is considered top secret. Most judges and legislatures have essentially decided that if the public has a legitimate interest in the information to be published then the press has wide freedom to proceed almost without fear of prosecution. So, for example, when a contractor for the National Security Agency decided to leak information about a massive surveillance program to the press, he was indicted and fled the country. All of the journalists who have received the information that Edward Snowden released are protected from prosecution even though without them Snowden's documents would never have become known to the public. It may seem unfair that the person who leaked a document may be prosecuted while a journalist who takes that document and reports it the world is free from fear, but the legal and structural history of watchdog journalism has created such a system.

Fair or not, it is a system that the American public has, for decades, supported. In fact, Snowden's leak of the NSA surveillance, coupled with other stories of the Internal Revenue Service targeting certain political nonprofits for investigation and stories of secret detention facilities run in the war on terror, has only built support for the concept of watchdog journalism. A 2013 report from the Pew Research Center found that nearly 70 percent of the American public concluded that press attention and criticism of government programs keeps political leaders from doing things that should not be done; only 21 percent said that scrutiny kept the government from doing its job. The number reflected a 10-point jump in just the last two years. This public support is bipartisan. According to the report, "About equal majorities of Republicans (69%), independents (69%) and Democrats (67%) view news organizations as a check on political leaders and there has been a significant rise in this view across nearly all demographic and political groups. Young people especially have become more likely to say news organizations keep political leaders from doing things that should not be done, a shift in opinion that has taken place concurrently with rising concerns about civil liberties" (Pew Research Center 2013).

The widespread support for the role of a watchdog press is impressive given the growing frustrations and distrust most Americans feel toward the press. In the same survey, only 26 percent said they felt the press gets its facts straight and only 20 percent said it was willing to admit its mistakes. These seemingly conflicting opinions reflect the complicated position the watchdog role puts a for-profit business like most media in. On the one hand, these journalists are tasked with holding politicians and bureaucrats accountable for what they do and how well it aligns with what they said they would do. Most Americans want them to be that fourth estate Burke described. Yet the public turns on the press when it falls short or is perceived to be biased. The press is left to navigate between what is popular and what the public wants to believe, and what it needs to know to make informed decisions. It is, at times, an unenviable position and yet most journalists will admit they take their role in the system, while unofficial, with seriousness and purpose.

Even in this era of journalism pressured for revenue streams and viable business models, watchdog reporting remains a touchstone for the industry. And yet what watchdog reporting looks like is far from monolithic. The most obvious branch of this accountability journalism is the investigative work done by major newspapers, some television, and many digital media outlets. Investigative reporting begins with a premise that the story put out by officials is usually not complete or even all that honest. Major investigations have dived into everything from the treatment of vets to environmental crimes and often explode in the media following a major publication by an outlet that devoted months or years to getting the story right. These investigative pieces are often controversial because they often take a stand that what is happening in this investigation is wrong and should be fixed. They do not rely, as much political reporting does, on getting multiple perspectives that debate the issue, rather the story comes from the angle that was is happening is wrong. As former Washington bureau chief of the *New York Times* Bill Kovach and American Press Institute's Tom Rosenstiel noted in their book on the media, "The news outlet is taking an implied stance on the issue that some wrongdoing has occurred. That is why investigative journalism has been called advocacy reporting, or as reporter Les Whitten called it, 'reporting with a sense of outrage,' and why the acronym for the professional association called Investigative Reporters and Editors spells out the word ire" (Kovach and Rosenstiel 2007). And many watchdog journalists can seem to be borderline paranoids, assuming the worst most of the time and seeing widespread conspiracy or neglect in many stories. Still, these investigators also are the ones who dig deeper on the story, pushing for the release of public documents and demanding that the government abide by the law. They are the descendants of the early muckrakers of the twentieth century who pushed the government to crack down on abuses by big business and machine politics. These crusading journalists often stop short, unlike many of the muckrakers, of proposing a solution to the problems they document, instead pushing the issue into the public sphere to be debated by the government and the public.

But some journalists have also sought to find other forms of reporting that abide by the spirit of the watchdog but perhaps take a less confrontational approach to the subject. For example, the Associated Press couched its effort at watchdog journalism in a less advocacy framework, declaring it "accountability" journalism. In explaining the idea, Washington bureau chief Ron Fournier said, "It's not opinionated journalism. It's not taking sides unless you count being on the side of the truth and being on the side of doing things right . . . It's no longer good enough when we hear a press secretary say a piece of what we call 'spin' where they are just kind of shading the truth and just laugh at it and say, 'that's just spin'—which is what we do in the newsroom, been doing for years. That's not good enough any more. We need to point it out" (Associated Press 2009). The AP effort highlights the road many journalists seek to pursue in their work, not assuming the worst, but also moving beyond the back-and-forth of a political debate.

One example of this form of watchdog work is the fact checking most news organizations do during campaigns. During these segments, journalists take the claims made by a campaign or an ad and explore the veracity of what is said, seeking the documents, pursuing the source of the financing, and seeking to educate the public as to the accuracy of the ad. Other forms of this less-confrontational, but still watchdog-oriented work include efforts to grade a candidate's performance on how well he or she delivered on the promises they made during the campaign. Again, the idea here is to hold the politician accountable for what they promised the public and what they then did when elected.

The watchdog role has also arrived more forcefully on the campaign trail in recent years as journalists seek to combat misinformation in elections. This stems from the dicey reality of post-truth politics where candidates can make a claim again and again and despite efforts from the press to clarify the misinformation, the facts themselves become debatable, making it difficult for the public to know what is true. This struggle to combat misinformation has led some to argue that simply having the strength to declare what is true and what is debatable may be becoming an act of watchdog reporting. Dan Froomkin worked for the *Washington Post* and eventually joined Glenn Greenwald, who broke the NSA story, at his service called The Intercept. Froomkin says, "To many people, watchdog reporting is synonymous with investigative reporting, specifically, ferreting out secrets. But there's another, maybe even more crucial form of watchdog reporting, especially in this age of relentless public relations and spin. It involves reporting what may well be in plain sight, contrasting that with what officials in government and other positions of power say, rebuffing and rebutting misinformation, and sometimes even taking a position on what the facts suggest is the right solution" (Froomkin 2013).

Throughout these different strands of modern reporting on politics—from investigative work to fact checking to simply standing up against political spin—there remains the central idea of serving the public's need for understandable information about their government. The service of watchdog journalism helped spur the initial inclusion of the press among the First Amendment rights Americans had. It helped develop the muckraking movement at the dawn of the twentieth century and played an important role in the increasingly confrontational reporting about the Vietnam War and the drumbeat of investigations into the Watergate break-in.

The goal of these reporters and editors is often summed up in a truism that was coined by a fictional Irish bartender conceived of by *Chicago Evening Post* journalist and humorist Finley Peter Dunne at the time of the muckrakers and has been a badge of honor for many journalists ever since that journalism at its best "comforts the afflicted and afflicts the comfortable." For the American system to work, voters need to be able to rely on sources of information that will warn them when the government has overstepped its bounds—federal courts have declared the NSA surveillance program unconstitutional and ordered it reined in, but only because it came out that it was happening. Similar watchdog reporting has uncovered political corruption and sex and financial scandals that have forced dozens of politicians out of office and changed the course of government. The role of journalism as watchdog is vital for the functioning of a free society. The trick for journalists—and the public—is to keep skepticism from descending into permanent cynicism.

See also: Advocacy Journalism; Muckraking; Post-Truth Politics; Trust in Journalism

Further Reading

Associated Press. 2009. "Associated Press: How to Do Watchdog Journalism." Associated Press. June 18. Accessed October 30, 2015. https://www.youtube.com/watch?v=Sxf90TXThY8.

Carlyle, Thomas. 1948. *Sartor Resartus, and On Heroes, Hero-Worship, and the Heroic in History*. London: J. M. Dent & Sons Ltd.

Froomkin, Dan. 2013. "Truth or Consequences: Where Is Watchdog Journalism Today?" Nieman Reports. June 13. Accessed October 30, 2015. http://niemanreports.org/articles/truth-or-consequences-where-is-watchdog-journalism-today.

Kovach, Bill, and Tom Rosenstiel. 2007. *The Elements of Journalism: What Newspeople Should Know and the Public Should Expect*. New York: Three Rivers Press.

Pew Research Center. 2013. "Amid Criticism, Support for Media's 'Watchdog' Role Stands Out." August 8. Accessed October 30, 2015. http://www.people-press.org/2013/08/08/amid-criticism-support-for-medias-watchdog-role-stands-out/#overview.

Washington, George. 1997. "George Washington to David Humphreys, 10 October 1787." In *George Washington, Writings*. Edited by John Rhodehamel. New York: Library of America.

THE *WEEKLY STANDARD*

One of the most recent additions to the array of intellectual journals on politics, the *Weekly Standard* has carved out a unique place in the journalism of political commentary, establishing its brand as closely associated with the conservative economics and assertive foreign policy often called neo-conservative. With a staff of 28 editors and writers and an array of conservative contributors, the magazine has established itself as an influential journal among Republican leaders and politicians.

The magazine, like many other journals of political thought, has never been a major financial success. It was founded with a budget of $3 million in 1995 given by News Corp. bigwig Rupert Murdoch and was edited by William Kristol. Kristol had made a name for himself as a political insider, having served as chief of staff to Vice President Dan Quayle. Kristol's father had also worked in magazines, having helped guide influential conservative magazines like *Encounter*, the *Public Interest*, and the *National Interest*. Kristol, in outlining the goals of the soon-to-debut journal, described the *Standard* as "a magazine of politics and ideas that helps frame the debate and is a forum for serious but also lively discussion of this new era. We'll be politically engaged, but not in a partisan way" (Berke 1995). When the magazine appeared less than four months later, it had to compete for attention. That same month, John F. Kennedy, Jr., debuted his glossy magazine *George*, sporting supermodel Cindy Crawford on the cover and promising to make politics sexy. The *Weekly Standard*, by comparison, launched with a cartoon of then-Speaker of the House Newt Gingrich swinging on a rope and armed for combat with his opponents. *George* got all the attention, but the *Weekly Standard* became an important source for the political leaders who had come to power with Gingrich. Within six years, *George* had ceased publication and the *Weekly Standard* was about to reach the heights of its influence.

The new magazine was based in Washington, D.C., in the same building as the influential American Enterprise Institute and, perhaps not surprisingly, many of the scholars at AEI would contribute to the new journal. The magazine took on Republican politics, foreign policy, and the judiciary while also examining art and literature. Its erudite, yet playful tone attracted readers from the left as well as the clear targets on the right and the circulation for the magazine soon grew to nearly 100,000. The magazine launched with Kristol and Fred Barnes, who had served a decade as a senior editor at the liberal *New Republic*, at the helm. The editors soon drew talented conservatives like Christopher Caldwell, P.J. O'Rourke, and Charles Krauthammer as contributors, and its influence seemed to be growing with each issue. The magazine's creation came at a time of resurgence in the Republican ranks, having just retaken the U.S. House for the first time in 40 years and having seen more and more state legislatures move to the right. But for all this political success, Kristol and the other founders of the magazine worried about the intellectual grounding of this newfound conservative success. He attracted a group writers and editors who looked toward Ronald Reagan, as well as tough-minded liberals like former U.S. senator Patrick Moynihan, for inspiration.

But for many critics of the new outlet, "this 'heterodoxy' is just a smokescreen for a sinister orthodoxy—neo-conservatism. The magazine has been Washington's noisiest champion of an assertive foreign policy that tries to link American power with American ideals (Mr. Kristol calls it 'neo-Reaganism'). And there is no shortage of material for conspiracy theorists who want to show the Iraq war was a Zionist plot . . . Mr. Kristol replies that neo-conservatism was more of a predisposition that shaped the magazine's response to events such as the genocide in Bosnia, rather than a pre-cooked ideology" (*Economist* 2005). But this connection to the so-called neo-conservative agenda would be one of the hallmarks of the *Standard*.

In 1997, the magazine published a famous essay, "Saddam Must Go," that illuminated the conservative argument that the Iraqi leader was a threat to democracy and stability in the region. The essay spoke to the *Weekly Standard's* strong activist foreign policy and actually foreshadowed many of the arguments that would be used six years later by the administration of George W. Bush to launch military action against Iraq. Throughout these years, the magazine was owned by Murdoch, who appeared unfazed by its inability to turn a profit. Most argued Murdoch was willing to lose a million dollars a year, the reported shortfall, for the amount of influence the journal seemed to have. This became especially true after the election of George Bush in 2000 and the terrorist attacks of September 11, 2001. White House speechwriter and conservative journalist David Frum would later tell the *New York Times*, "On foreign policy, *The Weekly Standard* had a lot of influence with the Bush administration. It was among the most consistent defenders of the broad outlines of Bush policy" (Arango 2009). Each week Vice President Dick Cheney received 30 copies of the magazine at his office alone, and the strong foreign policy arguments of the magazine's writers seemed to be playing out not just on the page, but in the real world as the United States battled al-Qaeda and later Iraq overseas.

But the 2003 Iraq invasion may have represented something of a high-water mark of influence and interest from its owner Murdoch. In 2007, Murdoch's News Corp. purchased the *Wall Street Journal* and the Australian's interest in the *Weekly Standard* appeared to ebb. By 2009, he decided to sell the magazine to another billionaire conservative, Philip Anschutz. Anschutz's Clarity Media Group publishes the *Examiner* paper in San Francisco, the *Washington Examiner* magazine in D.C., and the website examiner.com. Clarity Media Group had for years been interested in reaching the influential in Washington. Clarity purchased a series of suburban papers in the D.C. area in 2004 and relaunched them as the *Washington Examiner*, a local paper that served all those communities and the capital. Despite its success in covering the communities of D.C., the newspaper lacked political influence and in 2013 the papers were ended and the magazine, also called the *Washington Examiner*, was created with the aim of reaching "45,000 government, public affairs, advocacy, academia and political professionals in Washington, DC, and state capitals" (Tapscott 2013). It was this publisher who took over the *Weekly Standard* in 2009, seeking to bolster its D.C. influence. With its new ownership, the *Standard* still reports a circulation of about 100,000 and claims its website reaches some 3 million. Its new owners kept together the same team of Barnes and Kristol at the helm, and the politics of the journal remains intellectually conservative.

See also: American Enterprise Institute (AEI); The *National Review*

Further Reading

Arango, Tim. 2009. "New Owner for a Magazine as Political Tastes Change." *New York Times*. August 2. Accessed August 25, 2015. http://www.nytimes.com/2009/08/03/business/media/03standard.html?_r=0.

Berke, Richard. 1995. "Murdoch Finances New Forum for Right: A Leading G.O.P. Strategist to Run Washington-Based Magazine." *New York Times*. April 30.

"The Neocon Bible; The Weekly Standard." 2005. *The Economist*. September 17, 2005. Accessed August 25, 2015. http://www.economist.com/node/4405615.

Tapscott, Mark. 2013. "Washington Examiner Shifts Business Model from Daily Newspaper to Political Site and Weekly Print Magazine." *Washington Examiner*. March 18. Accessed August 30, 2015. http://www.washingtonexaminer.com/washington-examiner-shifts-business-model-from-daily-newspaper-to-political-site-and-weekly-print-magazine/article/2524796.

WHITE HOUSE CORRESPONDENTS' DINNER

If there is a lightning rod for the criticism about political reporters and their relationship with the politicians they are paid to cover, it is the annual black tie gala where Hollywood celebrities, Cabinet members, and the upper echelon of the Washington press corps gather to crack jokes and toast one another—the White House Correspondents' Dinner.

For those in Washington, D.C., the event has become known as "Nerd Prom," a night where the ink-stained wretches of the political press cut loose and have some fun with the people they cover. At least that was the idea, but what the dinner has come to mean for many journalists and political observers is the worst of excess. *New York Times* correspondent Mark Leibovich penned a full book that castigated the dinner and the elements of D.C. journalism that bask in the glory of "Nerd Prom," writing, "Three thousand tux-and-gowners rise as one in the ballroom of the 'Hinckley Hilton' and offer a solemn toast 'to the President of the United States' . . . [T]o the outside world, the dinner and its collateral goings-on present an image of Washington as one big game and costume party, everyone bathed in the same frothy mix of fame and fun and flattery and (most of all) belonging. It all looks terrible" (Leibovich 2013). This sense of the elite press and political powers-that-be sitting, dressed to the nines, and laughing at their own jokes as the political process remains hopelessly deadlocked has created real frustration inside and outside of Washington. But for many inside D.C., Leibovich's portrayal of one dinner as some shallow, cynical ball is overblown and misunderstands the benefits of journalist and politician seeing one another as people and not just problems.

The event, for all its current controversy, has actually been around for nearly a century. It started as a celebration at the rebirth of the association that runs it—the White House Correspondents' Association. The WHCA had gone dormant during the Woodrow Wilson years after their efforts to protect regular press briefings by the president failed. Fifty men gathered in May 1921 to toast the election of a new president—Warren G. Harding—who had already promised to revive the meetings with the press. With the press conferences back, the association reorganized the dinner to promote the freer flow of information from the White House to the press. According to the WHCA history of their dinner, "On a social level, the correspondents saw Harding, a newspaper publisher, as one of their own. One of his first acts as president had been throwing a dinner for the correspondents who had covered his campaign in Marion, Ohio. Now, it was time to reciprocate" (WHCA). That night the president was not in attendance—in fact Harding never attended a dinner—but his main liaison with the press was there as were many of his staff. By 1924 the first president made an appearance at the dinner—Calvin Coolidge.

The events tended to be informal affairs until 1941 when FDR used the dinner to deliver an important policy speech about the growing unity in opposition to the Axis powers of Germany and Japan, telling the reporters, "It differs from the press conferences that you and I hold twice a week, for you cannot ask me any questions tonight, and everything that I have to say is word for word on the record." The president went on to warn of war and to defend and explain the Lend-Lease Act he had just signed, which essentially put America firmly in the British camp and helped set the country on the path to war. His speech was a sobering warning of what was to come, and the audience of reporters appeared in a patriotic mood. "While today's journalists are trained never to react to a politician's substantive remarks, the reporters at that dinner interrupted the 35-minute speech 34 times with applause that often included whoops and cheers. But when it was done, and Roosevelt turned the microphone over to emcee Jay Flippen, a vaudevillian, popular singer, Broadway actor, and sometime radio voice of the New York Yankees, the correspondents did not rush to their typewriters. They poured more drinks, lit more cigarettes, and settled back for the rest of the entertainment" (Condon 2015).

Aside from that historic dinner, the event remained largely unremarkable, except for the overt sexism that also ran through its early history. Even though women could join the association, they were banned from the dinner. In 1950 Navy undersecretary Dan Kimball hosted a counter-dinner for "the underprivileged ladies" of the White House press corps to pressure the association to change. Still, the man-only rule stayed in place for more than a decade. By 1960, United Press International had assigned Helen Thomas to begin covering the newly elected president John F. Kennedy, and she stepped up the pressure to open the dinner to women. Steve Thomma, the head of the White House Correspondents' Association, recalled at her death in 2013, "At her urging in 1962, Kennedy said he would not attend the annual dinner of the White House Correspondents Association unless it was opened to women for the first time. It was. And in 1975–76, she served as the first woman president of the association. Women and men who've followed in the press corps all owe a debt of gratitude for the work Helen did and the doors she opened. All of our journalism is the better for it" (Mirkinson 2013).

For much of the next 30 years, the event remained a big deal in Washington and almost nowhere else: a very "inside baseball" dinner with some celebrity entertainment and a few scandalous moments. That began to change in 1993 when C-SPAN rolled in a camera and began broadcasting the event live. Suddenly the evening became something the entire nation could see, a grand ballroom where the national political reporting corps yucked it up with the men and women they were supposed to keep honest, all decked out in tuxedos and the finest gowns. The event soon morphed into the Washington Oscars, complete with a red carpet arrival area outside the Washington Hilton—where James Hinckley attempted to assassinate Ronald Reagan in 1981. Still, the association tried to downplay the dinner's pomp. In a 2014 video produced after Leibovich's book, the WHCA says, "The first and foremost mission of the White House Correspondents' Dinner is to promote journalism education through the scholarship fund." And the association does hand out $100,000 in scholarships—a sizeable amount. But some wonder if that really is the point of an event where some of the richest celebrities and most successful fundraisers on the planet flock to a hotel ballroom. And the event continues to grow in size, production value, and breadth. It's now merely the centerpiece of nearly a week of receptions, parties, and galas.

For all the criticism of its excess, the dinner still provides a unique moment where the world of politics and comedy—always intertwined—fully embrace one another. Bob Hope emceed in 1944, and entertainment has been a regular component of the evening since the 1950s. Both professional comedians and the sitting president now routinely turn in performances that can be controversial platforms for biting political commentary. In 2015, for example, President Obama joked, "For many Americans, this is still a time of deep uncertainty. I have one friend, just weeks ago, she was making millions of dollars a year, and she's now living out of a van in Iowa," referring to the recently launched presidential campaign of his former secretary of state Hillary Clinton. In 2006, Stephen Colbert brought his satirical conservative talk show persona to the dinner and delivered a stinging series of jokes about President George W. Bush, who appeared decidedly unamused as Colbert riffed, "Now, I know there are some polls out there saying this man has a 32 percent approval rating. But guys like us, we don't pay attention to the polls. We know that polls are just a collection of statistics that reflect what people are thinking in reality. And reality has a well-known liberal bias . . . Sir, pay no attention to the people who say the glass is half empty, because 32 percent means it's two-thirds empty. There's still some liquid in that glass, is my point. But I wouldn't drink it. The last third is usually backwash." Response to the controversial performance became, itself, a political story for days afterwards as people debated whether it was appropriate for Colbert to mock the president in front of him.

Many who attended the dinner said Colbert's jokes largely bombed in the room, but videos of the performance took off on the web, drawing hundreds of thousands of views. James Poniewozik later wrote of the incident, "This has become the political-cultural touchstone issue of 2006—like whether you drive a hybrid or use the term 'freedom fries.' For those of you who haven't seen the performance, Colbert, in character, launched into a scathing (by the standards of the dinner, not 'The Colbert Report') 'tribute' to President Bush that had the Commander in Chief grimacing and the room of reporters and dignitaries in largely uncomfortable silence." The Colbert performance and many of those that followed highlighted how the dinner had become a political video event as much as a Washington insider celebration.

By 2015 there were 112 reporters covering the arrival of dinner attendees, just one of the many spring galas that now mark the calendar. Most, like the Washington Correspondents' Dinner hosted by the congressional reporting organization, are far more tame affairs, but for some the entire week of events has become an emblem of a major problem in Washington journalism. D.C. reporter Patrick Gavin spent a year putting together a documentary about the events, called "Nerd Prom." He lashed out at in the excess in Politico, writing, "What started off decades ago as a stately formal celebration of the best of presidential reporting has morphed into a four-day orgy of everything people outside the Beltway hate about life inside the Beltway . . . four full days of signature cocktails and inside jokes that just underscore how out of step the Washington elite is with the rest of the country. It's not us (journalists) versus them (government officials); it's us (Washington) versus them (the rest of America)" (Gavin 2015). Thomma defended the dinner and the larger question of sources and journalists rubbing shoulders to public radio's *On the Media*, saying, "Every reporter in this town who covers a beat, we all take people out to lunch or dinner. Either cause we're already talking to them every day or we're hoping they'll return our calls and talk every day, and I just don't have a problem with it. It's up to every journalist what they do with their source. We're just not gonna get involved in that relationship" (Garfield 2015).

The White House Correspondents' Dinner remains one of the most controversial media events for reporters, a litmus test for many journalists who have grown to see the dinner as an abominable representation of the corrupt coziness of political reporters and politicians. Many worry that a dinner that puts these two groups in the same room and laughing at the same jokes makes the entire watchdog idea of reporting weaker. How can a reporter hammer a source for dishonesty one minute and pay for them to join them at a dinner the next? But for others there is an element of old world charm to the event. It is a way to hearken back to a time when reporters knew the men and women they covered, and the professional relationship of source and reporter did not artificially prevent two people from knowing each other socially. But these people who like the dinner as a chance to poke fun at the overheated politics and talk in Washington, and to actually get together to toast the president, tend to remain quiet in the face of the E! Hollywood-ization of politics that having Kim Kardashian and Barack Obama and U.S. Senate Majority Leader Mitch McConnell in the same room has become.

See also: Comedy, Satire, and Politics; Watchdog Journalism; White House Press Corps

Further Reading

Condon, George. 2015. "Magic, Music, and War: The Strangest White House Correspondents' Dinner Ever." *National Journal*. April 25. Accessed August 13, 2015. http://www.nationaljournal.com/magazine/the-strangest-white-house-correspondents-dinner-ever-20150424.

Garfield, Bob. 2015. "Watchdogs in Tuxedos." *On the Media*. April 17. Accessed August 12, 2015. http://www.onthemedia.org/story/watchdogs-tuxedos-revisit/transcript.

Gavin, Patrick. 2015. "Nerd Prom Is a Mess." *Politico*. April 23. Accessed August 14, 2015. http://www.politico.com/magazine/story/2015/04/white-house-correspondents-dinner-117287.html.

"History." White House Correspondents' Association. Accessed August 14, 2015. http://www.whca.net/history.htm.

Leibovich, Mark. 2013. *This Town*. New York: Blue Rider Press.

Mirkinson, Jack. 2013. "Helen Thomas Dead: Pioneering White House Reporter Dies at 92." Huffington Post. July 20. Accessed August 13, 2015. http://www.huffingtonpost.com/2013/07/20/helen-thomas-dead_n_3628151.html.

Poniewozik, James. 2006. "Stephen Colbert and the Death of 'The Room.'" *Time Magazine*. May 3. Accessed August 13, 2015. http://entertainment.time.com/2006/05/03/stephen_colbert_and_the_death.

WHITE HOUSE PRESS CORPS

The journalists who cover the president each and every day, often traveling at thousands of dollars of expense to their news organization to be with the leader of the free world, have evolved from a small, chummy group of political insiders who would meet privately with the president to a rhetorical dueling partner with the White House press secretary. The relationship between the hundreds of reporters credentialed to cover the president and the senior officials within the government has often been a source of concern and frustration for those outside of Washington, D.C.

There is no official White House press corps, as many of those who cover the president may be assigned on a case-by-case basis, but the bulk of the regular media that covers the president are members of the White House Correspondents Association. The organization formed in 1914 with an aim of pressuring then-president Woodrow Wilson from ending his regular press briefings. Wilson had a notoriously rocky relationship with the press and several reporters had heard a rumor, which turned out not to be true, that a congressional committee would be tasked with selecting whom among the press could cover the president. The association now boasts more than 250 members, including radio, television, print, and web news outlets, and works with the White House to ensure press access to officials and occasionally the president. The journalists who get the White House beat are often the rising stars of their respective news organizations and have made their way to the White House by building a name for themselves.

The corps of reporters who cover the president have often found themselves at the forefront of the debate over issues of access to political leaders and the behavior of the political press. One of those elements that receives much attention by both scholars of politics and the current political blogosphere and punditry is the influence a president can hold over the press or that the press can push on the White House. Whether in the animosity and mutual disdain that appeared between the Nixon White House and the press, or the friendships and off-the-record counsel that marked the FDR administration, the questions about what is the right relationship between the two is often debated. Roosevelt is credited with wielding enormous influence over the press because he brought them into his thinking about Depression-era policies, asking the advice of leading columnists, and offering unprecedented access to the press for interviews and press conferences. So what happened to the more easy, casual relationship between the press and President Franklin Roosevelt or even President Kennedy?

First, when television began broadcasting press conferences, both the president and the men (and increasingly women) who covered the White House became household names. This pushed both to step up their work and act more "professional." Also, events intervened that changed the relationship. One exhaustive study found that it was the press's increasing focus on objectivity as a critical component of its work and "Vietnam and Watergate-related presidential abuses that undermined journalistic trust in the president . . . [S]uch events appear to have led White House reporters toward a more fundamental reconsideration of their proper role" (Clayman, et al. 2010).

If there had ever truly been a love affair between the press and the White House (it was more likely an uneasy mutual necessity than an actual friendship), both the press and the politicians had ended it by the late 1960s. Politicians targeted the increasingly sharp-penned press as negative and abusive. Nixon vice president Spiro Agnew became noted for blasting the press as out of touch with the real concerns of Americans. He said the president ought to have the "right to communicate directly with the people who elected him . . . without having the President's words and thoughts characterized through the prejudices of hostile critics before they can even be digested . . . The views of a—the majority of this fraternity do not—and I repeat, not—represent the views of America" (Taylor 2015).

This combat between the White House and the press is now most evident in the daily press briefing by the press secretary. For decades, the press secretary would take to the podium in what is now called the James S. Brady Briefing Room in the West Wing of the White House to face the 49 seated journalists and the scores of cameras set up along the back row. The press secretary would take questions from the press about what the White House was doing that day, reacting to a news event overseas or getting a political assessment about administration negotiations with Congress. But as the Monica Lewinsky scandal exploded in 1998, a technical change was made to the press room; it was only later Mike McCurry, then-press secretary, came to understand its significance, saying, "The moment I realized I had made some kind of mistake was when the networks started using two cameras—one to shoot the briefing [i.e., McCurry at the lectern] and a second one, right near my shoulder, to shoot correspondents asking the questions . . . The dynamic changed. Now the briefings were television events rather than an opportunity to answer questions about the news" (Simon 2014).

But it was not just the relationship between the president and his staff and the press dispatched to cover them. The demands of the media also changed over time, affecting the types of stories the White House press corps produced and requiring the news organizations to develop new tools to address those needs. It is easy to see that the president is perhaps the single most covered public figure in the world. Leaning over a sneeze guard at a Chipotle in Washington triggered a deluge of stories about President Obama. President Clinton's running shorts were often a point of public discussion, and the press eagerly covered President Nixon walking on the beach in a full suit with dark socks and shoes. But with the advent of television coverage and then the shocking assassination of President Kennedy, the "body watch" became a central part of the White House press corps's job. Wherever the president went, the press would be there, capturing every moment in film and the written word. For some time the pressure on these journalists to generate a daily story about what the president did and the political ramifications of those actions stretched the journalists' ability to report. The press adapted to its strange new role with an innovation: the pool report.

Now a small team of reporters and photographers are tasked each day with supplying a blow-by-blow account of the president's actions. The account, the "pool report," is transmitted to all White House correspondents so they can include specific details to their respective readers and viewers. What is often not clear is this information is essentially second-hand since the reporter, unless selected that day to be the pool reporter, did not actually witness it. Liberal writer Matthew Yglesias called the pool report "basically a mutually agreed upon plagiarism pact. It's not feasible for all news organizations to get first-hand reports about the president's activities. But they want to *pretend* that they can. So they come up with the idea of the 'pool reporter' and then a convention that it's okay to mislead the audience about what happens by writing up information drawn from pool reports as if it's original reporting" (Yglesias 2009). The pool reports almost never make it into the final reports of the White House correspondents, but they often highlight the mundane reality of covering someone they rarely actually interact with. One pointed column that documented the early days of the Bill Clinton White House and how the inexperienced staff had mangled the press logistics of Clinton's visit to the 50th anniversary of D-Day in Europe included one section of the pool report that gives a sense of what the reporters who cover the president receive:

> Afterward, Clinton worked the rope line. He met a lot of ribbon-wearing veterans. We then followed Clinton on a small boat while he was on the HMY Britannia; couldn't see him. Our little ever-bobbing "chase" boat, by the way, was too slow to keep up with the Britannia, so we took a lot of shortcuts. Best color we saw was this: the presidential party watched an impressive flyover, including jets flying in a

> stunning precision formation reading "50." I believe Clinton gazed skyward at this display, although we were pretty far away. (Lewis 1994)

The pool reports helped expedite the evolution of the press corps feeling more and more disengaged from their job of tracking the president every day. With a heavy reliance on the pool for the most specific reporting about the president and an often-heavy-handed set of restrictions on where press traveling with the president can go and with whom they can interact, it is not as surprising that when continued budget cuts raised the question of whether to send reporters on trips with the president, more and more outlets started saying no. Traveling with the president, unless part of the pool, is not cheap. According to the WHCA, the press spent $18 million on travel in 2009. As more news outlets begged off traveling with the president, the higher the costs of paying for the charter flights became for the remaining organizations, which in turn prompted more to bail on the coverage. Now when a president travels or a presidential candidate hits the road, news outlets often attempt to cover them in the most cost-effective way, sending younger, more inexperienced staff onto the press busses and relying on the pool reports more and more.

Back in Washington, though, there is still an argument that the White House press corps has lost perspective as to what its real job is and what it should be focused on. This came into sharp relief after the resignation of Helen Thomas, the longest-serving White House correspondent, in 2010. Thomas, as tradition held, would ask the first question at every press conference with the president, peppering presidents from Kennedy to Obama with often tartly phrased jabs that aimed to provoke a response to the day's events. When Thomas was quoted making anti-Israel statements in 2010 she was forced to resign from her job reporting for Hearst newspapers and she left her spot in the White House press room. The news triggered a high school-style turf fight among the organizations and reporters covering the White House as to who would inherit her seat in the front row of the White House press briefing room. A frustrated *Nation* columnist Eric Alterman lamented the corps's "childish insularity and ego-driven myopia." He went on to declare, "The entire focus of the White House press corps is on what happens inside the White House. While that's not irrelevant, neither is it what's really important. Reporters climb over one another like gerbils in a crowded cage, and for what? It's rarely to examine the consequences of any given policy—'substance,' after all, is not their beat" (Alterman 2010).

This kind of criticism—that the press corps is as much interested in its own self-promotion and proximity to power as in the civic good—also fuels criticism of the press corps's most public moment: the annual White House Correspondents' Dinner. The black tie extravaganza attracts Hollywood celebrities and the elite press to hobnob with administration officials. The dinner has drawn fire for the coziness it seems to showcase between official Washington and the press.

Moreover, the White House now uses social media to communicate directly with the public, through an Instagram feed of official photographs, a YouTube channel, and countless tweets, Facebook posts, and web content about issues both international and domestic. This shift has forced the press corps to go public with its concerns. In 2015, the WHCA declared its "Practices and Principles of White House Coverage," that aimed to formalize the modern relationship of the press with the executive branch and reinforce the role and value of the press corps. The statement included demands that:

- The press must be able to see, hear, witness and question the President and his or her aides on a routine basis, in addition to the daily White House briefing.
- The press must have the ability to question the President in person on a regular basis, including through a full news conference at least once a month and in response to significant news developments.
- The President's events are by default open to the full press corps and, in the instance of legitimate space constraints, are at minimum open to the full press pool.
- The press has regular access to the President's aides, beyond those in the White House Press Office.
- Briefings by administration officials are on the record, as a general practice.
- Background briefings where officials are not identified by name are reserved for subjects of special sensitivity. (WHCA)

The statement was a striking admission of how the press has lost the authority that FDR sought to use to influence public opinion of his policies. Now as the use of the press has become only part of an overall communications strategy, the power of the White House press corps has waned to the point where it must itself publicly pressure the administration for access. A Politico survey of reporters who cover the White House reported that fully 80 percent of the White House press corps had not conducted a one-on-one interview with President Obama by late in the seventh year of his presidency. And the simple fact is he does not need to sit down with specific reporters to get his message out. Instead, between the orchestrated chaos of the daily White House briefing, the social media feeds of the White House, and the background briefing by various members of the administration, the message gets out to the public regardless of who is sitting in the West Wing briefing room or how often the chartered press plane accompanies the president to a foreign trip.

See also: White House Correspondents' Dinner

Further Reading

Alterman, Eric. 2010. "'Cutthroat' Crybabies." *Nation*. July 5. Accessed August 13, 2015. http://www.thenation.com/article/cutthroat-crybabies.

Clayman, Steven E., Marc N. Elliott, John Heritage, and Megan K. Beckett. 2010. "A Watershed in White House Journalism: Explaining the Post-1968 Rise of Aggressive Presidential News." *Political Communication* 27, no. 3: 229–47.

Lewis, Michael. 1994. "POTUS Operandi." *New Republic*. June 27.

"Practices and Principles of White House Coverage." White House Correspondents' Association. Accessed August 14, 2015. http://www.whca.net/2015WHCA_Declaration.pdf.

Simon, Roger. 2014. "Daily Combat at the White House." Politico. June 3. Accessed August 14, 2015. http://www.politico.com/story/2014/06/mike-mccurry-white-house-press-secretary-107339.html.

Taylor, Jessica. 2015. "Giving Some Rope: A Brief History of Tensions between Politicians and the Press." NPR. July 6. Accessed August 15, 2015. http://www.npr.org/sections/itsallpolitics/2015/07/06/420595547/giving-some-rope-a-brief-history-of-tensions-between-politicians-and-the-press.

Yglesias, Matthew. 2009. "The Pool." ThinkProgress. December 3. Accessed August 13, 2015. http://thinkprogress.org/yglesias/2009/12/03/184523/the-pool.

WHITE, THEODORE (1915–1986)

It took a foreign correspondent to see the historical sweep of campaigns for what they were: epic human dramas filled with flawed and very human characters. It took Teddy White to create the modern form of political reporting.

Theodore White started as a historian, fascinated by China's complex centuries-long story. Upon graduating from Harvard University, he landed a fellowship that allowed him to travel the world. He would end up in Chungking, the World War II-era capital of China as the country battled the Japanese. After working briefly for the government, he took an assignment as a correspondent for *Time* magazine, although he bristled at the lack of space and the rewriting his copy went through. He would later write of his wartime experience in the country in a book he co-authored in 1946 called *Thunder Out of China*. The book marked the first of many White would write and highlighted his uneasy relationship with contemporary journalism. He wanted to contextualize the events of war and diplomacy within the larger historical reality of the region. Daily journalism and even magazines like *Time* wanted more of the day-to-day action on the ground.

White also produced several works of fiction that caught the interest of Hollywood producers and stars. By 1959 he was able to choose the next book he wanted to write and was torn between two ideas—tell the story of the true dangers of nuclear weapons or chronicle a presidential campaign. Most advisers told him to go with the weapons book, but White disagreed. He would later write, "The idea was to follow a campaign from beginning to end. It would be written as a novel is written, with anticipated surprises as, one by one, early candidates vanish in the primaries until only two final jousters struggle for the prize in November. Moreover, it should be written as a story of a man in trouble, of the leader under the pressure of circumstances" (Porch 2015). The result would become one of the most important works of modern political journalism—*The Making of the Presidency 1960*. The book would chronicle the primary and general election campaign from the inside, with White tagging along with candidates, capturing telling moments, and turning them into novel-like scenes that took the readers into the psyches of the men seeking the office. He also paired that personal drama with a historian-like approach to the process of the election, documenting and explaining the evolution of the primary system, the role of conventions, and the historical significance of the first televised debates.

It was a narrative about American politics that had never been seen before and would spawn an entire genre of copycats. Noted conservative author William F. Buckley would credit White with singlehandedly "revolutionizing the art of political reporting" by focusing on the drama of the campaign and the poignancy of the candidate's personal struggle to convince voters to support him. Buckley noted White captured this "because his were the eyes of a journalist who could convey the inclinations of a small gathering of Americans who convened to hear a candidate by noting how much effort they put into wiping their own hands clean before accepting the politician's proffered hand. The voters spoke their intimate thoughts to him, his colleagues spoke their minds to him, presidents and presidential candidates sought him out" (Buckley 2008).

And it was this unique position as a historian-turned-journalist-turned-novelist that helped him see politics less as a daily slog of press releases and campaign meetings and more a story of the people running the campaign and their strategy for capturing the highest office in the land. White would become the benchmark for many editors who would demand the kind of intimate portraiture that White captured in his books, and those that would come after him would turn campaign strategy and internal workings into the stuff of high drama. The *New York Times*' Jill Abramson, in bemoaning what had become of the narrative form White really pioneered, would marvel at the uniqueness of the moment that the journalist had captured in 1960, writing, "White was writing at a time when television was just becoming the medium through which most Americans experienced political campaigns, though in a limited way. Much of the action still took place off camera, which enabled a respected journalist like White to gain direct but unpublicized access to the candidates as well as to their families and members of their staffs, who spoke openly about their hopes and ambitions" (Abramson 2010). Those that would come after White would try and emulate his prose, but would never gain the sort of access he managed in the era before campaigns became so carefully stage-managed. Works like *Game Change* that documented the 2008 campaign would aim for that insider feel, but would lack the direct access, relying on dozens of anonymous sources that captured elements of the story White did nearly 50 years earlier—few capturing the full breadth.

White would win the 1962 Pulitzer Prize for Nonfiction and would revisit the approach in 1964, 1968, and 1972, crafting popular works on the presidential campaign. These books helped drive the idea of campaigns as "narratives," a form that has become a central concept to the reporting about and the running of modern political campaigns. He would also document the Watergate scandal and would seek to stitch together the *Making of the Presidency* series while covering the 1980 campaign. But none of these later works could capture the originality and impact of that first 1961 book. It would become a must-read for many aspiring political reporters and campaign operatives.

White died suddenly from a stroke in 1986, but his body of work remains one of the influential in American political reporting.

See also: Access to Candidates; Campaign Narratives and Dramatization; Campaign Strategy Coverage

Further Reading

Abramson, Jill. 2010. "The Making of the President, Then and Now." *New York Times*. March 10. Accessed November 3, 2015. http://www.nytimes.com/2010/03/21/books/review/Abramson-t.html?pagewanted=all&_r=0.

Buckley, William F. 2008. *Happy Days Were Here Again: Reflections of a Libertarian Journalist*. New York: Basic Books.

Porch, Scott. 2015. "The Book That Changed Campaigns Forever." Politico. May/June. Accessed November 3, 2015. http://www.politico.com/magazine/story/2015/04/teddy-white-political-journalism-117090.

White, Theodore. 2009. *The Making of the Presidency: 1960*. New York: Harper Perennial.

WINCHELL, WALTER (1897–1972)

Walter Winchell had style. In the 1920s, wearing a fedora and with a cigarette dangling from his mouth, he invented the gossip column and wrote exhaustively about big-time marriages, divorces, new children, and the exploits of celebrities. And he did it using vivid and creative language. Couples were "welded" instead of married, had "blessed events" instead of babies, and went "phfft!" instead of divorced. People loved it. For some three decades, Winchell had a tremendous following, both in print and on the radio. It was a following that made him powerful not just in the celebrity circles of Hollywood, but also in the halls of power in Washington.

"By one estimate, fifty million Americans—out of an adult population of roughly seventy-five million—either listened to his weekly radio broadcast or read his daily column," wrote Neal Gabler in *Winchell: Gossip, Power and the Culture of Celebrity*. And those readers were loyal—it was once said that 200,000 readers switched New York papers when he did (Gabler 1994).

His work transformed journalism, dredging up scandal and gossip and helping to create the culture of celebrity that endures today. His fame flickered out long before he did, and most of his vast audience would turn away from him in his final years. His increasingly shrill embrace of McCarthyism in the 1950s turned off some loyal fans, as did unpopular attacks on certain celebrities. But in his prime, from the 1920s and into the early part of the 1950s, Winchell entertained—something he first learned to do as a kid on stage in New York City.

Born Walter Winchel (he later added the second L after seeing it on a theater marquee) in New York City in 1897, he grew up in a poor family. Desperate to make his mark, he went to a theater and became a song plugger, someone who sang before movies started. That led to a childhood career in vaudeville, including some time in a well-known duo with his first wife, Rita Greene. Being on stage prepared him in many ways for his journalism career. Gabler wrote that vaudeville made

Winchell "an entertainer for life and in life," writing, "For Walter, vaudeville had provided, as his Harlem childhood had, a lesson in fear, humiliation and resentment, and he brought those to his journalism too" (Gabler 1994).

Vaudeville led him into the newspaper business, too. His first writing gig was with the *Vaudeville News*, a trade paper where he wrote columns and sold ads. Next it was the *New York Graphic*, then William Randolph Hearst's *New York Daily Mirror.* He also embraced broadcast as it emerged as a powerful new media. In 1930, he began hosting a weekly radio show, and over the years he also appeared in movies and later narrated a TV show in the 1960s.

He wrote about—and feuded with—actors, actresses, reporters, and editors. Mobsters, athletes, and politicians courted him, too. Nobody wanted to be on Winchell's bad side. He wasn't shy about his political leanings either. "He adored the New Deal, supported civil rights and repeatedly denounced Fascism and Hitler far sooner than more Establishment journalists did," wrote Bernard Weinraub for the *New York Times* in 1998. But it was his political leanings that would lead to his downfall. An anticommunist, he embraced the ideas of U.S. senator Joseph McCarthy, who claimed communists had infiltrated the U.S. government. Even after McCarthy had been largely discredited, writes Gabler, "Walter continued to Red-bait, issuing warnings on everyone from a Broadway dance instructor . . . to playwright Arthur Miller to *The New York Times*" (1994). Winchell's once vast audience began to turn on him, the same way the country turned on McCarthy. He wrote for the *Daily Mirror* until it folded in 1963 and narrated *The Untouchables*, a 1960s TV show. But, by all accounts, he'd lost the fame he'd enjoyed for so many years. "Walter Winchell had been a veritable king and he had a good, long reign. Then fame ended. But he did not, doomed to years and years of has been-ism," wrote Dick Cavett for the *New York Times* in 2009.

He died in 1972 and his legacy is debatable. He served as something of an inspiration for gossipy Hollywood writers, and Internet sensation Matt Drudge has gone to extraordinary lengths to embrace the Winchell legacy, including the dapper hat. His lively prose and thirst for gossip changed journalism. Yet, at the end of his life, Winchell was a man more known for his flaws. "He had gone from a man who demonstrated the inspiring power of the press to one who demonstrated its terrifying dangers. No one could argue away that politically, at least, he had done good and evil in almost equal measure" (Gabler 1994).

Michael Wright

See also: Drudge Report; Infotainment

Further Reading

Cavett, Dick. 2009. "The Ghost Ship, 'W.W.'" *New York Times*. December 4. Accessed October 14, 2015. http://opinionator.blogs.nytimes.com/2009/12/04/the-ghost-ship-ww/?hp&_r=1.

Gabler, Neal. 1994. *Winchell: Gossip, Power and the Culture of Celebrity.* New York: Knopf.
Weinraub, Bernard. 1998. "He Turned Gossip into Tawdry Power; Walter Winchell, Who Climbed High and Fell Far, Still Scintillates." *New York Times.* November 18. Accessed October 14, 2015. http://www.nytimes.com/1998/11/18/arts/he-turned-gossip-into-tawdry-power-walter-winchell-who-climbed-high-fell-far.html?pagewanted=all.

WOMEN AND THE NEWS MEDIA

In terms of how political reporting has historically been overrun by men, it may be useful to look back to the 1972 presidential campaign. The election was a crushing defeat for Democrats and a resounding victory for President Richard Nixon. It also sparked a wave of campaign books, including Timothy Crouse's seminal campaign narrative, *The Boys on the Bus*. But as the name of Crouse's work implies, there were almost no women journalists on that campaign trail and their marginalization in reporting circles for decades is something that has colored political reporting and general news coverage ever since.

What's notable about the state of gender equality in the newsroom is that while a generation of pioneering women journalists carved a place in the nation's news organizations in the 1960s and 1970s, the effort appears to have stalled out in the past two decades. Every year, the American Society of News Editors produces a census of the country's newspaper newsrooms. The focus of the census is to explore how ethnically diverse the nation's newspaper staffs have become, but buried in the data sheets is some troubling information about gender. According to the 2015 census, the percentage of newspaper employees who are women has been stuck, essentially unchanged, since 1999. The 1999 report found that 36.9 percent of all editorial jobs at newspapers were held by women. Sixteen years later the number had inched up to 37.1. The picture is not much better in terms of newsroom supervisors, where women hold 35.3 of those jobs, up slightly from 33.8 percent in 1999. Among reporters, the picture actually worsened a bit. When the lens is broadened to global media, the news is even worse. According to the Global Media Monitoring Project, which advocates for more women in the media and has conducted audits of gender equality in reporting since 1995, only 25 percent of people heard, spoken of, or read about were women. Meaning only a quarter of the stories in print or broadcast were reported by women or featured women as expert sources.

The lack of gender equality in the United States or abroad has raised real concerns for women's rights activists who see the media as a core component of shaping and potentially changing public perceptions of men and women. Noted feminist Gloria Steinem has said, "It's hard to think of anything except air, food and water that is more important than the media . . . Literally, I've spent most of my life working in the media. That has made me hyperaware of how it creates for us the idea of normal, whether or not the normal is accurate. Especially for groups that have been on the periphery for whatever reason: If we can't see it, we can't be it" (Zernike 2014). Steinem helped organize the Women's Media Center to document the issue, and a 2015 report from the organization tracked some troubling trends generally within the news media and specifically in the area of covering politics. The survey found that 32 percent of evening news stories were reported by women and 37 percent of newspaper and magazine stories were authored by female writers. The news is even worse in political reporting. Julie Burton, head of the WMC, noted in the report that "with the 2016 presidential election already under way, it is particularly disturbing that Novetta research for WMC shows men reporting 65 percent of U.S. political stories. This is not progress from the 2012 presidential election, when Novetta research for WMC found that 71 percent of all front-page stories were written by men and that on cable and network TV, political news show guests and experts were 77 percent men" (State of Women in the U.S. Media 2015).

Women have had a place in the newsroom for more than a century, but their role was profoundly limited. With a few exceptions, women found a place in newspapers as those publications aimed to expand their readership. With a business model that relied on the widest possible circulation, news organizations began adding "society pages" in newspapers and "women's sections" in magazines to attract female readers. These new sections began hiring young women to report for them and soon female reporters were covering beats like fashion, cooking, and the home. There were exceptions to this limited role for female journalists. Women like Elizabeth Jane Cochrane, who would write a fiery letter to the editor denouncing a sexist column in a Pittsburgh paper and land herself a reporting job, taking on the pen name of Nelly Bly. Bly would talk her way onto the staff of Joseph Pulitzer's *New York World*, and would soon produce a groundbreaking exposé on the state of mental hospitals after she feigned mental illness and went through treatment in a New York asylum. The next year, 1888, Pulitzer sent her around the world in a publicity stunt to see if she could circumnavigate the globe faster than the fictional Phileas Fogg from the H.G. Wells book *Around the World in Eighty Days*. Other women would also carve out names as stellar journalists, including muckraker Ida Tarbell.

But for every Bly or Tarbell there were thousands of women who found themselves trapped in news organizations that relegated them to secretarial work or subjected them to sexual harassment. Throughout the 1950s and 1960s the number of women working in newsrooms grew, but it would take a series of lawsuits from women at the Associated Press, the *New York Times*, *Newsday*, and *Newsweek* to force many changes. In 1970, 46 women working at *Newsweek* sued the magazine accusing the organization of widespread sexual discrimination. Lynn Povich was one of those women, and some 40 years later she would recall the kind of environment that prompted the lawsuit, calling it "the 'Mad Men' era—married bosses had affairs with women who reported to them; a randy writer passed by the desk of one young woman and planted a kiss on her neck; a researcher was stalked by her senior editor, who had a crush on her. He told her if she didn't marry him, she would have to leave Newsweek—which she did" (Povich 2012). Povich and her colleagues timed their lawsuit to come out on the day the magazine published a feature on the women's movement called "Women in Revolt," with a picture of a naked woman in red silhouette, pumping her first in the air. That same day they filed a complaint with the Equal Employment Opportunity Commission under the charge that they had been "systematically discriminated against in both hiring and promotion and forced to assume a subsidiary role" due entirely to their gender. The lawsuit at *Newsweek*, the first by women against a media company, received mixed reactions in the press—New York *Newsday* headlined their article "Newshens Sue *Newsweek* for 'Equal Rights'"—but the magazine soon negotiated a settlement. Povich, five years later, would become the first female senior editor in *Newsweek* history.

Throughout the 1970s newsrooms began to change their behavior and offer more tracks for women to senior positions, but many woman still report a more subtle, but persistent form of sexism in the workplace. Slate writer Amanda Hess captured the view of many women in the modern newsroom when she revisited the *Newsweek* case, writing, "The Civil Rights Act of 1964 and the sex-discrimination lawsuits that followed successfully challenged such blatantly sexist displays in American newsrooms. They also cleared room for quieter, subtler forms of sexism to take their place. Today's sexist employer knows that he can no longer get away with pinching butts by the water cooler or explicitly barring women from the ladder's highest rungs. But between clearly actionable sex discrimination and full gender equality lies an extensive menu of workplace tactics by which employers can marginalize women" (Hess 2012). These lawsuits may have barred the most overt forms of discrimination, but as Hess notes and the statistics help support, a legal structure that bans overt gender discrimination has not led to an equal number of women being employed in journalism or an equal number of managers in positions of authority in most newsrooms.

The lack of female reporters and editors developing stories and selecting the political topics to focus on can have both clear direct and indirect effects. On the direct side of the equation, the paucity of female political correspondents has affected the stories told by journalists and how they choose to tell them. Kay Mills, a longtime journalist and author of the book *A Place in the News: From the Women's Pages to the Front Page*, tried to explain the effect in a report on the Harvard University Nieman Foundation site, noting, "Many women (not all) see stories in ways many men (not all) do not. In what topics they choose to cover, in how they decide to tell the story, and in their commentaries, men and women display different approaches. Gender can also play a role in reporters gaining access to or trust of sources" (Mills 2011). Mills notes that the different life experience and worldview of a female reporter can sometimes push her to approach a story differently.

Indirectly, the gender inequality in the newsroom can taint the way the news media handles even categorizing and describing issues affecting women. For example, 1996 marked the rise of the "soccer mom," a type of female voter who lived in the suburbs and often had an upper middle class lifestyle. The idea of the "soccer mom" as some sort of magical unicorn of swing voters in the country started with a woman who ran for city council in Denver in 1995. Susan Casey made her slogan "A soccer mom for city council" as a way to connect herself to those suburban parents she hoped to represent. She won, but the moniker of soccer mom soon became a term all about gender. As Casey told the *New York Times*, that was never the intent. "It has nothing to do with women or men—'soccer parent' just didn't sound like a good phrase. If I were a male I probably would have said soccer dad, but it wasn't meant to be an appeal to women. Soccer dads know that soccer moms are the same. Actually the dads I know are worse than the moms and kids—they are much more involved" (MacFarquhar 1996). The term became a touchstone for political reporting, serving as a target market for political messages from the Democrats and Republicans as well as a way to describe the persistent problem Republicans have had in attracting large numbers of white female voters. By the time of the 1996 Republican convention in San Diego, pundits, many of them men, were opining about the need for Senator Bob Dole to make in-roads to these voters if he hoped to defeat President Bill Clinton.

But behind this discussion lay a real disconnect, one exacerbated by the relative lack of women in newsroom leadership roles. Were suburban married women fundamentally different than suburban married men? Were they a voting bloc at all or simply a loose demographic group? Could they be swayed en masse with a key issue or targeted mailing? To talk about women voters, who make up more than half the electorate, as a sort of monolith is clearly misleading, but some critics argue the media's adoption of these descriptions can be more damaging than just being misleading. One feminist scholar argued that the term "soccer mom" soon morphed from a political force into a consumer market, be it for a candidate or a product. The result, Mary Douglas Vavrus argued, is that "her identity as a political force is far less important than her identity as a consumer with a solid, disposable income. Her political interests are only alluded to, or are cast in the vaguest of terms. When her politics are mentioned, they tend to reinforce essentialist, traditional, domestic concerns—concerns well suited to product, as opposed to policy, intervention. This tendency is one that can push women out of the electoral political power centers—such as the House of Representatives or the Senate—by suggesting that they are perhaps more appropriately situated in their homes, raising their children" (Vavrus 2002). Vavrus saw the media as the source of this misleading and disempowering term and then saw the marketing world embrace it and commercialize it. But for her, it was the news media that created this creature, too easily lumping women into a simplistic whole that could be then sold policies and beauty products. Critics argue this lazy categorization of suburban women was made possible, at least in part, by the still low number of women in the newsroom.

But that was changing. As more and more women rose through the ranks of news organizations, the reporters tasked with covering presidential campaigns began to change. Some news organizations have seen through staff changes and increasing seniority more women move into positions within the political reporting field. Anne Kornblut of the *Washington Post* has covered campaigns for the paper since 2000. When the 2008 campaign rolled around, with Senator Hillary Clinton running for the Democratic nomination and later Alaska governor Sarah Palin running as the

Republican vice presidential pick, she said she noticed a change. She told NPR in 2012, "When we had a female candidate on both tickets, there was a lot of talk about 'girls on the bus' instead of 'boys on the bus.' I think we did notice a higher percentage of women reporters gravitating toward the Clinton campaign and then we all reunited on the Palin campaign several months later. But I think in general that's true. I don't think it was just because there were two female candidates. We look around now and our political staff is almost half women at this point, which obviously would have been unheard of in 1972" (Inskeep 2012).

What's perhaps notable about Kornblut's point is those female political reporters were assigned to cover the female candidate, as if a decision was made in newsrooms to dispatch females to cover females—an almost unconscious throw-back to the era of the society page reporters of the nineteenth and early twentieth centuries. But whatever the cause, 2008, and later 2012, offered more women than ever before the chance to get out to report on politics. But as the Women's Media Center report notes, most news organizations are still offering women far fewer opportunities to report and to serve as expert sources for stories. The WMC survey did find that the *PBS NewsHour* nightly television program was heads and shoulders above other outlets in its use of women and minority sources and reporters, but according to the organization that is only because the program, co-anchored by two women, has made it a priority. Longtime political reporters Gwen Ifill and Judy Woodruff both said they know how any news organization can fall into the rut of having the same guests on to discuss an issue. Woodruff said, "It is a conscious decision every single day. We literally cast our reporters and producers to go out and actively look for people and make a triple effort to make sure they are finding people who are diverse in gender, race and age . . . If you don't do that, it's so easy to slip back into the trap and just say, 'Well, we used so-and-so last time we did this topic, so let's use them again.' Frankly, there's no excuse for that" (Taibi 2015).

See also: Palin, Sarah

Further Reading

Hess, Amanda. 2012. "What's Changed, and What Hasn't, Since the Women of Newsweek Sued Their Bosses." Slate. September 4. Accessed December 17, 2015. http://www.slate.com/blogs/xx_factor/2012/09/04/the_good_girls_revolt_what_s_changed_since_the_women_of_newsweek_stood_up_to_their_bosses_.html.

Inskeep, Steve. 2012. "'Boys on The Bus': 40 Years Later, Many Are Girls." NPR. April 12. Accessed December 16, 2015. http://www.npr.org/2012/04/19/150577036/boys-on-the-bus-40-years-later-many-are-girls.

MacFarquhar, Neil. 1996. "What's a Soccer Mom Anyway?" *New York Times*. October 20. Accessed December 17, 2015. http://www.nytimes.com/1996/10/20/weekinreview/what-s-a-soccer-mom-anyway.html.

Mills, Kay. "Measuring Progress: Women as Journalists." Nieman Reports. January 10. Accessed December 18, 2015. http://niemanreports.org/articles/measuring-progress-women-as-journalists.

Povich, Lynn. 2012. "Women in the Workplace: How 'Good Girls' Fight Back." *Los Angeles Times*. October 7. Accessed December 15, 2015. http://articles.latimes.com/2012/oct/07/opinion/la-oe-povich-newsweek-discrimination-gender-20121007.

"The Status of Women in the U.S. Media 2015." Women's Media Center. Accessed December 16, 2015. http://wmc.3cdn.net/7d039991d7252a5831_0hum68k6z.pdf.

Taibi, Catherine. 2015. "The Media Is Failing Women, but One Network Is Leading the Fight to Change Things." Huffington Post. June 18. Accessed December 18, 2015. http://www.huffingtonpost.com/2015/06/18/pbs-women-media-newshour_n_7587852.html.

Vavrus, Mary Douglas. 2002. *SUNY Series in Communication Studies: Postfeminist News: Political Women in Media Culture*. Albany: State University of New York Press.

Zernike, Kate. 2014. "Rutgers to Endow Chair Named for Gloria Steinem." *New York Times*. September 26. Accessed December 17, 2015. http://www.nytimes.com/2014/09/27/nyregion/rutgers-to-endow-chair-named-for-steinem.html?_r=0.

WONKETTE

Go into a bar on Capitol Hill while Congress is in session and you will hear a mix of policy critique, personality snark, and endless rumors of what might happen or who is up or who is down. Add a healthy dose of potty humor and pottier words, and this is the voice of the blog Wonkette.

If the Internet taught media anything, it was that you can succeed if you can find a niche and own it. In Washington, rumormongering is a full-time sport, so much so that in 1992 the venerable *Washington Post* launched a column called "Reliable Source." The column was part gossip rag and part D.C. celebrity column and was an instant hit. Gawker Media, the collection of blogs that focused on clicks and web traffic above all else, launched a competing service in 2004 called Wonkette.

The site was run by self-proclaimed "failed journalist" Ana Marie Cox and embraced a foul-mouthed mix of sex and politics as its daily fare. When a story of an alleged affair involving then-Democratic presidential nominee John Kerry leaked on the notoriously unreliable Drudge Report, Cox posted update after update on Wonkette, cataloguing every step of the story. When a former Hill staffer named Jessica Cutler started blogging under the pen name Washingtonienne about her sexual adventures in the nation's capital, including an affair with a staffer from Senator Mike DeWine's staff, Wonkette offered the later-to-be-sued Cutler a platform to expand her audience.

The Washingtonienne episode landed Cutler a book contract and scored Wonkette a huge surge in attention. The site "traffic shot up more than threefold, to more than 1.5 million visits in the month of May 2004" (Solove 2007, p. 53). The attention turned Cox into one of the city's new celebrities. She hit the town with Cutler and the two posed for photos posted later on Wonkette. She was soon asked by MTV to help cover the national political conventions that year.

Those who admired or disliked her work said Cox flourished in part because she was a product of the new media empire of Gawker and not tied to the more traditional outlets like the *Post*'s "Reliable Source." Former alternative weekly writer-turned-ABC news correspondent Jake Tapper said in 2004, "The difficulty with writing a gossip column from the moss-covered towers of any established media organization is that one's bosses are more often than not likely to be golfing and sipping port with your choice subjects. So Ana Marie has an advantage there" (Bosman 2004). And it was an advantage that she rode to a form of D.C. celebrity status.

By 2006 Cox had used the publicity of Wonkette to score two separate book deals and on the eve of the release of her first work, a novel that satirized life in Washington, D.C., she stepped down as Wonkette editor. The site then burned through a couple editors before, in 2008, Gawker Media Group announced it would spin off the site into its own business. In 2012 the site took on its latest iteration when former alternative weekly editor Rebecca Schoenkopf purchased the site and became its editor. Schoenkopf continued the site's tradition of liberal views mixed with a strong feminist stance, bringing on Kaili Joy Gray, a liberal blogger from California, to help run the site. The site has served as a model for some state-based services that follow the same mix of snark, sex, and liberal commentary on political matters. Schoenkopf continues to run the site, even after moving to Montana in 2014.

Wonkette maintains an irreverent voice that mixes humor with left-leaning commentary. It sells t-shirts emblazoned with a sexy version of U.S. senator Elizabeth Warren set in a definitely Soviet-era propaganda aesthetic. Its Facebook page lists the site as a "Newspaper" and a "Prison & Correctional Facility." But it has also lost much of its traffic it enjoyed during the heyday of Cutler's drama. It promises advertisers the ability to reach some 650,000 visitors a month (and a million on election months), with the additional promise that "Wonkette readers are born with an advanced degree and at least one third of them have jobs" (Wonkette 2015).

Throughout its incarnations Wonkette has stressed its role as living up to the stereotype of bloggers. Cox would often do interviews wearing slippers and in reporting on her departure from Wonkette, the *Washington Post* said "the writer who made Washington politics irresistibly naughty, is giving up her job as a full-time, pajama-clad blogger to become a full-time, pajama-clad author" (Argetsinger and Roberts 2006). Cox's slippers were retired into the Newseum in Washington, D.C., but it remains to be seen if Schoenkopf and her band of merry revolutionaries can help Wonkette achieve its past political scandal glories.

Further Reading

Argetsinger, Amy, and Roxanne Roberts. 2006. "Wonkette's Sex Change." *Washington Post*. January 4. Accessed February 2, 2015. http://www.washingtonpost.com/wp-dyn/content/article/2006/01/03/AR2006010301935.html.

Bosman, Julie. 2004. "First with the Scoop, If Not the Truth." *New York Times*. April 18. Accessed January 30, 2015. http://www.nytimes.com/2004/04/18/style/first-with-the-scoop-if-not-the-truth.html.

Solove, Daniel. 2007. *The Future of Reputation: Gossip, Rumor, and Privacy on the Internet*. New Haven, CT: Yale University Press.

Wonkette. 2015. "So You Want to Give Wonkette All of Your Money." Accessed February 2, 2015. http://wonkette.com/219557/advertising-on-wonkette.

WOODWARD AND BERNSTEIN: WOODWARD, BOB (1943–) AND BERNSTEIN, CARL (1944–)

They were not a natural team. In fact, they really didn't like seeing each other across the *Washington Post* newsroom, both chasing a Saturday story about a burglary at the Democratic National Committee headquarters at the Watergate complex in June 1972. Bob Woodward had heard about Carl Bernstein's penchant for nosing his way into a good story, and Bernstein thought Woodward was a prima donna who couldn't write. But there they were, working on the same story—along with a slew of other reporters—about a "third-rate burglary."

They had no clue then, but that burglary was the story that would trigger more than two years of investigative reporting that exposed a vast web of political tricks and crimes and a cover-up that pushed President Richard Nixon out of the White House and led to indictments of 40 White House and administration officials.

The two Metro reporters became famous and wrote two books about what became known as Watergate. Their legendary editor, the late Ben Bradlee, wrote in his autobiography that Woodward and Bernstein's work "put the *Post* (and me) on the map in ways that no one could have predicted" (Bradlee 1995). The investigation remains one of the most significant accomplishments in the history of journalism, and their names would hardly be uttered separately in the following decades. Despite that, the two men couldn't have been more different.

Carl Bernstein was born on February 14, 1944, in Washington D.C. At 16, he was a copy boy at the *Washington Star*. At 19 he became a full-time reporter. He went to the University of Maryland for a little while, but struggled with school and dropped out. But the *Washington Star* had an informal rule that reporters had to have college degrees. He had no interest in finishing his, so he left the paper in 1965. He joined the *Washington Post* in 1966 (Shepard 2007).

Bob Woodward was his straight-laced opposite. Woodward was born on March 26, 1943, in Geneva, Illinois. He went to Yale on a Navy Reserve Officer Training Corps scholarship, which required him to serve in the Navy after graduation. When he got out, he convinced the *Washington Post* to give him a quick try-out, which he failed. His editor said he didn't know how to tell a story. But, Woodward loved reporting, so he caught on at the *Montgomery Sentinel*, a weekly paper in Maryland. After just a year there, he was back at the *Post*, this time in a permanent job. He had only been on staff for nine months before the break-in.

Neither reporter had done anything terribly remarkable in journalism before five men wearing suits and surgical gloves were arrested in the Watergate that June night. Woodward had been writing about crime and unsanitary restaurants. Bernstein had covered courts and the city, sometimes wrote about music, and liked to do "long, discursive pieces about the capital's people and neighborhoods" (Woodward and Bernstein 1974). The Saturday story on the burglary at the Democratic headquarters was published with Alfred E. Lewis's byline, but the story belonged to Woodward and Bernstein for the years that followed. They kept pulling the threads and found a complicated web that linked the burglary to the White House and the re-election campaign for President Richard Nixon. They kept up the pressure with story after story, unveiling new details and new evidence of the president's connection on the front page of the *Post*.

Based on their work, the *Post* won the1973 Pulitzer Prize for public service journalism, but the story didn't end there. Nixon won the 1972 election and looked to be heading for another four years, but what Woodward and Bernstein uncovered would prevent that from happening. Under a great deal of pressure, Nixon resigned in August of 1974—the first sitting president to be forced to do so by work of investigative journalists.

Woodward and Bernstein wrote about their reporting in *All the President's Men*, which would become a movie starring Robert Redford and Dustin Hoffman. The film helped inspire a generation of new journalists to question authority. They also wrote a book called *The Final Days* about the months leading up to Nixon's resignation.

Their work was also notable in its use of an anonymous source. A man who became known as Deep Throat met secretly with Woodward and offered guidance and tips throughout the investigation. Deep Throat became the subject of widespread speculation on who it was, and nobody who knew said anything for 30 years. Then, in a 2005 *Vanity Fair* article, Deep Throat was revealed to be Mark Felt, a Twin Falls, Idaho, native who was the number two official at the FBI when Woodward and Bernstein were tracing the scandal (O'Connor 2005).

Watergate was the pinnacle of both reporters' careers. Woodward stayed on at the *Post* and has written a laundry list of books, but also has been the subject of controversy and criticism. Bernstein, too, has authored books—including a biography of Hillary Clinton—and written for a number of publications, but had a tumultuous personal life that inspired Nora Ephron, his second ex-wife, to write the novel *Heartburn*.

Despite their flaws, Woodward and Bernstein remain as icons of modern investigative journalism who showed just how mighty the pen can be. The University of Texas bought their notes and recordings from the Watergate scandal, giving others the opportunity to trace the corruption.

Michael Wright

See also: Anonymous Sources; *Washington Post*

Further Reading

Bradlee, Ben. 1995. *A Good Life*. New York: Simon and Schuster.

Inskeep, Steve. 2014. "40 Years On, Woodward and Bernstein Recall Reporting on Watergate." NPR. June 13. Accessed October 8, 2015. http://www.npr.org/2014/06/13/321316118/40-years-on-woodward-and-bernstein-recall-reporting-on-watergate.

O'Connor, John. 2005. "I'm the Guy They Called Deep Throat." *Vanity Fair*. July. Accessed October 8, 2015. http://www.vanityfair.com/news/politics/2005/07/deepthroat200507.

Shepard, Alicia. 2007. *Woodward and Bernstein: Life in the Shadow of Watergate*. New York: Wiley Publishing.

University of Texas. "The Woodward and Bernstein Watergate Papers." Accessed October 8, 2015. http://www.hrc.utexas.edu/exhibitions/web/woodstein.

Woodward, Bob, and Carl Bernstein. 1974. *All the President's Men.* New York: Simon and Schuster.

Woodward, Bob, and Carl Bernstein. 1976. *The Final Days.* New York: Simon and Schuster.

Y

YAHOO NEWS

Begun as a news aggregator, Yahoo News has emerged as one of the top news sites on the web, mixing original content with syndicated content it receives from partners. The site, while attracting some 175 million visitors a month, has also come under fire for aggressively using personalization filters to feed people the news they want to see rather than the most important information of the day.

Like its historic rival Google, Yahoo grew out of Stanford University. There at the electrical engineering graduate school, two students, Jerry Yang and David Filo, created a website in January 1994 called "Jerry and David's Guide to the World Wide Web." By March of that year they renamed the site Yahoo! and in January 1995 the site was launched at yahoo.com. Yahoo's idea was to create an index of the World Wide Web, so the site allowed new sites to apply to be listed on different topic pages that were organized in sections of the site.

As the site grew throughout the 1990s, adding new companies and countless subdirectories of web pages, the service launched a news aggregator that listed top newspapers and television stations that provided news. Over time, Yahoo decided to begin partnering with these sites to highlight individual stories versus general links to the front pages of news organizations. And with that, Yahoo News was born. The site's early sources of content included traditional wire services and the biggest news providers at the time and included Associated Press, Reuters, Agence France-Presse, Fox News, ABC News, NPR, *USA Today*, CNN.com, and BBC News.

From some of its earliest days, Yahoo was interested in highlighting what was popular and would draw traffic as well as the editorially most significant news of the day. In 2001, for example, it added a new feature that allowed people to see what stories were being emailed most frequently. The idea was both intriguing and a little terrifying to editors who had historically selected stories to highlight based on their editorial significance. Yahoo's innovation allowed people to see what interested each other, removing the traditional editorial gatekeeper from the equation. The result drew the attention of some of those gatekeepers, with the *New York Times* reporting at the time, "'Most-emailed' proved to be an immediate hit, and it has become something of a cult favorite among heavy consumers of news . . . The company also created another statistics-based feature, this one a bit more conventional: 'Most-viewed content,' a list of the headlines and photos most clicked on in the last hour. 'Most-viewed,' which began in August, is heavy on breaking news and entertainment stories, while 'Most-emailed' tends toward the quirky or bizarre" (O'Connell 2001). The *Times* and other coverage at the time said Yahoo, which produced no content of its own, was relying on its own internal statistics to create "cheap content" that could be automatically generated and drive traffic to less traditional articles. Despite its cool reception from some outlets, others, like MSNBC, soon followed in releasing their own versions of their "best of" lists and promoting the sharing of the news stories via email. It's important to remember this discussion of popular and most shared pre-dated social networks like Facebook and Twitter by several years, but the idea of computer aggregated and organized news was already loose within Yahoo.

Despite this interest in technology, which would continue throughout its history, Yahoo was increasingly interested in developing its own content in addition to featuring partner stories. In 2010, the site started adding its own reporters, scooping up reporters from Gawker, Politico, *Newsweek*, and elsewhere to begin reporting for the site. One of those reporters, David Chalian, who was hired away from the *PBS NewsHour* to go to Yahoo in 2012, landed in hot water after an ABC microphone picked up the correspondent cracking a joke about Republican nominee Mitt Romney and his wife being unconcerned about a possible hurricane striking New Orleans during their party's national convention. His comment, "Feel free to say, 'They're not concerned at all. They're happy to have a party with black people drowning,'" got him quickly fired by Yahoo who said his remarks did not reflect the professionalism of the site.

Yahoo's approach to news is to aggressively mix technology and tracking with the content itself. The company has made personalization a hallmark of its search and other services. Its CEO, former Google official Marissa Mayer, described the philosophy in a 2013 interview, saying, "We can think 'How do we take the Internet and order it for you.' There are all these newsfeeds all over the web that people will check, you know Twitter, Facebook, and the question is what order should people read these in the morning . . . To do that great job in discovery mode as well as search you need a terrific sense of personalization" (Bloomberg 2013). By the time Mayer said that, personalization had already become the normal approach to reporting on Yahoo News. The site sought to find the kind of stories that a person was interested in by monitoring what they clicked on and how long they spent on the article. One researcher noticed the degree to which the site now relied on personalization after a spur-of-the-moment decision prompted her to read a story about a murdered child. Soon Yahoo News was filled with injured and killed children and the researcher reacted in horror, writing, "Yahoo personalizes headlines for its audience of over 700 million people through its Content Optimization and Relevance Engine, an algorithmic system based on demographic data and reading behavior. As a researcher who studies digital media, I was aware that my news was filtered, but I had never noticed the filtering process in action, probably because, until now, Yahoo had guessed me right. (Or at least not so gruesomely wrong.)" (Kendzior 2012).

All of these tools, combined with Yahoo's continued efforts to hire top-name journalists, has turned the site into a formidable news destination. The site has usually ranked first or second in terms of audience, and Mayer has sought to beef up the talent pool even more. In 2013, the site added former chief political correspondent for the *New York Times Magazine*, and in the largest move to date, Mayer orchestrated the hiring of former CBS News anchor Katie Couric. The Couric deal, which was renewed for $10 million a year in 2015, has been called risky by many who see Yahoo's strength as organizing content. But Mayer feels it a good investment, saying, "You can do things like measure the ads that you've sold against those programs and the follow-on views. And they all mean this is a very profitable and good investment. But I will say, to me it was really more about raising that journalistic standard, getting our name out there as people who really want to participate in news and participate in the dialogue in a different way than just republishing content" (Primack 2015).

And this is the role that the site has settled in to, producing more and more original print and video pieces while also operating a heavily personalized news site that draws more than 100 million users a month. The site maintains a correspondent at the White House and has produced major live coverage of political events. Although it lacks the traditional media outlet of a broadcast or newspaper, Yahoo is not simply an aggregator of other people's content; it is a major news operation covering politics in its own right.

See also: Personalization and the Internet

Further Reading

Kendzior, Sarah. 2012. "The Day Yahoo Decided I Liked Reading about Child Murder." *The Atlantic*. April 17. Accessed September 2, 2015. http://www.theatlantic.com/technology/archive/2012/04/the-day-yahoo-decided-i-liked-reading-about-child-murder/255970.

O'Connell, Pamela LiCalzi. 2001. "New Economy; Yahoo Charts the Spread of the News by E-Mail, and What It Finds Out Is Itself Becoming News." *New York Times*. January 29. Accessed September 3, 2015. http://www.nytimes.com/2001/01/29/business/new-economy-yahoo-charts-spread-e-mail-what-it-finds-itself-becoming.html.

Primack, Dan. 2015. "Marissa Explains It All: Yahoo CEO on AOL, Katie Couric and Sergey Brin's Parting Advice." *Fortune*. May 19. Accessed August 31, 2015. http://fortune.com/2015/05/19/marissa-explains-it-all-yahoo-ceo-on-aol-katie-couric-and-what-sergey-brins-parting-advice.

"Yahoo's Mayer: Personalization Is Future of Search." Bloomberg. January 25, 2013. Accessed September 3, 2015. http://www.bloomberg.com/news/videos/b/5c3bf0c9-2f8e-4c23-8c5f-05aafa3f26db.

Z

ZOGBY ANALYTICS

From the moment John Zogby and his Zogby Poll entered the national political discussion, both have been controversial. Zogby, who started Zogby International in the 1980s and now works with his son at Zogby Analytics, is an American pollster based in upstate New York.

His polls have been famously accurate at times when others faltered and equally famous for their inaccuracies—he wrote in May 2004, "I have made a career of taking bungee jumps in my election calls. Sometimes I haven't had a helmet and I have gotten a little scratched. But here is my jump for 2004: John Kerry will win the election" (Cooper 2004). Kerry ended up losing by 3 million votes. But whether wrong or right, the pollster always attracts ink with his surveys and analyses.

His work first drew major national attention when he predicted the 1996 reelection of President Bill Clinton to within one-tenth of one percent, a far closer assessment than any of the traditional polling giants like Gallup. Zogby himself is quick to trumpet the *Washington Post* story about his 1996 prediction, which began "All hail Zogby, the pollster who conquered the 1996 election." What Zogby doesn't quote is what the director of polling at the Post wrote next, "*And may you burn in the fires of polling hell, you lucky dog,* hiss his competitors who say John Zogby is the newest bad boy of survey research" (Morin 1996, C5). And while many public opinion pollsters grumbled about questionable methodologies and an unhealthy penchant for publicity, John Zogby had arrived.

Although 1996 was something of a coming out party for Zogby, he had actually been running Zogby International since 1984 to conduct research on global attitudes and New York-based political issues. The son of Lebanese immigrants, Zogby's group made a name for itself by conducting some of the first focus group and other research into specifically Arabic views of the United States. As far back as 1991, Zogby was discussing the how Arab Americans needed to combat an increasingly negative stereotype in the United States, arguing, "What has been missing from this expanding body of scholarship and popular literature has been the weight of official statistics on demographics to offset the stereotypes left by images in popular culture" (Willford 1991, p. 69). But Zogby, who was also a professor of political science, was also expanding his political work and growing in regional and national attention.

Zogby's firm started doing marketing work and increasingly offered services to political candidates. His firm also began doing more and more political polls and predictions of elections. He accurately predicted in 1994 that George Pataki would upset three-term governor Mario Cuomo and soon his work was drawing national attention. Zogby's techniques make him one of the most controversial pollsters working in American politics. He argued that traditional pollsters were oversampling Democrats and set out to create a more accurate method for conducting phone polls.

But it was the advent of the Internet and the opportunities and pitfalls that presented to pollsters that made Zogby even more of a lightning rod. In the late 1990s he developed a controversial Internet polling method that allowed him to quickly and cheaply develop online surveys for marketing material and political issues. But many professional public opinion pollsters have blasted the technique as fundamentally flawed. In 2009, for instance, noted statistics modeler Nate Silver took to his site FiveThirtyEight to criticize a new Zogby poll that indicated that President Obama's approval rating had dropped ten points and stood at roughly 50-50—a result almost 10 points worse for the president than other tracking polls. Under a less-than-subtly titled post ("The Worst Pollster in the World Strikes Again"), Silver blasted the pollster's methodology, writing, "These polls are conducted among users who volunteer to participate in them, first by signing up at the Zogby website . . . and then by responding to an e-mail solicitation. These Internet polls, to the extent they rely on voluntary participation, violate the most basic precept of survey research, which is that of the random sample. And as you might infer, they obtain absolutely terrible results" (Silver 2009). This self-selection of survey participants is something Zogby's group says they can counter through the correct weighting and structure of the survey and its results, but many remain dubious.

Still, Zogby surveys, even the more scientifically questionable opt-in online polls, continue to drive serious coverage of politics. In early 2015, for example, as the Republican race for the nomination was still taking shape, Zogby released the results of an online survey with a whopping 6.6 percent margin of error that put the race at a dead-heat between many of the frontrunners. The survey was picked up by Newsmax, the *Miami Herald* (with a caveat that the survey was "experimental"), Forbes .com, and other outlets and speaks to the power of the survey to drive coverage for at least a short time.

Zogby sold most of his initial firm, Zogby International, in 2010 to a Brazilian public opinion research firm and fully divested himself in 2012, the year the multinational shut down Zogby's office in Utica, New York. The next month, he and his son launched Zogby Analytics, a full service marketing and public opinion survey company that moved into the same location as the former Zogby International. The new firm is far smaller than the one that closed in 2012, but Zogby continues to be a presence in the media and the Zogby Poll continues to influence political bloggers, even if other experts continue to worry about the scientific validity of some of the firm's work.

See also: FiveThirtyEight (538); Gallup; Public Opinion

Further Reading

Cooper, Horace. 2004. "Outside View: John Zogby Is Wrong." United Press International. May 15. Accessed February 22, 2015. http://www.upi.com/Business_News/Security-Industry/2004/05/15/Outside-View-John-Zogby-is-wrong/23571084600800.

Morin, Richard. 1996. "Poll-axed: The Maverick Predictor Who Beat Us All." *Washington Post*. November 10.

Silver, Nate. 2009. "The Worst Pollster in the World Strikes Again." FiveThirtyEight. March 24. Accessed February 23, 2015. http://fivethirtyeight.com/features/worst-pollster-in-world-strikes-again.

Willford, Catherine. 1991. "Arab American Institute Releases Demographic Study." *The Washington Report on Middle East Affairs*. March. Washington, D.C.: American Educational Trust.

Selected Bibliography

Aalberg, Toril, Jesper Strömbäck, and Claes de Vreese. 2012. "The Framing of Politics as Strategy and Game: A Review of Concepts, Operationalizations and Key Findings." *Journalism*. February.

Achenbach, Joel. 2014. "Journalism Is Aggregation." *Washington Post*. April 9. Accessed July 25, 2015. http://www.washingtonpost.com/blogs/achenblog/wp/2014/04/09/journalism-is-aggregation

Adatto, Kiku. 2008. *Picture Perfect: Life in the Age of the Photo Op*. Princeton, NJ: Princeton University Press.

Anderson, Brian. 2008. *Manifesto for Media Freedom*. New York: Encounter Books.

Anderson, Chris, Emily Bell, and Clay Shirky. 2014. "Post Industrial Journalism: Adapting to the Present." Tow Center for Digital Journalism. December 4. Accessed December 29, 2015. http://towcenter.org/research/post-industrial-journalism-adapting-to-the-present-2

Ansolabehere, Stephen, and Shanto Iyengar. 1995. *Going Negative: How Political Advertisements Shrink and Polarize the Electorate*. New York: Free Press.

Associated Press. 2009. "Associated Press: How to Do Watchdog Journalism." Associated Press. June 18. Accessed October 30, 2015. https://www.youtube.com/watch?v=Sxf90TXThY8

Atkin, Charles, and James Gaudino. 1984. "The Impact of Polling on the Mass Media." *Annals of the American Academy of Political and Social Science*. March.

Aucoin, James. 2007. *The Evolution of American Investigative Journalism*. Columbia: University of Missouri Press.

Baker, C. Edwin. 2006. *Media Concentration and Democracy: Why Ownership Matters*. New York: Cambridge University Press.

Banville, Lee. 2013. *Debating Our Destiny: Presidential Debate Moments that Shaped History*. Arlington, VA: MacNeil/Lehrer Productions.

Barker, Kim. 2012. "How Nonprofits Spend Millions on Elections and Call it Public Welfare." ProPublica. August 18. Accessed October 8, 2015. http://www.propublica.org/article/how-nonprofits-spend-millions-on-elections-and-call-it-public-welfare

Bateman, Robert. 2013. "Who Are the Anonymous Sources in DC Journalism?" *Esquire*. October 23. Accessed July 2, 2015. http://www.esquire.com/news-politics/news/a25367/anonymous-sources-in-dc-journalism-102413

Bennett, W. Lance. 2011. *News: Politics of Illusion*. Chicago: University of Chicago Press.

Bensman, Marvin. 2000. *The Beginning of Broadcast Regulation in the Twentieth Century*. Jefferson, NC: McFarland & Company, Inc.

Blöbaum, Bernd. 2014. "Trust and Journalism in a Digital Environment." Reuters Institute for the Study of Journalism. University of Oxford.

Boatright, Robert. 2011. *Interest Groups and Campaign Finance Reform in the United States and Canada*. Ann Arbor: University of Michigan Press.

Broh, C. Anthony. 1980. "Horse-Race Journalism: Reporting the Polls in the 1976 Presidential Election." *The Public Opinion Quarterly*. Winter.

Brown, Heath. 2015. *The Tea Party Divided: The Hidden Diversity of a Maturing Movement*. Santa Barbara, CA: ABC-CLIO.

Carter, T. Barton, Marc Franklin, and Jay Wright. 1989. *The First Amendment and the Fifth Estate: Regulation of the Electronic Mass Media*. Westbury, NY: The Foundation Press, Inc.

Chinni, Dante. 2010. *Our Patchwork Nation: The Surprising Truth about the "Real" America*. New York: Gotham Books.

Cohen, Marty, David Karol, Hans Noel, and John Zaller. 2009. *The Party Decides: Presidential Nominations Before and After Reform*. Chicago: University of Chicago Press.

Collins, Scott. 2004. *Crazy Like a Fox: The Inside Story of How Fox News Beat CNN*. New York: Penguin.

Corrado, Anthony. 2000. *Campaign Finance Reform*. New York: The Century Foundation Press.

Cotter, Cornelius, and Bernard Hennessy. 2009. *Politics Without Power: The National Party Committees*. Piscataway, NJ: Transaction Publishers.

Cowan, Geoffrey, and David Westphal. 2010. "Public Policy and Funding the News." USC Annenberg School of Communication & Journalism. Accessed December 18, 2015. http://www.niemanlab.org/pdfs/USC%20Report.pdf

Cramer, Richard Ben. 1992. *What It Takes: The Way to the White House*. New York: Random House.

Critchlow, Donald. 2007. *The Conservative Ascendency: How the GOP Right Made Political History*. Cambridge, MA: Harvard University Press.

Crotty, William, and John Jackson. 1985. *Presidential Primaries and Nomination*. Washington, DC: CQ Press.

Crouse, Timothy. 2013. *Boys on the Bus*. New York: Random House.

Dagnes, Alison. 2010. *Politics on Demand: The Effects of 24-Hour News on American Politics*. Santa Barbara, CA: Praeger.

D'Alessio, Dave. 2013. *Media Bias in Presidential Election Coverage 1948-2008: Evaluation via Formal Measurement*. Lanham, MD: Lexington Books.

David, Paul, Ralph Goldman, and Richard Bain. 1960. *The Politics of National Party Conventions*. Washington, DC: Brookings Institution Press.

Davis, James. 1980. *Presidential Primaries: Road to the White House*. Westport, CT: Greenwood Press.

Davis, Lanny. 2013. *Crisis Tales: Five Rules for Coping with Crises in Business, Politics, and Life*. New York: Simon & Schuster.

Davis, Richard. 2009. *Typing Politics: The Role of Blogs in American Politics*. New York: Oxford University Press, USA.

Dean, Walter. (n.d.). "The Lost Meaning Of 'Objectivity.'" American Press Institute. Accessed December 21, 2015. http://www.americanpressinstitute.org/journalism-essentials/bias-objectivity/lost-meaning-objectivity

Denton, Robert, and Jim Kuypers. 2008. *Politics and Communication in America: Campaigns, Media, and Governing in the 21st Century*. Long Grove, IL: Waveland Press, Inc.

Dewey, Donald. 2007. *The Art of Ill Will: The Story of American Political Cartoons*. New York: New York University.

Diamond, Edwin, and Stephen Bates. 1984. *The Spot: The Rise of Political Advertising on Television*. Cambridge, MA: The MIT Press.

DiFonzo, Nick. 2011. "The Echo-Chamber Effect." *New York Times*. April 22. Accessed October 23, 2015. http://www.nytimes.com/roomfordebate/2011/04/21/barack-obama-and-the-psychology-of-the-birther-myth/the-echo-chamber-effect

Dubois, Philip, and Floyd Feeney. 1998. *Lawmaking by Initiative: Issues, Options and Comparisons*. New York: Algora Publishing.

Dumenco, Simon. 2011. "What It's Like to Get Used and Abused by The Huffington Post." *Ad Age*. July 11. Accessed July 25, 2015. http://adage.com/article/the-media-guy/abused-huffington-post/228607

Dunaway, Johanna, and Robert Stein. 2013. "Early Voting and Campaign News Coverage." *Political Communication*. New York: Routledge.

Farrar-Myers, Victoria, and Justin Vaughan. 2015. *Controlling the Message: New Media in American Political Campaigns*. New York: New York University Press.

Farrell, Mike, and Mary Carmen Cupito. 2010. *Newspapers: A Complete Guide to the Industry*. New York: Peter Lang Publishing, Inc.

Faucheux, Ron. 2003. *Winning Elections: Political Campaign Management, Strategy & Tactics*. Lanham, MD: Rowman & Littlefield.

Filler, Louis. 1976. *Progressivism and Muckraking*. New York: R.R. Bowker Company.

Filler, Louis. 1993. *The Muckrakers*. Stanford, CA: Stanford University Press.

Fisher, Dana R. 2006. *Activism, Inc: How the Outsourcing of Grassroots Campaigns Is Strangling Progressive Politics in America*. Palo Alto, CA: Stanford University Press.

Foley, Elizabeth Price. 2012. *The Tea Party: Three Principles*. New York: Cambridge University Press.

Foley, John, Dennis Britton, and Eugene Everett. 1980. *Nominating a President: The Process and the Press*. New York: Praeger.

Formisano, Ronald. 2012. *The Tea Party: A Brief History*. Baltimore: The Johns Hopkins University Press.

Froomkin, Dan. 2013. "Truth or Consequences: Where Is Watchdog Journalism Today?" Nieman Reports. June 13. Accessed October 30, 2015. http://niemanreports.org/articles/truth-or-consequences-where-is-watchdog-journalism-today

Gans, Herbert. 2012. "Citizen News: A Democratic Addition to Political Journalism." Nieman Lab. November 28. Accessed October 25, 2015. http://www.niemanlab.org/2012/11/citizen-news-a-democratic-addition-to-political-journalism

Garry, Patrick. 1993. *An American Paradox: Censorship in a Nation of Free Speech*. Westport, CT: Praeger.

Ghiglione, Loren. 1984. *The Buying and Selling of America's Newspapers*. Indianapolis: R.J. Berg & Company.

Gibbons, Gene. 2010. "Statehouse Beat Woes Portend Bad News for Good Government." Nieman Reports. December 15. Accessed October 3, 2015. http://niemanreports.org/articles/statehouse-beat-woes-portend-bad-news-for-good-government

Gillmor, Dan. 2004. *We the Media: Grassroots Journalism By the People, For the People*. Newton, MA: O'Reilly Media.

Goodwin, Gene, and Ron Smith. 1984. *Groping for Ethics in Journalism*. Ames: Iowa State University Press.

Grant, J. Tobin, and Thomas Rudolph. 2004. *Expression vs. Equality: The Politics of Campaign Finance Reform*. Columbus: The Ohio State University Press.

Gray, Jonathan, Lucy Chambers, and Liliana Bounegru. 2012. *Data Journalism Handbook*. O'Reilly Media. Accessed June 25, 2015. http://datajournalismhandbook.org/1.0/en/introduction_2.html

Gray, Jonathan, Jeffrey Jones, and Ethan Thompson. 2009. *Satire TV*. New York: NYU Press.

Green, Donald, and Alan Gerber. 2008. *Get Out the Vote: How to Increase Voter Turnout*. Washington, DC: Brookings Institution Press.

Halperin, Mark, and John Harris. 2006. *The Way to Win: Taking the White House in 2008*. New York: Random House.

Hargreaves, Ian. 2005. *Journalism: A Very Short Introduction*. London: Oxford University Press.

Hess, Stephen, and Sandy Northrop. 1996. *Drawn and Quartered: The History of American Political Cartoons*. Montgomery, AL: Elliot and Clark.

Hill, David. 2006. *American Voter Turnout: An Institutional Perspective*. Cambridge, MA: Westview Press.

Hindman, Matthew. 2008. *The Myth of Digital Democracy*. Princeton, NJ: Princeton University Press.

Hohenstein, Kurt. 2007. *Coining Corruption: The Making of the American Campaign Finance System*. DeKalb: Northern Illinois University Press.

Hurwitz, Leon. 1985. *Historical Dictionary of Censorship in the United States*. Westport, CT: Greenwood Press.

Interactive Advertising Bureau. 2013. "The Native Advertising Playbook." Accessed August 14, 2015. http://www.iab.net/media/file/IAB-Native-Advertising-Playbook2.pdf

"The Invisible Primary—Invisible No Longer: A First Look at Coverage of the 2008 Presidential Campaign." Project for Excellence in Journalism and the Joan Shorenstein Center on the Press, Politics and Public Policy at Harvard University. October 29, 2007. Accessed December 1, 2015. http://www.journalism.org/files/legacy/The%20Early%20Campaign%20FINAL.pdf

Jamieson, Kathleen Hall. 1992. *Dirty Politics: Deception, Distraction, and Democracy*. New York: Oxford University Press.

Jamieson, Kathleen Hall, and Joseph Cappella. 2010. *Echo Chamber: Rush Limbaugh and the Conservative Media Establishment*. New York: Oxford University Press.

Jensen, Carl, and Project Censored. 1996. *Censored: The News That Didn't Make the News—and Why*. New York: Seven Stories Press.

Johnson, Dennis. 2007. *No Place for Amateurs*. New York: Routledge.

Johnson, Dennis. 2010. *Routledge Handbook of Political Management*. London: Routledge.

Johnson, Dennis. 2011. *Campaigning in the Twenty-First Century: A Whole New Ballgame?* New York: Routledge.

Johnson, Jason. 2012. *Political Consultants and Campaigns*. Boulder, CO: Westview Press.

Kahn, Si. 1991. *Organizing: A Guide for Grassroots Leaders*. Washington, DC: National Association of Social Workers Press.

Kaid, Lynda Lee, and Christina Holtz-Backa. 1995. *Political Advertising in Western Democracies*. Thousand Oaks, CA: Sage Publications.

Kaniss, Phyllis. 1991. *Making Local News*. Chicago: University of Chicago Press.

Katz, James, Michael Barris, and Anshul Jain. 2013. *The Social Media President*. New York: Palgrave Macmillan.

Keech, William, and Donald Matthews. 1976. *The Party's Choice*. Washington, DC: The Brookings Institution.

Key, V. O. 1961. *Public Opinion and American Democracy*. New York: Alfred A. Knopf.

King, Elliot. 2010. *Free For All: The Internet's Transformation of Journalism*. Evanston, IL: Northwestern University Press.

Kovach, Bill, and Tom Rosenstiel. 2001. *The Elements of Journalism: What Newspeople Should Know and the Public Should Expect*. New York: Crown Books.

Kraus, Sidney, ed. 1979. *The Great Debates: Carter vs. Ford, 1976*. Bloomington: Indiana University Press.

Kuypers, Jim. 2002. *Press Bias and Politics: How the Media Frame Controversial Issues*. Westport, CT: Praeger.

Ladd, Everett Carll, and Charles Hadley. 1978. *Transformations of the American Political System*. New York: W.W. Norton & Company, Inc.

Leibovich, Mark. 2013. *This Town*. New York: Blue Rider Press.

Levendusky, Matthew. 2013. *How Partisan Media Polarize America*. Chicago: University of Chicago Press.

Lilleker, Darren. 2006. *Key Concepts in Political Communication*. London: Sage Publications.

Lippmann, Walter. 1920. *Liberty and the News*. New York: Harcourt, Brace and Howe.

Lippmann, Walter. 1925. *The Phantom Public*. New York: Harcourt, Brace and Company.

Littlewood, Thomas. 1998. *Calling Elections: The History of Horse-Race Journalism*. Notre Dame, IN: University of Notre Dame Press.

Luntz, Frank. 1988. *Candidates, Consultants, and Campaigns*. New York: Basil Blackwell.

Magleby, David, and Candice Nelson. 1990. *The Money Chase: Congressional Campaign Finance Reform*. Washington, DC: The Brookings Foundation.

Mark, David. 2006. *Going Dirty: The Art of Negative Campaigning*. Lanham, MD: Rowman & Littlefield Publishers.

Marshall, Jon. 2011. *Watergate's Legacy and the Press: The Investigative Impulse*. Evanston, IL: Northwestern University Press.

McCue, Duncan. 2011. "Reporting in Indigenous Communities." Developed under the John S. Knight Journalism Fellowship at Stanford. Accessed January 20, 2016. http://www.riic.ca

McEnteer, James. 2006. *Shooting the Truth: The Rise of American Political Documentaries*. Westport, CT: Praeger.

McKinnon, Mark. 2012. "Gone Rogue: Time to Reform the Presidential Primary Debates." Joan Shorenstein Center on the Press, Politics and Public Policy. January. Accessed July 5, 2015. http://shorensteincenter.org/wp-content/uploads/2012/03/d67_mckinnon.pdf

McMillian, John. 2011. *Smoking Typewriters: The Sixties Underground Press and the Rise of Alternative Media in America*. New York: Oxford University Press.

Medvic, Stephen. 2001. *Political Consultants in Congressional Elections*. Columbus: The Ohio State University Press.

Meyer, Phil. 2009. *The Vanishing Newspaper: Saving Journalism in the Information Age*. Columbia: University of Missouri Press.

Mills, Kay. 2011. "Measuring Progress: Women as Journalists." Nieman Reports. January 10. Accessed December 18, 2015. http://niemanreports.org/articles/measuring-progress-women-as-journalists

Morozov, Evgeny. 2011. *The Net Delusion*. New York: Public Affairs Books.

Murrow, Edward. 1958. "Radio and Television News Directors Association Speech." Radio Television Digital News Association. October 15. Accessed January 4, 2016. http://www.rtdna.org/content/edward_r_murrow_s_1958_wires_lights_in_a_box_speech

Navasky, Victor. 2013. *The Art of Controversy: Political Cartoons and Their Enduring Power.* New York: Knopf.

Nelson, Keith. 2015. "The Citizen Journalist: How Ordinary People Are Taking Control of the News." Digital Trends. June 19. Accessed October 25, 2015. http://www.digitaltrends.com/features/the-citizen-journalist-how-ordinary-people-are-taking-control-of-the-news

Newman, Bruce. 1999. *Handbook of Political Marketing*. Thousand Oaks, CA: Sage Publications.

Nichols, John, and Robert McChesney. 2013. *Dollarocracy: How the Money-and-Media Election Complex Is Destroying America*. New York: Nation Books.

Norrander, Barbara. 2015. *Super Tuesday: Regional Politics and Presidential Primaries*. Lexington: University Press of Kentucky.

Nyhan, Brendan. 2012. "Breaking the Pack Journalism Paradigm." *Columbia Journalism Review*. October 3. Accessed July 16, 2015. http://www.cjr.org/united_states_project/how_to_avoid_pack_journalism_at_debates.php

Oberholtzer, Ellis Paxson. 1911. *The Referendum in America*. New York: Charles Scribner's Sons.

O'Connor, Rory. 2012. *Friends, Followers and the Future*. San Francisco: City Lights Books.

Ostler, Rosemarie. 2011. *Slinging Mud: Rude Nicknames, Scurrilous Slogans, and Insulting Slang from Two Centuries of American Politics*. New York: Penguin Books.

Overholser, Geneva, and Kathleen Hall Jamieson. 2005. *The Press*. New York: Oxford University Press.

Pariser, Eli. 2011. *The Filter Bubble: What the Internet Is Hiding from You*. New York: Penguin Books.

Parker, David. 2014. *The Power of Money in Congressional Campaigns, 1880–2006*. Norman: University of Oklahoma Press.

Parti, Tarini. 2014. "An Unlikely Survivor in the Digital Age: Direct Mail." Politico. August 3. Accessed June 14, 2015. http://www.politico.com/story/2014/08/an-unlikely-survivor-in-the-digital-age-direct-mail-109673.html

Patterson, Thomas. 2011. *Out of Order*. New York: Knopf Doubleday Publishing Group.

Paul, Norm. 1999. *Computer-Assisted Research: A Guide to Tapping Online Information*. Chicago: Bonus Books.

PBS NewsHour. 2014. "How 'Microtargeting' Works in Political Advertising." PBS. February 18. Accessed July 21, 2015. http://www.pbs.org/newshour/bb/how-microtargeting-works-political-advertising

Penenberg, Adam. 2009. *Viral Loop*. New York: Hyperion Books.

Perlmutter, David. 2008. *Blogwars*. New York: Oxford University Press.

Polsby, Nelson. 1983. *Consequences of Party Reform*. Oxford: Oxford University Press.

Polsby, Nelson. 2012. *Presidential Elections: Strategies and Structures of American Politics*. Lanham, MD: Rowman & Littlefield Publishers.

Postman, Neil. 1985. *Amusing Ourselves to Death: Public Discourse in the Age of Show Business*. New York: Penguin Books.

Prior, Markus. 2007. *Post-Broadcast Democracy: How Media Choice Increases Inequality in Political Involvement and Polarizes Elections*. Cambridge: Cambridge University Press.

Rae, Nicol. 1989. *The Decline and Fall of the Liberal Republicans From 1952 to the Present*. New York: Oxford University Press.

Ralph, Elizabeth, and Margaret Slattery. 2015. "Why Politicians Hate the Press." *Politico Magazine*. May/June. Accessed September 21, 2015. http://www.politico.com/magazine/story/2015/04/why-politicians-hate-the-press-117142

Ranney, Austin. 1975. *Curing the Mischiefs of Faction: Party Reform in America*. Berkeley: University of California Press.

Roberts, Michael. 2008. "Q&A With Daily Show Creator Lizz Winstead." Westword. April 23. Accessed January 14, 2016. http://www.westword.com/news/qanda-with-daily-show-creator-lizz-winstead-5892810

Rogers, Simon. 2014. "Data Journalism Is the New Punk." *British Journalism Review*. June.

Rosenberg, Howard, and Charles Feldman. 2008. *No Time to Think: The Menace of Media Speed and the 24-hour News Cycle*. New York: Continuum Press.

Rosenfield, Margaret. 1994. "Early Voting." *Innovations in Election Administration 9*. Washington, DC: National Clearinghouse on Election Administration.

Rosenstiel, Tom. 1994. *Strange Bedfellows: How Television and the Presidential Candidates Changed American Politics, 1992*. New York: Hyperion Books.

Rowan, Ford. 1984. *Broadcast Fairness: Doctrine, Practice, Prospects*. New York: Longman Inc.

Rutchick, Abraham, Joshua Smyth, and Sara Konrath. 2009. "Seeing Red (and Blue): Effects of Electoral College Depictions on Political Group Perception." *Analyses of Social Issues and Public Policy, Vol. 9, No. 1*. Accessed May 19, 2015. http://www.ipearlab.org/media/publications/rutchick_smyth_konrath_asap_2009.pdf

Sager, Ryan. 2006. *The Elephant in the Room: Evangelicals, Libertarians and the Battle to Control the Republican Party*. Hoboken, NJ: John Riley & Sons, Inc.

Samples, John. 2006. *The Fallacy of Campaign Finance Reform*. Chicago: University of Chicago Press.

Sasseen, Jane, Katerina-Eva Matsa, and Amy Mitchell. 2013. "News Magazines: Embracing Their Digital Future." Pew Research Center. Accessed November 20, 2105. http://www.stateofthemedia.org/2013/news-magazines-embracing-their-digital-future

Scheuer, Jeffrey. 1999. *Sound Bite Society: Television and the American Mind*. New York: Four Walls Eight Windows.

Schlesinger, Arthur. 1973. *History of U.S. Political Parties*. New York: Chelsea House Publishers.

Schmidt, Benno. 1976. *Freedom of the Press vs. Public Access*. New York: Praeger.

Schroeder, Alan. 2000. *Presidential Debates: Forty Years of High-Risk TV*. New York: Columbia University Press.

Schuman, David, and Esther Thorson. 2007. *Internet Advertising: Theory and Research*. Mahwah, NJ: Lawrence Erlbaum Associates.

Serrin, Judith, and William Serrin. 2002. *Muckraking!: The Journalism that Changed America*. New York: The New Press.

Sherman, Gabriel. 2014. *The Loudest Voice in the Room: How the Brilliant, Bombastic Roger Ailes Built Fox News—and Divided a Country*. New York: Random House.

Smith, Charles. 1939. *Public Opinion in a Democracy: A Study in American Politics*. New York: Prentice Hall.

Smith, Melissa, and Larry Powell. *Dark Money, Super PACs, and the 2012 Election*. 2013. Lanham, MD: Lexington Books.

Society of Professional Journalists. (n.d.). "SPJ Ethics Committee Position Papers: Anonymous Sources." Accessed July 1, 2015. http://www.spj.org/ethics-papers-anonymity.asp

Strachey, John St. Loe. 1924. *The Referendum: A Handbook to the Poll of the People, Referendum, or Democratic Right of Veto on Legislation*. London: T. Fisher Unwin Ltd.

Streitmatter, Rodger. 2015. *Mightier Than the Sword: How the News Media Have Shaped American History*. Boulder, CO: Westview Press.

Sutter, Daniel. 2006. "Media Scrutiny and the Quality of Public Officials." *Public Choice* 129, no. 1/2. October.

Tesh, Sylvia. 1984. "In Support of 'Single-Issue' Politics." *Political Science Quarterly* 99, no. 1.

Tewksbury, David, and Jason Rittenberg. 2012. *News on the Internet: Information and Citizenship in the 21st Century*. Oxford: Oxford University Press.

Thurber, James, and Candice Nelson. 2014. *Campaigns and Elections American Style*. Boulder, CO: Westview Press.

Toefel, Richard. 2012. *Why American Newspapers Gave Away the Future.* Now and Then Reader. http://www.nowandthenreader.com/why-american-newspapers-gave-away-the-future/

Tremayne, Mark. 2012. *Blogging, Citizenship, and the Future of Media*. New York: Routledge.

Trent, Judith, Robert Friedenberg, and Robert Denton. 2011. *Political Campaign Communication: Principles and Practices.* Lanham, MD: Rowman & Littlefield.

Trippi, Joe. 2004. *The Revolution Will Not Be Televised.* New York: Harper Collins Publishers.

Tushnet, Mark. 2013. *In the Balance: Law and Politics on the Roberts Court*. New York: W.W. Norton & Company.

Tuten, Tracy. 2008. *Advertising 2.0: Social Media Marketing in a Web 2.0 World*. Westport, CT: Praeger.

Vavrus, Mary Douglas. 2002. *SUNY Series in Communication Studies: Postfeminist News: Political Women in Media Culture*. Albany: State University of New York Press.

Viguerie, Richard, and David Franke. 2004. *America's Right Turn: How Conservatives Used New and Alternative Media to Take Power*. Los Angeles: Bonus Books.

Wallace, Aurora. 2005. *Newspapers and the Making of Modern America*. Westport, CT: Greenwood Press.

White, Theodore. 2009. *The Making of the President 1960*. New York: Harper Perennial.

Wilson III, Clint C., and Felix Guitierrez. 1995. *Race, Multiculturalism and the Media*. Thousand Oaks, CA: Sage Publications.

Wood, Stephen. 1990. "Television's First Political Spot Ad Campaign: Eisenhower Answers America." *Presidential Studies Quarterly*. Spring.

Zeller, Tom. 2004. "Ideas & Trends; One State, Two State, Red State, Blue State." *New York Times*. February 8. Accessed May 19, 2015. http://www.nytimes.com/2004/02/08/weekinreview/ideas-trends-one-state-two-state-red-state-blue-state.html

The Author and Contributors

The Author

Lee Banville is an associate professor of journalism at the University of Montana. He teaches political reporting as well as digital and social media reporting and journalism law. Prior to teaching, he spent 14 years at the *PBS NewsHour*, helping launch and then serving as editor-in-chief of the Online NewsHour. In that role, he helped develop and execute coverage of national political campaigns dating back to 1996. He is married to fellow professor and journalist Jule Banville and they have two daughters, Kate and Maggie.

The Contributors

Jule Banville is an assistant professor of journalism at the University of Montana. Before that she served as deputy managing editor at the *Washington City Paper,* was a daily news reporter at the *Erie Times-News* in Erie, Pennsylvania, and worked at WNYC in New York.

Jason Begay is an assistant professor of journalism at the University of Montana and president of the Native American Journalist Association. Jason has also served as editor of the *Navajo Times* and worked at the *Oregonian*.

Michael Wright is a reporter for the *Bozeman Daily Chronicle* and a writer whose work has appeared in *Modern Farmer* and newspapers around Montana.

Index

Note: Page numbers in **bold** indicate the location of main entries